AN ACCOUNT OF MY LIFE

(GOHUR-I-IKBAL)

AN ACCOUNT OF MY LIFE
(GOHUR-I-IKBAL)

SULTAN JAHAN BEGAM

TRANSLATOR

C. H. PAYNE

GYAN

Published by

Gyan Publishing House
5, Ansari Road
Daryaganj, New Delhi-110002
Phone: 011-47034999, 9811692060
E-mail: books@gyanbooks.com

Distribution Network
gyanbooks.com
India, USA, Canada, UK, Australia

ISBN: 978-93-6920-706-0 (PB)

First Published, 1910

2nd Impression 2025

Printed at: Gyan Press, Delhi.

AN ACCOUNT OF MY LIFE (GOHUR-I-IKBAL)
Author: SULTAN JAHAN BEGAM, Translator: C. H. PAYNE

AN ACCOUNT OF MY LIFE

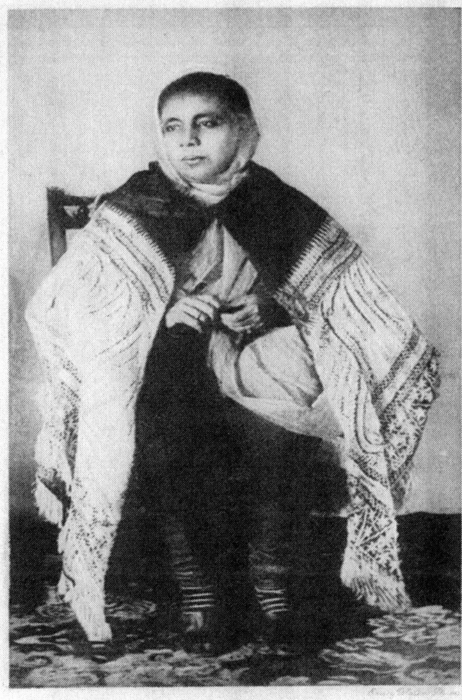

Her Highness
Nawáb Sultan Jahán Begam
1901

AN ACCOUNT OF MY LIFE

(GOHUR-I-IKBAL)

BY HER HIGHNESS
NAWAB SULTAN JAHAN BEGAM
G.C.S.I., G.C.I.E.
RULER OF BHOPAL

TRANSLATED BY C. H. PAYNE, M.A.
LATE EDUCATIONAL ADVISER TO H.H. THE BEGAM

WITH MAP AND ILLUSTRATIONS

LONDON
JOHN MURRAY, ALBEMARLE STREET, W.
1912

TRANSLATOR'S PREFACE

Some years before her death, the late Begam of Bhopal published a history of her State from its foundation down to the year 1872. This work is entitled *Táj-ul-Ikbál,* and was translated into English by Mr. H. C. Barstow of the Bengal Civil Service, and sometime Political Agent in Bhopal. *An Account of My Life,* called in Urdu *Gohur-i-Ikbál,* is a sequel to the *Táj-ul-Ikbál.* The objects with which it has been composed are sufficiently explained in the opening pages of the first chapter. Nawáb Sultán Jahán Begam does not claim to have written a book that will interest the general public. But perhaps her own remarkable personality, the unique position which, as a female ruler, she holds in the Muhammadan world, together with the simple and spirited manner in which she tells her story, and the insight it affords into life in one of the most interesting as well as one of the most loyal of the Feudatory States of India, may attract a wider circle of readers than Her Highness's modesty has allowed her to anticipate.

It will, I think, be admitted by the majority of those who have had experience in turning Oriental languages into English that a word-for-word translation not only results in disjointed and unnatural English, but is apt to produce an altogether distorted impression of the author's meaning and literary style. In the following pages I have endeavoured to convey to English readers the same meaning which, as far as I am able to judge, the Urdu original is intended to convey to Muhammadan readers. The translation is as literal as I could make it, consistently with this aim. In some cases correspondence and speeches originally in English were only available in Urdu translations; I have, therefore, had to retranslate them. All such are marked with an asterisk; and

I herewith offer to those who composed them my humble apologies for the liberty I have taken. I have to thank Maulavi Abdul Ghafúr Khán and Munshi Walí Muhammad for their patient assistance in the elucidation of many difficult passages.

The illustrations are a special feature of the English version. For their kindness in placing portraits at my disposal I am indebted to Lady Meade, Sir David W. Keith Barr, and Sir Arthur Wollaston, President of the Northbrook Society.

C. H. P.

Bhopal, 1911.

CONTENTS

PART I

CHAPTER I

INTRODUCTORY

Early history of Bhopál—First period—Second period—Shah Jahán Begam's *History of Bhopál*—I desire to follow my mother's example pp. 1–4

CHAPTER II

NAWAB SIKANDAR BEGAM

Sikandar Begam's place in the history of Bhopál—Birth and childhood—Bhopál at the commencement of her rule—Her military reforms—Her loyal services during the Mutiny—Incompetency of her predecessors—Administrative reforms—Bairasía added to the Bhopál territory—Durbar at Akbarábád—Pilgrimage to Mecca—Death and character—Ministers and nobles of her court—Maulavi Jamál-ud-dín—Rája Kishen Rám—Háfiz Muhammad Hasan Khán—British political officers . . . . . . pp. 5–19

CHAPTER III

MY CHILDHOOD

My birth—A memorable year—How I obtained my *jágír*—My grandmother's affection for me—My hours of study—Letters from Mecca—A happy meeting—Death of my father and of my grandmother—I commence to live with my mother—Changes in my education—My first speech—My *nashrah* ceremony—My mother's second marriage . . . . pp. 20–31

CHAPTER IV

NAWAB BAKI MUHAMMAD KHAN

The Mishti Khail—Ali Bayázid Khán—Wazír Muhammad Khán—The siege of Bhopál—Bahádur Muhammad Khán—Retires with Sikandar Begam to Islámnagar—My mother's marriage—My father's services during the Mutiny—Copies of dispatches—His illness—Performs the *haj*—His death . . . . pp. 32–39

CHAPTER V

My Marriage

My grandmother's anxiety concerning my marriage—Selecting the bridegroom—Some essential qualifications—Ahmad Ali Khán—His training in Bhopál—The choice approved—Marriage correspondence—A visit from the Agent to the Governor-General—Marriage sanctioned by the Viceroy—An unfortunate delay—The Kudsia Begam—The marriage ceremony—The *chauthi* ceremony—An impressive scene—Ahmad Ali Khán's family and character . . . . pp. 40–62

CHAPTER VI

A Royal Visit and Other Matters

Universal joy in India—Invitation to Calcutta—Correspondence regarding the royal visit—Preparations in Calcutta—The *purdah* question—Plans for the advancement of Sidik Hasan Khán—Arrival in Calcutta—Visit to Lord Northbrook—Reception by the Prince of Wales—A return visit—A royal Chapter—My indisposition and return to Bhopál—An account of the births of Bilkis Jahán Begam and of Nawáb Nasrullah Khán—Family dissensions—Widow re-marriage—Evil influence of Sidik Hasan Khán—An arbitrary proceeding . . . . pp. 63–80

CHAPTER VII

The Imperial Durbar at Delhi

Journey to Delhi—Visit to the Viceroy—A gift from the Queen—A return visit—Visit from Lady Lytton—Description of the Imperial Durbar—The royal Proclamation—More visits—Return journey—Halt at Agra pp. 81–89

CHAPTER VIII

1877—1881

An entertainment at Bhopál—The Kaisar Gang—A banquet—Sidik Hasan Khán's usurpation of power—A regrettable durbar—Birth of my second son—A marriage proposal—Seeds of dissension—My illness—Ill-requited generosity—My daughter's *nashra*—A happy festival—My daughter's second *nashra* . . . . pp. 90–100

CHAPTER IX

1881—1882

Short account of the Kudsia Begam—Her wrongs—Her death—General mourning—Death of Maulavi Jamál-ud-dín—Ahmad Raza Khán—Abdul Latif Khán—Colonel C. I. H. Ward—Journey to Calcutta—At Calcutta—Return journey—Illness of Nawáb Nasrullah Khán—My mother's displeasure pp. 101–108

CHAPTER X

The Bhopal State Railway

Central India in the sixties—Sir Henry Daly—A generous offer—Terms of agreement—Reception of visitors—Opening ceremony—The Begam's speech—Colonel Bannerman—Education of my sons . . pp. 109–119

CHAPTER XI

1883—1886

Sidik Hasan Khán's ascendancy—His dangerous writings—Investigation by Sir Lepel Griffin—Sidik Hasan Khán's disgrace—The blame thrown upon me and my family—A durbar—Speech by Sir Lepel Griffin—A distinguished statesman . . . . pp. 120–128

CHAPTER XII

1886—1888

Appeal to the Government on behalf of Sidik Hasan Khán—Interview with the Viceroy—Kindness of Lord and Lady Dufferin—A prolonged visit—Mischief-makers—Her Majesty's Jubilee—The Kaisar Embankment—Loyal messages—A useful memorial—Childhood of Bilkis Jahán Begam—My mother takes entire charge of her—A cunning scheme—Another marriage proposal—Bilkis Jahán's first illness—She returns to her own home—Second illness—Death of Bilkis Jahán Begam—Widespread sorrow . pp. 129–140

CHAPTER XIII

1889—1891

Visit of Lord Roberts—Review of the State troops—Death of Sidik Hasan Khán—His character and early career—"The late Nawáb"—Sáhibzáda Obaidullah Khán becomes a *háfiz*—A celebration in honour of the event pp. 141–146

CHAPTER XIV

The Visit of Lord Lansdowne to Bhopal

Preparations for the visit of Lord Lansdowne—Arrival at the railway station—State visits—A banquet—Her Highness's speech—Lord Lansdowne's reply—A unique display—A public appreciation—Lord Lansdowne's second visit—Entertained at the railway station—His Excellency's speech . . . . pp. 147–154

CHAPTER XV

Some New Institutions

The State's indebtedness to Lord Lansdowne—An appropriate memorial—Major Meade opens a hospital—The anniversary of the Queen's accession—A steam factory—A profitable undertaking for Imtiyáz Ali Khán—Her Highness pays a farewell visit to Lord Lansdowne at Simla—Formation of the Bhopál Imperial Service Lancers—A *kharita* from the Viceroy . pp. 155–161

CHAPTER XVI

The Death of Sahibzadi Asif Jahan Begam

Asif Jahán Begam is attacked by rheumatic fever—Doctor Abdul Rahím Sáhib—I remove my daughter to Samarda—Return to Bhopál—The sickness increases—Samarda a second time—Miss Mackenzie—Return once more to Bhopál—Major Meade—Death of Asif Jahán Begam—Sorrow and sympathy—Birth of Sáhibzáda Hamidullah Khán . . . . pp. 162–167

CHAPTER XVII

1895—1897

Welcoming Lord Elgin to Bhopál—State visits—State banquet at which Her Highness proposes the health of Their Excellencies—Lord Elgin's reply—Corrupt administration of Imtiyáz Ali Khán—His death—Extension of the Bhopál State Railway—Opening ceremony—Speeches delivered by the Begam and the Agent to the Governor-General . . . pp. 168–177

CHAPTER XVIII

The Last Years of my Mother's Reign

A durbar in honour of the Diamond Jubilee—A loyal speech—Introduction into the Bhopál State of the coinage of British India—Manner in which the exchange was effected—Arrival of Lord and Lady Curzon—An enthusiastic welcome—Her Highness's speech and His Excellency's reply—Two days in Bhopál—Proposals for the marriages of my two elder sons—I ask my mother's advice—The marriages are arranged—I endeavour to overcome my mother's displeasure—Celebration of the *nikah* ceremony—My mother falls sick pp. 178–189

CHAPTER XIX

The Death of Nawab Shah Jahan Begam

Alarming symptoms—Domestic troubles and afflictions—Ali Hasan Khán and his daughter's nuptials—Mián Alamgír Muhammad Khán—Servility and slander—My mother prepares to go to Mecca—Her purpose is frustrated—A pathetic message—Death of my mother—The silent palace—Funeral ceremony—A *Gazette Extraordinary*—Chief events in my mother's life—Her reign and character—In the pages of history—A vindication—Death of Her Majesty the Queen . . . . pp. 190–204

PART II

CHAPTER I

THE FIRST DAYS OF MY REIGN

Sad memories—The Táj Mahal—A visit from Colonel Meade—A Muhammadan custom—Ceremonial extravagance—I begin to feel my way pp. 205–209

CHAPTER II

MY INSTALLATION

Arrival of Colonel and Mrs. Meade—The durbar hall—A State procession—Installation ceremony—A *kharita* from the Viceroy—Colonel Meade's speech—My reply—Presentation of *khiláts*—State banquet—My early training and inexperience—My husband's title—How I entertained my guests—Nawáb Nasrullah Khán appointed heir-apparent—A comprehensive agreement pp. 210–222

CHAPTER III

THE DEATH OF NAWAB IHTISHAM-UL-MULK

My mother's administration—Sidik Hasan Khán—Ministers with full powers—Financial disorder—An anxious time—The Revenue Department—Land settlement—Reducing expenditure—My sons' *shádi*—A happy Ramazán—Death of my husband—A heavy sorrow—My husband's illness—Mourning and sympathy—My husband's estate . . . pp. 223–237

CHAPTER IV

THE DAYS OF MOURNING

The rules of mourning—My lonely position—I resolve to perform the *haj*—The duties of an orthodox Musalman—A petition to the Viceroy—Pilgrimage postponed—Major L. Impey—Land settlement—Condition of the Records Office—Collection of arrears—Munshi Isrár Hasan Khán—The Educational Department—My sons' *jagirs*—My sons go on tour—Results of the tours pp. 238–249

CHAPTER V

A MARRIAGE FESTIVAL

Preparations made by my husband—I decide to carry out his intentions—Presentation of *khiláts*—My durbar speech—*Risála Ihtishámia*—Presentation of *kalgi*—My speech on this occasion—Arrival of guests—The marriage party—Dinner to my European friends—I propose the health of Mr. and Mrs. Bayley—Mr. Bayley's speech—The furnishing of my sons' palaces pp. 250–259

CHAPTER VI

MINISTERIAL CHANGES

Resignation of Maulavi Abdul Jabbar Khán—I become my own Minister—The Judicial Department—The police—The Revenue Department—A joint ministry—*Moin-ul-muhám* and *Nasír-ul-muhám*—Munshi Mumtáz Ali Khán—Maulavi Nasír-ud-dín . . . . . . pp. 260–264

CHAPTER VII

THE CORONATION DURBAR

A *kharita* and a notification—The Bhopál camp—Arrival at Delhi—Welcoming the Duke of Connaught and the Viceroy—A happy coincidence—The durbar—I offer my congratulations—My address to His Majesty—A royal Chapter—Return to Bhopál—How the coronation was celebrated in Bhopál . . . . pp. 265–274

CHAPTER VIII

MY FIRST TOUR

Tours entail hardship on the villagers—A stringent order—Heavy work in camp—A village welcome—Friendly intercourse—Arrival at Raisen—A lucky escape—Four days in Bhopál—Return to Raisen—Plague precautions—I retire to Samarda—Tour completed . . . . pp. 275–281

CHAPTER IX

TWO YEARS' ADMINISTRATION

I am no stranger to hard work—The new settlement—Difficulties of the cultivator—Forest administration—State pensioners—Need for education—The court *vakils*—The police—The Roman Catholic Church—Receipts and expenditure—Plague regulations—An urgent order—Widespread alarm—I endeavour to restore confidence—Persuasive measures—Trust in God—The behaviour of the villagers—Effect of my presence—Malicious rumours—The disease subsides . . . . pp. 282–294

CHAPTER X

THE ANNIVERSARY OF MY ACCESSION

Previous anniversaries—A new departure—My durbar speech—I review my administration—My early difficulties—The new ministry—A short term settlement—Munshi Mumtáz Ali Khán—Regulating advances of grain—Tours of inspection—Plague operations—Police reforms—The coronation durbar—The Military Department—Háfiz Muhammad Hasan Khán—The Victoria Lancers—The State Cavalry . . . . pp. 295–302

CHAPTER XI

THE BIRTH OF BIRJIS JAHAN BEGAM

Good news—A visit from the Political Agent—More good news—His Majesty's letter—Miss Blong—Birth of my granddaughter—A lucky day for Abdul Husein—The *akika* ceremony—Congratulatory letters—Presenting *jora*—Nawáb Nasrullah Khán's liberality—An interesting procession—The *chhathi* ceremony . . . . pp. 303–311

CHAPTER XII

PROGRESS AND REFORM

Coronation durbar medals—Presentation by the Political Agent—My speech—Sáhibzáda Hamidullah Khán—Judicial reforms—The Majlis-i-mashwara—The Yunáni system of medicine—A neglected science—A memorial to my daughter Asif Jahán Begam—Address by the Yunáni medical officer—Nawáb Nasrullah Khán's speech—A drug store opened pp. 312–322

CHAPTER XIII

EDUCATIONAL PROGRESS

Female education—I decide to open a girls' school—The *purdah* difficulty—The duty of Muhammadan women—The school opened—Local self-government—The municipal committee—Education of Sáhibzáda Hamidullah Khán—Indian tutors—I undertake the duties of teacher—Studying the Korán—The Daly College at Indore—Mr. Payne's appointment pp. 323-329

CHAPTER XIV

THIRD YEAR'S ADMINISTRATION

The Alexandra Nobles' School—Backward state of the nobles of Bhopál—State pensions and their result—Lord Curzon and the chiefs' colleges—Laying a foundation stone—My speech—Police reforms—State schools—The Military Department—The Judicial Department—*Fatwa* decrees . pp. 330–337

CHAPTER XV

THE *HAJ*

Preparing for my pilgrimage—Nawáb Nasrullah Khán in charge of the administration—The uncertainty of life—Chartering a steamer—Quarantine regulations—Departure from Bombay—Arrival at Jedda—My escort—Attacked by Bedouins—At Bir Abbas—Arrival at Medina—Welcomed by the Governor—Medina to Mecca by road—The Keeper of the Sacred Curtain—Second attack by Bedouins—Arrival at Mecca—Origin of the *Haj*—Return journey—Arrival at Bombay—Return to Bhopál—A hearty welcome pp. 338–352

CHAPTER XVI

THE YEAR 1904

Birth of my grandson—The *akika* ceremony—Meeting with Lord Curzon—I am appointed a Knight G.C.I.E.—My second son takes command of the Imperial Service Cavalry—Durbar in honour of his appointment—Speeches by Mr. Bayley and General Beatson—I establish a military riding-school—Visit to Indore—Illness of my grandson—Banquet at the Residency—Mr. Bayley proposes my health—Return to Bhopál . pp. 353-368

APPENDICES . . . . pp. 369–379

GENEALOGICAL TREE OF THE BHOPAL FAMILY . . p. 380

INDEX . . . . pp. 381–383

In the spelling of proper names the system adopted by Sir W. W. Hunter in his *Imperial Gazetteer* has been followed as far as possible.

LIST OF ILLUSTRATIONS

HER HIGHNESS NAWAB SULTAN JAHAN BEGUM 1901 *Photogravure Frontispiece*

FACING PAGE

NAWAB SIKANDAR BEGAM 6
NAWAB SIKANDAR BEGAM WITH HER GRAND-DAUGHTER, SULAIMAN JAHAN BEGAM 6
NAWAB SIKANDAR BEGAM WITH HER FIRST AND SECOND MINISTERS 16
COLONEL J. W. WILLOUGHBY-OSBORNE 18
SIR RICHARD MEADE 18
SIR ROBERT HAMILTON 18
NAWAB SULTAN JAHAN BEGAM (AGED 11 YEARS) 28
NAWAB UMRAO DULA 32
CAPTAIN MATTU KHAN, AFTERWARDS NAIB BAKSHI 36
HAFIZ MUHAMMAD KHÁN NAIB BAKSHI 36
BAKSHI MURAWWUT MUHAMMAD KHAN 36
NAWAB SULTAN JAHAN BEGAM AT THE TIME OF HER MARRIAGE 44
NAWAB IHTISHAM-UL-MULK AT THE TIME OF HIS MARRIAGE . 56
H.R.H. THE PRINCE OF WALES, 1875 64
LORD NORTHBROOK 72
THE EARL OF LYTTON 84
THE COUNTESS OF LYTTON 88
THE TAJ MAHAL AND BE-NAZIR PALACES 98
NAWAB ABDUL LATIF KHAN, C.I.E. 104
HAFIZ AHMAD RAZA KHAN 104
THE EARL OF RIPON 108
SIR HENRY DALY 110
GADAROYA BRIDGE ON THE BHOPAL STATE RAILWAY . . 116
COLONEL C. I. H. WARD 124
SIR LEPEL HENRY GRIFFIN 128
THE MARQUIS OF DUFFERIN AND AVA 130
THE MARCHIONESS OF DUFFERIN 132

FACING PAGE

SAHIBZADI BILKIS JAHAN BEGAM 136
FIELD-MARSHAL LORD ROBERTS 142
NAWAB SIDIK HASAN KHAN 144
THE MARQUIS OF LANSDOWNE 152
THE MARCHIONESS OF LANSDOWNE 152
SAHIBZADI ASIF JAHAN BEGAM 162
THE EARL OF ELGIN AND KINCARDINE 172
THE COUNTESS OF ELGIN 172
SIR DAVID W. KEITH BARR 176
LADY CURZON 182
BARON CURZON OF KEDLESTON 184
ENTRANCE TO THE TAJ MAHAL 194
NAWAB SHAH JAHAN BEGAM 198
THE EARL OF MAYO 200
COURTYARD OF THE TAJ MAHAL 206
COLONEL MALCOLM J. MEADE 216
NAWAB NASRULLAH KHAN, HEIR-APPARENT IN BHOPAL . . 222
NAWAB IHTISHAM-UL-MULK WITH SAHIBZADA HAMIDULLAH KHAN 236
THE SADAR MANZIL PALACE 256
THE CORONATION DURBAR: A PORTION OF THE AMPHITHEATRE . 270
THE HAYAT AFZAH GARDEN 294
OFFICERS OF THE BHOPAL VICTORIA LANCERS 302
THE DURBAR MEDAL 312
SAHIBZADA HAMIDULLAH KHAN 326
THE NISHAT AFZAH GARDEN 340
THE SHAUKAT MAHAL 352
SAHIBZADA COLONEL OBAIDULLAH KHAN 362

IT is the duty of all right-minded men, at the commencement of their undertakings, to give praise and glory to Almighty God, who, in spite of the frailty of human nature, hath raised man to the foremost place amongst created beings, and hath adorned him with sense and understanding to learn, as he passes down the picture-gallery of his life, the lessons of wisdom that are there set before him. And more specially are we, who are Musalmans, bound to give Him thanks that He hath ordained us to be the followers of His chosen prophet, Muhammad, saying of us, " Of all mankind ye are My faithful servants," and that He hath for our guidance and protection in spiritual and temporal matters set before us His most excellent commandments, and for the sure continuance of the same hath ordained Kings and Princes to rule over us, establishing them in power and majesty by His most holy decree, " To God, His Prophet, and to lawful Kings shall ye render obedience." Yea, verily are His mercies unbounded and infinitely above all human gratitude.

O God unknown, unsearchable, in vain
We strive with human sense Thyself to scan;
Our striving done, unknown Thou dost remain,
Unutterable still Thy praise by man.

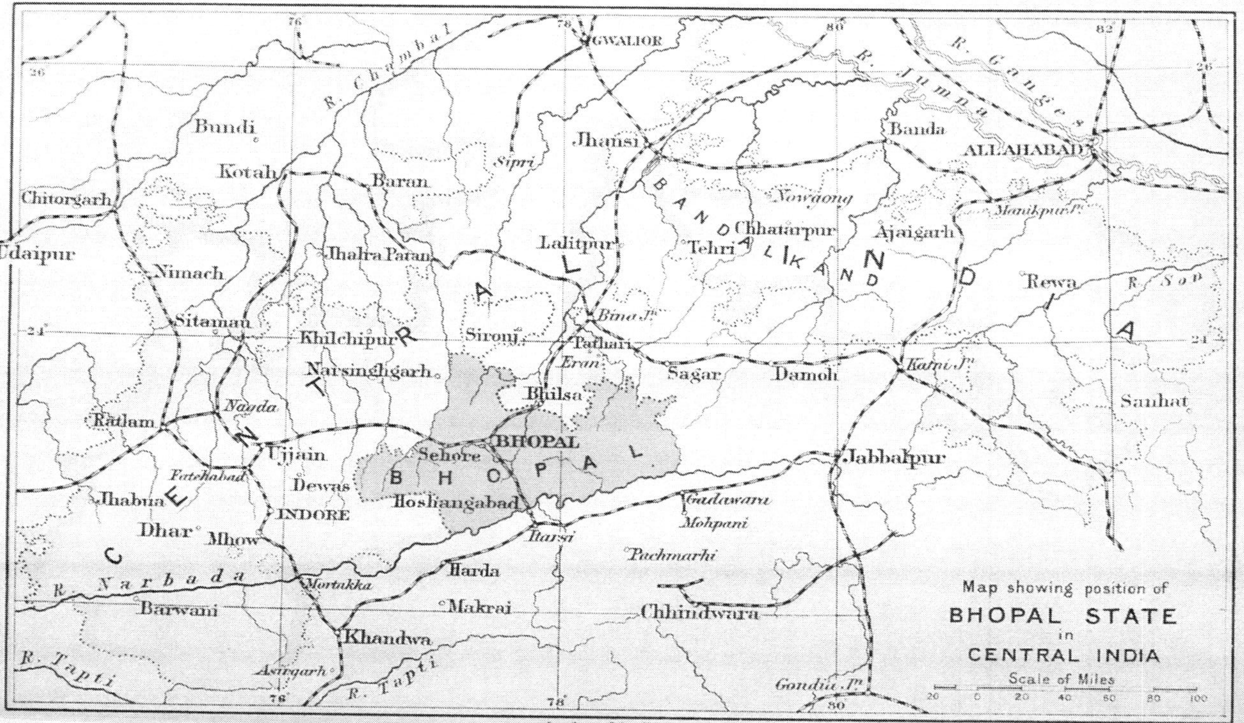
Map showing position of
BHOPAL STATE
in
CENTRAL INDIA
Scale of Miles
GWALIOR
Jhansi
Banda
ALLAHABAD
Bundi
Kotah
Baran
Chitorgarh
Udaipur
Nimach
Jhalra Patan
Lalitpur
Tehri
Chhatarpur
Ajaigarh
Nowgong
Manikpur Jn.
Rewa
R. Son
Sitamau
Khilchipur
Sironj
Bina Jn.
Pathari
Eran
Sagar
Damoh
Katni Jn.
Sanhat
Narsinghgarh
Bhilsa
Nagda
Ratlam
BHOPAL
Sehore
Ujjain
Fatehabad
Dewas
Hoshangabad
Jabbalpur
Jhabua
INDORE
Gadawara
Mohpani
Dhar
Mhow
Itarsi
Pachmarhi
Harda
Mortakka
Makrai
Chhindwara
Barwani
Khandwa
Asirgarh
Gondia Jn.
R. Narbada
R. Tapti
R. Chambal
R. Jumna
R. Ganges
Sipri
CENTRAL INDIA
BANDALKHAND
BHOPAL
London: John Murray

AN ACCOUNT OF MY LIFE
(GOHUR-I-IKBAL)

PART I

CHAPTER I

INTRODUCTORY

AFTER ascribing all honour and glory to God, I commence this work, in which it is my design to complete the history of Bhopál down to the present time. Although I shall concern myself mainly with the course of events in my own State, and the progress of its administration, I shall, I trust, be able to show how the history of Bhopál is connected with, and has been influenced by, the mighty movements that have taken place in the world outside. When those who have witnessed these scenes have passed away, and old records have been lost or destroyed, this book may serve to remind future generations of the debt they owe to those who have gone before them; and when they read of the brave deeds of their ancestors, of their faithfulness to the British Government, and of the eternal renown which is their reward, I trust it may serve to stir up in their hearts a desire to achieve a similar renown by an ever-increasing loyalty to the same Power, and an ever-increasing appreciation of the blessings which their country has enjoyed under its protection.

To the members of my family I hope that this book will be especially useful, and that they may lay to heart the many lessons it teaches on the conduct of life, whether domestic or public. It may also help them to detect and avoid those persons who, by flattery and servility, seek the favour of those who are above them, and who, having no end in view but their own advancement, care not if they destroy a thousand houses so they may build their own. I am not without hope, also, that the descriptions I have given of royal durbars and other State functions may be of use to my fellow Rulers in India, as well as to political officers and others to whose lot, from time to time, the arrangement of such matters may fall. That my book, dealing, as it does, solely with events connected with my family and my State, will be of interest to the general public, I cannot expect. If it prove of use and interest to my children and my subjects and the generations that are to come after them, the object of my task will be fulfilled.

The history of Bhopál may be divided into two periods, the first commencing with the life and conquests of Nawáb Dost Muhammad Khán, the founder of the Bhopál dynasty, and the second embracing the events subsequent to the treaty with the British Government.

The decay of the Mughal Empire was followed by a period of strife throughout the whole of Hindustán. The doors were shut on order and freedom, and contemporary history is little more than a record of war, massacre, and oppression. In the south and east the English, with science in their train, were step by step advancing their power, but in every other part of the country anarchy and confusion were rife. Although scarcely two centuries have elapsed, obscurity is already drawing her veil over these troublous times, for where war, bloodshed, and civil strife prevail history can shed but a feeble light. In Bhopál itself the pen, by comparison with the sword, was reckoned a thing of very small account. The nobles of the court were men who knew of nothing and cared for nothing but arms and warfare. No soil existed in which science or literature could grow, and the story of the State was left to be told in another generation.

The Bhopál dynasty had not long been established when

the Maráthás commenced their predatory campaigns. A few brave Patháns was all that the State could look to to oppose the constantly advancing bands of marauders who threatened to overrun the entire country. Gradually, however, the English, by the fertility of their resources, succeeded in getting this widespread conflagration under control; and peace and security, so long banished by bloodshed and strife, were again restored. The Bhopál State concluded a treaty with the British Government which guaranteed her immunity from all dangers and interference from outside, and with the signing of this treaty the first period of her history terminates. Although a full and connected narrative of this period was an impossibility, the account which we have of it in the *Táj-ul-Ikbál* is not without interest, and we owe a debt of gratitude both to Nawáb Sikandar Begam and to Nawáb Shah Jahán Begam; to the former for having amassed, with careful discrimination and after minute research, the materials for this work, and to the latter for having clothed them in the garb of history.[1]

The second period commences under happier auspices. With the restoration of peace, men's minds turned again to the cultivation of the soil, and the state of chaos which the events of past years had produced in the internal administration of the State gradually began to give place to order and reform. The need for arms and self-defence had passed away, and in its place, ushered in by an era pregnant with new aims and new enterprises, arose another need, little understood before—the need for political foresight and wisdom to guide the destinies of a State in times of peace. Government by means of law and justice is fraught with greater difficulties than government by means of the sword; and in a community where every law was likely to be looked upon as an infringement of personal liberty, these difficulties were increased tenfold. Amongst those to whom the task of overcoming them was entrusted none stands out more conspicuously than Nawáb Sikandar Begam. Endowed with all the sterner attributes of a ruler, she possessed, in addition, that softer quality, the love of peace and mercy, which only attains its full development

[1] For a summary of the events of this period, see Appendix G.

in a woman's heart, and by which alone true happiness can be spread. It must be regarded as a proof of God's special favour to the Bhopál State that for three successive generations He has placed the reins of government in female hands.

The story of the first period, with its wars and petty strifes, throws but little light on the actual development of the State; and as it has been treated of at length in the history compiled by my Mother, Nawáb Shah Jahán Begam, there seems no need to go over the ground again. But the reign of Nawáb Sikandar Begam, with which the second period opens, and which was also included in the above-mentioned work, forms an essential and instructive portion of the history of the State. And since this lady was the first, as well as the most capable, of the Begams of Bhopál, a recapitulation of the events of her life and the reforms of her reign cannot be without interest. It therefore seems to me fitting that the present work should open with an account of Nawáb Sikandar Begam, though the more detailed description of events must date from my own marriage.

Those who are acquainted with the responsibilities and manifold duties of the ruler of a State will easily understand my difficulty in finding time for the composition of this narrative. Since, however, it is my desire to follow in the footsteps of my ancestors, and to profit by the example which they have set before me, I have determined that the history which Nawáb Sikandar Begam commenced, and which Nawáb Shah Jahán Begam continued to the year 1872, shall be completed up to the present time by my own hand. In spite of interruptions due to state affairs, and to frequent journeys by land and sea, everything which I have recorded as a fact in this book has undergone the most thorough investigation. After reading the accounts of my journey to Mecca, and my visit to Delhi on the occasion of the durbar in 1903, my readers will be satisfied as to the labour I have bestowed on this part of my task. My late lamented Mother had in her lifetime collected material for a new volume; but, unfortunately, her manuscripts, through the carelessness of those in whose charge they were placed, were destroyed, and the work of repairing this loss has not been the least laborious part of my undertaking.

CHAPTER II

NAWAB SIKANDAR BEGAM

NAWAB SIKANDAR BEGAM holds the same place in the history of Bhopál that the Emperor Akbar holds in the history of India. When Akbar ascended the throne the state of the country was in the highest degree critical. By his political foresight and wisdom, the dangers threatening on every side were met and overcome; and the government was brought to such a high state of efficiency that, although centuries have passed away, the wisdom of his policy and the excellence of his administration continue to be recognized and praised in every civilized country.

Nor did Nawáb Sikandar Begam serve her country less worthily. Born and bred during the darkest days of its history, and surrounded from her cradle by men who, though brave-spirited, were ignorant and illiterate, she spent the first thirty years of her life amid scenes of conflict and the clash of arms, when the only tales that beguiled the time were those that told of battle and bloodshed, and the very atmosphere was hot with war and the rumours of war. There would have been nothing unnatural had the surroundings of her youth imbued her, too, with the turbulent spirit of the age. But she was by nature peace-loving, and from her earliest days deeds of blood and tales of blood were alike hateful and repulsive to her. The wise acts that subsequently characterized her reign mark her as one specially endowed by nature with the talents and qualities of mind necessary to make a great reformer; and as a great reformer she will go down to posterity in the pages of history. In Bhopál itself the events of her long and happy reign, the vigour and nobility of her mind, and the thoroughness of her work will ever be held in honourable remembrance.

The foundation of the Bhopál State was laid in dangerous times, times when the permanency of the administration necessitated the employment of bodies of armed men whose loyalty could be thoroughly relied upon. For this reason the early rulers gathered round themselves a number of military chiefs and nobles, each of whom supported a band of armed retainers, who in peace time were their personal servants, and in time of war fought under their leadership. The influence of these chiefs dominated every branch of the administration. When Nawáb Sikandar Begam began to rule, the State still contained many such men, and the durbar was a nest of warlike and quarrelsome feudatories, influential and independent, who regarded the new era of peace and order with anything but favourable eyes, and who desired nothing better than to live the same wild and exciting lives their fathers had lived before them. To remedy this state of affairs, and to introduce into an assembly of men who, for generations, had obeyed no will but their own, a reverence for law and constituted authority, was a delicate and difficult undertaking. But the Begam had early determined that reform should be the first object of her life. Disregarding the difficulties that lay before her, and relying upon God to strengthen her endeavours, she boldly faced the situation, and, opposing turbulency with firmness, and obstinacy with tact, she succeeded in bringing her refractory courtiers into subjection. Not only did this achievement bring credit and profit to Bhopál, but it raised the Begam, as a ruler, high above many of her contemporaries who could boast of wider and more ancient territories; and it showed to the world that a woman can rise superior to the weaknesses of her sex, and can challenge competition even in those spheres of action which demand qualities that men only are supposed to possess.

The remodelling of the State army was, therefore, the first of the many reforms undertaken by Nawáb Sikandar Begam. The conditions of military service were entirely changed. Out of the gangs of disorderly retainers which were scattered

NAWAB SIKANDAR BEGAM.

NAWAB SIKANDAR BEGAM WITH HER GRAND-DAUGHTER, SULAIMAN JAHAN BEGAM.

p. 6]

about the State a regular force was constructed, in which every man was the servant of the State, and drew his pay directly from the State treasury. Wise regulations for the management of this force were framed, and military instruction according to the system then employed in the British Army was introduced. The artillery, which was ill regulated and badly equipped, was also thoroughly reorganized. The result of these reformatory measures soon became evident, and what had before been a disorderly and refractory levy was transformed into an efficient and well-disciplined force.

It was due to these wise changes that, during the calamities of the year 1857, when bloodshed, murder, and devastation, consequent upon the mutiny of the native army, filled the greater part of Hindustán, the Bhopál State maintained itself in almost undisturbed tranquillity. The State army had not been so long remodelled that it could withstand altogether the evil influences which were abroad, and signs of wavering began, at one time, to be apparent in its ranks. But the tact and indomitable resolution of Nawáb Sikandar Begam, and the undaunted courage and fidelity of Nawáb Nazír-ud-daulah Báki Muhammad Khán, Commander-in-Chief of the State forces, not only quenched this smouldering unrest, but kindled in its place a spirit of vigorous loyalty to the British Government, and a keen desire to help in the restoration of peace; and, when mutiny spread to the Sehore contingent, it was subdued and stamped out by the Bhopál force. This force also crossed the frontiers of the State, and assisted in the maintenance of peace as far as the boundaries of Ságar and Bandalkand. It gave further proof of its loyalty by affording protection to many English people, who, in those days of blood, knew not where, or to whom, to turn for safety or protection.[1] These services were duly recompensed and appreciated by the British Government, and will long be remembered with pride by the people of Bhopál. I myself can never forget the bravery of my countrymen in those dark days; and I am proud to feel that not only am I the successor of a loyal and faithful ruler, but that my subjects, too,

[1] See Appendix A.

are the children of men who devoted themselves to the service of the British Government.

The difficulties against which Nawáb Sikandar Begam had to contend were, in many cases, the result of the neglect and incompetence of her predecessor, Mián Faujdár Muhammad Khán. On the death of Nawáb Jahángír Muhammad Khán, Nawáb Shah Jahán Begam was appointed his successor; but being too young to be entrusted with ruling powers, Faujdár Muhammad Khán was made regent, and for two years he was free to govern according to his own misguided will. And when Nawáb Sikandar Begam succeeded him as regent, she found herself confronted, not only with the task of restoring order in a chaotic administration, but of paying the interest on a debt of over twenty-three lákhs of rupees, nineteen lákhs of which were the legacy of Jahángír Muhammad Khán, the remaining four lákhs being the two years' contribution of his unworthy successor. At the same time, as the result of mismanagement and neglect, the revenue of the State had dwindled down to little more than eleven lákhs of rupees.

Her military reforms being completed to her satisfaction, the Begam next turned her attention to the economic and social side of the administration. She made a tour throughout her territories, halting in every district, and made herself acquainted with the nature and condition of the cultivation prevailing in each. The whole State was surveyed, the boundaries fixed, and the districts demarcated. Since the days of Akbar the Great, no Indian ruler had ever undertaken such a task. It was, however, successfully accomplished, and the State was divided up into three districts and twenty-one *parganas*. Under her personal direction, a new system for the collection of revenue was framed—a system which has been generally praised, and with which the ryots themselves expressed their satisfaction. Mr. Robert Hamilton, Agent to the Governor-General for Central India, in his dispatch of November 7th, 1854, writing in praise of the Begam's administration, said, "You are setting such an excellent example that it will be well for the State if the direction of its affairs continue in your hands."[1] By this system the condition of the ryots, who had previously suffered many hardships owing to the absence of any satisfactory or permanent policy, was greatly improved; debts amounting to several lákhs of rupees were cleared off, and the treasury was once more replenished. For the benefit of cultivators and *mustájirs*, an arrangement was made to facilitate the punctual payment and recovery of advances, which resembled somewhat the system of Agricultural Banks, by means of which the British Government is trying, in many parts of India, to help and encourage the agricultural portion of the population.

To improve the civil administration of the State, courts of justice were established, and a code of laws was drawn up for the protection of the rights of the people, and for the prevention of crime. Civil and criminal laws alike were framed to meet the necessities of the times, and were drafted with all the ability of an experienced legislator. They included regulations for the administration of the settlement and revenue departments, and defined the duties of collectors, *patwáris*, *jágirdárs*, and cultivators, and dealt with all matters connected with customs, forests, engineering, education, the police, and the State army. Modifications and changes have since been introduced, but the laws, as they were originally compiled,[2] would have met practically all the requirements of the present day.

[1] The Sikandar Begam was at this time acting as regent for her daughter, Nawáb Shah Jahán Begam. In 1859, she wrote to the Government of India claiming her right to be made ruler. She stated that, in accordance with the customs of Bhopál, which the Government were pledged to uphold, she, as the daughter of Nawáb Kudsia Begam, ought to have been that ruler's successor. Contrary to this custom, however, she had been made to resign her claims in favour of her husband. And now that he was dead, she looked to the Government to restore her to her rights. In 1860, her claims were acknowledged, and she was placed on the throne, her daughter, who willingly retired in her mother's favour, being recognized as heir-apparent. (See Appendix F.)

[2] Printing-presses, at the time of which I am writing, were rare in India, and every copy of these laws and regulations had to be hand-written. It was not until the year 1860 that the Sikandar press was set up and the printing of State papers commenced.

When we picture to ourselves the troubles and perplexities of her position, Nawáb Sikandar Begam appears like a skilful and experienced sailor navigating his almost sinking ship through the perils of a hurricane. Like her grandfather, Nawáb Wazír Muhammad Khán, she twice saved the State from impending ruin. But let us not forget that the former was a man, and the latter a woman: and that what the man brought about by means of the sword, the woman achieved by a policy of peace and justice.

When all her reforms were completed, and the wheels of the new administration had begun to turn smoothly and regularly, Nawáb Sikandar Begam turned her attention with more energy than ever to the interests of the *mustájirs*, and cultivators. Sympathy and affection characterized all her dealings with these people, and she was constantly searching for means to make them happy and contented with their lot. Whenever *mustájirs* or *patels*[1] visited the capital city, she used to show them her palaces and gardens, and provide them with every variety of amusement, while presents of toys and sweetmeats gladdened the hearts of their children. In the days of my childhood she would often give me wise counsel, and I well remember how her first and most earnest injunction was always to this effect: "The cultivators of the soil are our wealth; that we are able to rule, and to live in state and luxury, is owing to the labour and industry of these poor people. When you become the ruler of the State, look upon the fostering of this humble but useful class as your first and highest duty." I have always respected this advice, and endeavoured to live in accordance with it; and the well-being of the cultivator, and the protection of his rights, is a first charge on the administration, and the object to which my highest efforts are directed.

When the Mutiny, and with it the rule of the East India Company, came to an end, the services which Nawáb Sikandar Begam had rendered to the British Government were recognized and rewarded. In 1861, a state durbar was held at Jabbalpúr, in which Lord Canning, as the representative of

[1] See Appendix D.

Her Majesty the Queen, in a speech addressed to the Begam, acknowledged her loyalty and friendship during the Mutiny, and placed in her hands the grant in sovereignty of the district of Bairasía.[1] It was formally taken possession of on May 1st, 1861, when Nawáb Sikandar Begam, Nawáb Shah Jahán Begam, Nawáb Umrao Dula, Nawáb Kudsia Begam, Nawáb Sulaiman Jahán Begam, and I myself, with the chief nobles and officers of the State, went to Bairasía to take part in the ceremony. A salute of seven guns was fired from the Fatehgarh fort to announce the transfer. In the following year, at a durbar held at Allahábád, the Begam was invested with the Most Exalted Order of the Star of India.[2] In the same durbar, medals and titles were also conferred upon Mahárája Kyáji Rao Sindhia, the Nawáb Sáhib of Rampúr, and the Mahárája of Patiála. After this durbar, Nawáb Sikandar Begam visited Benáres, Fyzábád, Lucknow, and Delhi.[3] On her return, on November 1st, 1861, she gave a dinner to her European friends to celebrate the honour which had been conferred upon her. The entertainment, the arrangements for which had been in the hands of Dr. Thomson, the Agency Surgeon, was a magnificent one; and, notwithstanding the inconvenience of the journey to Bhopál, owing to the absence of railway connection, Major Meade, and a large number of other guests, were present. My *bismillah* ceremony, inaugur-

[1] Bairasía formerly formed part of the State of Dhár, but was afterwards confiscated.

[2] The law enjoins that the *insignia* of the Star of India shall be returned to the Government after the death of the recipient. The Star of Nawáb Sikandar Begam was, therefore, returned after her death; but three years later it was conferred upon her daughter and successor, Nawáb Shah Jahán Begam.

[3] In a description of this journey, Nawáb Sikandar Begam tells how she went to see the grand mosque of Shah Jahán. Its gates were closed, but as a special favour to her, the officers in charge caused them to be opened, and allowed her to enter. After describing the mosque, she writes nothing more on the subject. But Captain Hutchinson, formerly Political Agent in Bhopál, in a letter dated April 7, 1862, says that the mosque of Delhi had been closed by the orders of the Government of India on account of the behaviour of the Muhammadans of the city during the Mutiny, and that it was at the request of Nawáb Sikandar Begam that it was once more opened to the public. He also states that on its being reopened the Begam was the first person to enter and perform her prayers.

ating the commencement of my studies, was also performed at this time, and all the guests took part in the festivities connected with it.

In 1860, the Begam attended another durbar at Akbarábád, the famous capital of the Mughal Emperors, at which eighty-four Central Indian Chiefs were present. On entering the durbar hall, she was met by the Viceroy, who, after the usual formalities of welcome, said: "Lord Canning, on his return to London, spoke very highly of you to Her Majesty, who was greatly pleased, and said she would much like to see you!" In this durbar, she was also presented with a robe of honour, as a mark of appreciation of her wise and loyal government. Lord Lawrence, in the course of an able and instructive speech delivered in Urdu, and dealing with the principles of State administration, spoke as follows in praise of Nawáb Sikandar Begam and the Mahárája Sindhia: "The British Government will honour that Chief most who excels in the good management of his people, who does most to put down crime and improve the condition of his country. There are Chiefs in this durbar who have acquired a reputation in this way; I may mention the Mahárája Sindhia and the Begam of Bhopál."

I have not thought it necessary to describe these durbars at length, a full account of them being contained in my Mother's book. Nawáb Sikandar Begam, seeing her services so thankfully acknowledged and so liberally rewarded, determined to show her gratitude to Almighty God by making a pilgrimage to Mecca.[1] Accordingly, in 1280 A.H., her pious resolution was acccomplished, and, notwithstanding the difficulties and dangers of the journey, nearly fifteen hundred persons accompanied her. Thus, not only was she pre-eminent amongst contemporary Chiefs for the wisdom of her rule and the loyalty of her friendship to the British Throne, but she also enjoyed the distinction of being the first Muhammadan

[1] There is no duty more difficult for a Muhammadan lady than the performance of the *haj*; and history shows that, with the exception of Gulbadan Begam, the daughter-in-law of Akbar, no lady of the Timurian dynasty ever accomplished it.

ruler in India to perform the *haj*. The nobles and men of rank in Mecca showed her both honour and friendship, and the representatives of the Ottoman Empire received her with the respect and distinction to which her rank entitled her.

Nawáb Sikandar Begam lived for five years after her pilgrimage to Mecca. She departed this life on the evening of Friday, the 13th of the month Rajab, in the year 1285 A.H., and laid at the feet of her Creator the burdens of regency and sovereignty, which for twenty-three years she had faithfully borne.

God alone is immortal.

Nawáb Sikandar Begam, although born to rank and grandeur, loved simplicity, and was so averse from all forms of outward display that she even forbade the erection of a dome over her grave. To high and low alike she extended the same affable courtesy. Although a woman, she possessed all the soldierly qualities that had distinguished her predecessors. Her personality inspired both love and respect. In a word, the enlightened ability of her administration surpasses that of any other ruler whose lot it has been to govern unaided in times as critical. To this day her memory is cherished with honour and affection in the hearts of the people of Bhopál; and the grey-haired amongst them, who remember her days, delight to recount to their grandchildren stories of the fame, the power, the kindness, and the charity of her whom they love to call Sikandar the Good. During the twenty-three years of her reign, Bhopál was transformed into a new State. She saw the seed, which her own hands had sown, spring up, and become a goodly tree, and God lengthened her days that she might taste the fruit thereof. May her descendants, who dwell beneath its shade, so tend it that its leaves may ever remain green and its fruit become more and more abundant.

I have not space at my disposal to describe all the benefits of this happy reign. They may be summarized as follows: The State army was entirely remodelled; the revenue was increased from eleven to twenty-four lákhs; the debt of twenty-three lákhs left by Jahángír Muhammad Khán and Faujdár Muhammad Khán was paid off, and the mortgaged lands were redeemed; the State was divided up into *nizámats*,[1] and each *nizámat* was connected with the capital city by a metalled road; sanitary and other improvements were made in the city itself; the roads, which were before so narrow that only a *dooly* or a *sowár* could pass along them, were sufficiently widened to admit every kind of vehicle, and were properly illuminated at night; two large schools were opened; one, the Sulaimánia School, for the education of the inhabitants generally, and the other, the Victoria School, named after Her Majesty the Queen, for teaching trades and handicrafts; revenue and judicial laws were compiled, and a new and improved police force was organized for the detection of crime; and last, but by no means least, the administration of the *jágírs* was carefully and thoroughly reformed. Indeed, so successful was Nawáb Sikandar Begam in all her administrative undertakings, that Lord Lawrence, as we have already stated, in the presence of eighty-four ruling Chiefs, spoke of her as one whose example was worthy of imitation by all rulers of states. Ever attended by good fortune, her life was, indeed, one to excite men's envy. In return for the burdens of sovereignty she gained, not merely worldly prosperity and fame, but peace and everlasting rest for her spirit. Though she has passed away, her fair name remains. She is not dead, but living still in the hearts of her people, immortalized by her own good deeds.

Her desire for the firmness and permanency of British Rule was honest and sincere, and she lost no opportunity of giving practical proof of her good faith. After her death, Sir Henry Daly, Agent to the Governor-General, in his report to the Government of India, wrote as follows:

Perhaps in no Native State have the relations with the Government of India been accepted so cordially and firmly as in Bhopál. In the darkest hours of mutiny, with disaffection at her side, nothing turned the Sikandar Begam

[1] See Appendix D.

from her fidelity and allegiance. She possessed rare energy of character and capacity for government, and with all her energy and capacity she was true to British Rule. It was her pride to be known as the faithful Feudatory of the Queen of England; and almost her last breath was in prayer for the happiness of Her Majesty, her family, and Government.

On the news of her death, mourning was proclaimed at the Agency in Sehore, and on the day of burial all public offices and places of business in the city were closed. Through a letter addressed to Nawáb Shah Jahán Begam by the Duke of Argyll, Secretary of State for India, Her Majesty the Queen communicated her deep sorrow and regret at this "much-lamented event"; and, in offering her condolences to the family, expressed a hope that my Mother would endeavour to emulate the high virtues which had characterized the illustrious Princess whom she was succeeding.[1] Captain Hutchinson, Political Agent, Mr. Hamilton, Colonel Durand, Captain Eden, Colonel Meade, and many other gentlemen, including Sir Lepel Griffin, Agent to the Governor-General for Central India, have all, on many occasions, testified to the noble qualities of Nawáb Sikandar Begam, and to this day all communications from the supreme Government are preluded by a reference to her capacity and allegiance.

[1] The letter ran as follows:

INDIA OFFICE, LONDON, *July* 31st, 1869.

To HER HIGHNESS NAWAB SHAH JAHAN BEGAM OF BHOPAL.

MY ESTEEMED FRIEND,

I have received the commands of the Queen to communicate to Your Highness the sincere regret with which Her Majesty has learnt the death of your Mother, Her Highness Nawáb Sikandar Begam of Bhopál, and to offer to you her affectionate condolence on this much-lamented event. And I am, at the same time, to express to you Her Majesty's assurance that she feels every confidence that Your Highness will administer the country under your charge with the wisdom and benevolence which characterized the government of the illustrious Princess whom you have succeeded.

That Your Highness may enjoy length of days and continued prosperity is the heartfelt desire of

Your Highness's sincere friend and well-wisher,

(*Signed*) ARGYLL.

No account of the reign of Nawáb Sikandar Begam can be complete which does not make some reference to the chief nobles and Ministers of her Court. It is a happy thing for both ruler and ruled when those who hold high offices are men of integrity, diligence, ability, and enlightenment. And it is another instance of the good fortune which invariably attended Nawáb Sikandar Begam that her first and second Ministers, the Commander-in-Chief of her army, and her Private Secretary were all men endowed with the above-mentioned qualities.

Her First Minister was Maulavi Muhammad Jamál-ud-dín Khán Sáhib, a man known throughout Hindustán for the piety and simplicity of his life, and qualified in a unique manner for his important office. Besides being a theologian and a statesman, he possessed military talents of no mean order. History affords few instances of men so richly and so variously endowed. His piety was manifested by his zeal for religious instruction, and by his punctuality in the performance of religious rites. The assistance he gave to the Begam in the affairs of the State, and the impartiality and justice which he brought to bear on his ministerial functions, prove his ability and enlightenment. It is a sufficient proof of his soldierly qualities that at the time when railways, bicycles, and motor-cars were unknown, he thought nothing of mounting a camel at nine o'clock at night and riding to Indore, a distance of more than a hundred miles. Reaching this place in eight hours, he would transact his business with the Agent to the Governor-General, start on his return journey at three o'clock in the afternoon, and reach Bhopál the same night. For a considerable period of time he was obliged to perform this journey once, and sometimes twice, in a week. He enjoyed the full confidence of the Begam and the political officers, and his loyalty to the State was only equalled by that of his mistress to the British Government. A *jágír* of twenty-eight thousand rupees was conferred upon him. He survived the Begam by fourteen years, and witnessed many of those revolutionary changes by which her death was followed, changes by which he himself was

NAWAB SIKANDAR BEGAM WITH HER FIRST AND SECOND MINISTERS.

p. 16]

not a little affected. His old age was troubled by the envy and ingratitude of one of his own relatives, Muhammad Sidik Hasan Khán. The treatment which the old Minister met with at the hands of this man would have been esteemed inhuman had it been meted out to an alien and an enemy. Sidik Hasan Khán used every endeavour to undermine his power and influence, hoping thereby to drive him from his office and to become himself the First Minister of the State. Muhammad Jamál-ud-dín often, and with sorrow, confided to me the afflictions of his later days. He showed me much kindness, and taught me both Arabic and Persian, and I acknowledge, with all a pupil's gratitude, the excellence of his methods of instruction. He departed this life in the year 1299 A.H., without male issue, but leaving behind him daughters to perpetuate his race. The mosques and other buildings which he made are memorials of him that time may obliterate ; but his generous and kindly nature made for him other memorials in the hearts of his fellow men which time cannot spoil. Nor will his piety be forgotten ; rather will the memory of it be kept ever fresher and more fresh—not by the mosques which he built, but by the prayers of the pious by which five times daily those mosques will be beautified.

The name of the Second Minister was Rája Kishen Rám. He was a member of the Kayásth section of the Hindu community, and a clever *munshi*. He was also an able and sagacious revenue officer, and during his tenure of office he brought the revenue department, of which he was the head, to a high state of efficiency. Like Birbál, in the days of Akbar, he may be counted as one of the jewels of the Court.

Háfiz Muhammad Hasan Khán, Nasrat-i-Jang, was the Commander-in-Chief of the State army. He was raised to this office after having gained military experience under his predecessor, Bakshi Murawwat Muhammad Khán. At the time of the Mutiny, when his fellow officers were engaged in protecting the city, he was appointed to command that portion of the State army which was dispatched to help the English in maintaining peace in the neighbouring districts. It is enough to say that, by his distinguished services

2

in behalf of law and order, by his faithfulness to the State, and by the conscientiousness which characterized all his acts, he won the regard and honour both of the Begam and of the British Government. He was decorated with a medal, and made a Companion of the Star of India. Of the distinguished servants of Nawáb Sikandar Begam, Bakshi Muhammad Hasan Khán was the only one who survived till my own reign. He was a brave man, and of a generous and honourable disposition. He died in 1321 A.H. The Private Secretary was Munshi Husein Khán. He was my English teacher, and he also filled the post of Private Secretary to my Mother, Nawáb Shah Jahán Begam.

In this connection it is fitting that I should make mention of those political officers whose sympathy and single-mindedness contributed so largely to the success of the reign of Nawáb Sikandar Begam, and won for them the deep gratitude both of that ruler and of her successors. The memory of their friendship and honourable dealings will be an heritage to the people of Bhopál for many generations. When it became manifest that the administration of Faujdár Muhammad Khán was in the highest degree injurious to the State, Captain Eden and Captain Joseph Cunningham supported the claims of Nawáb Sikandar Begam, and, by expelling Faujdár Muhammad Khán from his office, caused her to be appointed regent in his stead. Her subsequent appointment as actual ruler of the State was brought about by Sir Richmond Shakespeare and Captain Hutchinson. These officers themselves placed her on the *masnad* on the 9th of Shawwál, 1276 A.H., and proclaimed Nawáb Shah Jahán Begam heir-apparent. There can be no doubt that this act was as wise as it was just. From Colonel Meade and Major Durand [1] she received both good advice and sympathy, and in the making of the settlement, and the reforms in the administration of *jágírs*, she owed much to their assistance. It is no mere figure of speech when I say that it is to officers such as these that England owes

[1] Major (afterwards Sir) Henry Marion Durand was acting for Sir Robert Hamilton as Agent to the Governor-General for Central India at the time of the Mutiny. The following is a list of the Agents to the Governor-

COLONEL J. W. WILLOUGHBY-OSBORNE.

SIR RICHARD MEADE.

SIR ROBERT HAMILTON.

p. 18]

her fame and her prosperity—men endowed with those qualities of heart and mind which it is the peculiar pride of the English race to possess, and which have gained for it superiority over every other nation in the world. In Bhopál their names will ever be remembered with respect, gratitude, and affection.

General during the reigns of Nawáb Sikandar Begam and Nawáb Shah Jahán Begam:

Sir Robert Hamilton	1854–1859
Colonel Sir Richmond Shakespeare	1859–1861
Colonel (afterwards General Sir) Richard Meade	1861–1869
Lieut.-General Sir H. Daly	1869–1881
Sir Lepel Griffin	1881–1888
Mr. F. Henvey	1888–1890
Mr. (afterwards Sir) R. Crosthwaite	1890–1894
Colonel (afterwards Sir) David W. K. Barr	1894–1900
Mr. C. S. Bayley, C.S.I.	1900–1905

CHAPTER III

MY CHILDHOOD

THE description of my early life contained in the *Táj-ul-Ikbal* is so brief and void of detail, that it seems to me better that I should myself give some account of my education and general training, and the way in which the days of my childhood were passed.

I was born in the year 1274 A.H. (A.D. 1858), and I cannot help recording this fact with feelings of pride, for it was a year rich in memorable events, and the forerunner of a prosperous and happy era. Before the year 1857, as my readers know, the English, although masters of India, left the administration of its affairs in the hands of a Company, and many parts of the country were still in a disturbed and lawless state. Railways and the telegraph had but just been introduced; trunk-roads and district highways were few and ill-maintained; higher education was scarcely thought of, and schools existed only in a few of the large cities. Backwardness was visible on every side; and, if the country was advancing at all, its progress was too slow to be apparent. But it pleased God that this state of affairs should come to an end. The Mutiny of '57 was not a mere chance event. It may be wiser to draw a veil over its dark tragedies; but let us not forget that it was a touchstone on which, if the loyalty of some turned to dross, that of many others showed bright and clear; and that, if its darkness was black, it was the darkness that came before the dawn.

The year 1858 is a memorable one in the annals of India. It witnessed the restoration of peace, the abolition of the Company, and the assumption by Her Majesty Queen Victoria of the reins of government. It witnessed the arrival of her Majesty's Dispatch, the Magna Carta of India, which, like a sun rising in the West, brought life and vigour to the fainting East, and dispersing the clouds of ignorance, insecurity, and distrust, spread in their stead the light of peace, progress, and knowledge. And it witnessed the beginning of that rule which, though ushered in by the sword, has won, by its beneficence and justice, the willing obedience of a loyal people. The year 1858 was, in fact, the standard-bearer, behind whom marched the armies of civilization and progress, led onward by Western thought and Western enterprise, to do battle against the darkness of this land. If my birth at this time is not a thing on which I have a right to pride myself, I must at least regard it as a high privilege, and one for which I shall never cease to thank Almighty God.

Before my birth even my own country was not free from the troubles of revolt. In the district of Gadhi Ambapáni a rising had taken place, set on foot by Fázil Muhammad Khán. Nawáb Sikandar Begam was greatly distressed at the prolongation of these disturbances, and was much concerned on account of the hardships which they entailed on her troops; for scarcely had they had time to draw breath after their services during the Mutiny, when this second revolt broke out, and threw the whole district once more into the wildest confusion. This happened about six months before my birth, and, as the Begam was one day meditating upon the difficulties which surrounded her, she made a vow that if, by the grace of God, the revolt could be put down ere these six months were past, the district of Ambapáni should become her grandchild's *jágír*. She prayed that it might happen according to her wish, and her prayer was granted. For it is written in His Holy Word, "Whatsoever ye shall ask in faith, ye shall receive." The insurrection was quelled; and when, on the 27th of the month Zil Kádah, in the year 1274 A.H. (July 10th, 1858), my birth took place, the above-mentioned district became my *jágír*.[1]

[1] *Jágír.* Persian *Já*, "a place"; *Gir*, "occupying." "A tenure common under the Muhammadan Government, in which the public revenue

Both the Kudsia Begam and Nawáb Sikandar Begam had looked forward to the birth of a son, for it was a matter of sorrow to them that for fifty-eight years no male child had been born in the family. When, contrary to these hopes, I made my entrance into the world, the Begam showed none of the regret which the birth of a girl might naturally have been expected to cause; and as soon as she saw me, animated by I know not what thoughts and emotions, she clasped me in her arms and said, "Thank God I am not one of those about whom it is written:

> "'And when any of them is told of the birth of a female, his face becometh black, and he is deeply afflicted.'[1]

This child is dearer to me than seven sons." Indeed, had a son been born, she could not have rejoiced more.

The news of my birth was proclaimed by a salute of guns, and entertainments and feasts were provided for all the servants of the State, as well as for the general public both in the city and in the districts, while presents of clothes were distributed among the poor. For six months these rejoicings continued, shared by nobles and commons alike. My birth, coinciding as it did with the advent of the new era, gave a double signification to the occasion, and on every side the air resounded with the music of peace and happiness.

Before I had reached the age of two years, Nawáb Sikandar Begam had been confirmed as the ruler of the State, and the law of succession had been established. At the Jabbalpúr durbar the district of Bairasía had been formally made over to the State, thus increasing both its area and its population: and the Begam had had the honour of receiving a *khilát*, and of being invested with the Most Exalted Order of the Star

of a given tract of land was made over to a servant of the State, together with the powers requisite to enable him to collect such revenue, and administer the general government of the district. . . . The assignment was either for a stated term, or, more usually, for the lifetime of the holder, lapsing, on his death, to the State, although not unusually renewed to his heir, and sometimes specified to be a hereditary assignment, without which specification it was held to be a life-tenure only" (Hughes' *Dictionary of Islam*).

[1] Sale's translation of the Korán.

of India. It is no wonder, then, that she regarded my birth as an auspicious event. Day by day she treated me with more and more kindness. Indeed, her love for me outweighed that of my parents and of all the other members of my family combined. I was the main object of her life, around which all her hopes and pleasures centred. Whenever she went on tour, she used to leave me in the care of my Mother, lest the difficulties of travelling through hilly regions and over rough roads might prove too much for me; but she never failed to arrange that news of my welfare should reach her daily. And although I was so young that I could neither read nor understand what was read to me, yet she continually wrote letters to me full of expressions of love and affection. After my marriage, these letters were given to me by my Mother, and, although I neither remember receiving them nor hearing them read, I never look upon them now without pleasure.

For the first five years of my life I experienced only my Grandmother's fostering care, play being the sole matter to which I gave any serious attention. At the close of this period the foundation of my education was laid, with the customary invocation of the divine blessing. A regular course of study was prescribed for me, and my daily routine was as follows:

Before Noon

From	5	o'clock	to	6.	Open-air exercise.
,,	6	,,	,,	7.	Morning meal.
,,	8	,,	,,	10.	Study of the Korán.
,,	10	,,	,,	11.	Breakfast with Nawáb Sikandar Begam.
,,	11	,,	,,	12.	Recreation.

After Noon

,,	12	,,	,,	1.	Handwriting lesson.
,,	1	,,	,,	3.	English lesson.
,,	3	,,	,,	4.	Persian lesson.
,,	4	,,	,,	5.	Arithmetic.
,,	5	,,	,,	5.30.	Pashtu lessons and fencing practice alternately.
,,	5.30	,,	,,	6.	Riding lesson.
,,	6	,,	,,	7.	Evening meal

And so at 8 o'clock to bed.

The following were my teachers:

Study of the Korán	Háfiz Syad Muhammad Surati.
Translation and *tafais* of the Korán	Maulavi Jamál-ud-dín.
Handwriting	Razá Ali Shírín Rakam.
English	Munshi Husein Khán.
Persian	Maulavi Bukhári.
Arithmetic	Guru Jí Pandit Ganpat Rai.
Fencing	Syad Amír Ali.
Riding	Ustád Hakdad Khán.
Pashtu	Akhánd Sáhib.

All the arrangements connected with my education, health, and guardianship were in the hands of my Grandmother, and I remained by her side day and night, three evenings only in each week being spent with my Mother. In 1280 A.H. my Grandmother performed the *haj*. Distressed at the idea of being separated from me, she had desired to take me with her on her pilgrimage, together with my Mother and my Father, Nawáb Umrao Dula. The Nawáb Sáhib was quite willing to go, but my mother was so terrified at the thought of a journey by sea, and made so many stipulations, that the idea of taking her had to be abandoned; and, consequently, the Nawáb Sáhib also was obliged to remain behind. The Begam set out from Bhopál on the 24th of Jamádi-ul-awwal, 1280 A.H. (November 5th, 1863), and the moment when she took her farewell of me is still fresh in my mind. There is no doubt that the parting was a great trial to her, and nothing but her desire to show her gratitude to God, and the knowledge that she was performing a religious duty, would have reconciled her to it. Every post brought letters from her, containing injunctions in regard to my education, besides numerous other instructions for my Mother, which clearly manifested the anxiety she was in on my account. The following are but a few out of the many that I received:

"ADEN, *7th Shábán*, 1280.

"I thank God that to-day, Saturday, the 7th of Shábán, 1280 A.H., at 2 p.m., our good ship *Indore* reached Aden in safety, and all of us are well. Whenever you think of me, make ablutions, and perform *namáz* on the prayer-mat which was sewn for you by Zafran, and pray for your Grandmother, and ask God to bring her back safe and well from the *haj*."

"ADEN, *8th Shábán*, 1280.

"I have bought for you, on board the ship, a box with a small space to hold an inkpot, and another to keep your letters in; also a small tooth-powder casket, a tea-kettle, a cup, a sweetmeat basket, and a bouquet of real sea flowers that grow in the sea; and I am sending them, together with similar presents for Sulaiman Jahán Begam, with this letter. Give your sister's share to her, and keep your own. The coloured ruler which I am sending is for you only, and not for Sulaiman Jahán Begam."

"MECCA, *17th Shawwál*, 1280.

"I have received your two letters of the 2nd Ramazán, and I heartily thank God to hear that you are quite well. But the letters are not signed by you. I understand that Nawáb Shah Jahán Begam Sáhiba has asked Kanwál Sen to write answers to my letters addressed to you; but he has neglected to make you sign them. In future, whenever you receive a letter from me, you should go to Rája Sáhib Bahádur, and dictate an answer to it with your own lips. Your seal that was with Injir Nána I am now sending you through Háji Husein, the Agent of Háji Ismail, and, God willing, you will soon receive it. I learn from the letter of Munshi Husein Khán that you still cry whilst reading the Korán, and that you have to be punished. You must remember that you are almost grown up, and that it is, therefore, a great shame for you to cry while you are reading, and to have to be punished. It is quite time that you gave up this bad habit. Whenever you are tired of reading, and you want to do something else, you should tell your teacher so, but do not cry. When you have finished reading you can go to Alík-ullah and practise handwriting. Always tell me about Sulaiman Jahán Begam in your letters."

"MECCA, *28th Shawwál*, 1280.

"To the fruit of the tree of my heart, the star of my prosperity and good luck, Sultán Jahán Begam. May God enhance her happiness and prolong her life.

"I learn from the letter of Munshi Husein Khán that you very often think of me, and grieve very much over our separation. Now, therefore, I write to tell you that when children are parted from their parents they should pray to God for reunion, and He will grant their prayer, and bring back their parents to them. I told you before I left Bhopál that, God willing, I should return after a year. Now there are 12 months in a year, and 30 days in a month; and if you go to the Rája Sáhib he will help you to find out how many days there are in a year, and then you will know when I am coming back. I should like to know what words you are learning to write now; so send me some of your copy-books. When you dictate your letters to me, say everything that comes into your mind: but, dear child, do not grieve for me at all. God willing, I will return as soon as I have performed my *haj*. Your Injir Nána performs the *tawáf*[1] oftener than any one else. He prays continually for your health, prosperity, and long life. He hopes you will finish the Korán before we return, and that you no longer cry whilst reading it, for it is our Sacred Book, and it is our duty to study it cheerfully."

These letters I read with the most eager joy; but how much greater was my pleasure when, after the expiration of a year, came the news of my grandmother's approaching return! On the day of her arrival, my Father, Nawáb Umrao Dula, together with all the nobles and chief officials of the State, assembled at Sikandarábád, three miles outside Bhopál, to bid her welcome; and, to my great joy, I was taken with them. As soon as her cavalcade came in sight, she saw me, though she was yet a long way off, for we were both mounted on elephants. Instinctively she stretched out her arms to me, and I remember how I wished that I had wings that I might fly to her. In a short time our elephants were side by side, and the next moment I was in her lap. Until the appointed halting-place was reached she continued to shower blessings and caresses upon me, while tears of joy and thankfulness fell from her eyes. Those, indeed, are pleasant days to recall, days when I was absolute monarch in child-

[1] *Tawáf* means making the circuit of the House of the Caaba at Mecca. It is one of the principal ceremonies connected with the pilgrimage, and is often repeated many times. "And let them pay their vows; and compass the ancient house" (Sale's Translation of the Korán, ch. xxii.).

hood's happy kingdom, with trouble, sorrow, and care banished from my dominions.

One of the first things Nawáb Sikandar Begam did after her return was to put me through an examination, to find out what progress my education had made during her absence. Since I had taken care to follow to the letter the injunctions she had given me, I passed this test with credit, and became a greater favourite with her than ever. My studies went regularly on, and whenever the Political Agent, or any other English gentleman, came to Bhopál, the Begam used to ask him to examine me in English, and to write me a certificate as to the result of the examination. The object of this expedient was two-fold ; it was meant to stimulate my own zeal for study, and to enable my Grandmother, who was not acquainted with English, to form a correct idea of the progress I was making. These certificates, of which the following will serve as examples, I have carefully preserved to this day.

"BOMBAY CASTLE, *May 8th*, 1866.

"*To* HER HIGHNESS SULTAN JAHAN BEGAM OF
"BHOPAL

"YOUR HIGNHESS,

"I have received your kind letter written in Persian and English, and was gratified to observe the progress you are making in your studies.

"Accept my best wishes for your welfare and happiness, in which Lady Frere joins me, and believe me,

"Your sincere friend,
(*Signed*) "W. E. FRERE."

"GWALIOR AGENCY, *New Year's Day*, 1867.

"I am greatly pleased to have had an opportunity of hearing the Princess Sultán Jahán repeat her lessons. Her Highness can read English in the First Reader fluently and correctly, has been well and carefully grounded in the first rules of Grammar, and altogether possesses a knowledge of the language which, considering her tender years, gives great promise for the future, and is very creditable to her instructor.

"I hope some day to have an opportunity of certifying to still higher attainments on the part of the Princess, who, having thus early begun the ascent of the ladder of learning, requires only continued diligence and attention to surmount every step, and thus to qualify herself for the exalted position she will one day occupy.

(*Signed*) "A. W. HUTCHINSON,
"*Political Agent, Gwálior.*"

In the year 1284 A.H., my renowned and honoured father, Nawáb Umrao Dula, died. My love for my Grandmother, combined with my tender age, did much to mitigate my grief, but my Grandmother herself felt the blow very keenly. Indeed, her heart never entirely recovered from this sorrow, and she never ceased to deplore the loss of one who had proved himself a loyal and obedient son-in-law, as well as a kind and loving husband. Who could have believed that, ere the expiration of sixteen months, she herself would have passed away from this world! My age at the time of her death, which, as I have already mentioned, took place in 1285 A.H., was 10 years and 7 months, but I can feel as plainly as if it were yesterday the grief which fell upon me. Her kindly deeds are ever in my mind, her wise counsels come daily to my aid, and I never cease to pray for the welfare of her soul.

I now commenced to live permanently with my mother, Nawáb Shah Jahán Begam, but my mind was constantly depressed with sad thoughts. My Mother sincerely sympathized with me, and gave me all the consolation in her power. I was now her only child, for her younger daughter, Sulaiman Jahán Begam,[1] died of small-pox at the age of five, in the year 1282 A.H. In these altered circumstances the arrangements for my education were entirely changed. The handwriting exercises were given up altogether, and my usual hours of study dwindled down to four a day. In my Mother's eyes it was much more important that I should acquire ex-

[1] Sáhibzádi Sulaiman Jahán Begam was born on the 12th of Jamádi-ul-awwal, about three years after my own birth. Although she had been vaccinated, she was attacked by small-pox. The physician who treated her, Hakím Ján Sáhib, mistook the nature of the disease from which she was suffering, and administered the wrong medicine, which did her great harm. She died on the 13th of Muharram, 1282 A.H.

p. 28]

NAWAB SULTAN JAHAN BEGAM.
(Aged 11 years.)

perience in domestic and official duties, than that I should progress in scholarly knowledge. The Korán I had read through before I was eleven years old; but I was now made to study it a second time, and for an hour daily Maulavi Jamál-ud-dín was employed in explaining to me the Holy Book and its commentaries. I read English for two hours a day, and Persian for one hour. These were the only actual lessons I had, but in addition to them I was made to read, and write orders upon various official papers which it was now Her Highness's practice to send me daily. The following *parwánahs*[1] which I received from time to time will give some idea of the system under which I was educated after my Grandmother's death:

(1) It has been brought to my notice that at the present time your studies are not being pursued with regularity, and it is not clear in what manner you employ your time from morning till evening. These are the hours which you should devote to study. You are, therefore, to draw up a time-table of the work that you are doing. On receiving this, I will myself send you a revised time-table for your daily guidance.

(2) You are to study the Holy Korán, with translation, from 7 a.m. till 9 a.m. with the Madár-ul-muhám Sáhib. You may then take your morning meal and rest. Between 2 and 4 p.m., you are to read the official papers which I shall send to you, and write on them any orders that you consider necessary. After 4 o'clock, your time is at your own disposal. You may go for a walk, or attend to household matters, or employ yourself in any way that you like.

(3) I am pleased to send you two certificates in English: one from Major Hutchinson, Political Agent in Gwalior, and the other from Major Wood. These certificates you should regard as a *sanad*. I hope that you will so persevere with your English studies that you may gain many more such certificates.

[1] The Persian word *parwánah* signifies, literally, a written order. It is a common term for any vernacular letter addressed to a subordinate officer.

(4) I have received your letter in which you say that you would like to send your files of official papers to me, so that I may see the orders that you have passed upon them. I am very glad to grant your request. Let all the papers, along with drafts of your orders, be sent to me. It will be still better if you yourself come to me, so that you may more easily understand the corrections that have to be made in them.

(5) You are to sign all urgent papers every day, and those that are not marked urgent twice a week, just as I myself am accustomed to do. I hope that you will strictly observe these instructions, so that the people concerned may not complain of delay.

On the first day of Shábán, in the year 1285 A.H. (November 16th, 1868), Nawáb Shah Jahán Begam ascended the throne, and I, at the same time, was proclaimed heir-apparent and received a *khilát* At a durbar held on this occasion, at which Colonel Meade, Agent to the Governor-General in Central India, and Colonel Osborne, C.B., Political Agent in Bhopál, were present, I made the first speech of my life. It was as follows:

"I thank God, who of His great goodness has advanced me to this dignity, and I thank the Agent to the Governor-General for Central India, and the Political Agent in Bhopál, who have appointed me heir-apparent, and my Mother ruler of Bhopál: I pray that the merciful God will keep me loyal to the British Government during the whole of my life."

All those who were present were delighted with my speech, and marvelled that one so young could speak with such clearness and confidence.

When a Muhammadan child has completed the reading of the Holy Korán it is customary to mark the occasion with great rejoicings, and for this purpose the ceremony of *nashrah* takes place. In the case of both my Mother and my Grandmother the *nashrah* had been performed with great splendour. So in 1288 A.H., my Mother decided that my own *nashrah* should be celebrated; and since this was the first occasion on which she had ever arranged a ceremony for me, it was performed on a grand and liberal scale. Invitations were sent to the European officers at the Residency and the Agency, and to the neighbouring Chiefs, and entertainments were also provided for the servants of the State and the citizens of Bhopál. Every night the streets were illuminated, and brilliant displays of fireworks took place. Festivities of various kinds were continued throughout a whole month, the entire cost amounting to Rs. 2,96,419. 9. 6.

In the same year Nawáb Shah Jahán Begam married her second husband, Sidik Hasan Khán, an event which marked the commencement of one of the unhappiest periods of my life. Intrigue became rife in the palace, and every kind of attempt was made to undermine my Mother's affection for me. The story of these days is best left untold, and I shall now pass on to the only event of interest which took place during the time that I remained in my Mother's charge, namely, my marriage, an account of which will form a fitting conclusion to the history of my early life.

CHAPTER IV

NAWAB BAKI MUHAMMAD KHAN

IT is necessary that I should, at this point, give a brief account of my Father and his family that my readers may be able to understand the reasons which led Nawáb Sikandar Begam to select as the husband of her daughter a stranger from the Mishti Khail. This Khail, or clan, like that of my Mother, the Mirázi Khail, was amongst the most famous in the Tirah country. The Afrídí, Aurakzai, and Mishti Khail usually lived in the same region, and enjoyed a reputation similar to many other brave and warlike tribes. The founder of the Indian branch of this family was my great-grandfather, Ali Bayázid Khán. He migrated from Afghánistán, and, as the Mirázi Khail were his friends and countrymen, he settled in Bhopál.

His advent was a great joy to every one, and particularly to Nawáb Wazír Muhammad Khán: for the times were stormy, and the arrival of Bayázid Khán was nothing less than a god-send to him. He was at once given a post in the army, as were also his two sons Bahádur Muhammad Khán and Bagh Muhammad Khán, who, though young in years, had the bearing of brave and high-spirited youths. Ali Bayázid Khán performed his military duties in a manner befitting a man of birth and courage, and day by day, until his death, the Nawáb's respect and affection for him increased. His death was soon followed by that of his son Bagh Muhammad Khán. Bahádur Muhammad Khán, the elder, proved to be a true son of his father, and continually gave proof of his loyalty and courage, while the Nawáb reposed such confidence in him that he selected him to be companion to his own son,

NAWAB UMRAO DULA.

p. 32]

Nazar Muhammad Khán. A short time afterwards, when Bhopál was besieged by Jagva Bapu,[1] he entrusted the defence of the gateway of the Old Fort to these two young men, whilst he himself looked to the defence of the other entrances. At this time the Nawáb had very few men at his disposal, and it had become necessary that every side of the fort and city should be defended. At each gateway, therefore, was posted a body of from fifty to sixty men under the command of two Sirdars. The Old Fort gateway, however, inasmuch as it was on the edge of a lake, was considered to be less vulnerable than the others, and a smaller force was set apart for its defence. This fact became known to the besiegers, who attacked the gateway in such large numbers that they forced an entrance into the city. Nazar Muhammad Khán and Bahádur Muhammad Khán displayed all the courage and warlike qualities characteristic of their race. Bahádur Muhammad Khán was wounded in many places, but with great bravery continued to maintain his ground, and, with only a handful of men to oppose the overwhelming odds against him, kept the fight going with such vigour that his enemies were filled with confusion. Intelligence of what was taking place in this quarter reached Nawáb Wazír Muhammad Khán, and his arrival in the nick of time with reinforcements turned their confusion into a complete defeat.

At the conclusion of this war Bahádur Muhammad Khán, in reward for the conspicuous services he had rendered, was raised by the Nawáb to the position of Commander-in-Chief of the forces of Bhopál. Day by day Bahádur Muhammad Khán added to the dignity of his office, and enjoyed till his last hour the reputation of a brave and skilful commander. The following instance of his loyalty and gratitude is worthy to be inscribed in letters of gold. When Jahángír Muhammad Khán took up the reins of government, a dispute arose between him and Nawáb Sikandar Begam, and to such lengths did

[1] Jagva Bapu was the General who commanded the forces of Sindhia. For an account of the siege of Bhopál by the combined forces of Gwálior and Nagpúr the reader is referred to *The History of Bhopál*, by Nawáb Shah Jahán Begam, and to Sir J. Malcolm's *Memoirs of Central India*.

the Nawáb carry his resentment, that he actually inflicted a sword wound on the Begam's person. With a view to putting an end to this unhappy feud, it was arranged that a *jágír* of five lákhs of rupees should be granted to Nawáb Kudsia Begam, and that she, together with her daughter, Sikandar Begam, should take up her abode at Islámnagar. Accordingly, when they were about to set out for this place, they inquired of Bahádur Muhammad Khán whether he would prefer to retain the office and rank of Commander-in-Chief of the Bhopál army, or whether he would abandon his high position and retire with them to Islámnagar and obscurity. Bahádur Muhammad Khán's reply, given with cheerful sincerity, was as follows: "That I have obtained rank and honours is due to the favour and goodness of Nawáb Wazír Muhammad Khán and Nawáb Ghaus Muhammad Khán. Neither I nor my children will ever stoop to such ingratitude as to desert the daughters of our benefactors in their hour of need. I count a cake of barley-bread at their hands in Islámnagar better than a thousand luxuries in this city, and a humble place in their service more honourable than to hold the command of the army of the State." The spirit of gratitude which animated the father manifested itself in no less a degree in the persons of his two sons, Sadar Muhammad Khán and Báki Muhammad Khán (afterwards Nawáb Umrao Dula), who likewise prized the friendship of the two Begams beyond all other honours. For seven years, therefore, Nawáb Kudsia Begam and Nawáb Sikandar Begam lived in retirement at Islámnagar; and when, at the close of this period, the latter assumed the regency, Bahádur Muhammad Khán was again restored to his office. On his death he was succeeded by his elder son, Sadar Muhammad Khán, and when he died without issue his younger brother, that is to say my own revered Father, became Commander-in-Chief of the forces of the State.

My Father was esteemed as well for his handsome appearance as for his noble disposition. Indeed, his bravery and comeliness have passed into a proverb. Even in his childhood the charm of his person and the grace of his manner captivated all who came in contact with him, and he possessed all the qualities necessary to make a fine General. From the first, Nawáb Sikandar Begam was deeply attached to him; and, indeed, he was worthy of her affection both on account of his own services and those of his family. The Begam was a shrewd and keen observer of human nature, and, judging Báki Muhammad Khán to be a proper man for her son-in-law, she deemed that his marriage with her daughter, Shah Jáhan Begam, and the consequent union of the two clans, would form a fitting recognition of the many services his family had rendered. Accordingly, with the knowledge and approval of the Government of India, this marriage was celebrated on the 11th day of the month Zikád, in the year 1271 A.H. (July 26th, 1855). The Government of India presented the Nawáb with a *khilát*,[1] and awarded him, at the Begam's request, a salute of seventeen guns. Orders were also issued for his suitable reception at public ceremonies, and the title Umrao Dula Nazír-ud-daulah was conferred upon him.[2]

No son could have been more devoted to his mother than was the Nawáb to Sikandar Begam. This devotion sprang as much from a sense of duty as from the natural warm-heartedness of his race. The Begam in her turn bestowed upon him all a mother's affection. At the time of the Mutiny, Nawáb Umrao Dula had, in consequence of his royal marriage, relinquished his position as Commander of the forces of the State, and the appointment had been conferred on Bakshi Murawwat Muhammad Khán, his sister's son-in-law. But since the Begam was aware of his intimate knowledge of military affairs, and of his influence over the troops, she used, even in times of peace, to take him into her counsel in all matters connected with the army; in fact, she looked upon him as her Minister of War. The outbreak of the rebellion filled him with anxiety and alarm, which were intensified by the dangers and perplexities of the Begam's position. He

[1] A *khilát* is a "dress of honour presented by a Ruler to an inferior, as a mark of distinction. A complete *khilát* may include arms, or a horse, or an elephant" (Hughes' *Dictionary of Islam*).

[2] It was on the strength of this precedent that a salute and similar honours were conferred upon Sidik Hasan Khán at the time of his marriage.

did all that lay in his power to keep the State free from disturbance, and to carry out Her Highness's desire to help the English, and to prevent the roads leading to the city from being blocked. To add to his difficulties, news was brought that Fázil Muhammad Khán and Adil Muhammad Khán, two Jágírdárs of Ambapáni, had joined the insurrection; and, at the same time, signs of unrest were becoming apparent amongst the troops in the city and the Fort. Under the instructions of the Begam, Nawáb Umrao Dula took immediate steps to cope with these difficulties, and worked day and night devising and directing plans of operation. Every day reports from the *mufassal* came pouring in upon him, each requiring his immediate instructions, while the officers entrusted with the task of maintaining tranquillity in the outlying districts were all looking to him for orders and guidance. His untiring energy at this juncture, and his skilful conduct of affairs, were admirably set forth in the records of the State; but, unfortunately, every paper bearing on the subject was destroyed by certain malicious persons who were envious of his fair name. Copies, however, of many of his orders are still to be found in the families of the officers to whom they were originally dispatched, being treasured as honourable relics and proofs of faithful service; and from these some idea of his presence of mind and promptness in times of emergency may be gained. I quote three of them:

Copy of an order of Nawáb Nazír-ud-daulah Umrao Dula, Báki Muhammad Khán, addressed to Muhammad Shams-ud-dín Ansári:

"*1st Muharram*, 1275 A.H.

"The communication of Háfiz Muhammad Khán, Naib Bakshi, dated 21st Zil Hijjah, has informed me that last night you, together with the said Naib Bakshi, came into collision with Adil Muhammad Khán and his followers, and, with great courage and military skill, inflicted on them a severe defeat, not only killing a large number, but capturing their provisions, arms, and beasts of burden. This signal proof of your loyalty and courage has given me the greatest satisfaction, and you have won the high regard both of Her Highness the Begam

CAPTAIN MATTU KHAN, AFTERWARDS NAIB BAKSHI. HAFIZ MUHAMMAD KHAN NAIB BAKSHI. BAKSHI MURAWWUT MUHAMMAD KHAN.

p. 36]

and of myself. Let it be your study to live up to the reputation you have gained, and to continue to deserve our high praise. Keep this order as a mark of my favour, and as a testimony to the good name you have won."

Copy of the orders of Nawáb Nazír-ud-daulah Umrao Dula, Báki Muhammad Khán Bahádur, dated 7th Muharram, 1275 A.H. :

" A copy of this petition, together with the orders passed thereon (dated 6th Muharram, 1275 A.H.), is to be forwarded to Nawáb Sikandar Begam for information ; the original is to be sent to Lálá Naubat Rai to be filed. A copy of these orders is also to be sent to Munshi Shams-ud-dín, who, with two patrols, should proceed to Ghairatganj, and with the help of the servants of the *mahal* and the *thána*, and in consultation with the Kámdár and his deputy, should endeavour to restore order in the town, and take steps to punish the rebels. He should keep Her Highness informed of all that takes place, and of any particulars which he can give concerning the whereabouts of the rebels, and of Adil Muhammad Khán. A second copy is to be sent to Gadhuri Lál, with instructions to furnish two patrols from the company of Jamadárs. Razá Husein is to accompany Munshi Shams-ud-dín to Ghairat-ganj. A third copy is to be sent to the petitioner Lálá Durga Parshád, Thánadár, with the information that Munshi Shams-ud-dín has been sent to his help with two patrols, and instructing him, with the aid of these men, and the servants of the *mahal* and the *thána*, to take the necessary steps for the restoration of good order in the town, for safeguarding the property of the inhabitants, and for protecting the chief buildings, roads, and gháts, and restoring confidence amongst the people of the town and the surrounding villages, so that the insurgents may not dare to show themselves again in that neighbourhood. The recipients of these orders must be day and night on the alert, and must show neither fear nor hesitation in the performance of the duty that has been entrusted to them, and must before all things put their trust in the Great Helper of mankind."

A copy of the orders of Nawáb Nazír-ud-daulah Umrao Dula, Báki Muhammad Khán Sáhib Bahádur, dated 19th

Rabi-ud-awwal, 1275 A.H., and endorsed on the application of Munshi Shams-ud-dín Ansári:

"A copy of this petition is to be forwarded with my endorsement to Nawáb Sikandar Begam Sáhiba. A copy is also to be sent to Munshi Shams-ud-dín, who is to be informed that his letter from Raisen, dated 9th Rabi-ul-awwal, regarding the insurgents, reached me this day some three hours before sunset. It is essential that he should inform Her Highness of any facts regarding the insurgents that may have come to his knowledge. He must, by any means that may be possible, reach Ghairat-ganj, and, having arrived there, he must take every precaution necessary for the protection of the town, and do his utmost to restore order and tranquillity amongst the inhabitants."

My Father dealt with the mutinous spirit of the troops in a very masterly fashion. Boldly, and without any sign of excitement or anxiety, he conducted Nawáb Sikandar Begam to the lines, and requested her to address the soldiers. She at once complied, and, briefly, but with great earnestness, exhorted them to be loyal to herself and to their duty. Her speech was followed up by a soldierly and eloquent oration from the Nawáb himself. Their words took effect with the speed of lightning. In a few moments every trace of insubordination had vanished, and the army, which had previously exhibited all the symptoms of mutiny, was brought to submission and obedience. But the Nawáb did not stop here. He called to mind, and acted upon, the well-known saying of the world-famed philosopher Sádi, "Give a soldier gold, he will give you his head"; and by a judicious and liberal distribution of *bakhsheesh*, the permanency of the newly restored allegiance was assured.

As I said above, my Father fully merited Nawáb Sikandar Begam's confidence and affection. Indeed, he bore away from her all the sorrow which the lack of a son usually creates in the female heart. She never attended a durbar without him, and her daily thought was how to increase his honour and dignity.

In the year 1283 A.H., the Nawáb was attacked by a severe form of dyspepsia, and for this reason he undertook a pilgrimage to Mecca, where he remained for a year under the care of Hakím Mulla Nawáb. He then went to Egypt to try the effect of the climate of that country; but, for lack of regular treatment, no benefit resulted, and his condition grew daily worse. He returned to Bhopál after seven months in a state of extreme weakness, and died on the 21st of the month Safar, in the year 1284 A.H. He was buried in his own garden.

My Father was married in all three times. His first wife was Malika Bíbí, the niece of Ghaus Muhammad Khán. She bore him a daughter, and died a year after her marriage. His second wife belonged to the Firoz Khail. She bore him four children, and is still living. Since the marriage with Shah Jahán Begam was contracted during the lifetime of this lady, a *jágír* of Rs. 6,000 was granted for her maintenance, and she is in possession of it to this day.

CHAPTER V

MY MARRIAGE

FROM what has been said in previous chapters, my readers will have seen that Nawáb Sikandar Begam treated me with rare kindness, and that my welfare, both present and future, was constantly before her mind. I have told how, notwithstanding the cares and responsibilities of her high office, she took upon herself the entire charge of my training and education; and how, in her leisure hours, it was her habit to call me to her side and supplement my general studies with kindly advice and wise instruction (from which, more than from any part of my education, I still continue, both in my public and private life, to derive light and guidance).

But in addition to my general upbringing, there was another matter about which Nawáb Sikandar Begam was equally solicitous, and that was my marriage. Her anxiety on this account was intensified by the consideration of my position as heir-apparent to the throne of Bhopál, as well as by the recollection of certain unfortunate complications which had arisen in connection with the arrangement of former marriages in the family. Although, therefore, I was still very young, having barely reached my seventh year, she was determined to select a husband for me before she died, and to choose a youth of tender age, that she might herself watch over his training, and teach him to sympathize with and understand the ways of the people amongst whom his life would be passed. This plan, she believed, would not only afford me ample opportunities of studying his character and temperament, but would also render him fitter to be my helpmate and counsellor in the life that lay before me.

In making her choice, it was necessary to look outside

the territories of Bhopál.[1] Her own husband had belonged to the Mirázi Khail, and she was, therefore, intimately acquainted with all the families of that clan who resided in the State, and from none of them did she consider that a suitable selection could be made. Recollection of the difficulties experienced in connection with the marriage of her daughter also added to Nawáb Sikandar Begam's anxiety on my account, and she determined to do all in her power to settle matters in such a manner that no subsequent troubles or impediment could arise. She entered into correspondence on the subject with the Political Agent, and the Agent to the Governor-General, in the course of which she intimated that there were four families in Bhopál from any of which it would be in the highest degree impolitic and dangerous to select my husband. These were the families of Faujdár Muhammad Khán (*i.e.* the family of Ghaus Muhammad Khán), Jamál Muhammad Khán, Muazzam Muhammad Khán, and Fázil Muhammad Khán; and she urged the Government, in the event of her dying before my marriage, to bear her wishes in mind, since all the four families above mentioned were enemies to the State, and particularly the last-named, that of Fázil Muhammad Khán, who, in the days of the Mutiny, had fought against the Government, and was captured and handed over to the English by the Bhopál army. A full account of this affair was sent to the Agent to

[1] Similar considerations had prevailed in connection with the marriage of my Mother, and many difficulties of a political nature had arisen. These difficulties were not overcome without considerable trouble, but they were not unproductive of good; for it was in consequence of them that the British Government issued a decree to the effect that husbands of the Begams of Bhopál, though styled Nawábs, should have no right to interfere in the administration of the State. The letter of the Government settling this matter was dated November 7th, 1854, and immediately after its receipt the search for a husband had begun. Boys from many of the most notable families in India were summoned to Bhopál, and choice was eventually made of Kudrat Ullah Khán, who was the uncle of Nawáb Ihtishám-ul-mulk. This family had its home in Jalálábád, and was connected by blood with the Bhopál family, each being descended, though in a remote period, from common ancestors. For various reasons, however, this marriage was never celebrated, and my mother, as the reader knows, took as her husband Bakshi Báki Muhammad Khán, Nasrat-i-jang.

the Governor-General by the First Minister, in his letter dated 24th Rabi-ul-awwal, 1290 A.H., and formed a part of the correspondence above referred to. At this juncture, Nawáb Sikandar Begam set out for Mecca, and it was only on her return from this pilgrimage that she was able to take active steps towards the accomplishment of her desire.

It may not be out of place if I state very briefly the chief considerations which a marriage in a Muhammadan family of rank gives rise to; for we change rapidly in these days of higher education and social reform, and should our grandchildren be anxious to know how such matters were settled in the middle of the nineteenth century, they will probably find the pages of history their only source of information. In most Indian families it is still customary for parents to arrange the marriages of their children. And it is right that they should do so. For happiness in later life depends upon the existence of sympathy and love between husband and wife; and since none can understand the nature and temperament of a child or forecast its future more clearly than its own parents, it follows that they alone are competent to decide a matter on which the welfare of their children so largely depends. In well-to-do families of the upper classes it is considered more important that the husband should be of good birth than that he should possess wealth and learning, since the former is a surer guarantee of nobility than the latter, and offers a truer support amidst the difficulties of life; and it may often be observed that the traditions which accompany noble birth will save a man from the evils into which illiteracy and poverty might otherwise plunge him. For this reason the pedigree of a would-be son-in-law is always investigated with the greatest care; and although this task is often beset with many difficulties, its performance is not only expedient, but is strictly enjoined by the laws of Islám.

Next to gentle birth, the most desirable quality in a son-in-law is thrift; and on this point, too, the doctrines of Islám lay considerable stress; extravagance being stigmatized as a crime of sufficient blackness to justify a wife in leaving her husband. And there can be no doubt that prodigality on the part of a husband destroys the peace of mind of the wife, brings desolation on the household, and saps the joys of married life. But if extravagance is a crime in a private individual, how much more is it so when displayed by the consort of a ruler, who, besides being responsible for the well-being of her own household, has also the control of public revenues, and is therefore indirectly, if not directly, responsible for the happiness and well-being of every family in her territories?

In selecting my husband, therefore, noble birth and a frugal disposition were the first considerations which Nawáb Sikandar Begam kept in view, though a handsome appearance and the habits and manners of a gentleman were in her eyes by no means unessential. If these qualities could be found combined in one not too old to undergo training and education, then other considerations, such as wealth or learning, would be of very minor importance. In these circumstances her thoughts turned towards Jalálábád, a place with which she was intimately acquainted; and she entered into communication with Háji Ahmad Karím, who lived in that neighbourhood, and who was the son-in-law of her First Minister, Maulavi Jamál-ud-dín. On his recommendation she wrote, on the 13th of the month Zikád, 1281 A.H., to one Ata Muhammad Khán, a respected resident of Jalálábád, and requested him to give her information about the families of the Fatima Khail (a branch of the Mirázi Khail), who dwelt either at Islámnagar or Jalálábád. After the necessary inquiries had been made, it was decided that a few of the most eligible boys should be selected and presented to Her Highness at Agra, for it was her intention to be present at the durbar shortly to be held in that city. And should one of the candidates meet with her approval, he was to be removed to Bhopál, where arrangements for his training would be made, and, after the lapse of sufficient time to enable a just estimate of his habits and temperament to be formed, a final decision in regard to him would be given. Accordingly, in the month Jamádi-us-sáni, 1283 A.H., Ata Muhammad

Khán brought several boys to Agra and presented them to the Begam. Her Highness's choice fell upon Ahmad Ali Khán, the son of Báki Muhammad Khán,[1] who, in birth, manners, and appearance excelled all the other suitors. Ahmad Ali Khán was accordingly brought to Bhopál, and his training under the supervision of the Begam was commenced, an allowance from the fund for State pensions being made to his mother, Muhammadi Begam.

Nawáb Sikandar Begam was not destined to see the realization of her plans for my future happiness. A year after the visit to Agra she fell ill, and Muhammadi Begam, seeing that her condition was critical, said to her: "You are ill; let me take the boy to my home, and when God grants you recovery I will bring him back to you." But Nawáb Sikandar Begam decided that he should be left to the care of Nawáb Shah Jahán Begam, with whom suitable arrangements had already been made. These instructions were complied with, and on the death of Nawáb Sikandar Begam, Muhammadi Begam returned to her own country in order to look after the *jágír* which the Government had granted to her, as well as to make arrangements for the marriage of her daughter.

The system devised for the upbringing of Ahmad Ali Khán by Nawáb Sikandar Begam was followed for the next four years—that is, to within a year of the time of my marriage. During this period we were constantly together both in study and play. We took our meals together, and only our sleeping-rooms were separate. Indeed, the only time we spent apart from each other's society was the half-hour after our lessons, which Ahmad Ali Khán used to pass with his mother, Muhammadi Begam, and after the departure of the latter to her home even these short partings ceased.

Since no ceremony had as yet confirmed my betrothal to Ahmad Ali Khán, it is not surprising that, after the death of

[1] Báki Muhammad Khán was the son of Imám Ali Khán, who was the son of Diláwar Khán, who was the son of Muhammad Yár Khán, who was the son of Sálár Mír Muhammad Khán, and hence a representative of one of the noblest and most ancient families of Jalálábád.

NAWAB SULTAN JAHAN BEGAM
At the time of her marriage.

my Grandmother, many letters containing proposals for my hand were received from various parts of the country; and at last my Mother decided to take the advice of her nobles and councillors, and she called a meeting at which the following persons were present: Mír Bakshi Háfiz Muhammad Hasan Khán; Mír Hátim Muhammad Khán, brother of the Kudsia Begam; Mattu Khán, who was Second-in-Command of the State army; Munshi Husein Khán; Bakshi Kudrat Ali Khán, Second Minister, and the First Minister. At this meeting, it was unanimously decided that no person was more suited to be the husband of the Nawáb Sultán Jahán Begam than Ahmad Ali Khán. No pressure was brought to bear on any of the voters, and their consensus of opinion was the natural outcome of a general admiration for the good qualities of Ahmad Ali Khán. Had it been otherwise, many of these nobles would have tried by any means and at any cost to secure for their own families so coveted an alliance. Nawáb Shah Jahán Begam, who loved Ahmad Ali Khán like a son, heartily desired the match. And Sidik Hasan Khán, of whom mention has already been made, also gave his approval. That he ever did anything so conducive to my happiness is a miracle, and only shows how, by the help of God, even our enemies may become instruments for our good.

This matter being satisfactorily settled, Nawáb Shah Jahán Begam, in conformity with the custom of the times, sent a letter to Nawáb Kudsia Begam, informing her that Ahmad Ali Khán had, with her own approval and that of the nobles of her Court, been chosen to be the husband of her daughter, Nawáb Sultán Jahán Begam. In reply, the Kudsia Begam sent her congratulations, but from the way her letter was worded it was plain that she resented the fact that she had not been consulted. The correspondence concerning my marriage has no direct bearing on the events to be recorded, but I have decided to insert some portion of it that my readers may be able to form an idea of the manner in which such correspondence was conducted thirty or forty years ago—a manner which is rarely to be seen in these days, and which, before many more years of this strenuous age have passed, will probably be altogether obsolete.

Letter from the Kudsia Begam to Nawáb Shah Jahán Begam, dated 8th Rajab, 1279 A.H.:

"To my beloved Shah Jahán Begam, fountain of prosperity and excellence, light of the lamp of glory and goodness, to whom God grant long life, prosperity, and honour. Be it known to you that your letter of the 6th day of Rajab, 1289 A.H., informing me of the proposal for the marriage of Sultán Jahán Begam with Ahmad Ali Khán of Jalálábád, and of your and her approval thereof, and that of the nobles and Jágírdárs of your State, has come to my hand. Since your letter is merely one of information, I have nothing to do but to acknowledge its receipt. May any proposal which is for the good of yourself and Sultán Jahán Begam receive the blessing of God Almighty."

On the 17th Shábán, 1289 A.H. (October 21st, 1872) the following letter was dispatched to Colonel John William Willoughby Osborne, C.B., Political Agent in Bhopál:

"Concerning the betrothal of my beloved daughter Sultán Jahán Begam, may her life be long and her prosperity unbounded:—This is to inform you that, with her own and my consent, together with the approval of the nobles, Jágírdárs, and learned men of this State, a husband has been chosen in the person of Ahmad Ali Khán, the son of the late Báki Muhammad Khán, belonging to a family of the Mirázi Khail, resident in Jalálábád. And I send herewith a copy of a letter, dated October 21st, 1872, corresponding to 17th Shábán, 1289, A.H., addressed to His Excellency the Viceroy of the Indian Empire, with a view to obtaining his consent to, and approval of, the said union; also I send a copy of the marriage proposal, attested by the seal and signature of my beloved daughter, of myself, and of the nobles and distinguished personages above referred to, the original of which document you yourself saw on the occasion of your recent visit to Bhopál; and also a copy of the letter of Nawáb Gauhar Sáhiba Kudsia, which was sent in reply to my own letter. I trust you will be kind enough to forward my humble letter to His Excellency the Governor-General."

Copy of the *kharíta*[1] addressed to His Excellency the Viceroy and Governor-General of the Indian Empire:

"Now that the age of my dear daughter Nawáb Sultán Jahán Begam Sáhiba has reached 15 years, anxiety on account of her marriage overshadows all other affairs. To find her a suitable husband I have searched both amongst the members of my own family and among all the Afghán families of Bhopál, but I could find no one whose fitness was wholly beyond question. Of all the suitors who have appeared before either the late Begam or myself, there is, in my opinion, none more worthy to be my daughter's husband than he whom my mother brought from Akbarábád at the time of the durbar which was held in that city. With the consent of his elders, who journeyed from their homes to meet Her Highness in Akbarábád, this boy has been brought up in my Mother's palace. He is now 16 years of age, and his name is Ahmad Ali Khán. He is the son of the late Báki Muhammad Khán, an Afghán of the Mirázi Khail, who lived in Jalálábád, in the district of Muzaffarnagar. He is handsome in appearance, and of noble birth both on the side of his father and on the side of his mother. The latter is still living, and pays periodical visits to Bhopál from her home in Jalálábád, where she resides with her daughter. Besides this daughter and Ahmad Ali Khán she has no other children. In the course of his education here, Ahmad Ali Khán has read the whole of the Holy Korán, and has studied both Persian and English. In Jalálábád his ancestors have been honoured and respected for many generations. In order to find out what the general opinion in regard to this matter might be, I caused the qualifications of the various suitors to be written down, and copies to be sent to the nobles and the elders of the State, as well as to Sultán Jahán Begam, so that each might state whether, in his or her opinion, there was any boy in the list who seemed in all respects worthy of selection. All these persons, including Sultán Jahán Begam, placed their seals and signatures against the name Ahmad Ali Khán. Since, therefore, Sultán Jahán Begam, with whom alone the final decision rests, has given her approval, and since the members of my family, the nobles, Jágírdárs, and learned men of the State have unanimously

[1] *Kharíta*, lit. a bag, or packet. The silken bag in which a letter is sent from one ruler to another is called a *kharíta*, but the word usually signifies the letter itself.

signified their agreement with my humble opinion, I now desire to have the consent and approbation of Your Excellency, whose presence bestows grace upon this land, and whom the State of Bhopál looks up to as its patron and protector. I trust that Your Excellency will honour my humble letter with a favourable reply, so that the anxiety which is now preying upon my mind may be taken away, and that we may proceed to the selection of an auspicious day for the celebration of this happy event."

As more than three months elapsed, and no reply to the above letter was received, the Begam, who was anxious that the marriage should be celebrated with as little delay as possible, wrote again to the Political Agent to inquire when an answer might be expected. Her letter was dated February 2nd, 1873:

"My anxiety for an answer to my *kharíta* to His Excellency the Governor-General, concerning the marriage of Nawáb Sultán Jahán Begam, must be my excuse for again troubling you on this matter. Kindly let me know whether the *kharíta* has been dispatched, and, if so, on what date. If it is still in your hands, I beg that it may be dispatched on the earliest possible date, and that notice of the same may be sent to me."

The reply to the above was received on February 13th:

* "Your letter inquiring about the dispatch of the *kharíta* concerning the marriage of Nawáb Sultán Jahán Begam, addressed to His Excellency the Governor-General of India, has reached me, and this letter of mine is to inform you that the delay in the dispatch of the said *kharíta* was due to the necessity of having it translated into English. This has now been done, and the *kharíta* was forwarded on February 7th to the Honourable the Agent to the Governor-General in Central India. Information will be given to you as soon as a reply is received."

A letter, dated May 7th, 1873 (9th Rabi-ul-awwal, 1289 A.H.), was also received from Colonel Watson, Acting Agent to the Governor-General in Central India, from which the following is an extract:

* "In regard to your representations concerning the urgent necessity for performing the marriage of your daughter, the Princess Nawáb Sultán Jahán Begam, His Excellency the Viceroy and Governor-General has informed me that he considers it desirable that I should myself come to Bhopál and discuss the matter with you. I therefore propose, in accordance with His Excellency's instructions, to visit you during the ensuing week."

On May 9th, 1873 (11th Rabi-ul-awwal, 1289 A.H.), the following reply to the above letter was written:

"Your letter has reached me this day. Your visit to Bhopál will be a source of great pleasure to me. The wish to see you has long been in my heart, but until now no circumstance has occurred to give rise to our meeting. My thanks are due to God for thus unexpectedly granting my desire. It will give me great pleasure to talk personally with you on the subject of the marriage of my daughter Sultán Jahán Begam. Nawáb Muhammad Sidik Hasan Khán and Muhammad Jamál-ud-dín, the First Minister of the State, will, in accordance with established custom, take part in the interview, but besides these two gentlemen no other person will be present."

After the conclusion of this correspondence, the Agent to the Governor-General fulfilled his promise and came to Bhopál, where he was received with the customary formalities. On the 24th of Rabi-ul-awwal, 1290 A.H., at 6 o'clock in the evening, he visited the Begam, and in the course of conversation informed her that the Viceroy much regretted that, owing to great press of work, he had been unable to send an early reply to her *kharíta* regarding the marriage of Sultán Jahán Begam. Seeing that a month had now elapsed since the dispatch of the *kharíta*, His Excellency desired to know whether, during this time, any change had taken place in Her Highness's views on the subject. My Mother replied that the opinion expressed in the *kharita* had been formed after much consideration, and with the help of the best advice she could obtain, and that nothing had since transpired to alter her determination. Her inquiries amongst the families of Bhopál had produced no one better fitted than Ahmad Ali Khán to be her son-in-law. The Agent to the Governor-General then asked the Begam whether she could answer for it that Ahmad Ali Khán would not make trouble in the State. The Begam replied that, as far as she had been able to judge, the manners and conduct of Ahmad Ali Khán gave rise to no such apprehensions. She explained that he had been brought to Bhopál at the age of 7 by Nawáb Sikandar Begam, with whom, as well as with herself, the responsibility of his upbringing and education had rested. His family had always been respected by the British Government, and it gave her great pleasure to say that his own behaviour left nothing to be desired, while his progress in his studies was, considering his age, more than satisfactory. He had now reached his eighteenth year, and the age of Sultán Jahán Begam was 16. On hearing this the Agent to the Governor-General said: "Since this is an important affair, and one with which the welfare of Sultán Jahán Begam is so closely connected, I should like to have an opportunity of hearing her approval from her own lips, and the Viceroy, too, is anxious that I should converse with her personally on the subject." "That," said my Mother, "is my own wish also. For although her seal and signature have already manifested her wishes, it is better that you should meet her and gauge her sentiments for yourself. I myself will retire, and she shall speak with you from behind the *purdah*." So saying, My mother went to rejoin Mrs. Humphrey and her other lady guests, while I was sent to the Agent of the Governor-General. After a few general remarks he said to me: "The document relating to your proposed marriage has been sent to me. May I ask if your seal and signature, which the document bears, were placed there of your own free will?" Although a verbal reply to this question was a considerable shock to my oriental sense of modesty, yet since my Mother had told me that amongst Europeans and Muhammadans it was not a matter about which the least shame need be felt, I answered frankly that it was by my own will and pleasure that I had affixed my seal and signature to the marriage proposal. The Agent to the Governor-General then said to me in English: "Is it your wish that I should forward this document to His Excellency the Viceroy?" I answered with the single word "yes," and remained silent. He then inquired if there was anything else that I wished to say. To divert the conversation from myself, I said that I had only to request him to be good enough to convey my compliments to His Excellency the Viceroy and his daughter. With this the interview came to an end, and I went into the room where Mrs. Humphrey and other ladies were sitting.

On the 24th of Jamádi-ul-awwal, 1291 A.H., Mrs. Humphrey wrote to Nawáb Shah Jahán Begam, giving her the pleasing intelligence that the negotiations with the Government had been brought to a favourable termination, and offering at the same time her sincere congratulations. On the 7th of the same month, the Political Agent himself came to Bhopál, and with his own hand delivered to Her Highness the *kharíta* of His Exellency the Governor-General. It ran as follows:

* "To my well-beloved and respected Nawáb Begam Sáhiba: may Almighty God keep her under His protection.

"I much regret that, owing to heavy work, I have been unable to reply earlier to your letter of October 21st, 1872, in which you request sanction for the marriage of your daughter Nawáb Sultán Jahán Begam with Ahmad Ali Khán, son of the late Báki Muhammad Khán. I should have been glad, and I think it would have been for the advantage of the State, if a suitable choice could have been made from among the nobles of your own family. But inasmuch as you assure me that you know of none better fitted to be your son-in-law than Ahmad Ali Khán, and that the elders of your family and the nobles of the State have given him preference over all other suitors, and since Nawáb Sultán Jahán Begam herself approves of the choice you have made, and has signified the same to my Agent at a personal interview which took place by my own instructions—taking all these facts into consideration, I have no hesitation in giving my consent to the marriage; and I trust Ahmad Ali Khán will, by his wisdom, his learning, his manners, and his habits, show himself to be worthy of the high position he will occupy as the husband of the heir-apparent to the State of Bhopál, and that he will so conduct himself as to win your daughter's affection and respect; for it is only with the assurance that this important step meets with her full approbation that my assent is now given. It is my earnest desire that this union may realize the advantages you anticipate from it, and that it may conduce to the life-long happiness and prosperity of your daughter, and to the welfare of the State. Be assured that I am ever solicitous for your own health and welfare, in regard to which I beg you will from time to time keep me informed."

In accordance with the custom of the State, information of the receipt of this *kharíta* was sent to the Nawáb Kudsia Begam:

"A *kharíta* has arrived from the Governor-General and Viceroy of the Indian Empire, dated June 2nd, 1873, to the effect that His Excellency approves of the marriage which we have arranged between Nawáb Sultán Jahán Begam and Ahmad Ali Khán, the son of the late Báki Muhammad Khán. May God, in His mercy, bring it to a happy fulfilment. It seems to us fitting that you should be informed of this matter, and we therefore send you this letter."

The Begam sent some *purdah* ladies to convey the intelligence to Muhammadi Begam, who presented the messengers with handsome robes of honour, and sent a letter of congratulation to the Begam, begging her at the same time to accept, on behalf of the bride, the gift of a wedding costume, a request which was graciously acceded to. On the 10th of Jamádi-ul-awwal, 1290 A.H., Ahmad Ali Khán was granted an allowance of Rs. 1000 a month, as pocket-money, until he should be finally settled in his own home, and instructions were sent to the Naíb Bakshi to appoint a *sowár* and an orderly to be in attendance on him. On the 20th of Shábán, 1290 A.H., the betrothal ceremony was performed with all due rites, and this was followed by the ceremony of ***namak chashi***, which took place after evening prayer on the 13th of Ramazán-ul-mubárak.

The Begam then issued orders that according to Indian usage a festival should be held on every holiday in the calendar, so that for the further space of one year the character of my betrothed husband might be watched and tested. Although my Mother's intentions were perfectly good, this delay proved unfortunate, for it afforded Sidik Hasan Khán abundant opportunities for harassing Ahmad Ali Khán, whose life from that time began to resemble that of a State prisoner. Sentries were posted outside his sleeping-apartment, and no one was permitted to have access to him, while he himself could not go forth without permission. To such an extent was his freedom curtailed that he was not allowed to hunt, ride, walk, or to enjoy any form of recreation whatever. But he bore all these trials with such exemplary patience, that even his worst enemies could find no blot on his behaviour. Everything possible was done to trouble and provoke him, but he never lost his self-control, and displayed all through this period of probation tact and wisdom far beyond his years. Fate willed that Ahmad Ali Khán should be my husband, and all the machinations of Sidik Hasan Khán and his friends could not alter Fate's decree.

The months passed rapidly away, and the time came to make final preparations for the wedding, which was now definitely fixed to take place on the 23rd of Zil Hijjah, 1291 A.H. (February 1st, 1874). Invitations were sent to many distinguished Europeans and Indians, as well as to near and distant relatives of the family. But Nawáb Kudsia Begam, the wish of whose heart was to see my marriage, and who had expended lákhs of rupees on jewellery and other wedding gifts, was not included amongst the number. The Agent to the Governor-General was away on tour, and could not be present; but Colonel Osborne, the Political Agent, and Mrs. Osborne accepted the invitation, and came to Bhopál some days in advance to assist in the entertainment of the European guests.

At the various halting-places between Itarsi and Bhopál, arrangements were made to make the visitors as comfortable as possible on their journey; and in Bhopál itself an extensive camp was pitched for their accommodation on the Jahángírábád parade-ground, where entertainments of every kind were provided to make the days pass pleasantly. On the 22nd of Zil Hijjah, the Political Agent and Mrs. Osborne paid visits at different hours to the Kudsia Begam. At these visits, the conversation naturally turned on the marriage festivities, and Mrs. Osborne told the Begam that she ought to be taking part in them. "Nay," she replied sorrowfully; "do you go and enjoy them! Had I been invited, I too would gladly go, for what else should I wish to do if not to rejoice with those who are dear to me?" And to Colonel Barstow she said, "Yes, sáhib, I also take delight in the marriage of Sultán Jahán Begam. How her Grandmother would have rejoiced to see this day! But she has passed away, and her death broke my old heart." I do not know how her words affected the Political Agent, but the State Vakil, who was present at both these interviews, was so deeply moved that on the same day he wrote an account of what had passed to Shah Jahán Begam, beseeching that the invitation might even then be sent, for in the time of Nawáb Sikandar Begam no public function ever took place at which the Kudsia Begam was not present. But this appeal was unheeded, and the very existence of the oldest and most venerable representative of the Bhopál family was ignored. My readers can judge how keenly she must have felt this treatment, and what sadness must have filled her heart as, seated alone in her home in the Shaukat Mahal, the merry din of the marriage festivities was borne to her ears. The Kudsia Begam was an affectionate and peace-loving lady. For many years she had shown no desire to take part in public affairs. Since the death of her daughter, for whom she never ceased to grieve, she had lived the life of a recluse. She asked no one for help, and indeed, as far as the things of this world were concerned, she needed none, for she was herself rich; she loved nothing better than to give pleasure to others, and her charity and liberality were unbounded. It was a cruel deed to make my marriage an opportunity for needlessly wounding so generous and gentle a nature.

The marriage ceremony itself took place on the afternoon of the 23rd of Zil Hijjah. The palace was elaborately and skilfully decorated. Detachments of the Bhopál State army were drawn up on either side of the courtyard, and the band of the 22nd Regiment was in attendance. Inside the palace were assembled the relatives of the family, the chief servants of the State, and the native guests, all wearing durbar dress. At 4 o'clock, the European guests arrived. As they were received on the steps of the palace by Sidik Hasan Khán, the troops presented arms, and the band played a wedding march. When all of them had alighted, they were conducted to the guest-chamber, where the gentlemen were assigned seats on the right-hand side of a screened doorway behind which Nawáb Shah Jahán Begam was seated, while the ladies passed behind the screen into the inner apartment. Shortly afterwards, the bridegroom arrived, attended by the chief members of his family. The guard of honour presented arms as he alighted from his carriage, and the band played the national air of Bhopál. *Chobdárs* in gold-laced liveries, with gold sticks in their hands, conducted him into the presence of the assembled guests, and announced his approach by chanting in a loud monotone his names, titles, and virtues. All the guests rose to greet him as he entered, and he acknowledged and returned their salutations with a dignified courtesy which well became the occasion. His dress was of coloured Benáres silk, and was surmounted by a richly coloured and costly turban. He wore a necklace of topazes, pearls, and diamonds, and from a jewelled belt about his waist hung a magnificent Ispahán sword. This dress had been, in accordance with the customs of Bhopál, presented to him by the State. His handsome appearance and dignified demeanour made a great impression on the whole assembly, and spontaneous congratulations and good wishes were showered upon him, and prayers for his future happiness were heard on every side. Sidik Hasan Khán shook hands with him, and conducted him to a chair next to his own, the *chobdárs* again raising their chant until he became seated. After the reception of the bridegroom, Maulavi Muhammad Jamál-ud-dín Khán Sáhib, with Sidik Hasan Khán, and Latíf Muhammad Khán, my half-brother, came to my apartment (I was not *purdah* to these three gentlemen), and, in accordance with Muhammadan law, asked me if I were prepared to take Ahmad Ali Khán as my husband. I replied that such was my will, and the three gentlemen then withdrew, and, going before the bridegroom, repeated the same question. He was at this time seated on a golden throne, over-shadowed by a canopy of rich cloth embroidered in gold and silver. He answered with the single word *kubúl*, that is, 'agreed,' whereupon Kázi Zain-ul-abedín approached the throne, and read the marriage *khutbah*. Other religious formalities followed, and a sum of two crores of rupees was settled upon me as my marriage portion. This brought the ceremony to an end, and all present, with loud cries of *bismillah*, raising their hands above their heads, prayed to the great God to vouchsafe to bridegroom and bride lives full of happiness and prosperity. Then, amidst shouts of applause, the bridegroom left the golden throne, and seated himself again by Sidik Hasan Khán.

A purse of *ashrafís* and other gifts were presented to the Kázi by the bridegroom. Each of the bridegroom's friends who had come from his country to take part in the marriage received a *khilát*, and *'itr* and *pán* and *mukáish* were distributed.[1] According to established custom, Ahmad Ali Khán had to sign a marriage agreement,[2] to which the signature of the Political Agent as witness was also attached. Many of the clauses of the agreement were such as could never be legally enforced, but they serve as an illustration of the skilful attempts made by Sidik Hasan Khán to obtain a hold over my husband. In the evening an assault-at-arms

[1] According to Indian etiquette, no reception is complete which does not conclude with the time-honoured custom of distributing *'itr* and *pán* (*i.e.* perfume and betel) among the guests, the most honoured of whom should receive it from the hand of their host.

[2] See Appendix B.

NAWAB IHTISHAM-UL-MULK
At the time of his marriage.

p. 56]

was given by the State army, after which the city was illuminated, and a display of fireworks brought to a close this long-to-be-remembered day.

The palace which was fixed upon as our residence was the same that I had always lived in, and was only separated by a doorway from that of my Mother, so that it was possible to pass from one to the other without the trouble of driving. On the 24th of Zil Hijjah, the bridegroom entertained all the Indian and European guests at a banquet. The bridegroom received from Shah Jahán Begam the title of Nazír-ud-daulah Sultán Dula. The title "Nawáb" was not given, as it had already been conferred on Sidik Hasan Khán. He received also the *jágírs* of Mahalpúr, Ambapáni, and Rámgarh, the united revenues of which amounted to Rs. 40,002. 14. 6. These *jágírs* adjoined my own.

On the wedding festivities the sum of Rs. 6,57,612. 14. 3. was expended, as follows:

The Bridegroom's outfit	Rs.	1,68,787	7	9
The Bride's trousseau	Rs.	4,38,028	8	3
General expenses of the marriage	Rs.	50,796	14	3
Total	Rs.	6,57,612	14	3

My own *jágír* consisted of some fifteen villages from the *parganas* of Gadhi-ambapáni, Bamhori, and Bilkisganj, of which the total revenue amounted to Rs. 80,382. As this amount was sufficient for my personal expenses, no addition was made to it.

On the 25th of Zil Hijjah, my Mother caused the ceremony of *chauthi* to be performed in the Bágh Nishát-Afzah (the Garden of Delight). By 8 o'clock in the morning the whole of the State forces, horse, foot, and artillery, with the *máhi marátib*,[1] were assembled in gallant array, occupying the entire length of the road from the Shaukat Mahal to the Pír Darwáza. Shortly after 8 o'clock, I myself in a *palki*, and the Nawáb Sáhib mounted on a handsomely caparisoned

[1] *Máhi marátib* (*máhi*, a fish, and *marátib*, dignities) are certain honours of which the privilege is especially conferred on princes and great nobles; they are denoted by the figure of a fish, two balls, and other *insignia*, and are carried, in State processions, upon elephants.

elephant, went in procession to the garden, attended by the nobles and chief officials of the State. The whole city came out to witness the sight, and our route was lined with crowds of enthusiastic and joyous spectators. When we arrived at the entrance to the garden, and the Nawáb Sáhib was about to descend from his elephant, Maulavi Jamál-ud-dín Sáhib, the First Minister, came forward, and bidding him tarry, addressed him in the following words:

> " Hear me, beloved ! Hear, and understand !
> For he whose life on noble lines is planned,
> Will spurn the World's red wine, and take, instead,
> The cup of wisdom from the sage's hand.

" The high rank to which you have been raised, these outward signs of dignity and power which you behold around you, and which are assembled here to do you honour, the lands and the wealth which are now in your possession—all these you owe to the favour and goodness of God ; and it is your duty to render thanks to Him not only with your lips, but in your life, that your gratitude may be manifest to all men through the righteousness of your conduct and the wisdom of your words. Be not puffed up with the pomp of power, but walk always in the paths of virtue and humility.

> " A man, indeed, is he whose heart,
> When Fortune smiles, from pride is free ;
> Whose simple faith in God remains
> Unshaken in adversity.

" High duties and responsibilities lie before you. Seek, therefore, after wisdom, and let patience, sympathy, and honesty characterize all your dealings. Above all, keep continually in your mind this sacred precept : ' Show honour to thy parents and thy elders, and let arrogance and conceit be far from thee.'

" I have read the Holy Korán with you, and therefore I may style myself your teacher, and it is in the character of a teacher as well as a friend that I offer you this advice."

The bridegroom bowed his head, in token that his teacher's words had not fallen on heedless ears. And, indeed, this sage's advice was accepted in the same earnest spirit in which it was given; it remained indelibly engraven on my husband's heart, and as years went by its good effect became more and more evident. The veteran Minister, who had grown grey in the service of the State, standing in the presence of the assembled troops and nobles, and gravely admonishing the handsome young bridegroom, was an impressive sight, and one not easily to be forgotten, while the words which he uttered deserve, for their simplicity and their wisdom, to be written in letters of gold.

In Bhopál the *chauthi* is usually followed by another ancient ceremony called *jumah*, in which bride and bridegroom are invited to a feast by some near relative, and are presented with *khiláts* and other gifts. The Kudsia Begam, although she had taken no part in the marriage, desired to entertain us in this fashion, but we were not permitted to accept her invitation; and when she again begged that we might be allowed to go, since all her preparations were complete, and her desire to present us with the gifts she had made ready was very great, she received from my Mother the following reply:

"I have on several occasions informed you that there is no necessity for you to put yourself to this trouble. God, in His bounty, has satisfied all the wants of Sultán Jahán Begam, and she stands in need of nothing more."

The pain that this reply must have inflicted on her proud and generous heart can easily be conceived. And what was the reason of it? Simply this—that Sidik Hasan Khán, knowing that her days could not be many in this world, did not choose that so much valuable property should go out of her house, for he intended that it should find its way into his own possession, as, indeed, it eventually did. Would that he had helped himself to my money instead, and that the last days of this pious and venerable lady had been allowed to pass in peace!

In the course of the wedding festivities, Shah Jahán Begam did not forget the poor. Money was liberally distributed amongst them, and many orphan girls who were old enough to marry received money sufficient to enable them to bear the heavy burden of expense which, even amongst the poorest families, a marriage always entails.

I cannot conclude this chapter better than by giving some account of the habits and eminent virtues of my husband.

The Nawáb Sáhib was the fourth in descent from the famous Sálár Mír Muhammad Jalál Khán, of whose family, and the honourable connection it has always had with the Government, a full description may be found in the *Tárikh Jalál*. As I am anxious not to burden my readers with unnecessary matter, I shall omit all details of family history and confine my description to the Nawáb Sáhib himself. He was born in the month of Rabi-us-sáni, 1270 A.H., at Jalálábád, in which city his childhood was spent. In 1283 A.H., Nawáb Sikandar Begam brought him to Bhopál, where, as has already been told, he received his education and his military training. For the latter, special instructors were engaged, under whom he quickly acquired proficiency and skill in all military exercises. The accompanying portrait affords a good idea of his handsome countenance and manly figure. In conversation his voice was gentle, and his courteous manner commanded the respect of all, whether young or old, with whom he came in contact. He was of a simple and contented disposition, humble in his own estimation, and quick to recognize merit in others. He possessed all the courage characteristic of his race, combined with an unusual amount of self-control and a natural fitness to command. Had he lived in less peaceable times, he would, doubtless, have won rank and fame as a military leader. A firm friend and a generous foe, he was ever ready to succour those in distress, and to pardon the wrong-doer. In his own family, and particularly amongst his children, he always bore a cheerful and happy countenance, and even strangers found it difficult to resist the charm of his manner, which at once placed them at their ease and compelled their admiration. Hunting, shooting, and *chaurang* were his favourite recreations, and he was a bold and accomplished horseman. Of the more intellectual pursuits, architecture had for him, as it has had for so many of the Musalman rulers of India, a strong fascination, and many of the buildings which he left show that he possessed not only scientific knowledge but elegant taste. The buildings in the Bágh Hayat Afzah and the Sadar Manzil (House of Council, so named because it is here that I hold my council meetings), are examples of his architectural skill, as well as of his real love for such works; for the cost of both these buildings was defrayed from his and my *jágírs*. He had a keen appreciation for natural scenery, and frequently retired for a week at a time to a beautiful place named Samarda in his own *jágír*, where he had built himself a shooting-box and a capacious villa. Zia-ud-dín Tekri, where I have now built my own residence, was the place which pleased him beyond all others, and for this reason I have named it Ahmadábád; and, indeed, it would be hard to find a more lovely spot.

The Nawáb Sáhib fully appreciated the high rank to which he had been raised by his marriage with me, but he never presumed upon his position, nor was his behaviour ever inconsistent with it. To me he was a true and faithful helpmate, and I derived the greatest benefit from his wisdom and experience. He was esteemed and respected by every Political officer connected with State. Colonel Barr[1] and Colonel Meade, Agent to the Governor-General, were particularly struck with his ability; and they used to say that, were he in England, he could aspire to the highest offices, and become a distinguished statesman. One statesman-like quality he certainly possessed in a pre-eminent degree, and that was tact, and nowhere did he display this more than in his attitude towards family feuds. These often assumed large and complicated dimensions, but he kept aloof from them himself, and desired that I should do the same; and thus, although they were a source of grief and annoyance to him, his enemies could never turn them to account against him. Towards Nawáb Shah Jahán Begam he showed all the affection and respect due from a son to a mother, and she, on her side, so long as Sidik Hasan Khán abstained from his machinations, treated him with conspicuous

[1] Now Colonel Sir David W. Keith Barr, K.C.S.I.

kindness. It was the Nawáb Sáhib's boast, and a matter for which he thanked God, that he envied none, but was rather an object of envy to all other men. By his refined manners and habits, his nobility of character, and his high abilities, he did more than justify the choice which Nawáb Sikandar Begam and Nawáb Shah Jahán Begam had made.

CHAPTER VI

A ROYAL VISIT AND OTHER EVENTS

TOWARDS the end of the year 1875, it was known that His Royal Highness the Prince of Wales was about to visit India. It would be difficult to convey an adequate idea of the pleasure with which this intelligence was received in all parts of the country. More than a century had elapsed since the English had laid the foundations of their Eastern Empire, and during that period neither the king nor the heir-apparent to the throne had set foot on Indian soil. But the name of Queen Victoria had long been a household word amongst all sections of the people, and the prospect of welcoming to their own land the eldest son of their beloved ruler filled them with unbounded joy. From time immemorial Eastern races have been accustomed to see authority vested in the hands of a single individual, and to regard the person of a king as the incarnation of power and dignity, an attitude which is both sanctified by tradition and enjoined as a religious belief. This is particularly true of the peoples of India; for although British rule has resulted in the growth of Western modes of thought, yet the worship of "the hero as king" is as natural to them now as it was in the days of Akbar the Great. They love their Emperor with a deep and sincere love, and whatever democratic principles have found their way into the administration of India they look upon as subordinate part of a whole which he alone has fashioned, and which he alone controls.

To no part of India did the tidings of the royal visit bring greater joy and satisfaction than to Bhopâl; for from the very first days of its existence the relations of the State with the dominant Power have been of the closest and most cordial nature. Nawáb Shah Jahán Begam at once instructed the State Vakíl to write to the Political Agent for official confirmation of the report, so that a *kharíta* of welcome might be dispatched to the Governor-General. On June 26th, 1875, the Political Agent wrote in reply that the report was true, but that he was not yet in possession of any details. On August 4th of the same year, Sir Henry Daly, C.B., Agent to the Governor-General for Central India, sent a letter to Her Highness, informing her that the Prince would arrive in India at the end of December, and that His Excellency the Viceroy, by order of Her Majesty the Queen, would hold a Chapter of the Order of the Star of India in Calcutta, and that His Excellency invited Her Highness, as a Knight Grand Commander of the Order, to be present on the occasion. Nawáb Shah Jahán Begam's reply to this communication was dated August 5th, and was to the following effect:

"Before the receipt of your letter I sent, through you, two *kharítas* to His Excellency the Governor-General; one to express my joy at the news of the approaching visit of the Prince, and the other to say that I would very gladly attend the Durbar in question, should nothing occur to prevent my doing so."

On August 16th Sir Henry Daly sent the following reply:

"Since writing your *kharíta* of 28th ultimo to the Viceroy, my note, announcing that the Prince of Wales will hold a Chapter of the Star of India in Calcutta, will have reached you. You will remember that on such occasions the members of the Order only take part in the Ceremony, and that this is not a Durbar or assembly for any other purpose.

"Should Your Highness be prevented from attending in Calcutta at the Investiture, I am sure your unavoidable absence will be regretted. There will, however, be other opportunities during the visit of H.R.H. the Prince of Wales of Chiefs meeting him. I will write distinctly on this matter directly the programme is settled. It is the intention of

H.R.H. THE PRINCE OF WALES, 1875.

p. 64]

the Viceroy to fix several places at which Chiefs and Nobles may pay their duty to the Queen's Heir. But the assembly in Calcutta will be, I believe, confined to the members of the Order of the Star of India.

"Under these circumstances, you will probably prefer that I should not forward your *kharíta* of the 28th ultimo. I will, therefore, keep it till I hear from Your Highness."

In the course of her reply Nawáb Shah Jahán Begam wrote:

"I did not decline to be present at the Durbar, for I am most desirous to meet His Royal Highness on that occasion, and, God willing, I shall do so. But I stated that in case the confinement of my daughter Sultán Jahán Begam should prevent me from leaving Bhopál, I would send my husband to Calcutta to represent me. Since, however, you, as my friend, advise me to go, it will be better to return the *kharíta* to me, so that the necessary emendations may be made. That portion in which I ask for information regarding the Prince's visit may stand as it is, for the preparations which I may have to make depend on the answer I receive to these inquiries. There is no one who at this time does not wish to give evidence of his loyalty to the heir-apparent to the throne, and this must be specially true of one who is bound, as I am, by the strongest ties of affection to the British Government."

After a few days, the following *kharíta*, dated August 16th, was received from His Excellency, Lord Northbrook, Governor-General of India:

* "Your letter of friendship, dated July 12th, 1875, in which you express your joy and pleasure at the forthcoming visit of His Royal Highness the Prince of Wales to India, and in which you desire me to convey to His Royal Highness your warm and loyal greetings, has reached me through my Agent in Central India. These renewed assurances of your fealty, and of your desire for the increase of the honour and prosperity of the British Throne and the Empire, are a source of great gratification to me. It will give me much pleasure to convey your greetings and felicitations to His Royal Highness on the first opportunity. A letter from you is always

5

welcome to me. I hope I may often have the happiness of hearing from you of your welfare and prosperity, for which, be assured, I am deeply solicitous."

Shortly after the receipt of this *kharíta*, a copy of a communication, addressed to the Agent to the Governor-General for Central India, by the Secretary to the Government of India, was sent to Nawáb Shah Jahán Begam. In this it was stated that ruling chiefs might, when visiting the Prince of Wales, present to him any articles of manufacture peculiar to their own States, provided that they were not of great value. In forwarding this communication,[1] the Political Agent requested the Begam, in the event of her wishing to

[1] The communication of the Secretary of State to the Government of India was as follows:

From the Secretary to the Government of India, to the Agent to the Governor-General for Central India, dated August 5th, 1875 (3rd Rajab, 1291 A.H.), No. 2179.

1. It is the desire of His Excellency the Governor-General in Council that the following directions should be communicated to you, concerning the presentation of *nazarána*, and the receiving of *khiláts* by Ruling Chiefs when paying visits to His Royal Highness the Prince of Wales.

2. His Excellency desires that the Chiefs who visit His Royal Highness at Bombay, or Calcutta, or at any other place, should not be put to more expense than is necessary. His Excellency does not intend to hold State Durbars, and the presentation of *nazarána* and *khiláts*, which is usual at such times, will not take place. He will, however, receive visits from the Chiefs, and pay visits in return, on which occasions all the customary formalities will be observed.

3. The same procedure will be followed in regard to visits paid to, and received from, His Royal Highness the Prince of Wales.

4. It is probable that the Rulers of States may wish to present to His Royal Highness specimens of the products or manufactures of their own territories.

5. His Excellency the Governor-General sees no objection to such a procedure, provided the articles presented are not of great value or of large size.

6. Chiefs availing themselves of this privilege should furnish His Excellency, through Political Agents or other official channels, with a list describing, and giving the approximate values of, such articles as they may wish to present, so that the consent of His Royal Highness may be obtained. No presents offered under conditions other than those stated in the foregoing clauses will be accepted by His Royal Highness.

7. These presents will be placed in the Royal Museum, and they should therefore consist of such articles as may serve as mementoes of His Royal Highness's visit to India.

take advantage of this privilege, to furnish, as soon as possible, a list of the articles which she proposed to present, with their approximate values.

The Political Agent in Bhopál, in a memorandum dated August 30th, informed Her Highness that all Knights attending the Chapter of the Order of the Star of India should wear the robes and insignia of the Order, and that these could be renewed if necessary. He also recommended the dispatch of a trustworthy agent to Calcutta to make arrangements for Her Highness's lodgings. A *kharíta* was also received from Lord Northbrook stating that the Chapter would take place on January 1st, 1876. The official invitation to the same was sent by the Secretary to the Order of the Star of India.

In her second *kharíta* to His Excellency the Viceroy, the Begam had made inquiries about the arrangements that would be made for her lodging in Calcutta. As a considerable time elapsed without any reply being received to these inquiries, a reminder was sent to the Political Agent. On September 20th, however, a letter was received from that officer, stating that a house would be engaged for Her Highness in Calcutta, the rent of which would not be charged to the State, and that Her Highness's private apartments would be supplied with furniture by Government. But if, in addition to these, a public reception-room was required, arrangements for its decoration and furniture would have to be made by the officials of the State, who, however, would be helped with supplies from the government *tosha-khána*.[1]

A second letter from the Political Agent stated that the Prince of Wales would hold no Durbar in Calcutta, but only a Chapter as above stated, at which only those persons who were Knights of the Order were qualified to take a prominent part; and that it was, therefore, all the more necessary that

[1] *Tosha-khána*, lit. a wardrobe, or storeroom. "Each Native State and the Foreign Office of the Government of India has a *tosha-khána*, where stores of costly robes, jewellery, trappings, and housings are kept. It is from such stores that *khiláts* are given, and State processions are provided by Native States" (*Táj-ul-Ikbal*, p. 126, n.).

the Begam of Bhopál should be present. The Secretary to the Order also wrote a second time, saying that if anything should prevent Her Highness leaving Bhopál, she would have other opportunities, either at Jabbalpúr or at Akbarábád, of meeting the Prince of Wales. But he hoped that she would, according to her original intention, and according to the strong desire expressed in her letter of September 18th, come to Calcutta in time to attend the Chapter, at which, he felt sure, Her Highness would consider it an honour to be present.

These matters having been so far settled, the Begam wrote to inform the Political Agent that she proposed to send the State Vakíl to Calcutta to superintend the arrangements for her lodging. She requested the Political Agent to provide him with a letter of introduction to the Foreign Secretary, stating that accommodation would be required for about two hundred and fifty people, besides horses and carriages. The Vakíl, accompanied by the Darogha of the *kár-khána* proceeded, on the 1st of Ramazán, to Calcutta, with instructions to inspect and report fully upon the house which should be selected, as well as to take measures for its adornment. Accordingly the Vakíl, on arrival in Calcutta, with the assistance of the Foreign Secretary and the Superintendent of the *tosha-khána*, was enabled to see the house and the manner in which it had been arranged, a detailed account of which, together with a plan of the building, he sent to the Begam. This house occupied one of the best sites in the Matia Burj.

On October 23rd, 1875, the State Vakíl asked the Political Agent if he could ascertain the opinion of His Excellency the Viceroy in regard to the propriety of the Begam's remaining *purdah* during her stay in Calcutta, and in regard to her paying and receiving visits, as no answer had been received to the *kharíta* in which information on these points was requested. The Political Agent happened to come to Bhopál at this time to inspect the robes and insignia of the Order of the Star of India, which Her Highness was proposing to wear at the Chapter, and in the evening of the same day he had a private audience with her, at which only Nawáb Sidik Hasan Khán and the First Minister of the State were present, and the *purdah* question was discussed. The Begam, anxious for more reasons than one to conform to the requirements of Oriental etiquette, quoted the examples of many Ránees and Begams to support her view of the question. But the Political Agent pointed out that if she remained *purdah* at the time of the visits of the Prince of Wales and the Viceroy, these visits would be deprived to a large extent of their official significance. For some time the matter was warmly debated, but at last my Mother decided to bow to the necessity of the occasion, and consented to appear at the Chapter and at other functions wearing a *burkha*. It must not be supposed that Nawáb Shah Jahán Begam in any way lacked the loyal sentiments which have always distinguished the Begams of Bhopál, or that she underrated the honour of being received by the Prince of Wales and the Viceroy. Her sole motive in raising the *purdah* question was to promote the honour and dignity of Sidik Hasan Khán by appointing him her representative; so that, in fact, he might occupy a position similar to that of former Nawábs who were actual rulers of the State. With this object alone she wished, first of all, to send Sidik Hasan Khán to welcome the Prince, on her behalf, in Bombay, and afterwards to make him her representative on public occasions in Calcutta, for which latter the *purdah* difficulty was to be the excuse. As a matter of fact, her plans for the advancement of Sidik Hasan Khán were impossible of fulfilment, nor was the fact of her being *purdah* a legitimate excuse, for the laws of Islám do not prohibit a Musalmán lady from appearing at public assemblies in a *burkha*, nor is there any reason why the ruler of a State should not go abroad clad in this fashion if she wishes to do so. Her Highness had, however, been induced to believe that to allow Sidik Hasan Khán to represent her and act for her, in the manner proposed, could in no way detract from her own dignity, while it would very materially add to that of her husband, and, in her anxiety that he should receive all the honours that Government could bestow upon him, she was willing to put herself in the background, and to forgo her own share of the advantages and honours which this unique occasion would afford. That this was so can be easily seen from the following communication, which at this time Her Highness sent to the Madár-ul-mohám:

"The *kharita* received from His Excellency the Governor-General states that His Royal Highness the Prince of Wales will disembark at Bombay. As many Indian Chiefs will be present there to bid His Royal Highness welcome, I am anxious that my own greetings and good wishes should not be wanting at such a time. Owing to the approaching confinement of my daughter, Nawáb Sultán Jahán Begam, it will be difficult for me to go to Bombay myself, and I therefore desire to send the Nawáb Sáhib in my stead. But should the Agent to the Governor-General for Central India sanction this arrangement, it is necessary that the Government should show to the Nawáb Sáhib, in Bombay, the same marks of distinction as would be shown to myself, so that the dignity of the State may be upheld in the presence of the other Chiefs."

A great deal more correspondence on the same subject took place between Her Highness and the Political Agent, which it is not necessary to reproduce. From what I have already said, and from what follows, my readers can easily perceive my Mother's design, and the methods by which she endeavoured to accomplish it.

Although there is no real necessity for the ruler of a State to be accompanied by the heir-apparent when attending public durbars, and although only twenty days had elapsed since the birth of my daughter, so that I was in too weak a state to bear the fatigues of a long journey, my Mother decided that I was to go with her to Calcutta, for it was neither practicable, nor in accordance with her wishes, that I should remain alone in Bhopál. She also told me that the same arrangements would be made for me as had been made for herself by Nawáb Sikandar Begam on a like occasion, and that there would be no necessity for me to appear in public in a *burkha.* As it had always been my habit to act according to the orders of my parents, I signified my readiness to comply with her desire. This conversation took place in the morning, and on the evening of the very same day my Mother again came to me and said that, as she herself was going to appear in a *burkha*, it was fitting that I, too, should adopt the same course. I had no choice but to agree, and at once set about making the necessary preparations for the journey.

The secret of these contradictory orders was this. Sidik Hasan Khán, finding that his plans for making himself the Begam's representative had come to nought, determined that, if he could not occupy the highest place, he would at any rate try to occupy the next highest, and the possibility of my being unwilling to go to Calcutta, or of my refusing to appear in public in a *burkha*, seemed to offer the chance for which he was looking. It was, therefore, at his instigation that the order for the *burkha* was given.

These controversies being settled, I prepared for my departure, and dispatched to Calcutta all such necessaries as were not likely to be available there. On the 1st of Zil Kádah, 1292 A.H. (November 30th, 1875) Ghulám Mahbub Khán, Mohtamim of the State *kár-khána*, was sent on in advance with the heavy luggage, tents, carriages, and a large staff of attendants. He reached Itársi on the 5th of Zil Kádah, and, proceeding thence by rail, arrived at Calcutta on the 10th, and took up his quarters in a bungalow close to that which the Government had selected for ourselves.

On Monday, the 7th of Zil Kádah, Her Highness, myself, Nawáb Ihtishám-ul-mulk, and Nawáb Sidik Hasan Khán, with about a hundred retainers and servants, set out from Bhopál. We reached Itársi in three days, and met the Political Agent there. From Itársi we went by rail to Calcutta, where we arrived on Wednesday, December 16th. We were met at the station by Captain Medif, A.D.C., and Mr. Keary, Under-Secretary to Government, who made kind inquiries after our welfare, and then Her Highness, myself, and Sidik Hasan Khán drove in a closed carriage to our lodging. As we were the guests of His Excellency the

Viceroy all the arrangements for our meals were in the hands of the Government, and during our month's stay in Calcutta we were entertained in a most sumptuous fashion.

On the 23rd of Zil Kádah (December 23rd), the Begam paid a state visit to the Viceroy, accompanied by the following nobles and officials of the State: Nawáb Sidik Hasan Khán; Nawáb Ihtishám-ul-mulk; Mián Nazar Muhammad Khán; Munshi Jamál-ud-dín Khán Sáhib, late Prime Minister; Mián Núr-ul-hasan Khán; and Mián Alamgír Muhammad Khán. In the afternoon of the same day His Excellency returned the visit at our lodging, Sidik Hasan Khán escorting him from the house of Sir Sálár Jang. Owing to ill-health I was not present on this occasion, but I took part in all the other receptions. December 23rd was the happy day on which His Royal Highness the Prince of Wales arrived in Calcutta. All the ruling Chiefs present in Calcutta assembled at the landing-place to bid him welcome. By the special favour of His Excellency the Viceroy, the Begam and I, instead of being at the landing-place, were permitted to await His Royal Highness at Government House, in company with His Excellency's daughters, where we had the privilege of paying our loyal respects.

On December 24th, Her Highness and I, attended by a few of the nobles of the State, paid a state visit to His Royal Highness at Government House. A guard of honour was stationed at the entrance and presented arms as we drove up, and the Foreign Secretary and the Under Secretary received us at the door of our carriage, while guns were fired by the saluting battery. We were then conducted to the audience hall, which was about fifty yards from the carriage. This chamber was furnished partly in European and partly in Eastern fashion. It contained many costly and beautiful ornaments, and the roof was hung with glass chandeliers of great beauty and fine workmanship. The entire floor was covered with rich carpets; and down the centre a pathway was formed of scarlet cloth, along which we walked, and on either side of which *chobdárs*, in liveries of red and gold, stood at intervals. His Excellency, wearing full durbar

LORD NORTHBROOK.

p. 72]

dress, was seated in the chair of state. When Her Highness had approached to within forty paces, His Excellency advanced to meet her, and shaking her by the hand inquired after her health. The Political Agent acted as interpreter, and Her Highness inquired after the health of His Excellency. The latter then shook hands with me, and said that he hoped I had not suffered from the fatigues of my long journey to Calcutta. I replied to his inquiries with befitting modesty, and, since I was able to converse somewhat in English, my answers did not require to be translated. After His Excellency had spoken to Nawáb Sidik Hasan Khán, Nawáb Ihtishám-ul-mulk, and others of our party, we all took our seats, my Mother on the Viceroy's right, myself next, and the others in the order of their rank, the chairs on the left being occupied by the members of the staff. We were all greatly delighted at the courteous and affable manner in which Lord North-brook entertained us. He talked to my Mother for nearly ten minutes, making many inquiries about Bhopál and our journey to Calcutta. We were then conducted by the two Secretaries and the Political Agent to another chamber, and ushered into the presence of the Prince of Wales. As we entered, His Royal Highness rose from his chair and bowed to us with princely dignity. He then shook hands with my Mother, and expressed a hope that she had recovered from the fatigues of her journey; then, extending his right hand to her, and his left to me, he led us to our seats. After conversing for some minutes with Her Highness the Prince turned to me, and said, with great good-humour, "You and I are in similar positions, for you are the Crown-Princess of the State of Bhopál, and I am the Crown-Prince of England." When I recall these words I cannot but regard it as a strange coincidence that the death of Her Majesty Queen Victoria took place in the same year as that of my own Mother, and that His Royal Highness the Prince of Wales became the ruler of the British Empire in the same year that I became the Begam of Bhopál. The visit was brought to a conclusion by the distribution of *'itr* and *pán*.

On December 29th, His Royal Highness honoured us by

returning our visit. He was met by Sidik Hasan Khán at the house of the Maháràja of Gwálior, and conducted thence to our residence. The Prince talked with my Mother in a most friendly manner, and clearly manifested his royal favour. At the close of the visit, the following gifts were exchanged :

From His Royal Highness the Prince of Wales to Her Highness Nawáb Shah Jahán Begam :

A gold medal bearing the image of His Royal Highness.
A diamond ring.
A portrait of Her Majesty Queen Victoria.
A gold chain.
A portrait of H.R.H. the Princess of Wales.
A portrait of His Royal Highness.
A gold seal.

From Her Highness Nawáb Shah Jahán Begam to His Royal Highness the Prince of Wales :

A gun of Bhopál manufacture.
An Indian scimitar.
A shield.
Two caps embroidered with gold thread.
A perfume box of silver filigree work.
A pair of Indian bracelets.
A pair of gold earrings.
A kerchief embroidered by Her Highness.
A copy of *The History of Bhopál*.
A book containing a description of Mecca, written by Nawáb Sikandar Begam.

Owing to indisposition I was unable to be present at this interview. I made the attempt, but was too weak even to reach the stairs which led to the reception-room. I was therefore obliged to remain in a lower apartment, where the members of the Prince's staff came to see me.

On January 1st, the Chapter of the Order of the Star of India took place. The spot selected for the assembly was the lawn in front of Government House, where arrangements had been made on a large and magnificent scale. A place was assigned to each member according to the number of his Star. Nawáb Shah Jahán Begam, clad in a *burkha*, occupied the place immediately on the left of His Royal Highness, and next to her came the other Knights, in the order of their creation. His Royal Highness then invested the various Chiefs and European gentlemen with the titles and orders that had been conferred upon them.

The birth of my daughter Sáhibzádi Bilkis Jahán Begam had left me in such a weak state that I ought never to have undertaken the journey to Calcutta. I went in obedience to my Mother's will, and it was only the thought that I was to see the heir-apparent to the throne of England that gave me the strength to bear the sufferings which my obedience entailed. I did, indeed, have the honour of visiting His Royal Highness, but, after that, I was too ill to take part in anything. Even this royal Chapter I was unable to see—a misfortune which I shall never cease to regret. After the Chapter, several other social functions took place, the most important of which was the visit paid by my Mother to the Viceroy and Lady Northbrook, and a visit paid by Their Excellencies in return. On the 18th of Zil Hijjah, we set out from Calcutta on our return journey. Our departure was private, and no official formalities took place. We halted at Benáres, where we visited the Mahárája and the Mahárání of Vizianágram, and again at Cawnpore.

During this visit to Calcutta, Nawáb Sidik Hasan Khán tried his best to get himself made *mukhtár*, or regent of the State. The question of my Mother remaining *purdah* had been raised solely with this end in view. It was, however, like all his other plans, unavailing; for, even had he been able to show that, by remaining *purdah*, my Mother was seriously hampered in the work of administration, he would have still required the consent of the heir-apparent before he, or any one else, could be appointed regent.

Before proceeding to an account of the Imperial Durbar at Delhi, which forms the subject of the next chapter, I will briefly narrate the circumstances connected with the births of two elder children.

My daughter Bilkis Jahán Begam was born at 1.37 a.m. on the 24th day of Ramazán-ul-mubárak, 1292 A.H. (October 25th, 1875). In honour of the event, five convicts were, according to the custom of the State, liberated from gaol, and money and corn were distributed amongst the poor. Early in the morning the newly born child received the salutations of all who were assembled at the Shaukat Mahal, and was afterwards taken to the mosque of Mahji Sáhiba to be blessed. The *akíka* ceremony was performed at 9 o'clock on the morning of the seventh day (30th of Ramazán-ul-mubárak), and the Sáhibzádi was named Muzaffar Begam, the letters of which denote the date of her birth. On this day the nobles and chief officers of the State broke their fast at my palace.

When the Sáhibzádi was forty days old, Nawáb Shah Jahán Begam desired to perform the *chatti* ceremony. But Nawáb Sidik Hasan Khán, who was learned in such matters, was opposed to its performance, telling my Mother that such ceremonies were not sanctioned by the Muhammadan religion. My Mother allowed herself to be guided by his advice, but she showed her affection for me by sending *jora* to my house (the Hamid Manzil), and by coming there herself and presenting my husband and myself with robes of honour, which she placed upon us with her own hands. Besides the usual presents given on such occasions, the midwife received a sum of two thousand rupees, and ornaments worth another thousand. A monthly sum of Rs. 250 was sanctioned for the Sáhibzádi's maintenance from the day of her birth. Nawáb Shah Jahán Begam dispatched *kharítas* to the Agent to the Governor-General and the Political Agent, who sent congratulatory letters in reply.

My second child, Nawáb Muhammad Nasrullah Khán, was born at 3 o'clock on the morning of the 17th day of the month Zil Kádah, 1293 A.H. (December 3rd, 1876). The news was received with great joy by all classes of the population. Perhaps no one was more genuinely delighted than

Nawáb Kudsia Begam, for, after four generations, a male child was born in the family of which she was then the oldest and the most distinguished member. It is almost a law of nature that the birth of a son gives more joy to a mother's heart, and is regarded by the other members of the family as a more auspicious event, than the birth of a daughter, and such feelings would naturally be intensified in the case of a family to which for a period of seventy-six years God had vouchsafed no male representative. The Kudsia Begam shared most heartily in the general rejoicings. According to custom, her retainers showed their happiness by firing off guns around her palace, and she accepted these and all other congratulatory demonstrations with great good-humour and kindness, distributing money and sweetmeats with her usual liberality. But the happiness which prevailed about her was not to be unclouded; and in the midst of the merry-making a peremptory order was received to the effect that all firing of guns was to cease, and this order was worded in a manner so offensive that it not only wounded the feelings of the Kudsia Begam in a most cruel manner, but did much to perpetuate and intensify the estrangement which already existed between her and my Mother.

One of the chief causes of this estrangement was my Mother's remarriage. This was an act contrary to the customs of the Afghán race, and the offence was aggravated by the fact that she had chosen to marry a man of an alien family. As a matter of fact, second marriages and the remarriage of widows are contrary neither to Muhammadan custom nor to the Muhammadan religion. For a considerable number of years, however, the Muhammadans of India had rigidly adhered to the custom of the Afgháns, and this had now taken such a hold on society that any breach of it was regarded as a heinous sin. This feeling was shared by men and women alike; even those whose ideas had been modified by Western education never permitted second marriages in their own families, and up to the present day the practice is viewed with disfavour by nearly all Muhammadans of Afghán descent. It was only natural, therefore, that the Kudsia Begam should support the traditions of her family and race. But this I can say with certainty, that, however strong her prejudices may have been, she would never have allowed them to become the cause of family dissensions, or to destroy her affection for her own flesh and blood. What offended her in my Mother's case was not so much the unlawfulness of the act itself, but the fact that the husband was a man of alien race, and qualified neither by rank, position, nor character to be the consort of the ruler of a State. She never publicly gave vent to her displeasure, but she was of too frank a nature to be able to disguise altogether her feelings towards Sidik Hasan Khán. He, too, knew the light in which he was regarded, and, instead of trying to gain her good-will by conducting himself with tact and courtesy, cherished resentment against her in his heart, and deliberately set himself to foment the family feud.

In carrying out these designs, he kept another purpose constantly before himself, and that was to trouble me and my family in every way that lay in his power, and in both his plans he was only too successful. Both I and my children were forbidden to enjoy the privilege of the Kudsia Begam's society and friendship. How painful this was to me only those can understand who are accustomed to look to their elders for affection and love, and to regard their friendship as one of the most precious things in the world. This treatment was the more hard to bear since it was altogether void of reason, and since we endured it at the hands of a stranger who never scrupled to sacrifice the happiness of others in order to compass his private ends. This was not the only injury I suffered. At the time of my marriage, the Kudsia Begam spent two and a half lákhs of rupees on jewellery and various household articles, which she intended as a marriage present for me. Many times she begged me to accept her gift, but my Mother, acting solely under the influence of Sidik Hasan Khán, would not permit me to do so. Her benevolent designs being thus frustrated, she resolved to wait for my *pirchath* ceremony, and to make her presentation to me on that occasion; but she only met with a similar disappointment. Until the day of her death she was the victim of schemes of this description, and then did Sidik Hasan Khán secure the prize which had formed the object of all his previous designs; for practically the whole of her property fell into his hands, a nominal share only finding its way into the State treasury.

But to return to the birth of my son. I received congratulatory letters from Colonel Kincaid, Political Agent, the Agent to the Governor-General, and many other English gentlemen. Colonel Osborne, formerly Political Agent, who had been specially intimate with my family, wrote to me from London telling me of the pleasure which the news had given him, and congratulating me in the most hearty manner. My Mother sanctioned a monthly allowance of Rs. 250 for the maintenance of my new-born son, as well as a lump sum of Rs. 3,000 to defray the cost of the birthday and *akíka*[1] ceremonies.

The *akíka* ceremony took place on the seventh day, and my Mother named the child Muhammad Nasrullah Khán. On the same day, according to custom, *jora* and other gifts were distributed at my expense amongst the retainers and servants of my household. On this occasion another event took place to mar our joy. My people were giving expression to their happiness in the usual manner by firing off guns, when the head *chobdár* made his appearance, and, approaching Nawáb Ihtishám-ul-mulk, said, in the presence of all who were gathered there, "An order has been given that these people are to disperse at once." The feelings of resentment which this order, and the manner of its delivery, aroused in us can easily be imagined. The Nawáb Sáhib, however, exercised his usual self-control, and merely said, "Very well; as soon as these people have received their presents they shall go away." But the matter did not end here. No sooner

[1] This is "a custom observed by the Arabs on the birth of a child: namely, leaving the hair on the infant's head until the seventh day, when it is shaved, and animals are sacrificed—namely, two sheep for a boy and one for a girl. It is enjoined by Muhammadan law, and observed in all parts of Islam" (Hughes' *Dictionary of Islam*). It is usual to name the child on this day.

had the *chobdár* gone away, than he reappeared accompanied by the Subhadár commanding the Body-guard, who said, in a loud and peremptory voice, "Dismiss these people instantly." There was nothing for it but to comply; and the Nawáb Sáhib reluctantly requested all who were present to depart, and at once sent a report of the whole affair to the Begam, the only result of which was that he himself was severely reprimanded. However distasteful the doings at my palace may have been to my Mother, she would never, of her own accord, have issued such an order. All her acts at this time were controlled by the specious arguments of her husband, and, not infrequently, orders were issued in her name and carried into effect before she had so much as heard of them.

CHAPTER VII

THE IMPERIAL DURBAR AT DELHI

In 1876, the newspapers announced that, on January 1st of the following year, a royal durbar would be held at Delhi, at which Her Majesty the Queen was to be proclaimed Empress of India. On October 13th, 1876 (24th of Ramazán, 1293 A.H.), a communication arrived from the Political Agent enclosing a formal invitation to the durbar. The invitation was, of course, accepted, and extensive preparations for the journey and the camp at Delhi were made. Her Highness's retinue was divided into three detachments, two of which consisted of the troops and camp equipment, and the third, which was the last to leave, of Her Highness's attendants and personal baggage. My own arrangements I had to commence two days after the birth of Nawáb Nasrullah Khán. My European friends, as well as many of my relatives, were altogether opposed to my going. But Sidik Hasan Khán had made up his mind that I should not be left behind, and he was, as usual, supported by my Mother. The reason of this determination was plain enough to me. Sidik Hasan Khán feared that, in the absence of my Mother, my former intimacy with the Kudsia Begam would be renewed, and all that he hoped to achieve by keeping us apart from each other might be lost.

In spite of my weakness, I obeyed my Mother's instructions, as indeed it was my duty to do, and set about preparing for my departure. We set out at 7 o'clock on the morning of the 27th Zil Kádah, 1293 A.H., the caravan consisting of Her Highness, myself, Sidik Hasan Khán, Nawáb Ihtishám-ul-mulk, and various nobles and State officials, numbering in all one hundred and sixty-three people. Hoshangábád was reached on the 30th of Zil Kádah, 1293 A.H. (December 17th, 1876). We were met here by the officer commanding the

Hoshangábád detachment with a guard of honour, besides several European officials. We left Hoshangábád the same day and reached Itársi in the evening. Here we were joined by the Political Agent, who had gone on in advance, and we embarked on the special train which was to convey us to Delhi. We had to stop at Jabbalpúr, Allahábád, and Aligarh, as, owing to my indisposition, special food had to be prepared for me at these stations. At 11 o'clock in the morning, we arrived at Delhi. A company of British soldiers formed a guard of honour, and presented arms as we alighted from the train. The Commissioner of Delhi and two Secretaries welcomed us on behalf of His Excellency the Viceroy, and various other European gentlemen were present on the platform.

As soon as Her Highness entered the camp, a salute of nineteen guns was fired. Since cholera was prevalent at this time, the Government had passed an order limiting the retinues of the Chiefs attending the durbar, the number of persons to accompany each Chief being fixed according to his rank. My Mother's retinue consisted of five hundred people, and the Bhopál camp was arranged to accommodate this number. The spot selected was near the village of Azádpúr, a healthy situation, and one that commanded a fine prospect. At 7.30 a.m. on Friday, 5th Zil Hijjah, Colonel William Kincaid, the Political Agent, called upon Her Highness to discuss the share which Bhopál should take in welcoming His Excellency the Viceroy on his arrival at Delhi, and on the following day Sidik Hasan Khán visited Sir Henry Daly, Agent to the Governor-General for Central India, to consult with him concerning the arrangements to be made for the reception of His Excellency at Her Highness's camp. Lord Lytton arrived in Delhi on the morning of the 7th, and the Chiefs assembled at the railway station to receive him. His Excellency, fearing that my Mother would be inconvenienced by so large a concourse of people, had excused her from being present at the railway station, and Bhopál was, therefore, represented by Sirdars of the State and a detachment of the State troops. The following day, His Excellency sent his Secretary to make inquiries after my Mother's health and welfare, and similar messages were received from the Rája of Nabha and the Rája of Samthar. Later on in the day, my Mother dispatched a messenger to the Nabha Camp to inquire after the health of the Rája.

In the evening, intelligence was received from the Political Agent that the Viceroy would receive Her Highness on December 27th, and that she was to be accompanied by not more than eight Sirdars; a programme of the procedure to be observed at this interview was also sent, together with eight tickets, on which the names, rank, and designation of the Sirdars accompanying Her Highness were to be written in English. All the arrangements for the visit were duly completed, and on the following day, *i.e.* December 27th, 1876, the Political Agent conducted the Begam to the Viceroy's camp, those accompanying her being Nawáb Sidik Hasan Khán, Nawáb Ihtishám-ul-mulk, Muhammad Jamál-ud-dín Khán Sáhib, First Minister of the State, Mián Núr-ul-hasan Khán, Mián Akil Muhammad Khán, Mián Nazír Muhammad Khán, Mián Alamgír Muhammad Khán, and Munshi Syad Abdul Ali Khán, the State Vakíl. I was unable to go owing to my indisposition, which the cold in camp had tended to aggravate. Her Highness was received with the usual salute of nineteen guns. The Chief Secretary, the Under Secretary, and Sir Henry Daly met her at the door of her carriage, and everything took place as arranged in the programme. His Excellency greeted my Mother in English, and asked her about her journey from Bhopál. He then inquired after me and Nawáb Nasrullah Khán, and expressed his surprise that I was able to undertake so trying a journey. "I am very pleased," he said, "that in spite of the very recent birth of your grandchild you have yet been able to come here and take part in this imperial durbar. I have heard much of your venerable Mother, the Nawáb Sikandar Begam, and of the many and high honours which were bestowed upon her. The history of her travels in Arabia written by herself, a copy of which you were kind enough to send to me, I have read with real pleasure. I, too, belong to a family of authors, and my whole life has been passed amongst men of learning, so I hope you will regard my appreciation of the book as a guarantee of its merits." At this moment the flag which had been sent to my Mother by Her Majesty the Queen was brought, and unfolded near His Excellency's throne. Whereupon, His Excellency descended from his seat, and, leading my Mother up to the flag, explained its high significance, and said, "This flag is a symbol of the friendly relations which exist between the Bhopál State and the English Government. Let it be carried in the State processions of Bhopál from generation to generation." He then presented my Mother with a gold medal, on which was inscribed, in English and Persian, the words "Empress of India." In doing so he said, "It gives me great pleasure to present to you, on behalf of Her Majesty the Queen-Empress, this medal and flag. I trust that you will honour them, and that you and your successors will regard them as tokens of the friendship of the Empress of India towards you, and as mementoes of this imperial durbar, at which Her Majesty the Queen has taken the title Empress of India. Whenever this flag is unrolled, you will remember, not only that your loyal State is joined by the bonds of friendship to the English throne, but that it is the real desire of the Ruler of Great Britain that your family should long continue to be great and prosperous. I have also the pleasure to inform you that the Nawáb Sáhib has been granted a salute of seventeen guns throughout India." After this announcement, he shook hands with the Nawáb Sáhib, and the interview came to an end. The Private Secretary, the Under Secretary, and the Agent to the Governor-General for Central India conducted my Mother and Sidik Hasan Khán to their carriage, and congratulated them upon the honours which they had received. As they left the Viceroy's camp, salutes of nineteen and seventeen guns were fired. On reaching her quarters, Her Highness dispatched a messenger to carry her *saláms* to the Rája of Samthar, and the same evening complimentary messages were received from the Rájas of Gwálior, Datia, and Benáres.

On the afternoon of January 28th, His Excellency the Viceroy paid a return visit to Her Highness. He was met half a mile from the Bhopál camp, and escorted to the entrance,

THE EARL OF LYTTON.

p. 84]

where the Begam, in person, received him as he alighted from his carriage, while a salute of thirty-one guns was fired. The Viceroy was accompanied by the Foreign Secretary, the Military Secretary, the Private Secretary, the Agent to the Governor-General for Central India, the officer commanding the Body-guard, and other European officers. After the usual greetings, His Excellency took his seat, with the Begam on his right hand, and the members of his staff, in order of rank, upon his left. On the Begam's left sat the Political Agent, and the Sirdars of the State. After *nazarána* had been presented, the Begam gave His Excellency a copy of *The History of Bhopál*, and also a book entitled *Shams-i-Anjuman*, which had been compiled by her husband, Nawáb Sidik Hasan Khán. His Excellency looked at this book with much interest, and, rising from his seat, shook the Nawáb by the hand, saying, "I thank you for this book." In reply the Nawáb said, "I am highly honoured by your acceptance of this poor gift." His Excellency then inquired if the book contained extracts from the works of the poet Sádi, and on being informed that it did he expressed much pleasure. *'Itr* and *pán*, together with fresh and dried fruits, were then distributed, and Her Highness presented the Viceroy with a fan, inlaid with gold, as an example of Bhopál workmanship, and purses ornamented with gold embroidery and filled with cardamoms were given to each member of the staff. This concluded the interview, and His Excellency and party left, being escorted, as on his arrival, to a distance of half a mile from the camp. On this occasion, the soldiers of the artillery composing the saluting battery received from Her Highness a present of five hundred rupees.

The following day, Nizám-ul-mulk Asif Jah sent Nawáb Imád Jang, with other Nobles, to carry his compliments to Her Highness, and to inquire after her health, and similar greetings were also received from other Chiefs, all of which were suitably acknowledged and returned. Besides the officers of Central India, many other European ladies and gentlemen visited my Mother, and were all much impressed by the affability and courtesy with which they were received.

On the 13th Zil Hijjah, the flag which had been presented by Her Majesty the Queen was brought from the Political Agent's quarters by Ghulám Mahbub Khán, Mohtamim of the *kár-khána*, and received with all due honour. The same day Her Highness paid a visit to Her Excellency Lady Lytton, by whom she was most cordially welcomed. His Excellency was also present, and talked with my Mother in a very friendly manner, the Political Agent acting as interpreter. At her departure, His Excellency shook hands with my Mother and with Nawáb Sidik Hasan Khán, and presented each with a copy of one of his own works.

Her Highness also sent through the Political Agent, and the Agent to the Governor-General, copies of *The History of Bhopál* to the Governors of Bombay and Madras, the Mahárája of Gwálior, the Lieutenant-Governor of the Punjab, the Khán of Khelát, Nawáb Imád Jang, and the Mír Munshi to Sir Sálár Jang. On this day the Political Agent sent twenty-three tickets for the durbar. Of these, one was for Her Highness; eight were for the following: Nawáb Sidik Hasan Khán, Nawáb Ihtisham-ul-mulk Ali Jah Bahádur, Maulavi Jamál-ud-dín Sáhib Bahádur, the First Minister, Mián Núr-ul-hasan, Mián Alamgír Muhammad Khán, Mián Ali Hasan Khán, Mián Sadar Muhammad Khán, and Syad Abdul Ali, the State Vakíl; and the remaining fourteen were for various Sirdars, to whom third-class seats had been assigned. Her Highness was assigned a seat close to the Agent to the Governor-General for Central India, and to the Mahárájas of Gwálior and Indore.

January 1st was the ever-memorable day for which all these elaborate and magnificent preparations had been made, in honour of which this great concourse of ruling Princes had assembled, a day which brought joy to every heart in India, and the record of which makes one of the most brilliant pages in her history. At 10 o'clock in the morning, Her Highness went in state to the durbar. She drove in a carriage drawn by four horses, and was escorted by her nobles and retainers and a detachment of the State troops. The assemblage was held in an enormous pavilion situated at the foot of the famous ridge, from which the British forces bombarded Delhi during the Mutiny. The seats of the ruling Chiefs were arranged on a semicircular platform, painted white and gold, and facing the Viceregal Throne. Indian nobles, who were not ruling Chiefs, and government officials, were accommodated in rows behind the Throne, and in the very centre of the pavilion was displayed the royal Crown, surrounded by the flags of all the Feudatory States of India. The platform for the accommodation of the Chiefs was divided into thirty-six blocks, and to the block of each Chief was affixed the flag of his State. The middle of the semicircle was occupied by His Highness the Nizám, and the Mahárájas of Mysore and Baroda, the Chiefs of Rájputána being on their right, and those of Central India on their left. The Chiefs of the Punjab occupied the extreme right of the crescent, and the lesser Chiefs the extreme left. The Governors of Madras and Bombay, the Lieutenant-Governors of the Punjab, Bengal, and the North-West Provinces, and the Commander-in-Chief in India were also seated on this platform. Each of these was attended by his staff, and each Chief by the nobles of his State; and, as the durbar filled, the handsome and many-coloured uniforms of the West, mingling with the barbaric splendour of the East, formed a spectacle as unique as it was brilliant. All the troops assembled at Delhi were drawn up on either side of the pavilion, the European portion on the north side, and the Indian portion on the south.

His Excellency Lord Lytton arrived at noon, and was received with a royal salute without guns. He was wearing the robes of a Grand Commander of the Star of India, and was accompanied by Lady Lytton and his daughters. Heralds announced his approach with a flourish of trumpets, and massed bands played the National Anthem. Having taken his seat on the Viceregal throne, His Excellency commanded the Chief Herald to read the proclamation "of the assumption of the Imperial title by Her Majesty the Queen." This having been done, a translation of the same in Urdu was read by the Foreign Secretary, after which the Royal Standard was hoisted, a salute of a hundred-and-one salvos of artillery and a *feu-de-joie* were fired, and the bands again played the National Anthem. His Excellency the Viceroy and Governor-General then rose and addressed the assembly. The speech which he delivered, worthy in every way of the greatness of the occasion, does not need to be reproduced here. It forms, together with the Proclamation and Her Majesty's gracious message to her Indian subjects, a permanent part of the history of the Empire, and there must be few amongst my readers to whom it is not familiar. When the Viceroy and Governor-General had concluded his address, the assembly spontaneously rose and joined the troops in giving repeated cheers; His Highness the Mahárája Sindhia, His Highness the Mahárája of Jaipúr, on behalf of the Chiefs of Rájputána, His Excellency Sir Sálár Jang, on behalf of His Highness the Nizám, Her Highness the Begam of Bhopál, His Highness the Mahárája of Cashmere, and other Chiefs, also rose and gave expression to sentiments of loyalty and congratulation; massed bands played the National Anthem, and at His Excellency's command the Assembly was dissolved.

The same evening a State banquet took place, at which His Excellency proposed, for the first time, the toast of the Queen-Empress. Nawáb Sidik Hasan Khán represented my Mother on this night, and His Excellency requested him to inform Her Highness that he had already cabled her congratulations, with those of the other Chiefs, to Her Imperial Majesty in London.

On the day after the durbar, Her Highness called upon Lady Lytton at the Viceregal camp. The visit was returned the following day, Her Excellency being accompanied by the Viceroy's Secretary and the Political Agent. Nawáb Ihtishám-ul-mulk and the First Minister escorted Her Excellency to the Bhopál camp, at the entrance to which she was received by Nawáb Sidik Hasan Khán, a detachment of the State Lancers forming a guard of honour. As mementoes of this visit, Lady Lytton gave my Mother a ring set with diamonds, and photographs of herself and Lord Lytton. My Mother's gifts to Her Excellency consisted of a fan, a pair of jewelled earrings, and a jewelled necklace. The next day, when my

THE COUNTESS OF LYTTON.

p. 88]

Mother was paying her farewell visit, His Excellency, on behalf of the Queen, presented her with a sword and belt,[1] and sent to me and to Nawáb Ihtishám-ul-mulk silver medals which had been struck in memory of the durbar. On January 5th, Her Highness visited the Nizám. She was received by Sir Sálár Jang, and, after a brief meeting with His Highness, entered the Zenana and saw the Begams. The return visit took place on January 6th, and, *'itr* and *pán* having been distributed, the Nizám, who was at that time very young, was taken into the Zenana tents, while Sir Sálár Jang was entertained by Nawáb Sidik Hasan Khán.

During our stay at Delhi I had suffered much on account of the cold, and so, at the close of the durbar, Her Highness decided, for the sake of my health, to leave our camp at Azádpúr, and seek accommodation in the city. Two houses were accordingly engaged, and we moved into them on January 7th. Before our departure we visited the Fort, the tomb of Humayun, and many other places of historic interest, and pilgrimages were made to the tombs of Hasrat Kutub-ud-dín Bakhtiyar Kháki, and Sheik Nizám-ud-dín Ahmad Baiauni, as well as to other sacred spots. Many of the European residents of Delhi called upon us, and we spent a considerable time making purchases in the shops of the city. We left Delhi on January 22nd, our party being divided into three detachments as on our outward journey. A halt of a few days was made at Agra. We were received on our arrival by a guard of honour and a salute, and we took up our quarters at the house of Sait Lakshmi Chand. As at Delhi, we visited the chief buildings and shops, and Her Highness subscribed Rs. 500 towards the repairs of one of the city mosques. Whilst we were in Agra, presents amounting to Rs. 6000 were distributed amongst our retainers and servants, and Sait Lakshmi Chand, who had shown us great politeness and attention, was presented with a *khilát*. We left Agra on the 14th of Muharram, and, travelling *viâ* Cawnpore, reached Bhopál in five days.

[1] This sword was afterwards presented to Sáhibzáda Colonel Obaidullah Khán, on his assuming command of the Forces of the State.

CHAPTER VIII

1875—1877

IT had been Her Highness's intention to entertain her European friends at a banquet during her visit to Delhi. But, so numerous were the engagements during the durbar week, that the project had to be abandoned, and Her Highness determined to invite them to Bhopál instead. Orders were, therefore, sent to Bhopál that arrangements should be made without delay for the accommodation of the guests, as well as for their conveyance by road from Itársi; and, by the time Her Highness had returned from Delhi, the invitations had been sent out, and the preparations were well advanced. On February 21st, the Political Agent came to inspect the arrangements, and on the following day the visitors began to arrive. Sir Henry Daly, Agent to the Governor-General, reached Bhopál on the 25th. He was met at the Lál Gáthi by Nawáb Sidik Hasan Khán, with the chief nobles of the State, and a guard of honour from the State army, and a salute of seventeen guns was fired as he entered the city. In the evening, Her Highness held a durbar in her city palace, at which she formally bade her guests welcome.

The next morning, Nawáb Sidik Hasan Khán paid a visit to Sir Henry Daly, who, in the course of conversation, urged the necessity of introducing vaccination into the State, and recommended that arrangements for doing so should be entrusted to Munshi Ragab Ali Khán. Her Highness cordially welcomed the suggestion, and the appointment of Ragab Ali Khán was at once sanctioned. Members of Her

Highness's family had always been vaccinated by a European doctor, but as soon as I heard of the new arrangement that had been made, I asked permission to have my eldest son Nawáb Nasrullah Khán vaccinated by the newly appointed officer, for I thought that his example would do much to encourage others, and to dispel the fear which the new remedy was likely to inspire among the ignorant classes. At 4 o'clock the same afternoon, Sir Henry Daly, accompanied by all the European guests, went to Shahjahánábád and laid the foundation of the Kaisar Gang, which Her Highness had decided to build in commemoration of the Imperial Proclamation. Both Her Majesty the Queen and the Viceroy were informed of this event, and signified to Her Highness the gratification which the intelligence gave them.

In the evening, a banquet took place in the Jahángírábád Kothi. On this occasion, both English and Indian dishes were served, and many of the latter were greatly appreciated. At the conclusion of the repast, the toast of the Queen-Empress was drunk, and speeches were made by Her Highness and Sir Henry Daly. The principal event of the next day was a military review, in which both the Imperial Service troops and the State army took part. Every one praised the precision with which the various evolutions were executed, and the uniform of the troops and the horses of the cavalry were generally admired. In the afternoon, the mint, the gaol, and the hospital were visited, and at night the guests were entertained at dinner by Nawáb Sidik Hasan Khán. The Nawáb Sáhib himself proposed the royal toast, and Colonel Kincaid, the Political Agent, proposed the health of the Nawáb Sáhib. Sir Henry Daly then made a short speech, in which he congratulated Sidik Hasan Khán on having received the honour of a salute, and spoke of the friendship which the Queen-Empress always displayed towards the Bhopál State. He concluded by praising the administration of the Begam, making particular reference to the help she was giving towards the construction of the railway from Itársi, and the bridge over the Narbadda at Hoshangábád. The Nawáb Sáhib briefly responded, and after *'itr* and *pán* had been distributed, and each guest had received a present of a *battua*,[1] the party broke up.

The next day was occupied in visiting the Fatehgarh Fort, the Old Fort, the High School, and the Press. In the afternoon, the Bhopál troops gave an assault-at-arms, and in the evening, in spite of a gale of wind, a grand display of fireworks took place in the Nishát Afzah garden, at the conclusion of which *'itr* and *pán* were again distributed, and each lady was presented with a handkerchief of Bhopál manufacture. Sir Henry Daly left the next morning, and the remaining guests the day after. Previous to their departure they paid a farewell visit to the Begam at the Shaukat Mahal, when Her Highness gave to each of them her photograph and *The History of Bhopál*, every copy of which bore her own signature.

It was not long after these festivities, that a very regrettable event took place. My readers have been told how Sidik Hasan Khán came to Bhopál an ordinary individual, possessing neither rank nor fame, and how by the help of fortune, he gradually rose to a position equal in importance and dignity to that of a ruler of a state. The Government of India, ever mindful of the ancient and unbroken loyalty of the Bhopál State, and ever ready to treat its rulers with consideration, conferred on Sidik Hasan Khán, at the earnest entreaty of Nawáb Shah Jahán Begam, the same titles and distinctions and the same salute as had previously been granted to Nawáb Umrao Dula. In the reign of Nawáb Sikandar Begam, it had been enacted by the Government of India that the husband of the ruler of Bhopál should be allowed no share in the administration of the State. This enactment Sidik Hasan Khán systematically ignored. For some time, the political officers at Indore and Bhopál, desirous of deferring as far as possible to the wishes of my Mother, overlooked this conduct, until at last his interference passed all reasonable limits. After the entertainment described above, his behaviour grew worse and worse, and he committed

[1] A *battua* is a small bag made of embroidered silk, and used to hold betel, cardamoms, or tobacco.

such acts as would assuredly have brought about the interference of the political officers, had it not been for the well-known loyalty of Nawáb Shah Jahán Begam. So great, however, was Sidik Hasan Khán's influence over her, that she became absolutely blind to his intriguing nature. She would oppose him in nothing, and would never hear a word breathed against his character. That he possessed learning and ability is beyond question; but he abused both. His lot fell to him in a fair ground, but neither to the State nor to the British Government did he manifest the smallest signs of gratitude. His disloyalty to the State found vent in an attempt to vilify the Government and blacken the reputation of Nawáb Sikandar Begam, the wisdom of whose administration has been, and continues to be, eulogized by statesmen and politicians of the highest rank. The attack which he made on the good name of this ruler was so gross and unwarranted that it outraged the feelings of every one who possessed any sense of decency or justice.

The occasion selected by Sidik Hasan Khán for the promulgation of this slander was a large durbar held, apparently, with no other object than his own glorification. It was attended by all the leading nobles and officials of the State, and the proceedings opened with a proclamation, in the course of which the administration of the late Begam was subjected to the most offensive criticism, her reign being described as a period of barbarism and oppression. With the exception of his own adherents, all who were present were disgusted at the tone of the proclamation, and took no pains to conceal their contempt for its originator. It was followed by a speech from the Nawáb Sáhib himself, of such prodigious length that to give even a summary of it would tax a far better memory than mine. But there were some passages in it which, by reason of their very malignancy, I can never forget. In attempting to draw a comparison between the present reign and the past, he stigmatized the Sikandar Begam as a despot, and described the whole State as groaning under the tyranny and injustice of her rule. My Mother he praised in the most extravagant terms. She was the most enlightened, generous, and capable administrator of her day, and her reign was the reign of peace, justice, and mercy. Then, as though he were a magistrate addressing an unlawful assembly, he warned his audience not to mistake clemency for weakness. He was well aware, he said, that a number of evilly disposed persons were attempting to make mischief and to stir up sedition in the State. Amongst others he mentioned Latíf Muhammad Khán and Majíd Muhammad Khán, the two sons of Nawáb Umrao Dula, who, he stated, were known to be in the habit of paying secret visits to Nawáb Ihtishám-ul-mulk, and, by working on his inexperience with evil advice, were endeavouring to form a party hostile to the Begam and to the State. But by the Grace of God —and his own prowess—their base designs would soon be frustrated. Much more followed in the same strain, and he eventually brought his harangue to an end with an outburst of self-glorification, and a fulsome expression of his gratitude and devotion to the Begam and the British Ráj.

Although the charges brought against my husband and the sons of Nawáb Umrao Dula were without a particle of foundation, it may well be imagined that such words, spoken as they were at a public durbar, and by one who was to all intents and purposes a stranger to the State, inflicted on me, and many others, wounds which time will not easily heal. Out of regard for Nawab Shah Jahán Begam, we refrained from giving expression to our feelings, and heard both the proclamation and speech in silence. In this durbar, Sidik Hasan Khán attempted to imitate the proceedings at the Imperial Assemblage at Delhi, he himself being the "Viceroy" of the occasion; and he evidently thought that the best way of showing his appreciation of the honours that had been bestowed upon him was to heap insults upon other people.

By this magnificent display of his greatness, as well as by the proclamation and his own speech, in both of which his services to the State, his titles, and his honours were elaborately set forth, he thought to win the respect and admiration of the whole population. But true respect is not to be gained by self-praise and intimidation, and any claims to admiration which Sidik Hasan Khán may have possessed were far from being strengthened by this ill-judged and unseemly proceeding. The proclamation read in this durbar was in the name of Nawáb Shah Jahán Begam, but it would be altogether unjust to hold her responsible for it. Those who act under compulsion merit pity and sympathy rather than condemnation. That my Mother acted under compulsion I have no doubt, and I believe that no one who knew her will think otherwise, or lay the events of that unhappy day to her charge.

On the 7th day of the month Zil Kádah (November 30th), the birth of my second son, Sáhibzáda Muhammad Obaidullah Khán, occurred, and was the cause of general rejoicing. The customary demonstrations of joy, however, did not take place. My readers will remember the unfortunate circumstances attending the celebration of the birth of my eldest son. I was determined to take every precaution against a repetition of such an experience; and, except that I distributed presents to the various members of my household, no festivities were held. On the third day, my Mother came to see her grandson, and sanctioned for him an allowance of Rs. 250 a month, besides defraying the cost of his birthday and *akíka* ceremonies.

It was about this time, that another event occurred which aggravated, to a considerable extent, my Mother's displeasure with me. This was the marriage of Mián Alamgír Muhammad Khán. It was my Mother's desire that a marriage should take place between the daughter of this person and my eldest son, and my consent to the proposal was asked. I knew that to refuse was to provoke my Mother's wrath, so I avoided giving a direct reply, which, indeed, was not difficult, seeing that Alamgír Muhammad Khán was only just married, and did not as yet possess a daughter. Time went on, and I was beginning to hope that the matter had been forgotten, when, unfortunately, a daughter appeared. The proposal was at once renewed, and Sidik Hasan Khán did his utmost to further it. He was well aware of Her Highness's attachment to Alamgír Muhammad Khán. He also knew that I should object to the match on account of Alamgír's parentage,[1] and that my refusal would greatly inflame the Begam's anger against me. The subject was continually talked about, and my Mother daily sent her female attendants to me in the hope that they might elicit my views about it. I, however, maintained a rigid silence, and, even had I approved of the proposal, nothing definite could possibly have been settled, as my son was barely two years old, and the girl only just born. At last, my Mother, unable to comprehend what my silence signified, asked me, point-blank, whether I consented to the proposed marriage or not. I told her, plainly, that I did not. She was extremely displeased, and said, "What! Are you unwilling that your son should be allied to the family of Wazír Muhammad Khán?" I replied that, had that family been noble on both sides, then neither in the case of my marriage, nor her own, would it have been necessary for Nawáb Sikandar Begam to search for husbands outside the circle of her own relatives; and I added that I looked to her to exercise no less circumspection in arranging the marriages of her grandchildren than had been used in her case and mine. Shortly after this, the daughter of Alamgír Muhammad Khán died, and her mother also; and all possibility of an alliance between our families was at an end. But my answer had made my Mother extremely angry, and it long remained one of the chief causes of her ill-will towards me.

On Tuesday, 25th Shábán, 1297 A.H. (August 3rd, 1880), at 8 o'clock in the morning, my youngest daughter, Asif Jahán Begam, was born. My Mother honoured us with her presence at the *akika* ceremony, and I distributed *jora* and other gifts to my dependents and servants. At this time, I was in a very bad state of health. I had fallen ill before the birth of my daughter, and, after that event, my sickness increased to an alarming extent. I was placed under the treatment of Hakím Muazzad-dín. The whole city became alarmed, prayers for my recovery were offered up in all the

[1] Alamgir Muhammad Khán's father was an illegitimate son of Jahangir Muhammad Khán, who was the grandson of Wazir Muhammad Khán.

mosques, the Holy Korán was read through from beginning to end, and the prayer that God "would keep the light of Bhopál kindled" was on every lip.

Nawáb Kudsia Begam, being in disfavour with my Mother, was at first diffident about visiting me. But her anxiety became more than she could bear, and, during the latter part of my illness, she came two or three times in every week to see me. I had always been a favourite with her, and she was much distressed on account of my illness, and distributed lákhs of rupees in charity for my restoration to health. At length, after three long months, I was pronounced convalescent. I took the "bath of recovery," and was invested by my Mother with the "robe of health."

My recovery was the signal for general rejoicings and thanksgivings. The joy of the Kudsia Begam was beyond description; and the benevolence and liberality she displayed on this occasion will long be remembered. To me she sent a "robe of health" and a lákh of rupees in cash, while to each of my children she presented a like sum of money, as well as to my Mother and Sidik Hasan Khán. The latter, however, caused the whole amount to be returned, with a message to the following effect: "Her Highness desires me to state that, as you are displeased with her, she is unable to accept your money, and, as she cannot accept it, neither is it fitting that her children should do so." That a quarrel existed is true, but this was not the reason why the money was returned, a transaction with which my Mother probably had little or nothing to do. Sidik Hasan Khán was, in reality, furthering a plan of his own, which only became apparent after the Kudsia Begam's death. And when that sad event took place, this large sum went to swell the amount which, as I have already narrated, found its way into Sidik Hasan Khán's pocket. The property which the Kudsia Begam left was neither inspected by my Mother, nor was any correct valuation of it ever made. There was a considerable sum in cash, and this was invested in railway shares, but of the rest only a very small portion was ever accounted for.

When my eldest daughter reached her fourth year, Nawáb

Shah Jahán Begam took entire charge of her. At the *akíka* ceremony, a grant of Rs. 250 a month had been made to defray the cost of her upbringing. From this allowance, however, only the pay of the Sáhibzádi's personal servants was taken. The remainder was allowed to accumulate in my *deorhi*, all other expenses being borne by my Mother. Until her sixth year, my daughter's ceremonies were performed in the ordinary fashion. But, in the beginning of her seventh year, the *nashra súra bakr* was celebrated on an unusually large scale. The *nashra súra bakr* is usually preceded by the ceremony of *bismillah*,[1] and this custom had been followed in my own case, as well as in the case of my sister, Nawáb Sulaiman Jahán Begam. Unhappily, this sister died only a month after the *bismillah* had taken place; and this sad event was so fresh in my Mother's mind, and the performance of the ceremony would have recalled so many painful memories, that she determined to omit it in the present instance, and to prepare for the *nashra súra bakr* instead.

The celebration took place on the first day of Muharram, 1299 A.H. All the relatives of the family and the nobles of the State were presented with *jora*, and the Ministers and other State officers were entertained at a banquet. The relatives of the family also presented *jora* to my daughter, and all these *jora* were carried in procession to the Táj Mahal palace. My Mother, at this time, lived in the city, but, since a procession was a necessary part of the function, it was decided that it should take place at the Táj Mahal, as the

[1] Properly speaking, the *bismillah* ceremony should take place when the child is four years, four months, and four days old. It consists in teaching the child to recite the inscription which is found at the commencement of the Korán, *bismil-láhir-rahmán-nir-rahím*, "In the name of God the Merciful, the Gracious." After this ceremony, the child is sent to school and taught the alphabet, and to recite certain passages from the Korán. In all, there are seven important ceremonies for children. The birthday ceremony, which takes place on the day of birth; the naming ceremony and the *akíka* ceremony, which take place on the seventh day; the purification of the mother on the fortieth day; the *bismillah*; circumcision, usually in the seventh year; and the ceremony which takes place when the child has completed the reading of the Korán.

THE TAJ MAHAL AND BE-NAZIR PALACES.

p. 98]

route thither lay through the main thoroughfares of the city. On this festive occasion, Her Highness presented *khiláts* to my husband and myself, and to all the members of the families of the Wazír Khail, the Báki Khail, and the Jalál Khail.[1] I received my *khilát* in the *zenána*, my Mother robing me in it with her own hands, while my husband, who was unable to enter this portion of the palace, as many *purdah* ladies were present, received his in the reception-room of the *mardána* from the hands of Sidik Hasan Khán. I never saw my Mother in better spirits than at this time. For a whole month, festivities were kept up, and every day her liberality and good-humour seemed to increase.

In the families of ruling Chiefs, the beginning of a child's education is usually marked by the presentation of a *jágír*, or by an increase in his or her monthly allowance; and, accordingly, Sáhibzádi Bilkis Jahán Begam was now given a *jágír* worth Rs. 12,000 a year. The *sanad* of this *jágír* was sent to me, but my Mother continued to keep its management under her own control. The *nashra súra bakr* takes place when a child begins the reading of the Korán, and when the Holy Book is finished the event is marked by another ceremony. My daughter was eleven years old when the latter took place—the reading of the Korán having occupied her four years. During this time, my Mother's attitude towards me had undergone a complete change, and her disfavour was now as apparent as her favour had been before. No greetings were ever exchanged between us, and the doorway that connected her palace with mine was never opened. The news that my daughter's second *nashra* was to be celebrated, of course, reached my family, but we never had any information of it from my Mother, nor were we invited to take part in it; and I, my husband, and my children remained in our palace

[1] It is customary amongst Afgháns to regard men who become famous in the world as the founders of new families, or Khails, which are named after them. Thus, the Wazír Khail takes its name from Nawáb Wazír Muhammad Khán; the Báki Khail from my father, Nawáb Báki Muhammad Khán; and the Jalál Khail from my husband's ancestor, Salár Mír Muhammad Jalál Khán. An account of all these families is to be found in the *Táríkh-i-Bhopál*.

as though we had been strangers. It was some satisfaction to us to know that Bilkis Jahán Begam still enjoyed Her Highness's favour and affection, yet we felt this public slight very keenly. The celebration took place in the Shaukat Mahal, and a large number of relatives and friends gathered there. In the evening, the doorway between our palaces was opened, and my daughter, gaily dressed and bedecked with jewels, was sent to us. She made her *salám* very prettily to the Nawáb Sáhib and myself, and then, with a due display of respect, presented her *nazar*. We both embraced her warmly, and, almost before we had done so, she was recalled, and the doorway was again closed.

CHAPTER IX

1881—1882

On the 24th of Muharram, 1299 A.H. (December 14th, 1881), the death occurred of the Kudsia Begam. This venerable lady was born in the year 1801, the period of her childhood being one of the stormiest in the history of Bhopál. She ruled the State for eighteen years, and then abdicated in favour of her son-in-law, Jahángír Muhammad Khán. She herself retired into private life, and never again took any active part in public affairs. A *jágír* of Rs. 4,98,682 was conferred upon her, the management of which remained in her own hands till the day of her death. After her retirement, the Government of India continued to show her every mark of respect, and she retained all the honours to which her previous position had entitled her. She received a personal salute of fifteen guns, and, after the Delhi Durbar, by the special command of Her Majesty the Queen, she was invested with the order of the Crown of India. The Agent to the Governor-General and the Political Agent visited her whenever they came to Bhopál; and they did so not merely as a mark of respect, but because they considered it a privilege to converse with a lady of such rare piety and virtue. The Kudsia Begam was renowned for her liberality, kindness of heart, and the simplicity of her life. To the people of Bhopál she was more than a mother, and she won not only their respect, but their gratitude and love. During the period of her seclusion, she witnessed the vicissitudes of no less than three reigns. No changes, however, affected the tranquillity of her life, which would have remained undisturbed to the end had it not been for the malevolence of Sidik Hasan Khán.

I have already referred to the troubles which darkened

the last years of her life, and to the estrangement that grew up between herself and my Mother after the latter's second marriage. Perhaps she resented nothing more bitterly than a memorandum which, shortly before her death, was sent to the Agent to the Governor-General, in which it was stated that she had grown too old to administer her *jágír*; that she could no longer control even her own servants, who were guilty of all kinds of mischievous acts: and that it was, therefore, meet that her affairs should be brought under the management of the State. It is almost needless to say that the Agent to the Governor-General refused to entertain the proposal. The full story of this and her many other wrongs, which I heard from her own lips, is too long and too sad to be repeated here. The Government of India eventually stepped in, and endeavoured to bring about a reconciliation. Their efforts were so far successful that, in November 1881, a *kharíta* was sent to the Viceroy, informing him that friendship had been restored. It was, however, little more than a formal reconciliation, and grief and affliction followed the Kudsia Begam to her grave. One great consolation she had, which was that God permitted her to live long enough to see two male children amongst her descendants—namely, her two great-great-grandsons, Nawáb Nasrullah Khán and Sáhibzáda Obaidullah Khán.

On the morning after her death, her body was carried, in mournful silence, to a garden[1] outside the city, where she was laid by the side of her husband, in a grave which she herself had had constructed. There was general mourning in the city for three days, all business being suspended, and all courts and offices closed. The sad news was communicated to the Political Agent, and, through him, to the Agent to the Governor-General and to the Viceroy. From each, letters of condolence were received, expressing sorrow for the loss which the State had sustained, and paying a high tribute to the departed Begam's generosity, ability, and loyalty

[1] This garden, which is situated about a quarter of a mile from the city, was made by the Kudsia Begam herself, and is named after Nawáb Nazar Muhammad Khán.

to the British Throne. By the orders of the Political Agent, a day of public mourning was proclaimed at Sehore. All public and private places of business were closed, and the British flag at the Agency flew at half-mast throughout the day.

The Kudsia Begam had not been buried many days when death deprived me of another old and valued friend in the person of Maulavi Muhammad Jamál-ud-dín, First Minister of the State. He died on the 27th of Muharram, 1299 A.H., after a long and honourable career. He entered the service of the State during the regency of the Kudsia Begam. Every year furnished new proofs of his ability and faithfulness, and the period of his ministry was marked by many important reforms. In his latter days, he made the one big mistake of his life in marrying his daughter to a son of Sidik Hasan Khán, and labouring for the latter's promotion. Gratitude was not among the virtues of Sidik Hasan Khán, as Maulavi Jamál-ud-dín found to his cost ; for his last days were embittered, and his life made a burden to him, by the very man whom he had advanced and befriended. The troubles which Sidik Hasan Khán brought on the old Minister were unconnected with public affairs, and there is no need to describe them here. Suffice to say, they were borne with patience and fortitude, and served to bring out more strongly than ever the true nobility of Jamál-ud-dín's character. His loyalty and valuable services to Bhopál will never be forgotten, and his life will remain an example to all future Ministers of the State. His death was followed by disorder in every branch of the administration. A description of the confusion, intrigue, and corruption which prevailed would fill a volume, and would be of very little interest. I shall, therefore, content myself with a brief notice of the Ministers who held office during the period of Sidik Hasan Khán's ascendancy.

Maulavi Jamál-ud-dín was succeeded by Maulavi Muhammad Mobin. This person had been Sidik Hasan Khán's tutor, and secured his appointment through his pupil's influence. But he held office for only a few months, and was succeeded by Háfiz Ahmad Raza Khán, an honest and capable man, who set to work with energy to restore the government to a state of order and efficiency. Before many days, however, clouds began to gather. Sidik Hasan Khán was determined to be the first person in the State, and Háfiz Ahmad Raza Khán was equally determined to have a free hand. Both were strong men, and both obstinate, and each strove to bring about the other's downfall. Peace between such rivals was out of the question. Had their quarrel been confined to themselves no great harm might have resulted. But the behaviour of the Minister gave much trouble and annoyance to my Mother, and was, at times, altogether incompatible with his position as the first officer of the State. At last, he aroused her displeasure to such an extent that he was dismissed from his office.

By the orders of the Government of India, Nawáb Abdul Latíf Khán Bahádur, C.I.E., was next appointed Minister, and my Mother was advised to trust, in all important matters, to his guidance. But she was jealous of her prerogatives and dignity, and the idea of ruling under the directions of a native of India was not to her taste. She therefore sought to bring about the appointment of a European Minister, in which she was strongly supported by Sidik Hasan Khán. The Government of India eventually acceded to her request, and selected Colonel C. H. Ward for the post. Nawáb Abdul Latíf Khán served the State for just three months, and promised to be a very able administrator. He was withdrawn on Colonel Ward's appointment.

In December 1881, a few days before the death of the Kudsia Begam, Her Highness received an invitation to attend a Chapter of the Order of the Star of India, which was to be held the following March in Calcutta. The invitation was accepted, and by the beginning of February all the necessary preparations were completed.

That I should be taken to Calcutta I had never for a moment doubted. At the time of the Prince of Wales's visit I had been ill, it was the cold season, and both the First Minister of the State and the Kudsia Begam were in Bhopál, and I could easily have been left in the charge of one or the other of them.

NAWAB ABDUL LATIF KHAN, C.I.E.

HAFIZ AHMAD RAZA KHAN.

Yet my going was insisted upon. This time I was in perfect health, the season was temperate, the Kudsia Begam was, alas! dead, and the First Minister was to accompany Her Highness. What was my surprise, then, to find that my name did not appear in the list of those who were to form the party! I was unable to understand it, but supposed that a separate order would be sent to me. When this did not come, I made inquiries of Her Highness personally, and, after a great deal of persuasion and argument, at length obtained permission to go. How the proposal to leave me behind came to be made will become apparent as the story goes on.

A telegram from the Political Agent informed us that we should reach Calcutta in the first week of March. The 4th of Rabi-ul-awwal, 1299 A.H. (February 23rd, 1882) was, therefore, fixed upon as the day of our departure. As on the previous occasion, all the arrangements for our lodging in Calcutta were made by the Government of India, and the Political Agent chartered a special train for the journey from Itársi. The party consisted of Her Highness, myself and my children, Nawáb Sidik Hasan Khán, Nawáb Ihtishám-ul-mulk, and about 240 retainers.

On our arrival at Calcutta railway station, we were met by Captain How, the Under-Secretary, and Captain Baker, A.D.C. A guard of honour was also present, and a salute of nineteen guns was fired. In the evening we were visited by Colonel Ridgeway, Under-Secretary to the Government, the Aide-de-camp in Charge, and Captain Taylor, who came to inquire after our welfare on behalf of the Viceroy. Four o'clock on the following afternoon was the time fixed for Her Highness to pay a State visit to His Excellency. A programme of the procedure to be followed was drawn up, and a copy was sent to us from the Foreign Office. Besides myself, ten other people accompanied Her Highness. We were escorted by a squadron of British cavalry, and on reaching Government House we were met by the Military Secretary and the Foreign Secretary, a salute of nineteen guns again being fired. His Excellency welcomed us as we entered, and after shaking hands with us led us to our seats. Her Highness's chair was on His Excellency's right hand, the Political Agent's next, then mine, then the Nawáb Sáhib's, and those of the remainder of the party in the order of their rank. What took place at the visit is sufficiently indicated in the programme, which, in order that my readers may have some idea of the detailed manner in which such functions are arranged, I give below.[1]

[1] "FOREIGN DEPARTMENT.

"FORT WILLIAM, *March 2nd*, 1882.

"*Reception of Her Highness the Begam of Bhopál, G.C.S.I., by His Excellency the Viceroy and Governor-General at Calcutta.*

"At 4.45 p.m. on Thursday, March 2nd, 1882, His Excellency the Viceroy and Governor-General will receive a private visit from Her Highness the Begam of Bhopál, G.C.S.I., in the Throne Room of Government House.

"The Brigadier-General Commanding the Presidency District and the District Staff will be requested to be present on this occasion.

"A carriage containing the Military Secretary, the Under-Secretary in the Foreign Department, and an Aide-de-Camp to His Excellency the Viceroy, will start from Government House at 4.5 p.m. for the purpose of escorting Her Highness from her private residence.

"On alighting from the carriage Her Highness will be conducted up the stairs of the Grand Entrance by the Military Secretary and the Under-Secretary, and will be received at the top of the stairs by the Foreign Secretary, by whom she will be conducted to the Throne Room. The Viceroy and Governor-General will receive Her Highness midway between the Throne and the entrance to the Throne Room, and will show her to a seat at his right hand.

"Immediately to the right of the Begam will sit the Political Officer on duty with Her Highness, next, the Nawáb Consort, the Nawáb Sultán Jahán Begam, and such of Her Highness's Attendants, not exceeding seven in number, as are entitled to a seat in the Durbar. On the left of the Viceroy and Governor-General will be seated the Foreign Secretary, the Brigadier-General Commanding the Presidency District, the Private and Military Secretaries to the Viceroy, the Under-Secretary, His Excellency's Personal Staff, and the District Staff.

"The Begam will present a *nazar* of 151 gold mohurs, which will be touched and remitted.

"After a short conversation, the Nawáb Consort, Nawáb Sultán Jahán Begam, and Her Highness's Attendants, will be presented to the Viceroy by the Political Officer on duty with Her Highness, and will, each, offer a *nazar* of one gold mohur, which will be touched and remitted.

"*'Itr* and *pán* will be served to the Begam at the close of the interview by the Viceroy and Governor-General, and to the Nawáb Consort and the Nawáb Sultán Jahán Begam by the Foreign Secretary, and to the other Attendants by the Under-Secretary.

"The Viceroy and Governor-General will take leave of the Begam at the

On March 2nd, we had the honour of receiving Lord Ripon at our residence. The formalities observed were much the same as those I have just described. My Mother presented His Excellency with a copy of *The History of Bhopál*, a Muhammadan head-dress, a silver *betel*-box, and a silver perfume-box, all of which were graciously accepted. All the officers who took part in the interview presented *nazarána*. In addition to my own, I presented, by my Mother's order, *nazarána* on behalf of my son Sáhibzáda Obaidullah Khán and my daughter Asif Jahán Begam, who were too young to make their appearance. Later in the day, Her Excellency Lady Ripon returned my Mother's visit. I was present on this occasion, and my Mother presented Her Excellency with a gold *guláband*, or jewelled necklace. While we were in Calcutta, my Mother visited many important institutions, and helped each of them with a subscription.[1] At different times, the Lieutenant-Governor of Bombay, His Excellency

same point at which His Excellency received her, the Foreign Secretary will conduct Her Highness to the top of the Grand Staircase, and the Under-Secretary and Aide-de-Camp to His Excellency will accompany Her Highness back to her residence.

"Her Highness will be escorted to and from Government House by a party of Cavalry.

"The Marble Hall will be lined by a party of the Body-guard.

"During the interview a Band will play at the head of the Grand Stairs.

"A Guard of Honour will be drawn up in front of Government House, and will salute on the arrival and departure of Her Highness.

"A salute of nineteen guns will be fired from Fort William on the arrival and departure of the Begam.

"Undress uniform will be worn.

"J. W. Ridgeway, *Lieut.-Col.*,
"*Offg. Under-Secretary to the Government of India.*"

[1] The following is the list of institutions visited by Her Highness, with the amount of her subscription to each:

	Rs.
The Zenána Hospital	1000
The Bengal Asiatic Society	500
The Calcutta Madrissa	300
The Rest House	250
The Mayo Hospital	250
The Campbell Hospital	250
The Indian Agricultural Society	250
The Zoological Gardens and Museum	1000

the Commander-in-Chief of the British Forces, Lady Grant, Captain Prade, and many other people of distinction called at our quarters, but I was not allowed to meet any of them.

It was while we were at Calcutta that we read in the newspapers of the attempt on the life of Her Majesty Queen Victoria.[1] The news of this outrage created a great sensation in Calcutta, and in all places of worship in the city prayers of thanksgiving that Her Majesty's life had been spared were said. Her Highness, through the Political Agent, cabled her congratulations to the Queen on her miraculous escape.

On 22nd Rabi-us-sáni, we left Calcutta for Bhopál by special train. Early in the day, my Mother and I paid a farewell visit to Their Excellencies Lord and Lady Ripon, and drove straight from Government House to the railway station. We were escorted by a squadron of native cavalry, and the Under-Secretary, the Foreign Secretary, and an Aide-de-camp were present on the platform to bid us farewell. We reached Itársi in four days, and journeyed thence by road to Bhopál, our arrival being announced by the usual salute.

[1] Her Majesty had alighted from the train at Windsor railway station. and was about to drive to the Castle, when some villain discharged a revolver at the carriage in which she and Princess Beatrice had taken their seats. By the Grace of God the bullet missed its mark, and the would-be assassin was overpowered by two Eton boys before he could fire a second time. The royal carriage then proceeded on its way, Her Majesty praising her daughter for the coolness she had displayed.

Photo by W. & D. Downey.

THE EARL OF RIPON.

p. 108]

CHAPTER X

THE BHOPAL STATE RAILWAY

COLONEL H. DALY, in his *Memoirs of General Sir Henry Dermot Daly*, thus describes the state of Central India in the middle of the last century: "In the Central India of 1868 there was an entire lack of railway communication. The Great Indian Peninsular Railway extended only as far as Khandwa, while the terminus on the northern side of the province was Agra. In roads also Central India was deficient. With the exception of the Grand Trunk road from Bombay to Agra, which passes through Indore, Goona, Sipri, and Gwâlior, there was practically not a yard of metalled road in the Agency."

It was a fortunate thing for the Province when, in 1868, Sir Henry Daly was appointed Agent to the Governor-General. It was a time of great distress. For two whole years the country had been devastated by famine, the horrors and hardships of which were increased tenfold by the absence of means of communication, which rendered any effective system of relief an undertaking of the utmost difficulty. The wretched people fled from district to district, but only to find, on every side, starvation and death awaiting them. In the words of Sir Henry Daly's official report (quoted in the *Memoirs* referred to above): "Thousands perished from sheer starvation, and thousands from cholera and sun-stroke. Villages, and even districts, were depopulated, and there were none left to tell how many of the inhabitants had sunk under the miseries that oppressed them. Scindia computes the casualties in the neighbourhood of Gwâlior at 92,987. Bodies and bones were found in *nâlas*, and on the plains, under trees, and upon the wayside: and this over a vast space." In urging the

Government to open up this portion of the country, Sir Henry Daly wrote: "This province, which yields an annual revenue of three millions sterling (two of which are received by the Government of India on account of opium exports), is without a mile of communication which can be used in the rainy season. Malwa, as regards the extent of cultivation, is still in a backward state: population is scanty, lands which would bear cotton and opium lie waste. With roads and a line of rail, Malwa would be to Central India what Bengal is to the North-West Provinces."[1] It was entirely through the influence and unceasing efforts of Sir Henry Daly that the Chiefs of Central India began to realize how essential railway communication was to the development of their territories. The Mahárája Holkar led the way by constructing a line from Khandwa to Indore, and his example was soon followed in Gwálior and Bhopál. In less than ten years' time, Sir Henry Daly had the satisfaction of seeing Central India traversed by a network of roads and railway lines, made and laid down at the expense of the Chiefs themselves, who thus became, by his instrumentality, the pioneers of the trade and prosperity of their province. The people of Central India will never forget what they owe to Sir Henry Daly. It is given to few people to win the confidence of an Indian community as he won theirs. The qualities that made him succeed are best described in the words of Colonel H. Daly. "He possessed," says that writer, "an extensive knowledge of the history of India generally, and of the States of Malwa in particular. He had a clear and precise conception of the Indian character, and, above all, he possessed a perfect temper, a buoyant good-nature, and the faculty of impressing his own high spirits and bonhomie upon those with whom he was brought into contact. Personal influence was the keynote of his success."[2]

[1] During this famine, Bhopál did not suffer so heavily as other places, and much grain could have been exported to the stricken districts had the means for doing so existed.

[2] Among the many evidences of the interest which he took in the ruling families of Central India, and of his anxiety to promote their welfare, is the College which he established at Indore for the sons of the Chiefs of the Province. That Colonel Daly now occupies the place which his father filled

SIR HENRY DALY.

p. 110]

It was during an interview with Sir Henry Daly, who came to Bhopál for the purpose, that Her Highness finally agreed to the construction of a State Railway from Itársi to Bhopál, promising to contribute funds from the State treasury, and to persuade the Kudsia Begam to advance money from her private purse. Soon afterwards, a letter was received from the Agent to the Governor-General, in which, after thanking Her Highness for her offer to provide funds for the railway, he informed her that His Excellency the Viceroy was only awaiting the decision of the Kudsia Begam before giving his sanction to the undertaking. It was then decided that a sum of thirty-five lákhs of rupees should be guaranteed, of which twenty-five lákhs should be contributed by the State in annual instalments of five lákhs, and ten lákhs by the Kudsia Begam in instalments of two láhks, the whole amount to be advanced free of interest. Information to this effect was sent to the Government of India, and it was settled that interest at the rate of 4 per cent. should be paid to the State and to the Kudsia Begam from the profits of the railway, and that should any surplus still remain, it should be divided between the aforesaid parties and the Government, the latter being responsible for the execution of this contract, which was to hold good in perpetuity.

The Chief Engineer of the Great Indian Peninsular Railway prepared and forwarded to Her Highness two plans, each showing a different route for the new line, one passing through Chauka Bishankhéra, and the other through Bhut Plassy and Yár Nagar. The choice was left to Her Highness, and she decided in favour of the former, as it would pass through a more thickly populated area, and would command a heavier carrying trade.

These preliminaries being concluded, other details regarding

with such distinguished ability, is a happy circumstance for Central India. Of the many characteristics of his father that are reflected in Colonel Daly, none is more conspicuous than his desire to advance, to the utmost of his power, the intellectual and social well-being of the ruling Chiefs and their families: and there is good reason to hope that the Daly College will, under his fostering care, develop into a great Indian Public School, to the lasting benefit of this important Province.

the making of the line, its boundaries, and the sites for the stations were arranged; and it was agreed that any disputes that might arise between the State and the railway authorities should be referred to the Government for settlement, and that the decision then given should be regarded as final. His Excellency Lord Lytton wrote to Her Highness, expressing his satisfaction with the arrangements that had been made, and stating that the Agent to the Governor-General had been instructed to draw up an agreement. On December 29th, 1877 (23rd Zil Hijjah, 1294 A.H.), this document was received through the Political Agent, and was duly signed, sealed, and returned, a copy being preserved in the State office.

At this juncture Her Highness foresaw that a branch line connecting her capital with Itársi would be of no great advantage to the State unless it could be continued beyond Bhopál to join the Gwálior State Railway at Ujjain, or be carried on through Bhilsa to Gwálior, thus opening up direct communication with Agra and the north of India. After much correspondence, it was agreed that the survey should be continued through Bhopál as far as Sehore, and that, on the completion of the line from Agra to Gwálior, Bhopál should be connected with it. At the same time the State and the Kudsia Begam agreed to advance fifty lákhs of rupees instead of thirty-five, the former contributing thirty-five lákhs and the latter fifteen. A plan of the Bhopál station was next prepared. Her Highness, however, objected to the proposed site, owing to the instability of the soil and the difficulty of obtaining a good water-supply. It was, accordingly, decided that the Political Agent and Nawáb Sidik Hasan Khán should select a site together, but that no further steps should be taken in this direction until the survey of the line should be completed.

In November 1878, the Agent to the Governor-General sent his First Assistant, Captain Barrow, to Bhopál with a letter to Her Highness, in which he again thanked her on behalf of the Viceroy for her liberality, and forwarded for her perusal a copy of the amended agreement. Her Highness accepted all the terms, but made certain suggestions in regard to the size of the waggons to be used on the new line, and stipulated that the work should be commenced on the first day of January 1880. A favourable reply having been received, preparations were made by the State to assist the work in any way that might be necessary, a special officer being appointed for this purpose. On October 14th, the agreement, which had been returned to the Government of India for ratification, was sent to Her Highness by the Political Agent, together with a request that the first instalments for the year 1880 might be paid to avoid all possibility of delay. Some years later, owing to the death of the Kudsia Begam, and to other altered circumstances, this agreement had to be considerably modified. The arrangement as to the division of profits was finally settled in a supplementary agreement, dated October 14th, 1890. The clause runs as follows:

"The profits accruing on the aforesaid railway shall be divided in perpetuity between the British Government and the Ruler of Bhopál in proportion to the capital contributed by each party at the close of the period for which the accounts are made up. In the event of the railway being worked at a loss during any half-year or other period for which the accounts may be made up, such loss shall be borne by the British Government and the Ruler of Bhopál in the same proportions. This agreement shall take effect from January 1st, 1891."

It was on June 12th, 1882, that a private letter from the Chief Engineer of the railway informed Her Highness that trains had already begun to run between Itársi and Hoshangábád, while, at the same time, intelligence was received through the State Vakíl that the Agent to the Governor-General would come to Bhopál to open the line, and that the ceremony would take place on November 18th, (29th Muharram, 1303 A.H.). Her Highness at once set about preparing for his reception, and orders were issued for decorating the city in a manner worthy of so great an event. Invitations were sent through the Political Agent to the Chief Commissioner of the Central Provinces, the Deputy Commis-

8

sioner at Hoshangábád, the Chief Engineer of the Railway, and to all the officers at the Residency and the Agency. Special instructions were given to the Mohtamim of the State *kár-khána* to arrange conveyances for the various visitors, and to see to their comfort on the journey from Itársi to Bhopál.

The Political Agent arrived on November 11th, and the Agent to the Governor-General on the evening of the 16th. Official etiquette prohibits the firing of salutes after sunset, and visitors whose arrival takes place at such an hour are not usually accorded a public reception. The Political Agent, however, informed Her Highness that in the Gwálior State public receptions had taken place after sunset, and, though such had never been the custom in Bhopál, he considered that the unique character of the occasion and the rank of her visitors would justify a departure from ordinary rules. Her Highness willingly consented to this proposal, and the necessary orders were given for carrying it into effect.

On November 12th, the Political Agent, accompanied by Mr. Cook, the State Engineer, and the Mohtamim of the *kár-khána,* went to the railway station to select a place for the opening ceremony. It was agreed that the large goods-shed would lend itself admirably to their purpose, and extensive arrangements were made for its adornment. Colonel Bannerman, Agent to the Governor-General, with his staff, reached Bhopál at 7.30 p.m. He was met at the Aish Bágh by the Political Agent and the Naib-ul-riyásat, the State troops, with the band and the *mahi-marátib,* forming a guard of honour. Colonel Bannerman shook hands with those present, and the Naib-ul-riyásat apologized for the absence of Her Highness, who, on account of the indisposition of the Nawáb Sáhib, was unable to receive him in person. A procession was then formed, and the visitors were escorted to the camp which had been pitched for their accommodation, the entire route being brilliantly illuminated and decorated with triumphal arches. The salute announcing their arrival was fired on the following morning. On the next evening, the Commissioner of the Central Provinces arrived, and he too was accorded a public reception. On the morning of the 18th, Colonel Bannerman called upon Her Highness at the Shaukat Mahal, while the Nawáb Sáhib paid a visit to the Commissioner. Later in the day all the other guests visited the palace and paid their respects to Her Highness.

The opening ceremony took place at 4 o'clock in the afternoon. As stated above, the place selected for the assembly was the goods-shed, and, so well had the decoration committee done its work, that it may safely be said that no goods-shed ever wore a more impenetrable disguise. It was surrounded without by troops: the State cavalry on the eastern side, the infantry on the west, a battery of artillery at one end, and a line of elephants, magnificent in their State harness, at the other. Her Highness's seat was in the centre of the building: the Agent to the Governor-General and the other European guests occupied the space on her right, and that on her left was reserved for officers of the State and *purdah* ladies, for whom special accommodation had been made.

As soon as Colonel Bannerman had declared the line open, a salute of thirty-one guns was fired, and Her Highness, having received the hearty congratulations of her many friends, arose and delivered the following speech:

"Colonel Bannerman, Ladies and Gentlemen,—I render a thousand thanks to Almighty God that He has permitted the State of Bhopál and its Ruler to enjoy the benign protection of Her Most Gracious Majesty the Queen-Empress of India, through the benevolence of whose rule the light of Western science is now shining on this land, and through whom and the wise statesmen and brave soldiers sent to govern and protect us, we are able to look back upon years of peace and progress—years that have transformed the pathless jungles of Hindustán into rich and fertile plains, vying in beauty with the gardens of Cashmere. When I think of the interest Her Majesty has always taken in the welfare of this State, of the friendship which she displayed towards my august Mother, Nawáb Sikandar Begam, and of her unfailing kindness to myself, I seek in vain for words to express my gratitude. Nor am I less grateful for the kind and courteous treatment I have always met with from the

Viceroys of India, their Agents in Central India, and the Political Agents in Bhopál. To you, Colonel Bannerman, my special thanks are due. I thank you most heartily for your congratulations on the completion of this Railway, and for your great kindness in coming here to-day to perform the opening ceremony. It is to yourself, to Sir Henry Daly, and to Mr. Griffin that congratulations should be paid on this memorable day, by whose advice this great work has been undertaken, and under whose supervision it has been carried out. I am very grateful to Colonel Kincaid for the good advice he has given to me and to the Wallájah-Amír-ul-mulk Nawáb Sáhib, and for his constant help in all matters connected with the making of this line. Let all praise be given to God who has permitted us this day to see the realization of our hopes, and to taste the first-fruits of our labours. I trust that the Bhopál State Railway will in every way prove a success, and that it will lead to as big an increase in the revenue of the State as was predicted when its construction was first contemplated. I now look forward to the time when the Bhopál line will be connected with the Great Indian Peninsular Railway at Bhilsa, which, besides conferring a great benefit on the travelling public, will, I am confident, make a very considerable increase in our profits.

"But the advantages of the Bhopál State Railway are not all in the future. It has given to me and my people the great advantage and pleasure of welcoming to Bhopál the Agent to the Governor-General for Central India, and the many other distinguished guests who have come here to grace this occasion. In the name of the State, I bid you all a most hearty welcome to Bhopál, and I thank you for the honour you have done me in accepting my invitation. To those officers who have taken part in the construction of this railway, I once more offer my congratulations on the successful completion of their labours. I am sending a telegram to His Excellency Lord Ripon to inform him that the Bhopál State Railway is now an accomplished fact. His Excellency will, I am sure, receive the intelligence with great satisfaction, and will regard this day as one worthy to be remembered in the history of his Viceroyalty. In conclusion, I pray for the everlasting prosperity of the great empire of Her Majesty the Queen, and I trust that, by the Grace of God, the friendly relations that have always existed between my State and the Crown may be strengthened day by day, and that Her

GADAROYA BRIDGE ON THE BHOPAL STATE RAILWAY.

p. 116]

Majesty will never cease to regard me as her grateful and loyal servant."

At the close of this speech, a telegram was dispatched to His Excellency the Viceroy, informing him that the line was open. All the visitors then embarked on a train which had been kept in readiness, and were conveyed to the railway station, where they found their carriages awaiting them. In the evening, a banquet took place at the Lal Kothi, Her Highness, according to her custom, joining her guests at the conclusion of the repast. As soon as she had taken her seat, the health of Her Majesty the Queen was drunk, after which Colonel Bannerman rose, and, in a brief but interesting speech, described the great political and commercial advantages which the new railway would confer not only upon Bhopál, but upon the whole of Central India. He spoke in high terms of the enterprise which Her Highness had displayed in providing, without security and free of interest, practically all the money required for making the line. He had no doubt, he said, that the future would prove this outlay to be a sound financial transaction, and he expressed the hope that Her Highness's example would be followed by many other ruling Chiefs. After referring to the proposed extension of the line through Bhilsa to Agra, and the impetus which would thereby be given to the trade and agriculture of the districts through which it was to pass, he asked his hearers to join him in drinking to the health and long life of Her Highness the Begam, and to the success of the Bhopál State Railway.

Colonel William Kincaid, Mr. Crosthwaite, Chief Commissioner of the Central Provinces, and Colonel Thomson, also made congratulatory speeches, and, on their own behalf and that of the other guests, thanked Her Highness for the hospitable welcome which had been extended to them. The evening terminated with a display of fireworks. Colonel Bannerman and the Chief Commissioner left for Hoshangábád the next morning, and the other visitors departed in the course of the day.

The construction of the railway coincided with one of

those periods when my Mother's displeasure with me was most marked. I, personally, therefore, was little acquainted with what was taking place, and my account is based upon what I have been able to glean from State records. In those days, all my time was occupied with domestic affairs, and particularly with the education of my children, of which I will give a brief account before passing on to the events of the next chapter.

Between the ages of my two sons, Nawáb Nasrullah Khán and Sáhibzáda Obaidullah Khán, there is a difference of only two years; and, though the elder began to study first, I was able to have them both educated together. Tutors were appointed to teach them Urdu, Persian, and handwriting, as well as to give them religious instruction; and they underwent, at the same time, a thorough training in military exercises. Moral instruction—without which education can never bear good fruit—they received at the hands of my husband and myself. It had always been our desire that one of our sons should become a Háfiz, not only because amongst Muhammadans such persons are highly esteemed, but because to become a Háfiz is, in itself, an act of great piety. Seeing, therefore, that our younger son was gifted with an unusually good memory, we decided that he was the better fitted to undertake the sacred task; and whilst he was engaged in committing the Holy Book to memory, his elder brother commenced to study English. Both of them worked hard and with zeal; and, in addition to the ordinary subjects of study, they read many Persian and Arabic books, from which they gained considerable knowledge of the world, as well as much wise counsel in regard to the conduct of life. Throughout the period of their education, the preservation of their health, and the cultivation in them of good manners and habits, ranked with me above all other considerations.

By the Grace of God, this system of education proved successful. My sons have grown up strong in mind and body, and their behaviour and habits are those of well-bred Muhammadan gentlemen. The manner in which they are able to discharge their duties, whether civil or military, shows that their early training was well suited to their needs. The study of English did not form a part of Sáhibzáda Obaidullah Khán's education. But he has since, with the help of my youngest son's English tutor, acquired a very serviceable knowledge of that language, and is able to converse in it freely and fluently on all ordinary topics.

CHAPTER XI

1883—1886

It has already been told how, on the occasion of my Mother's first marriage, the Government of India had ordained that the husbands of the Begams of Bhopál should, from that time forward, be Nawábs only in name, and should have no title to interfere in any matters connected with the administration of the State. It has also been told how, after her second marriage, this ordinance was neglected, and how Sidik Hasan Khán was permitted to raise himself, step by step, until he became the virtual ruler of Bhopál. Enough too has been said about the character of this man to enable my readers to form some idea of the disastrous results which his illegal assumption of authority produced. But it was not the evil influence of one man alone that brought the State to the verge of ruin. Sidik Hasan Khán surrounded himself with a band of adherents who, besides being utterly unscrupulous, had no personal interest in the welfare of the State, and no sympathy with the people; and to these men he gave, one by one, every high office that fell vacant, with the result that corruption and mismanagement spread into all branches of the administration.

Amongst his other occupations, Sidik Hasan Khán devoted considerable time to literary work, and possessed some reputation as an author, chiefly on account of his contributions to the controversial literature of the day. This was a field which provided him with ample scope for his talents, but was, at the same time, one in which it was impossible for him to conceal his true character; and he soon achieved for himself a notoriety which contributed in no small degree to his downfall. Amongst his other writings there were three books entitled *Majmua Khutub, Hadáyat-us-Sáil*, and *Iktarábat-us-Sáat*, which, though purporting to be religious treatises, constituted in reality an attack upon the British Government. These books were published just at the time when the British Army was pursuing the Mahdi in the Soudan, and it was not long before they were brought to the notice of the Government of India, who at once dispatched them to Sir Lepel Griffin, Agent to the Governor-General in Central India. On receipt of the books, Sir Lepel Griffin, through the Political Agent in Bhopál, explained to Sidik Hasan Khán the evil consequences of such writings, and warned him against committing such an offence again. To this warning Sidik Hasan Khán paid no attention whatever, and in the course of the next two years published several more books of an equally questionable character. Sir Lepel Griffin, who had in the meantime gone to England on leave, found these books awaiting him on his return; and, hearing at the same time reports of the unsatisfactory condition of affairs in the State, he came to Bhopál to inquire privately into all these matters.

On August 27th, he had an interview with Her Highness, at which there were present Colonel Kincaid (the Political Agent), Munshi Dharam Naráyan, Mír Munshi of the Residency, Syad Abdul Ali, second Náib of the State, Syad Asgári Khán, and Syad Ináyat Husein Khán, the State Vakíl. All the charges to which Sidik Hasan Khán had laid himself open were explained in detail to Her Highness, but such was her confidence in him that she declined to believe any of them. The next day another interview took place, at which all the books written by the Nawáb Sáhib were produced for examination. This time the Nawáb Sáhib himself was present. A large number of passages which had been previously noted were read aloud, and the Nawáb was asked what he had to say in reply. He attempted an explanation, but he was altogether unable to refute the accusations brought against him.

Six weeks later, Sir Lepel Griffin again came to Bhopál, and on the 16th of Muharram, 1303 A.H., a durbar was held at the Shaukat Mahal, which was attended by all the chief officers of the State, as well as by Nawáb Ihtishám-ul-mulk, and my three elder children. The Agent to the Governor-General arrived, accompanied by his Staff and the Political Agent; and, after a brief and formal greeting, he turned to my Mother and said:

"His Excellency the Viceroy has directed that Nawáb Sidik Hasan Khán be deprived of his titles and his salute, and that he shall in future abstain from all interference, direct or indirect, in the affairs of the State; and that, in the event of his disregarding this order, a punishment of a much heavier kind shall be dealt out to him. Seeing that by his usurpation of authority, and by the oppression that has characterized his acts, the condition of the State and its administration is in the highest degree unsatisfactory, His Excellency directs the appointment of a duly qualified Madár-ul-muhám who is to be given full administrative powers."

I need not tell my readers that this punishment was a heavy blow to Sidik Hasan Khán. My Mother felt his disgrace hardly less keenly. Although, throughout the proceedings, nothing had been done which cast any reflection on her character, or which implied that she was in any way responsible for the evils that had arisen, she, nevertheless, felt that the orders of the Government touched both her dignity and her honour. Sidik Hasan Khán had no one to thank for his punishment but himself, yet he imputed the whole blame to me and the members of my household. He did all in his power to convince my Mother that we had plotted his downfall, and to encourage in her the idea that it was in reality herself upon whom the orders of the Government had brought disgrace, inasmuch as the titles and salute of which he had been deprived were honours belonging not to himself, but to the position that he held as the husband of the Ruler of Bhopál.

On February 16th, 1886, in accordance with the Order

above referred to, Nawáb Abdul Latíf Khán, C.I.E., was, on the suggestion of Sir Lepel Griffin, and with the approval of His Excellency the Viceroy, appointed First Minister of the State. He held the post for only four and a half months. He introduced many useful reforms into the judicial and revenue departments, and arranged for the transfer of an experienced officer from the British service to take charge of the latter. The accounts were disentangled and audited, and the true financial position of the State ascertained, after which a budget for the coming year was prepared. Nawáb Abdul Latíf Khán displayed both energy and ability, and, had he remained longer in Bhopál, would, in all probability, have brought the administration to a high state of efficiency. But Sidik Hasan Khán had set his mind on the appointment of an English Minister, thinking, for what reason I know not, that this would give him a better chance of regaining his lost powers and honours; and he induced Her Highness to apply to the Government for the appointment of Mr. Brook, Deputy Commissioner in Khandwa. Moved by Her Highness's repeated solicitations,[1] the Government at last consented to the appointment of a European, but selected for the post Colonel C. I. H. Ward, an officer with a high reputation for revenue work. He took charge from Nawáb Abdul Latíf Khán on July 1st, 1886.

Colonel Ward was an able administrator and a thorough English gentleman. He was intimately acquainted with the Indian character, and rapidly gained the sympathy of the people. From the day of his appointment, he gave his whole heart to the task before him, bringing to bear on it an enormous capacity for hard work, a wide and practical knowledge of Indian law and finance, a quick insight, and a shrewd judgment, while in all matters that came before him he gave the fullest possible consideration to the interests and wishes of the people. His ministry was a period of uninterrupted progress. A forest department was opened, a survey of the State was executed, new roads were made, strong and effective measures

[1] This was in direct opposition to the advice of Sir Lepel Griffin, who disapproved of the appointment of a European Minister.

were taken to suppress bribery, and the police force was thoroughly reorganized.[1] As a result of these reforms, the revenue of the State showed a substantial and steady increase.

But even Colonel Ward did not succeed in pleasing everybody, and amongst the few who viewed his administration with disapproval was Sidik Hasan Khán. The *régime* of an English Minister had not resulted in that rapid restoration to rank and power to which he had been looking forward, and he soon became as anxious for his removal as he had before been to bring about his appointment. His efforts were, as usual, seconded by Nawáb Shah Jahán Begam, and the Government of India, only too glad to have the services of Colonel Ward again at its disposal, withdrew him after he had served the State for two and a half years.[2] Colonel Ward's

[1] In the reorganization of the police, very valuable assistance was rendered by Munshi Isrár Hasan Khán. He was one among the many able officers who took service in Bhopál during Colonel Ward's ministry, and he now holds the post of Nasír-ul-muhám, or Chief Judicial Minister of the State. He came to Bhopál as Superintendent of Police, and by his hard work, his strict integrity, and his indifference to the opinions of all except his own superior officers, he gained the respect both of Her Highness and of Colonel Ward. Unfortunately, there were others who by no means appreciated Isrár Hasan Khán's high sense of duty, and the very qualities I have mentioned procured him so many enemies that, on the retirement of Colonel Ward, he, too, resigned his appointment, and returned to the service of the British Government, from which he had been transferred.

Khán Bahádur Isrár Hasan Khán is a member of a well-known family of the Háfiz Khail, in Shahjahánpúr. During the Mutiny, his father and uncles served the British Government with bravery and distinction. The former had his house burnt to ashes, and two of the latter were killed. Mr. Carmichael, Senior Member of the Board of Revenue in the United Provinces of Agra and Oudh, concludes a short account of this family with these words: "Every member of this loyal family is entitled to our consideration and respect." The Government of India has not forgotten its obligations, and to this day any member of this branch of the Háfiz Khail who desires service is sure of an honourable post. Muhammad Isrár Hasan Khán was a Deputy Collector in the district of Unao when his services were transferred to the State. In the year 1906 he received the title "Khán Bahádur" in recognition of his personal qualities and meritorious service.

[2] Muhammad Isrár Hasan Khán tendered his resignation at the same time. Her Highness, being fully aware of the excellent work he was doing, at first refused to accept it; but, as he would not be persuaded to change his mind, she was compelled, with great reluctance, to let him go. My husband had a very high opinion of Isrár Hasan Khán, and often spoke of

COLONEL C. I. H. WARD.

p. 124]

successor was Munshi Imtiyáz Ali Khán, a Vakíl from the province of Oudh. He assumed charge of his office on the 17th of Rabi-us-sáni, 1306 A.H.

Soon after the degradation of Sidik Hasan Khán, Sir Lepel Griffin again came to Bhopál, this time for a very different purpose, namely, to present to Háfiz Muhammad Khan, Mír Bakshi of the State troops, the badge of a Companion of the Indian Empire. The ceremony was performed at a durbar held in the Shaukat Mahal on February 20th, 1886. There were present Her Highness the Begam, myself, Nawáb Ihtishám-ul-mulk, Colonel Kincaid, Political Agent, the First Assistant to the Agent to the Governor-General, and a large number of nobles and State officials. Sir Lepel Griffin made an eloquent and interesting speech, which was afterwards read in Urdu by his First Assistant, and then, with his own hand, fastened the badge to the Mír Bakshi's breast. Muhammad Hasan Khán had previously been decorated for his services during the Mutiny, but his medal had been lost or stolen, and the Government of India had permitted a duplicate to be made in Calcutta. This medal also Sir Lepel Griffin presented to him; and he was likewise the recipient of a *khilát*, or robe of honour, from Her Highness as a special mark of her favour.

The speech which Sir Lepel Griffin made on this occasion is too long to quote in full. From the extract which follows it will be seen how little my Mother is to be held responsible for the disorders which sprang up in the State during the period of her husband's control. Previous to her second marriage, the excellence of her administration had been constantly acknowledged by the highest officers of the Government. Those in whom she afterwards reposed her confidence would have deceived the ablest ruler. She lost none of the high qualities of heart and mind for which she had been pre-

him to me. Evidence of his ability reached me from other sources, and, when I became the ruler of the State, I applied to the Government of India for the transfer of his services. He has since risen step by step, and now holds one of the highest appointments in the State, a position which he fills in a manner that fully justifies the estimate I had formed of him.

viously distinguished; but, the marriage with Nawáb Sidik Hasan Khán once being accomplished, it became impossible for her to escape the destinies which that step involved.

At the commencement of the speech in question, Sir Lepel Griffin spoke in the highest terms of Her Highness's loyalty, and of the loyalty and bravery which had so often been displayed by previous members of her house. He then explained at considerable length the policy of the British Government in its dealings with Native States, and showed how much had been done by Great Britain, both in India and elsewhere, to protect and further the interests of the Muhammadan race, instancing the support which had been given to Turkey during the Russo-Turkish war, and the protection which had been afforded to pilgrims to Mecca. Turning next to the State of Bhopál, he said:

* "For reasons to which I need not refer the administration of the State became thoroughly contemptible. Every class of the population, Hindu and Muhammadan alike, felt the hand of the oppressor, and lived in a perpetual state of fear. In the city all authority was vested in a few individuals, each of whom exercised simultaneously the powers of a magistrate, a policeman, and a gaoler. Neither life nor reputation was safe. Two of these magistrates, who had been guilty of oppression and cruelty, were at my suggestion, and with the consent of Her Highness, charged with their crimes in the Court of the Political Agent, where they were convicted, and sentenced to rigorous imprisonment. The assessment of village lands was increased to such an extent that a large number of *mustájirs* and cultivators were ruined, and seven thousand of the latter migrated from the State, and settled in the neighbourhood of Bhilsa in the territory of the Mahárája Sindhia. Lawsuits were won by those who could offer the biggest bribes, and the complaints of the poor passed unheeded."

After referring to Her Highness's endeavours to bring about a better state of things, Sir Lepel Griffin continued as follows:

"On a happy occasion such as the present I should not

refer to a subject painful both to Her Highness and to myself, were it not that I wish to take this opportunity of proclaiming publicly Her Highness's wise and courageous resolution to put down every evil that is brought to her notice, and to introduce such reforms as will result in the permanent benefit of her subjects. She has appointed a Muhammadan gentleman [1] of distinguished ability and high reputation to be the Minister of the State, and has placed the control of all departments and offices in his hands. He will be subject to no outside interference, but will deal in all matters directly with Her Highness. I am sure that when the people of Bhopál become acquainted with this reform and its beneficial results they will congratulate themselves on their good fortune in living under the sway of a Ruler who is ready to hear a complaint or to redress a wrong the moment she becomes aware of its existence.

"There is no State in India which Her Majesty the Queen and His Excellency the Viceroy regard with more friendly interest than the State of Bhopál, which, whether in peace or adversity, has always remained the true friend of the British Government. This loyalty will be all the more appreciated when it becomes known how Her Highness the Begam has determined to legislate for the good of her people, and to root out, once and for all, oppression and corruption from her territories.

"On behalf of His Excellency the Viceroy, I beg to congratulate Her Highness on the wise course she has adopted, and I trust her good fame will advance, step by step, with the happiness of her subjects and the prosperity of her State."

The events just narrated show how closely Sir Lepel Griffin is connected with the history of my family, and how keen an interest he took in the affairs of the State. He was a statesman of unusual ability, possessing bold determination and a deep, if somewhat stern, sense of justice; while in all matters that came before him, whether for advice or decision, he displayed both patience and sympathy. The smallest detail never escaped his notice, and his opinion once formed was seldom altered. In the case of Sidik Hasan Khán he acted with forbearance and kindness; and it was not until

[1] Nawáb Abdul Latif Khán, C.I.E.

these means had proved unavailing that he had recourse to the sterner measures I have described. Throughout these painful proceedings, he showed the greatest consideration for my Mother, and carefully avoided any step which might cast a slur upon her character. Indeed, he spoke highly of her at all times, for he fully recognized her many good qualities. He rightly held Sidik Hasan Khán and his adherents responsible for the evils which had sprung up in the State, and he saw that my Mother was blind to the deceptions that were practised upon her, and powerless to escape from the network of intrigue by which she was surrounded.

After his retirement, Sir Lepel Griffin continued to take an active interest in the affairs of the land he had served so well, and his opinion, whether spoken or written, on Indian matters was always considered of the highest value. The friendly relations that exist to-day between India and Afghánistán were largely of his making. The late Amír, Abdul Rahman Khán, in his autobiography writes:

> "I consider the present friendly situation to be largely due to the wise and politic manner in which negotiations with me and the people of Afghánistán were conducted by Sir Lepel Griffin, and I do not think that the services that he rendered to his Government have been adequately rewarded. If General Roberts deserved to be created Lord of Kandahár, he equally deserves the title of Lord of Kábul."

The news of Sir Lepel Griffin's premature death was a heavy blow to his many friends in India, where he will be remembered as one who devoted his life to the advancement and protection of British interests, and to the strengthening of British power.

From a drawing by C. W. Walton.

SIR LEPEL HENRY GRIFFIN.

p. 128]

CHAPTER XII

1886—1888

Her Highness felt the degradation of Sidik Hasan Khán so keenly, and was so convinced that he was the victim of a conspiracy set on foot by her own enemies with the ultimate object of overthrowing her rule, that she determined to go to Calcutta, and, in a personal interview with the Viceroy, ask for a reinvestigation of the whole affair. Sidik Hasan Kḥán had decided to go also; but the Agent to the Governor-General, hearing of his intention, informed him, through the Political Agent, that this could not be allowed. He was accordingly left behind, and Her Highness, accompanied only by Bilkis Jahán Begam and a few retainers, set out from Bhopál on March 8th, 1886. On her arrival at Calcutta she was met by the Secretary to the Government of India and an Aide-de-camp. A carriage drawn by four horses was waiting at the railway station, in which she drove with Bilkis Jahán Begam to Chauringhi Road, where a house had been engaged for her accommodation.

On March 12th, Her Highness paid a State visit to the Viceroy at Government House, being accompanied by Bilkis Jahán Begam, Mián Akbar Muhammad Khán, Mián Ashík Husein, Syad Abdul Ali, second Náib of the State, the State Vakíl, and Munshi Diu Diál, Mír Munshi of the Sehore Agency. The following day, His Excellency paid a return visit, in the course of which my Mother explained the object of her journey to Calcutta, His Excellency listening, but making no comment. On March 14th, a visit was paid to Lady Dufferin, which was also returned the following day. During her sojourn in Calcutta, many other ladies and gentlemen called on my

Mother, amongst them being Mrs. Durand, wife of the Foreign Secretary, and the wife of the Lieutenant-Governor of Bengal.

On March 18th, a second and private interview with His Excellency took place, at which my Mother presented a *kharíta*, dealing with the affairs of Sidik Hasan Khán, and concluding with a request that the Deputy Commissioner of Police in Calcutta might be appointed Minister of the State. His Excellency accepted the *kharíta*, and said he would give his reply after submitting it to Sir Lepel Griffin. Shortly afterwards, Mr. Durand came to see my Mother, and in a kind and courteous manner gave her to understand that no alteration in the orders of the Government was possible. Mr. Durand was intimately acquainted with the character and customs of the Afghán people, and, as his father had been Agent to the Governor-General for Central India during the rule of Nawáb Sikandar Begam, he was specially interested in the Bhopál State. He expressed great sorrow on account of the troubles which had befallen my Mother, and with much friendly sympathy pointed out to her that they were the direct consequence of her departure from the traditions of her race in contracting a second marriage, and in selecting for her consort a man of alien race and low degree.

Although His Excellency had found it impossible to comply with my Mother's request, he showed her every mark of respect and friendship. To Bilkis Jahán Begam he was specially kind. On one occasion she was taken by Colonel Kincaid to a Flower Show, at which both His Excellency and Lady Dufferin were present. His Excellency greeted her in the kindest manner, and said, "Do you know that I have actually risen from a bed of sickness to have the pleasure of seeing you here to-day?" Bilkis Jahán thanked him for his kind words, and then Lady Dufferin took her to see the aviary and other interesting features of the show.

Her Highness remained in Calcutta for twenty-five days. Her arrival had been announced in most of the papers; and one of these, a Bengali organ called *The Indian Mirror*, went so far as to state that the Begam of Bhopál had come to Calcutta to consult the Viceroy on the reorganization of her

THE MARQUIS OF DUFFERIN AND AVA.

p. 130]

Government. As a consequence of this, a large number of Bengali pleaders, and others who apparently thought that the situation offered opportunities, found their way to Chauringhi Road. They met with no success, however, for not one of them was granted an interview. Her Highness subscribed liberally to many institutions in Calcutta: Rs. 10,000 was given to the Lady Dufferin Fund, Rs. 1,500 to the Bible Society, and Rs. 2,000 to the Islámia Madrissa, besides a scholarship of Rs. 6,000 to enable a student to study either Law or Medicine in England for three years, with an additional Rs. 1,200 for the expenses of his journey. On April 7th, Her Highness left for Bhopál.

There is one other incident connected with this visit to Calcutta which deserves to be recounted because it shows that, in spite of the constant efforts that were made to embitter the relations between my Mother and my family, yet her affection for me never wholly disappeared from her heart. It happened that when preparations were being made for the journey, I fell sick, and, though I was much better by the time the day of departure arrived, I had not fully recovered. My Mother had been in the habit of receiving reports of my health from Bilkis Jahán, and her anxiety on my account was made known to me by the same means. I used to call Bilkis Jahán my little fairy ambassador, and looked forward to her daily visits with infinite pleasure; for I was always anxious to see her, as well as to hear what intelligence she might bring me. God rest her gentle spirit: many a time, like an angel of mercy, she came to me with tidings that filled my heart with thankfulness and joy; and it was a sad day for me when I learnt that my little ambassador had been deprived of her office.

As I have already said, my health was improving rapidly when my Mother set out for Calcutta. As days went by, and the period of her absence became unusually prolonged, there were certain people who began to feel anxious lest by the influence and advice of those in high places, and by associating with European ladies of high rank, Her Highness's ideas and inclinations might be changed or modified in a manner that would be by no means acceptable to them. They accordingly contrived a plan by which they knew that she would be thrown into a state of great anxiety and agitation. Their object was twofold: first, to induce her speedy return to Bhopál; and, secondly, to increase the disfavour with which she already regarded my husband, Nawáb Ihtishám-ul-mulk.

The plan was a simple one. Letters purporting to be from various quarters were sent to Calcutta, giving a most alarming account of my health, and accusing the Nawáb Sáhib of neglecting me to such an extent that there was very little hope of my recovery. These letters reached my Mother, and caused her the greatest uneasiness. She sent at once for Joan Bourbon, a highly connected French lady,[1] who was governess to Bilkis Jahán Begam, and with tears of sorrow on my account, and violent manifestations of anger against the Nawáb Sáhib, told her of the news she had received. Joan Bourbon proposed to write at once to Bhopál for further particulars. Her Highness agreed, but thought it better that the letter should be written by Bilkis Jahán. "She is her child," she said, "and it will appear only natural that she should inquire after her mother's health." It was decided that the letter should be addressed to the Nawáb Sáhib, as I was apparently so dangerously sick. The following letter was therefore dispatched:

"To the *Kiblah* and *Kábah* of both the Worlds, Sultán Dula Sáhib Bahádur,—

"The news of the grievous sickness of my honoured Mother, which has reached us through letters from Bhopál, has plunged us all in the deepest anxiety. For the love of God, do not leave us, who are absent, in suspense, but send us tidings with all the speed possible, that our hearts may be comforted."

When this letter reached Bhopál, it was brought to me

[1] For an account of the Bourbons of Bhopál, see Vol. III. of the *Central India State Gazetteer*, pp. 106–7.

THE MARCHIONESS OF DUFFERIN.

p. 132]

by the Nawáb Sáhib, and the following reply was at once sent:

"Light of my eyes, your letter shows that you have received news about my health which has caused you anxiety, letters from Bhopál having informed you that I am dangerously ill. Your letter was shown to me by your Father, and that you may be the more comforted, I am writing the reply to it with my own hand. The weakness which you saw in me has disappeared, and by the Grace of God I am now in perfect health, and looking forward to the return of Her Highness and yourself. I pray that your journey may be a safe one."

When my Mother returned to Bhopál, we learned from Bilkis Jahán Begam and from Joan Bourbon how real her anxiety on my account had been, and I rejoiced to think that, whatever troubles might come upon me through the malice of others, the ties of blood could never be wholly severed.

During the succeeding two years, only one public event occurred which calls for notice—namely, the Jubilee of Her Majesty the Queen-Empress. In India, the celebration took place on February 16th, 1887, a day that will always be remembered as one of universal joy. The date was officially communicated to Her Highness some weeks beforehand, and she decided to commemorate the great event, not only by holding a durbar and general festivities, but by the erection of a memorial which should confer a permanent benefit on the people of Bhopál. It was decided that this memorial should take the form of a *band* to the Shahjahánábád lake, and should be called the Kaisar Embankment. Orders were issued by Colonel Ward that the day was to be observed as a general holiday, and arrangements were made for a review of troops, illuminations, a banquet to the European residents, and the release of a number of prisoners. A sum of a hundred rupees was sent to the Political Agent for feeding the poor in the Sehore cantonment, and a full report of all the preparations was sent to the Agent to the Governor-General.

On the appointed day, a salute of 101 guns was fired from the Fatehgarh fort, and a review of the entire Bhopál army took place on the Jahángírábád parade ground, at the close of which a sum of five hundred rupees was distributed among the soldiers. Twenty-four prisoners were released from gaol, five of whom were under life sentences, and two others had their sentences reduced. Colonel Ward, on behalf of Her Highness, laid the foundation stone of the Kaisar Embankment, and at night the entire city was illuminated, forts, palaces, offices, private houses, and bazars glittering with all the colours of the rainbow. The Jahángírábád lake was also illuminated, and a brilliant display of fireworks took place in front of the Purána Kothi, where the European guests were being entertained. During the day, Her Highness sent a congratulatory cablegram to Her Majesty the Queen, to which the following reply was received through the Agent to the Governor-General:

"Her Imperial Majesty has directed His Excellency the Viceroy to thank you very warmly for your congratulations."

A few days later, Her Highness received a *kharíta* from His Excellency in confirmation of this message, containing many expressions of kindness and good-will. By Her Highness's order, this *kharíta* was read out to the troops on the parade ground, and a *kharíta* was sent in reply, gratefully acknowledging His Excellency's kindness, and containing an account of the rejoicings which had taken place at Bhopál.

The Jubilee was not celebrated in England till June 21st. This day was also observed as a holiday in Bhopál, and a salute of 101 guns was again fired. Her Highness sent a second cablegram to Her Majesty, through the Agent to the Governor-General, which was as follows:

"The Begam of Bhopál sends her most hearty congratulations to Her Majesty the Queen-Empress on the completion of fifty years of her reign."

A reply was received on August 1st:

"Her Majesty the Queen-Empress heartily thanks you for your congratulations."

Soon after the making of the Kaisar Embankment had commenced, Her Highness decided to have another memorial of Her Majesty's Jubilee, on an even larger scale, which was to take the form of an extension to the city water-works. On more than one occasion, Dr. Dane, the Agency Surgeon, had condemned the water of the lower lake as being unfit for household use. It was, therefore, decided to make this water available for irrigation in the gardens and fields to the north of the town, and at the same time to supply drinking-water from the Táláb Kalán, or large lake, to Jahángírábád and other quarters unconnected with the existing works. The water for irrigation was to be conducted to its destination by means of a channel starting from the Pukhta Pul, or northern *band* of the lower lake, while the drinking water for the city was to be conducted in pipes from the Táláb Kalán to the entrance to the new channel, where a large water-wheel would pump it up into the city. The plans and estimate, amounting to over three lákhs of rupees, were prepared by Mr. Cook, the State Engineer, and as soon as they had been approved by Her Highness the work was commenced. It was completed in three years; and on Ramazán 21st, 1308 A.H., water flowed into Jahángírábád and the Nishát Afzah garden. Many new branches have since been opened, and water is now carried as far as Islámnagar, a distance of more than six miles from the city.

In the year following the celebration of Her Majesty's Jubilee, there took place one of the saddest events of my life, the death of my beloved daughter Bilkis Jahán Begam. Let me acquaint my readers very briefly with the main circumstances of her life, for they throw some light on the events recorded in this history, and explain, to a large extent, the hostile attitude towards me of Sidik Hasan Khán, of whose machinations she was for some time the innocent and unconscious centre.

When only four months old, Bilkis Jahán Begam was

vaccinated for small-pox. She was at that time living with me, and my Mother had clearly told me that she did not propose to follow the example of Nawáb Sikandar Begam (who, as my readers will remember, took upon herself the entire responsibility of my up-bringing), and had no intention of removing my daughter from my care. When, however, the vaccination had taken place she came to me and said, with great kindness, " You yourself are still very young. I will take care of Bilkis Jahán until she has quite recovered her health." And my daughter was accordingly removed to her house. The effects of the vaccination soon passed off, but, in the meantime, my Mother had grown so fond of Bilkis Jahán, and was so averse from parting with her, that I was obliged to consent, though with great reluctance, to the prolongation of the arrangement for an indefinite period. In spite of her coldness towards me, Her Highness treated my daughter with great kindness and affection, and this, combined with the knowledge that Bilkis Jahán was very fond of her grandmother, did much to reconcile me to the parting.

Sidik Hasan Khán's influence over my Mother was now very strong. It had always been a sore point with him that his sons were in a more or less inferior position in the State, and possessed none of the privileges belonging to members of the ruling family. It was also a bitter disappointment to him that Her Highness bore him no son, for the birth of a child, and particularly of a male child, would have added greatly to the importance of his own position, and would at the same time have rendered him a far more powerful and formidable antagonist. Long ago he had sought to bring about a marriage between myself and one of his sons, but, finding that he had not sufficient influence to upset the plans of Nawáb Sikandar Begam, he considered discretion the better part of valour, and posed as the supporter of the marriage which she had arranged, although it seemed to give the death-blow to his ambition. The birth of Bilkis Jahán Begam, however, opened up new possibilities, and he was not long in laying his plans, of which the removal of the child to my Mother's control—and therefore to his own—was the first step. This he contrived with such

SAHIBZADI BILKIS JAHAN BEGAM.

p. 136]

skill that we saw in it nothing more than the evidence of a grandmother's affection, and even my Mother herself was probably unaware that she was being influenced by anything but her own inclinations. Had we seen through Sidik Hasan Khán's design—namely, the marriage of my daughter with his son, Ali Hasan—it is doubtful if we could have done anything to frustrate it; for if, without being able to assign any adequate reason, we had rejected my Mother's offer, made apparently with the kindest intentions, our action would have been generally condemned, and my Mother would have felt herself grievously affronted.

Sidik Hasan Khán used all his influence and all his resources to further his cherished object. Although the son in question already had a wife, and not only a wife but children also, he was made the constant companion of Bilkis Jahán Begam, and, whether in play-time or lesson-time, was always to be found at her side. At the same time Her Highness commenced to reside permanently at the Táj Mahal in Shahjahánábád, as a result of which I seldom saw my daughter more than once a week.

Matters continued thus until Bilkis Jahán Begam reached her eleventh year, and then her marriage with Ali Hasan Khán began to be openly discussed. Finding our suspicions confirmed, and learning that Her Highness, in spite of the fact that Ali Hasan Khán had a wife and children living, and was a stranger by birth, had given her consent to the betrothal, my husband and I were in great consternation, and determined, at all costs, to get our child back to her own home, lest she might consent to the proposal through fear of my Mother's anger; for it is the custom throughout the East for children to abide, in such matters, by the decision of the elders of the family. Whilst we were seeking means to combat the difficulties, intrigues, and even dangers which now began to surround us, Bilkis Jahán Begam fell seriously ill. For several days continuously she was in a high fever, and suffering acute pain in her chest. She was attended by a native Hakím, and neither I, nor any one belonging to me, was allowed to see her.

For the space of two weeks, all kinds of contradictory

reports reached me, and my state of mind can better be imagined than described. At the end of this time, to my unbounded relief, my daughter came to see me. She was better, but so weak that she could scarcely walk. There were deep black lines under her eyes, and her skin was the colour of saffron. We learnt for the first time that she had been suffering from pneumonia. For the sake of her health and our own peace of mind, as well as on account of the marriage question, we made up our minds that she should not again leave our house. We knew that this would rouse afresh my Mother's resentment, as indeed it did. But we placed the future happiness of our daughter above all other considerations, and, in spite of fierce and persistent opposition from Sidik Hasan Khán, we kept our resolution. At first, Bilkis Jahán fretted for her grandmother, to whom, as I have already said, she was deeply attached. But she soon recovered her health and spirits, and commenced to live a happier life than she had ever known before. At the Táj Mahal there had been none to play with her, and, with the exception of her grandmother, none who had any real affection for her. She now found herself surrounded with loving friends and happy playmates, and everything that could make her childhood pleasant. Moreover, as she grew older and her character developed, she began to view the world from a less childish standpoint, and her opinions and actions often showed shrewd judgment as well as considerable will power. She no longer desired to return to her grandmother's house, and steadily withstood all the efforts that were made to tempt her to go there. She still loved the Begam, but she was able to see, and she felt as keenly as any of us, the injustice with which her family was being treated, and she declared that she would not go to Shahjahánábád until her Mother could go with her. She made many earnest and pathetic appeals to the Begam on my behalf. But an appeal to the Begam was only another name for an appeal to Sidik Hasan Khán, and the will of the former, and not the inclination of the latter, dictated its reply.

But little more than a year after her return to me, Bilkis Jahán Begam was again attacked by a severe fever. My house, which was situated in the heart of the city, was small and ill-ventilated. Even when I had lived alone with my husband, it had barely sufficed for our accommodation; and now that I had four children, and, in consequence, a much larger number of servants, all of whom lived on the premises, the building was most unhealthily crowded. I, therefore, removed my daughter to the Háyat Afzah garden, hoping that the change to a purer atmosphere would restore her to health. It soon became apparent that she was suffering from typhoid fever, and by the advice of Colonel Ward, from whom, as well as from Mrs. Ward, I received unfailing help and sympathy, I called in Dr. Dane from Sehore, and, at his request, Dr. Hannyngton, Civil Surgeon at Indore, was also summoned.

The disease developed with terrible rapidity. We tried every remedy that our poor human skill could devise. But who can stay the hand of Death? On Friday, the 15th of Rabi-us-sáni, 1305 A.H., the lamp of her life was extinguished, and the doors of Paradise opened to receive her gentle spirit. I will not attempt to describe our grief. Its heaviness only those will understand who have encountered a like sorrow. It was the will of God, and we submitted to it with whatever patience we could command. As soon as the sad news reached the city, people of all classes came thronging to the Háyat Afzah garden to express their sympathy with us in our distress. The Sáhibzádi's death caused widespread grief. To the people of Bhopál she had been dear, not only on account of her loving and happy disposition, but because they had looked upon her as the future ruler of the State, and one who would secure for them a continuance of those special blessings they had so long enjoyed under a woman's rule. The funeral ceremony was performed by Mufti Muhammad Yahza, and was attended by dense crowds of people, so that the roads to the garden were blocked. Bilkis Jahán Begam was laid to rest beneath the trees on the north side of the garden, where a tomb has been erected to her memory.

All the political officers connected with the State sent us letters of condolence. His Excellency the Viceroy, who had treated my daughter with so much kindness, wrote to me as follows :

" Lady Dufferin and myself are deeply grieved at hearing of the sad loss you have suffered. I know how dearly you loved this child. Let the knowledge that God has taken her comfort you in your distress. The news of her illness filled us with anxiety, and we are greatly shocked at its sad termination."

My daughter's *jágír*, which was worth Rs. 25,000 a year, reverted to the State, and her personal servants, who had attended her from infancy, were pensioned.

CHAPTER XIII

1889—1891

ON February 25th, 1889, Bhopál was visited by Lord Roberts, Commander-in-Chief of the Indian Army. Her Highness received previous notice of this event through a letter from the Political Agent:

"His Excellency," the letter stated, "will be accompanied by Lady Roberts and Miss Roberts, General Ellis, an Aide-de-camp, and Dr. Dane. He will remain for one day in Bhopál, and then proceed to Sehore for two days, passing through Bhopál again on his return journey. Several distinguished military officers wish to take the opportunity of meeting the Commander-in-Chief at Bhopál, and Your Highness will, doubtless, be kind enough to extend your hospitality to them also."

The Political Agent and several military officers came to Bhopál on February 24th, and His Excellency Lord Roberts arrived at 4.30 p.m. on the following day. The Begam was present at the railway station, and, on the arrival of the train, Lord and Lady Roberts and Miss Roberts were conducted by the Political Agent to the carriage in which she was seated. The guard of honour presented arms as His Excellency alighted, and a salute of seventeen guns was fired from the Fatehgarh fort. After having formally welcomed her visitors to Bhopál, Her Highness returned to her palace, and the First Minister escorted the party to Lál Kothi,[1] the route thither being lined

[1] This *kothi* is situated in Jahángírábád. It is a spacious and pleasant house, built on European lines. It was commenced in 1886, and completed in three years. The situation is healthy, and the views from the house and garden are remarkably fine. It was constructed under the supervision of Mr. Cook, the State Engineer, at a cost of Rs. 72,878. 3. 6.

on either side by troops. A State banquet took place in the evening. Her Highness, accompanied by the First Minister, joined her guests at the conclusion of dinner, and distributed *'itr* and *pán* with her own hands. The officers of the Bhopál Battalion were also invited to this dinner, but, as the Battalion was about to be inspected, they were unable to be present. In the morning, Lord Roberts, attended by his Aide-de-camp and the Political Agent, witnessed a parade of the State troops. His Excellency asked the Officer-in-Command, Bakshi Háfiz Muhammad Hasan Khán, C.I.E., many questions concerning the strength and constitution of the Force, and spoke with the officers individually about their length of service, pay, quarters, and other details. Then, riding up to the colours, he asked the Bakshi Sáhib if his men could march past. The necessary orders were at once given, and after this and various other evolutions had been performed, His Excellency called out the officers, and congratulated them on the smart appearance of their men, and the precision with which their orders had been obeyed—"in which respect," he said, "your regiment compares favourably with any that I have seen in India."

After the parade, Lord Roberts, escorted by the Bakshi Sáhib and Munshi Abdul Ali Khán, Second Judicial Minister, drove to the Táj Mahal to see Her Highness. He then visited the Fatehgarh fort, where he was received with a salute of seventeen guns. Lady Roberts and her daughter, and Mrs. Kincaid, also called upon Her Highness, and later in the day all the guests met in the Nishát Afzah garden, where tea and other refreshments were provided. At 7.30 p.m., Her Highness returned the visits of Their Excellencies at the Lál Kothi, and bade them farewell. According to the programme, Lord Roberts spent the next two days at Sehore, and, returning to Bhopál on February 28th, left in the evening for Ujjain.

The next visitor of distinction whom the State had the honour of welcoming was His Excellency Lord Lansdowne. But before I proceed to the description of this, the first visit of a Viceroy of India to Bhopál, there is another event to be chronicled, an event of considerable moment both to the State and to myself—namely, the death of Sidik Hasan Khán.

FIELD-MARSHAL LORD ROBERTS.

p. 142]

After the confiscation of his titles and salute, Sidik Hasan Khán carefully abstained from all open interference in State affairs, for his one ambition was to get his lost honours restored, and he never ceased urging my Mother to some new effort on his behalf. Her first attempt was a petition, submitted through the Minister of the State, to Lord Dufferin, which met with a peremptory refusal. Her second, the journey to Calcutta, was, as the reader knows, equally unsuccessful. But she was in no way daunted, and scheme after scheme, each as fruitless as the one that preceded it, was devised. How long she would have persevered it is impossible to say, for, in the midst of her endeavours, Sidik Hasan Khán was transferred to a sphere where titles and salutes would stand him in very little stead. He succumbed to an attack of dropsy on the morning of the 2nd Rajab, 1307 A.H. He was buried, by his own desire, in strict conformity with the rites of Islám, though the funeral was a public one, and was conducted with considerable pomp. It was attended by both the Agent to the Governor-General and the Political Agent, and amongst the chief mourners was Sáhibzáda Obaidullah Khán Sáhib, Minister of the State of Tonk.

The exposure of the character and ways of Sidik Hasan Khán was no part of the object with which I undertook the writing of this book. Both on account of the esteem in which he was held by my Mother, and the position which, as her husband, he held in my family, I would gladly have pictured him to my readers in a less disadvantageous light. Moreover, when I think of his rise to power, dramatic alike in its rapidity and its brilliance, and then of the even greater suddenness and completeness of the Nemesis which overtook him, all feelings, save one of pity, vanish from my heart. But, as I have set myself to tell the story of the Bhopál State, in which public and private matters are so intermingled that it is impossible to separate them, I must record events as they took place, the good and the pleasant with the bad and the unpleasant, only using in respect of the latter such briefness as may be consistent with a connected and truthful narrative.

Sidik Hasan Khán was a native of Kanouj in the district

of Farukhábád. He used to say that his grandfather, Syad Aulád Ali Khán, Sáhib Bahádur, Anwar Jang, had been a great noble of Hyderábád, and belonged to the *Shiah* sect; but that his father, by reason of his having become a *Sunni*, was disinherited and forced to leave Hyderábád, and that he settled in Kanouj, and became a religious teacher. Sidik Hasan Khán was educated at Delhi, and came to Bhopál in the reign of Nawáb Sikandar Begam. He was given a subordinate post in the secretariat, and was afterwards placed in charge of the Records Office. In my Mother's reign, he became Superintendent of Education, and, after holding this post for a short time, was promoted to be Mír Munshi, with the titles "Mír Dabi" and "Khán." After his marriage with Her Highness, a *jágír* of Rs. 24,000 was conferred upon him. Her Highness, however, did not consider his titles consistent with his new position, and, after repeated solicitations, prevailed upon the Government of India to confer upon him the same rank as had been held by her late husband, and he was accordingly made Nawáb Walájah Amír-ul-mulk. Previous to his marriage with my Mother, he had taken to wife the daughter of Munshi Jamál-ud-dín Sáhib, First Minister of the State, thereby connecting himself with an ancient and respected family. Munshi Jamál-ud-dín, who was a wise and learned man, attracted by Sidik Hasan Khán's literary abilities, and particularly by his theological researches, approved of the marriage, and recommended his son-in-law to my Mother for the post of Mír Munshi. The story of his subsequent career is familiar to my readers, and needs no repetition. Bereft of his rank and grandeur, he found himself deserted by many of his former friends and adherents, and his latter days were passed in comparative loneliness. The heaviness of his retribution would seem to indicate sins of no ordinary magnitude; but human judgment is liable to err, and the ways of God are inscrutable. The taint of sin is over us all, and only in His court is there perfect justice.

Death having put an end to my Mother's plans for reinstating her husband, she determined that, although the Government of India had refused to honour him living, respect should,

NAWAB SIDIK HASAN KHAN.

p. 144]

at any rate, be shown to his memory. She therefore dispatched a *kharita* to the Viceroy, begging that in all future correspondence, Sidik Hasan Khán should be referred to as "the late Nawáb and husband of the Ruler." After some deliberation, His Excellency Lord Lansdowne granted this request; and the fact was communicated to Her Highness by Mr. Henvey, Agent to the Governor-General. His letter was dated October 12th, and was as follows:

"It gives me great pleasure to state that the Government of India has acceded to your Highness's request that your late husband may be referred to in official documents and correspondence as 'the late Nawáb and husband of the Ruler.'"

On receipt of this letter, the Minister was directed to issue a notice to all the heads of departments, and to the nobles and *jágirdárs* of the State, informing them of the orders of the Government of India, and directing that the same should be observed from that time forward.

It was not long after the death of Nawáb Sidik Hasan Khán that my second son, Sáhibzáda Muhammad Obaidullah Khán, completed his task of learning by heart the Holy Korán. The work had occupied him three whole years, during which time he received constant assistance from Nawáb Ihtishám-ul-mulk. I need not tell my readers how our hearts rejoiced when we knew that success had crowned his endeavours. His own joy was no less than ours, and we thanked Almighty God that He had vouchsafed to us a son thus capable of winning honour and blessings for himself and his family. We had, indeed, cause to be grateful to Him; for was not our son a Háfiz, and was not this the fulfilment of one of the dearest wishes of our hearts?

Since my Mother's anger had first displayed itself against us, we had abandoned the performance of all ceremonies except such as were strictly necessary, and even these we conducted with the utmost simplicity. When, however, we considered the long labours our son had undergone, we determined to celebrate his success in as complete a manner as possible. We, accordingly, determined that, during the blessed month of Ramazán, which was then approaching, he should publicly recite the whole Korán, and that none of the demonstrations of joy customary on such occasions should be omitted. There are few events in my life that I recall with greater pleasure. The only cloud on our happiness was the absence of my Mother: and for twenty-seven years I enjoyed no pleasure over which that same cloud did not cast its shadow.

On the first day of the Fast, at the hour of evening prayer, the Sáhibzáda commenced his recitation, and continued it daily at the same hour until, on the twenty-first evening, his pious task was completed. All the members of my family, and every servant from the highest to the lowest belonging to my household, attended night after night to hear him. When the last chapter had been recited, the greatest happiness prevailed, and my son, as well as my husband and myself, received the warmest congratulations. Sweetmeats, rose-water, and *kewara* [1] were distributed, and handsome presents were given to each person who had attended the recitation. The mosque which my family attended for prayer was brilliantly illuminated, and for several nights large numbers of poor people were fed at our expense. To perpetuate the date of this happy event, a chronogram stanza of four lines was composed, of which the following is a literal translation:

"Truly, he does an excellent work who commits to memory the Holy Book:
For such are high places reserved in heaven.
Why should not the head of Iblis be cut off?
For the heart of Obaid is become as a guarded tablet." [2]

[1] A perfume extracted from the flower of the *kevra* plant (*Pandanus odoratissimus*).

[2] The dates of notable events are often signified in this manner. To every letter in the Persian Alphabet a certain numerical value has been assigned. This is technically known as *abjad*, from the first four letters of the table, *a* = 1, *b* = 2, *j* = 3, *d* = 4. If a couplet or stanza is correctly composed, the value of all the letters contained in it, when added together, gives the required date. Should the exact date not result, the excess or defect must be signified in the verse. Thus, the total given by the above-mentioned stanza shows the year *after* the event which it commemorates. The number 1, therefore, has to be subtracted from the result. The third line of the stanza signifies this. The head of Iblis has to be cut off; that is, the first letter of his name, which in Persian is the letter *a*, has to be omitted from the calculation.

CHAPTER XIV

THE VISIT OF LORD LANSDOWNE TO BHOPAL

ON October 22nd, 1891, the Honourable Mr. Crosthwaite, Agent to the Governor-General in Central India, informed Her Highness that His Excellency the Viceroy had started on tour from Simla, and intended visiting Bhopál on November 20th, and to remain three days, with the object of meeting Her Highness and the other Chiefs of the Bhopál Agency. Her Highness was greatly pleased at this intelligence, and wrote to His Excellency, thanking him for the honour he was about to confer upon her. Preparations for his entertainment were made on an unusually extensive scale. Lord Harris, the Governor of Bombay, and Lady Harris, besides many other European guests, were invited to Bhopál for the occasion; and the native guests included the Chiefs of Rájgarh, Narsinghgarh, Khilchipúr, Kurwái, Basoda, Pathári, Muhammad-garh, Dhábla Dhamar, Dhábla Ghosi, Dariakéri, and Rámgarh.

On the 20th, the greatest excitement and enthusiasm prevailed in the city, and as the hour of His Excellency's arrival approached, the populace gathered in crowds at every spot from which a view of the great man might be obtained. The roads from the railway station to the Lál Kothi, and from the lower lake to the palace in Shahjahánábád, were elaborately decorated. Triumphal arches and floral gateways were erected along their entire lengths, and the sky itself was almost hidden by festoons of flowers and bunting. In front of the barracks in Jahángírábád the road was spanned by an enormous arch formed of ancient and modern weapons of warfare, cunningly arranged in floral devices. Another arch, in front of the Táj Mahal, was composed entirely of glass mirrors, on which were painted flowers and fruit of every imaginable colour. From this arch to the gateway of the palace the ground on either side of the road was laid out in flower-beds, backed by towering masses of palms, ferns, and foliage plants. The beautiful grounds of the Lál Kothi were illuminated each evening; and as the house barely afforded sufficient accommodation for the large number of guests, a large *shamiána*, of cloth of gold, was set up on the lawn, and furnished as a drawing-room. Much trouble had been taken in planning and carrying out these arrangements, and the result amply proved Her Highness's desire to accord to the representative of Her Majesty the Queen a loyal and magnificent welcome.

At 5 o'clock in the evening, Her Highness drove in full state to the railway station. The road on either side was lined with troops, and the State artillery was posted on the west side of the line opposite to the platform. The station gateway was flanked by two rows of elephants, resplendent in scarlet *jhools*, and bearing on their backs silver howdahs. As His Excellency's special train steamed into the station, the artillery fired a salute of thirty-one guns, and the band played the National Anthem. Her Highness advanced to the door of the railway carriage to welcome her guests, and escorted them to her private waiting-room. After a formal exchange of greetings, the following had the honour of being presented to His Excellency: the First Minister of the State, Mián Alamgír Muhammad Khán, Mián Sadar Muhammad Khán, Mián Núr-ul-hasan Khán, and Mián Abdul Hai Khán. Lord and Lady Lansdowne then took their seats in a carriage drawn by four horses, and drove off from the station. Her Highness's carriage, also drawn by four horses, came next, the remainder of the party following in procession. On reaching the lower lake, Her Highness left the procession and returned to her palace.

On the next day, at 11 o'clock in the morning, Her Highness, accompanied by eleven Sirdars, paid a State visit to the Viceroy. She was accorded a private interview, at the conclusion of which she presented her *nazar*. The eleven Sirdars were then introduced, and each in turn presented his *nazar*. Before leaving, Her Highness was conducted to another apartment, where she was received by Lady Lansdowne and other ladies. At 5.30 p.m., His Excellency received visits from Mián Alamgír Muhammad Khán, Háfiz Bakshi Muhammad Hasan Khán, C.I.E., Commander-in-Chief of the Bhopál army, and the Assistant Revenue Minister. At 6 p.m., according to the programme, he returned Her Highness's visit at the Táj Mahal, expressing, as he drove along, his keen appreciation of the manner in which his route to the palace had been decorated. He was received at the outer gate by the Political Agent and the First Minister, and at the inner gate by Her Highness in person. The following fourteen Sirdars were present at this Durbar: Munshi Syad Imtiyáz Ali, First Minister; Mián Alamgír Muhammad Khán; Mián Sadar Muhammad Khán; Mián Núr-ul-hasan Khán; Mián Ali Hasan Khán; Mián Akil Muhammad Khán; Mián Nazar Muhammad Khán; Mián Abdul Hai Khán; Mír Bakshi Sáhib Bahádur, Nasrat-i-jang; Mián Akbar Muhammad Khán; Munshi Abdul Ali Khán, Mohtamin of the Daftar Huzúr; Munshi Hakím-ud-dín, Mír Munshi; Munshi Ahmad Hasan Khán, State Vakíl; and the Assistant Revenue Minister. The proceedings were of a strictly formal character, and terminated with the distribution of *'itr* and *pán*, His Excellency, the Foreign Secretary, and the Agent to the Governor-General receiving it from the hands of Her Highness, and the remainder from the First Minister.

In the evening, a State banquet was given at the Lál Kothi. The health of the Viceroy was proposed by Her Highness in person, who spoke as follows:

"Your Excellencies, Ladies and Gentlemen,—I have no words to express either the pleasure which it gives me to welcome to Bhopál His Excellency the Governor-General of India and Lady Lansdowne, or the gratitude I feel for the honour which their visit has conferred upon me and upon my State. I heartily thank Their Excellencies and my other guests for the kindness they have done me in accepting my poor hospitality. I have long cherished the hope that the unbroken loyalty which, from the earliest days of its history, this State has always displayed towards the British Government, and my own endeavours, since the time of my accession, to live up to the traditions of my ancestors, would procure me the honour which His Excellency has now conferred upon me, the honour of welcoming within my territories the representative of Her Most Gracious Majesty the Queen-Empress.

"Unfortunately, the means of communication between my State and the outside world have, until recently, been such as to render a journey to Bhopál a long and tedious undertaking. But that my hopes have been deferred by this or by whatsoever cause, only makes me appreciate more fully their realization to-day. And I can assure Lord Lansdowne that the 21st of November, 1891, will always be regarded by me as one of the happiest days of my life, and one of the most important in the history of Bhopál. Since His Excellency's appointment to the high office of Viceroy of India, the greatest sympathy and consideration have characterized all his dealings with this State. To him, and to the Government of which he is the head, I am deeply grateful, and I beg that, when the opportunity may be forthcoming, he will assure Her Majesty the Queen of my loyalty and devotion, and of my readiness to expend not only my utmost means, but my life itself, in her service."

Her Highness's speech was greeted with loud applause; and, the toast having been duly honoured, His Excellency rose and made the following reply:

"Your Highness, Ladies and Gentlemen,—I am deeply sensible of the honour which Her Highness the Begam has done me, an honour which possesses the greater value in my eyes because I believe I am the first Viceroy who has had the advantage of being received as Her Highness's guest in Bhopál. I appreciate Her Highness's kindness the more because she is still suffering from a severe domestic affliction, and it must have cost her an effort to emerge from her retirement; but I feel sure that upon this, as upon other occasions, Her Highness would allow no private feelings of her own to prevent her from manifesting, by word and by deed, the respect for Her Majesty the Queen-Empress which she has expressed in such eloquent and earnest words. I shall not fail to make known to Her Majesty the manner in which Her Highness has referred to her this evening. As for myself, it is a source of the greatest satisfaction to me to hear from Her Highness's own lips that I have, in her opinion, treated the different questions connected with the State of Bhopál which have come before me with that consideration to which Her Highness is entitled; and I can promise her that my friendly respect for her will be, if possible, strengthened by the manner in which she has received me on this interesting occasion. The Rulers of Bhopál have always been conspicuous for their loyalty, their administrative ability, and their magnificent charity. The services rendered to the British Government by the Mother of Her Highness, the Sikandar Begam, during the Mutiny, when such services were most needed, are not and can never be forgotten. Her Highness, the present Ruler of the State, is a worthy inheritor of those traditions; she has shown herself to be a wise and sagacious Ruler, and she has contributed largely towards the welfare of the State by her generous support of many good and useful works. She has assisted liberally in the development of the railway system of this part of India, she has constructed roads, built hospitals, secured for the people of Bhopál an invariable supply of good water, and, only to-day, she has intimated to me her desire that the Government of India should take advantage of an offer which she had made some time ago, to place a part of the military forces of the State at the disposal of the Government for the purpose of Imperial defence. Ladies and gentlemen, I ask you to join with me in drinking Her Highness's health, and in expressing the hope that any trouble or anxiety which she may have had may in time pass away and be forgotten, and that she may long be spared to continue a reign which has been fruitful of good to the people of her State, and which has merited the support and approbation of the Government of India."

The next evening, the Táj Mahal and the adjoining lake were illuminated. Much thought and labour had been expended on this feature of the programme, which was executed with great skill, and proved a complete success. Thousands of coloured lights flashed from every part of the great palace, thousands more illuminated the margin of the lake, varied at intervals with cascades and fountains of fire, and weird and fantastic boats, birds, dragons, and fishes, like jewelled shapes from fairy-land, floated hither and thither over the surface of the water, in which the entire scene was reflected with dazzling brilliancy. The spectators were accommodated on the roof of the Dil Kusha palace, and were greatly delighted with this unique entertainment. Lady Lansdowne, as she bade Her Highness good-night, said that she had not seen in any Native State a more brilliant and effective display.

On November 22nd, His Excellency visited the Buddhist remains at Sánchi, and on his return inspected the Prince of Wales's Hospital, the Zenana Hospital, the Fatehgarh Fort, and the Bala Kila. The same day Her Highness called at the Lál Kothi to bid His Excellency farewell. The visit was returned by Lady Lansdowne at the Bahar Afzah palace. I also called at the Lál Kothi the same day. My husband and my two sons accompanied me, and we were received by His Excellency with great cordiality. After a short conversation, an Aide-de-camp was sent to inform Lady Lansdowne of our visit. Her Excellency came at once to see us. She talked to us in the pleasantest manner, telling us how much she had enjoyed the illuminations and other incidents of her visit to Bhopál. We then received *'itr* and *pán* from Lord Lansdowne, and took our departure. In the evening, His Excellency and party left by special train for Indore.

On the occasion of this visit, the Viceroy conferred a special honour upon the State by exempting its ruler from that time forward from the obligation of presenting a *nazar*, and a proclamation to that effect was issued by the Government of India. That Her Highness's loyal welcome and hospitality were fully appreciated by Lord Lansdowne is manifest from the following extract from a speech delivered by him at the Town Hall, Calcutta, at the close of his tour:

"In the course of my tour, I visited no less than four Chiefs, and it would be ingratitude on my part if I did not acknowledge the warmth of the reception I met with at their hands, and if I did not bear testimony to the spirit of loyalty by which they were animated. I had the pleasure of visiting Her Highness the Begam of Bhopál, and I was astonished at her enlightenment, prudence, and ability. The loyalty of the State is proved both by its traditions and its history, and the Begam herself has always been a true friend and firm supporter

THE MARQUIS OF LANSDOWNE.

THE MARCHIONESS OF LANSDOWNE.

p. 152]

of the English Throne. In spite of a private sorrow, which at the time of my visit was weighing heavily upon her, her cordial and friendly welcome is something I shall not easily forget."

When the programme of His Excellency's tour for 1892 was published, it was seen that he would pass through the Bhopál railway station on October 28th. Her Highness, thereupon, through the Agent to the Governor-General, invited Their Excellencies and party to accept her hospitality on that day. The invitation was gratefully accepted, and a grand dinner was arranged in a pavilion at the station. Their Excellencies arrived by special train at 8 p.m., and, after dinner had been partaken of, Her Highness, who had watched the proceedings from an adjoining tent, entered the pavilion, and in a brief speech proposed the health of her guests. Her Highness's words were loudly cheered, and after the toast had been drunk His Excellency rose and said :

* " Ladies and Gentlemen,—I cannot sufficiently thank Her Highness for the very kind words in which she has proposed my health and that of Lady Lansdowne. For a second time we have the great pleasure of enjoying the hospitality of Bhopál. The previous occasion was twelve months ago. It was one that I shall never forget, and I am quite sure it will never be forgotten by those who accompanied me. Since I came to India, nothing has left a deeper impression on my mind than the eloquent and sincere manner in which Her Highness, at the conclusion of the State banquet, expressed her devotion to the Government of India, and her loyalty to Her Majesty the Queen. In accordance with the promise I then made, I communicated these sentiments to Her Majesty, by whom they were very highly appreciated. For Her Highness's kindness to us to-day we feel especially grateful. Our route happens to take us through the State of Bhopál, but it is not possible for us to break our journey. Notwithstanding this, Her Highness was no sooner informed that we should reach Bhopál this evening than she invited us to alight, if only for a few minutes, and partake once more of her hospitality.

" Thus again is Her Highness's loyalty publicly manifested : and I can assure her, though I am confident that no such assurance from me is necessary, that there is no Chief in

India on whose devotion the British Government places more reliance than on that of the Begam of Bhopál. And if ever that Government can be of service to her it will always be a pleasure to me to see that its assistance and support are forthcoming.

"Ladies and gentlemen, I ask you to join me in drinking to the health of Her Highness the Begam, with every good wish for the happiness of her life and the welfare of her State."

CHAPTER XV

SOME NEW INSTITUTIONS

Of the many works of public utility which the State owes to Nawáb Shah Jahán Begam, none has conferred a more lasting benefit on the people than the Lady Lansdowne Hospital, which was built in memory of the visit of Lord and Lady Lansdowne, described in the previous chapter. Her Highness had special reasons for being grateful to His Excellency, for he had done all that lay in his power, consistent with the policy of the Government, to console her for the unhappiness which the degradation of Sidik Hasan Khán had caused her. Having granted her request regarding her late husband's title, he came himself to Bhopál, thus conferring upon her the honour of being the first ruler of the State to entertain the representative of the Sovereign of the Empire ; and to mark his favour still further he exempted her, and all future rulers of the State, from the obligation of presenting *nazarána*. To show her gratitude for these favours and privileges, my Mother determined to found an institution which, while being of permanent benefit to her people, should serve to keep alive in their minds the memory of a Viceroy to whom the State was so deeply indebted.

There was at this time in Bhopál no hospital worthy of the name for the treatment of *purdah* women. Lady Lansdowne had herself spoken of the need of such an institution, and it was, therefore, decided that no memorial would be more suitable, or more generally appreciated, than one which supplied this want. The site selected was a piece of ground close to the lower lake, on the north side of the road leading to the railway station. Plans and estimates were quickly prepared and sanctioned, and in a little more than a year the building was completed. By Her Excellency's permission it was named "The Lady Lansdowne Hospital for Women." It is a well-designed and handsome edifice, possessing abundant accommodation.[1] The opening ceremony was performed by Major Meade, the Political Agent, on May 26th, 1892, the anniversary of Her Majesty the Queen's accession. Besides Her Highness and the Political Agent, there were present the First Minister, Nawáb Munnawar Ali Khán, Chief of Kurwai, the leading nobles and Jágírdárs of the State, and the Vakíls from many other States in the Agency. Major Meade opened the proceedings by reading a congratulatory *kharíta* addressed to Her Highness by the Viceroy. Her Highness then addressed the assembly, and having explained the origin and object of the Hospital, concluded her speech with these words :

"I regard it as a most happy circumstance that we are holding this opening ceremony on the anniversary of Her Most Gracious Majesty's accession. I am very grateful to Her Excellency Lady Lansdowne for the interest she has taken in this institution, and for her kindness in permitting it to be named the Lady Lansdowne Hospital. I request Major Meade to open the Hospital, and I trust it may prove a permanent boon to the people of Bhopál."

The opening ceremony then took place, and Major Meade made a short speech describing the accommodation of the building, and the general arrangements for its supervision and management. After this *'itr* and *pán* were distributed, and the meeting dispersed.

Later in the day, a durbar in honour of the Queen's accession was held, and a salute of a hundred and one guns was fired. In the evening, the State troops gave an assault-at-arms, which was witnessed by a large crowd of spectators. The day's rejoicings were brought to an end by a banquet at the Lál Kothi, at which Her Highness proposed the health of the Queen-Empress.

Another building opened by Major Meade in the same

[1] Children of both sexes are admitted to this hospital, and instruction is given in midwifery.

year, was the steam factory in Shahjahánábád. It had been commenced as far back as the year 1882, a sum of Rs. 7,00,000 having been sanctioned for its construction. No steam machinery of any kind yet existed in the State, and Her Highness believed that the factory would be a source of considerable profit, and would at the same time afford employment to a large number of work-people. It took nine years to complete, and was opened in 1310 A.H., in the presence of a large gathering of nobles, State officials, and merchants. It is situated in the eastern part of Shahjahánábád, and is surrounded by an extensive compound containing go-downs, and a *kothi* for the manager. Munshi Imtiyáz Ali must have found the erection of this factory an undertaking of considerable profit. The building may have cost as much as two lákhs of rupees, possibly a good deal less; the engine was purchased for Rs. 50,000. The furniture ordered for the *kothi* was suitable for a palace. Whether it was ever placed in the *kothi* or not I cannot say; it is not there now, nor is there any trace of it either in the *kár-khána* or the *ferásh-khána*. In the busy season—that is, from December to May—nearly two hundred hands are employed in the factory, and the engine, when working at full pressure (50 horse-power), drives sixty different machines. Of these, the large majority are for cleaning and pressing cotton, and the remainder for sawing timber, grinding grain, and weighing and pressing grass. The cotton comes from all parts of the State, and after being cleaned and made up into bales is exported to Bombay.

The period of Lord Lansdowne's Viceroyalty was drawing to a close, and Her Highness, being anxious to bid him farewell before his departure for England, determined to visit Simla for this purpose. Accordingly, she instructed Munshi Imtiyáz Ali, the State Minister, to inform the Political Agent of her intention, and to request him to accompany her and to arrange the preliminary formalities. In reply to the Minister's letter, the Political Agent stated that the proper course was for Her Highness, first of all, to inform His Excellency of her desire to visit him. A *kharíta* was therefore dispatched through the Agent to the Governor-General for Central India, and on

December 5th, 1893, through the same source, the following reply was received:

"It will give Lady Lansdowne and myself great pleasure to see you again before we leave India. It will be most convenient for me if you can come on or about the 23rd of September, as it is my intention to leave Simla for some days on the 29th."

On receipt of this reply, Her Highness completed the preparations for her journey, and on September 21st left by special train for Simla, being accompanied by eight Sirdars, Munshi Imtiyáz Ali Khán, Hakím Muaz-ud-dín, Chief Medical Officer, and a hundred and one attendants and servants. Kalka was reached on September 24th, and Simla on the following day. Three miles outside the city Her Highness was met by two Aides-de-camp and a military escort, and a salute of nineteen guns was fired as she entered the city. She drove at once to the *kothi* which had been engaged for her reception. Here two more Aides-de-camp waited upon Her Highness, and informed her that His Excellency would be pleased to receive her visit at 2.25 p.m. At 2.13 p.m., Her Highness, accompanied by the Political Agent, the Minister of the State, and six Sirdars, set out for Viceregal Lodge. She was received by His Excellency with every mark of kindness. In accordance with the recent proclamation, Her Highness did not present a *nazar*, but the formality was observed by the members of her retinue.

On September 27th, His Excellency paid a return visit. The Minister, with Mián Alamgír Muhammad Khán, Mián Nazar Muhammad Khán, and Mián Akil Muhammad Khán, escorted him from Viceregal Lodge, and a guard of honour was drawn up in front of the *kothi*. The visit was conducted in accordance with a previously arranged programme, and terminated with the usual distribution of *'itr* and *pán*. During her stay in Simla, Lady Lansdowne showed my Mother much kind attention, and on one occasion honoured her by accepting an invitation to luncheon. Her Highness had also the honour of meeting His Excellency the Commander-in-Chief and the Lieutenant-Governor of the Punjab. Before her departure, she visited many places of interest in and about Simla, and also attended the Simla races. On the return journey, she halted at Lahore, Delhi, and Agra, and reached Bhopál on the 1st of Jamádi-ul-awwal, 1311 A.H.

Another important feature of Her Highness's reign, and belonging to the period we have now reached, was the establishment of the Imperial Service Lancers. In 1885, when Russia made an attack on Punjdeh, it was generally believed that the British Government would be forced to declare war, and many of the ruling Chiefs requested the Viceroy, Lord Dufferin, in the event of a campaign against Russia, to permit the troops of their States to take the field. War was, however, averted, and the Government had no opportunity of complying with this request. Lord Dufferin was succeeded by Lord Lansdowne, and during the latter's Viceroyalty the question of the formation of an Imperial Service Force was again brought forward; and it was decided that any ruling Chief who wished to do so should maintain a body of troops, trained and equipped according to the regulations of the Indian Army, and that these troops should be inspected by British officers, and should be called upon to take the field should the need for their services arise. Her Highness at once declared her desire to maintain a regiment of cavalry; and at her request Captain G. Edwards, who had been appointed Inspecting Officer for Central India, was sent to Bhopál to arrange the necessary details. The estimate prepared by him for the formation and upkeep of the regiment was as follows:

For uniforms, transport, and hospital	Rs. 125,000
For building lines	Rs. 100,000
For maintenance, a monthly sum of	Rs. 16,986

This estimate provided for the enrolment of 900 persons, as follows:

Officers and sowars	500
Syces	283
Menial servants	74
Hospital Staff	11
Dhobies, barbers, etc.	32
Total	900

As the Bhopál State still used its own coinage, it was provided that, in the event of the regiment being called upon for Imperial service, officers and men should be paid in the coin of British India, without any deduction being made.

Her Highness approved of the estimate, and proposed to Captain Edwards to transfer to the new regiment all the men of the State army who belonged to the old fighting families of Bhopál, as they were likely to make good soldiers, and would welcome a life alike congenial to their inclinations and in accord with the traditions of their race. To this proposal Captain Edwards agreed; and 138 men, officers and *sowars*, were selected from the State army, and formed the nucleus of the Imperial Service regiment. Forty-two other *sowars* were recruited at the same time, and two writers and twenty-two menial servants were engaged. Major Hasan-ud-dín Khán, a Risáldár from the Hyderábád Contingent, was placed in command; and thus, with a complement of 205 persons, the Bhopál Victoria Lancers, as the regiment is now called, came into being. The fact was announced to the Government of India, and, in acknowledgment, a *kharíta* was received from His Excellency the Viceroy:

"SIMLA, *May 15th*, 1894 (1312 A.H.).

* "MY DEAR FRIEND,

"Some years have passed since the proposal to utilize a portion of the armies of Native States for the purposes of defence first came before the Government of India. The part you have taken in furthering that proposal is an additional manifestation of the loyalty and devotion to the British Government for which your State has so long been famous. It is, I know, your desire that the regiment of cavalry maintained by you should be thoroughly efficient, and ready, at any time when their services may be required, to take the field with the regular Forces of the Empire. The Government of India is deeply concerned in all matters affecting friendly States and their rulers; and the reports submitted by the Inspector-General of Imperial Service Troops have been perused with attention and pleasure. I am desired by Her Majesty's Secretary of State for India to inform you that the vigorous efforts made by the Chiefs of India for the success of this movement have afforded him much gratification. The Government is fully confident that the regiment that you are raising in Bhopál will be completed in the same admirable fashion in which its formation has been commenced. It will, I am sure, give you great pleasure to hear that the co-operation of the Native States in the work of forming an Imperial Service Force has been sincerely appreciated by Her Majesty Queen Victoria, and I am desired to convey to you, and to other Rulers, Her Majesty's gratitude."

At the same time, it was made known to Her Highness through the Political Agent, that the Government of India had decided that the Imperial Service Troops were to be considered of the same standing, to serve under the same conditions, and to enjoy the same privileges as the native Indian army.

Not long after the formation of the regiment, Major Hasan-ud-dín was succeeded by Major Karím Beg, also of the Hyderábád Contingent. Under this officer a marked and rapid improvement took place in the strength, discipline, and efficiency of the regiment. Her Highness was most liberal in supplying funds, every expenditure that was recommended being speedily and willingly sanctioned.

The maintenance of a regiment of cavalry is a costly undertaking. But there is no doubt that, had due economy been observed, the State might have been spared a great deal of expense without sacrificing efficiency. But outside the regiment Her Highness had no military advisers, and the senior officers, being all strangers to Bhopál, were not the men to study the financial needs of the regiment in their relation to the general needs of the State. The military department has since been entirely remodelled, as will appear later on. But it is still a matter for regret that so few of the natives of Bhopál are to be found in the ranks of the Victoria Lancers. Troop and squadron commanders naturally like to see vacancies filled up by their own countrymen: and as long as these officers have to be imported from outside, it is unlikely that the *personnel* of the force will undergo much change.

CHAPTER XVI

THE DEATH OF SAHIBZADI ASIF JAHAN BEGAM

WHEN Sáhibzádi Asif Jahán Begam was only twelve years old, she was attacked by rheumatic fever. At the commencement of her illness, she was attended by Hakím Núr-ul-hasan, who was formerly a servant of my *deorhi*, but had since been appointed Chief Medical Officer of the State. After a short time, as her condition grew worse, Doctor Joshi, Assistant Surgeon, was also summoned. The Sáhibzádi was suffering great pain in her chest, and it was the opinion of both doctors that the rheumatism had begun to affect the heart. When another week's treatment brought no relief, Hakím Abdul Majíd Khán was summoned from Delhi; but, owing to the death of his father, he was obliged to return at the end of a week. His fee was a thousand rupees a day, and, as his treatment proved ineffectual, he was not recalled. Doctor Abdul Rahím Sáhib, a man of considerable reputation, was then sent for from Lucknow. His fee was five hundred rupees a day, and he treated my daughter for nearly two months. His diagnosis confirmed the opinion of the other doctors, but his treatment was more beneficial, and his medicines afforded the patient considerable relief. The pain came on only at intervals, and was severe twice in the day and twice in the night for about fifteen minutes. It was a time of great anxiety for me and for Nawáb Ihtishám-ul-mulk, and for many days and nights we scarcely slept at all. Gradually, however, an improvement took place, and after she had been in the hands of Doctor Abdul Rahím Sáhib for two months, the pain had almost entirely left her. My husband and I were greatly comforted, and the doctor told us that the humming noise of the heart, which the other doctors had also noticed, would probably never cease,

SAHIBZADI ASIF JAHAN BEGAM.

p. 162]

but that he did not consider it an alarming symptom so long as the patient remained unmarried—a warning which we determined we would never neglect. When Doctor Abdul Rahím Sáhib returned to Lucknow, he received a present of two thousand rupees in addition to his daily fee. His treatment was continued by Miss Mackenzie, a lady doctor of high qualifications and great nobility of character, and she was ably assisted by Doctor Joshi.

I had obtained permission from my Mother to avail myself of the services of Miss Mackenzie and Doctor Joshi, so long as my daughter's illness continued. We were, therefore, well off as far as medical aid was concerned. After Miss Mackenzie had watched her patient for some time, she advised a change of climate, and asked me to take her to some place where the air was purer and more invigorating than in Bhopál. I, therefore, decided to remove her to Samarda, a healthy and bracing spot, where my husband had built himself a shooting-box. My Mother's permission was obtained, and the plan was carried into effect. Miss Mackenzie was unable to accompany us, but she continued to advise us by letter, and to send us all the medicines we needed.

The change of air and the treatment combined produced a beneficial effect, and my daughter began rapidly to regain strength. The symptoms of her disease were, however, still apparent, and the absence of the daily supervision of a skilled doctor inclined me not to prolong our stay at Samarda. Miss Mackenzie, in her letters, strongly advised us to try the effect of sea air, and the Nawáb Sáhib and I formed the plan of taking our daughter to Bombay. My Mother gave her sanction (for without this we could not set foot outside Bhopál), and also gave me permission to write to Major Meade and inform him of our plans, and to request him to obtain sanction from the Government of India for an English officer to accompany us. In reply to my letter, Major Meade wrote to say that he believed the Government would have no objection to granting my request, which he had forwarded to Mr. Crosthwaite, Agent to the Governor-General. In a subsequent letter he gave the name of the officer who was to accompany us and the date of his arrival. I, therefore, made preparations for his reception at Samarda, and at the same time arranged all the details of our journey to Bombay, my Agent being sent on in advance to engage a house. No officer arrived on the date fixed, but instead, a few days later, a letter came from the Agent to the Governor-General, stating that the Government was unable to accede to my request for the services of a European officer, as this was a privilege only granted to ruling Chiefs. In these circumstances, we decided to abandon altogether our plan of going to Bombay, and, after having been three months at Samarda, we returned to Bhopál.

In a very short time, my daughter's condition again became alarming, and she grew even weaker than she had been before. We therefore returned once more to Samarda, and this time my anxiety was greatly increased by the departure of Miss Mackenzie from Bhopál. She had been acting for Miss Neibel, and on the latter's return to duty, she went to Alwa, where she was given a permanent appointment. The people amongst whom Miss Mackenzie works are indeed fortunate. Her mere presence gives her patients fresh life, and her unremitting attention and her womanly sympathy turn despair into confidence and hope. I never think of Asif Jahán Begam without calling to mind Miss Mackenzie's affectionate care of her. She would sit for hours by her little patient's bedside, and with pleasant stories charm away her pains, and bring happy smiles to her face. I think her presence comforted me almost as much as it did my child.

This time we were two months at Samarda, but the change did not benefit my daughter as much as on the previous occasion. Doctor Muhammad Syad, my own private medical adviser, was with us, and by his advice we once more returned to Bhopál, and immediately on our arrival sent for Miss Neibel. This lady was in every way a contrast to Miss Mackenzie; she was neither courteous in her manner nor attentive in her treatment. The disease steadily advanced, and for a week Asif Jahán Begam took no nourishment, any attempt to do so being followed by violent sickness. When Miss Neibel's opinion was asked, she said that she could discover no specific disease from which my daughter was suffering, and, as far as she could see, there was nothing serious the matter. And yet it was plain that death was near. Doctor Joshi was again called in, and, as soon as he approached the invalid's bedside, he pronounced the case hopeless.

It was on a Saturday that her condition became desperate. On the Sunday morning, Major Meade called to make inquiries and to offer his sympathy. On hearing Doctor Joshi's report he was greatly shocked. Major Meade was more than Political Agent; he was a true and kind friend to me and my family. It was the continuation of a friendship which had been commenced by his father, who had been Agent to the Governor-General in the time of Nawáb Sikandar Begam, and on whose advice and assistance my Grandmother used to set the highest value. By my invitation, Major Meade entered the sick chamber, and spoke words of sympathy and comfort to Asif Jahán Begam. She was quite conscious at the time, but it was easy to see that she was sinking. She lived on till 4 o'clock the next afternoon, and then darkness took possession of my heart, for the light of her love and her goodness had ceased to shine. On the day of her death, the 18th of Muharram, 1312 A.H., she had reached the age of 14 years 4 months and 22 days.

We are God's, and unto Him shall we surely return.[1]

Since the death of our beloved elder daughter, Asif Jahán Begam had been our main consolation and comfort. And now that she too was taken away, the burden of our grief seemed almost more than we could bear. That my Mother felt the blow almost as keenly as we did, I have no doubt; but she bore her sorrow as we had to bear ours—alone. Her displeasure added greatly to our gloom, and the presence of our two sons was our only ray of light; for of our other relatives, not a single one came near us. I must not, however, forget the kindness which was displayed towards us by many officers of the Government: the letters of sympathy we received from them were to us a real source of courage and consolation.

[1] Sale's translation of the Korán.

But though our earthly comforters were few, God did not abandon us. He gave us strength and patience, and we bowed ourselves in submission to His will. The funeral took place in the Hayát Afzah garden; and, although we had given no notice of the hour, and had invited no one to attend the ceremony, a large crowd of people joined the procession as soon as it left the Sadar Manzil. A peculiar sadness always attaches itself to the death of the young, and my double bereavement evoked genuine and widespread sympathy among the people of Bhopál.

Sáhibzádi Asif Jahán Begam was a pious and sweet-tempered girl. During her long illness of two and a quarter years, she never omitted her daily prayers, and on each occasion she kept the fast of Ramazán for half the month. In addition to her religious exercises, she had learnt to write Urdu, and had commenced to study English and Persian. She loved her parents and brothers deeply, and was never truly happy unless she saw that they were happy too. Her cheerful and affectionate disposition won for her the love of every member of my household, and her untimely death will ever be lamented.

I have said that God remembered me in my affliction. Let me, then, close this chapter by telling of the special manifestation of His goodness and mercy which was vouchsafed to me.

On the 8th of the month Rabi-ul-awwal (September 9th, 1894), I gave birth to my youngest son, Sáhibzáda Hamidullah Khán. My Mother did not visit me on the occasion, nor were there any demonstrations of joy on the part of the State. The necessary religious ceremonies I performed in a simple manner in my own house, and when the *akika* ceremony took place, I myself selected the name Muhammad Hamidullah Khán. My own joy at the birth of this child was unbounded. For since the death of Asif Jahán Begam, I had been depressed and melancholy, and there seemed to be no pleasure for me in life any more. How welcome, then, was this timely gift from God, which, straightway, put new vigour into my heart, and new joy into my life. I felt as the withered and parched grass of the desert must feel when, after long months of drought, it is again watered by the blessed rain from heaven; and I looked upon this child as an angel of mercy sent by the Great Consoler of human hearts, to minister to me in my time of need, and to be to me in the place of those two whom He had seen fit to take away.

CHAPTER XVII

1895—1897

On October 12th, 1895, the Political Agent sent information that Lord Elgin, accompanied by Lady Elgin and his Staff, would visit Bhopál on November 4th, arriving at 9 a.m., and departing the following evening at 11 p.m. The preparations for his reception and entertainment were similar to those which had been made on the occasion of the visit of Lord Lansdowne. The leading Chiefs of the Agency were invited to meet His Excellency, besides a large company of English ladies and gentlemen. The Foreign Secretary and the Political Agent arranged the programme, all the details of which were carefully carried out.

His Excellency was received at the railway station by Her Highness, the Agent to the Governor-General, the Political Agent, the Chiefs of the Agency, together with the European guests and the high officials of the State, and a guard of honour was drawn up on the platform. On the arrival of the train, Her Highness came out from her waiting-room and welcomed Their Excellencies as they alighted. At the same time, the guard of honour presented arms, and a salute of thirty-one guns was fired by the State artillery. The Viceregal party drove at once to the Lál Kothi, escorted by a detachment of the Imperial Service Lancers. At 11 o'clock, the Minister, Mián Alamgír Muhammad Khán, Mián Sadar Muhammad Khán, and Mián Núr-ul-hasan went to the Lál Kothi to make the *mizáj pursi*. They were received by the Foreign Secretary and the Military Secretary, who presented them with *'itr* and *pán*, and informed them that the Viceroy would be ready to receive Her Highness at 12 o'clock.

At 11.15, the Military Secretary, the Under-Secretary, and an Aide-de-camp drove to the Táj Mahal to escort Her Highness to the Lál Kothi. They were met by the Political Agent, and on being informed by him that Her Highness was ready, the whole party returned forthwith to the Kothi, reaching there punctually at noon. As Her Highness's carriage approached, a salute of twenty-one guns was fired. An Aide-de-camp received her at the door of her carriage, and the Foreign Secretary at the foot of the steps leading to the entrance, the guard of honour drawn up on either side presenting arms. As she mounted the steps, His Excellency advanced to meet her, and, leading her into the drawing-room, seated her in a chair on the right-hand side of his own. The Political Agent then introduced the Minister, Mián Alamgír Muhammad Khán, and the other nobles by whom Her Highness was accompanied. Each of them presented his *nazar*, which His Excellency touched and returned. After a brief conversation, *'itr* and *pán* were distributed, Her Highness receiving it from the hands of His Excellency, and the others from the Foreign Secretary. Her Highness then paid a short visit to Her Excellency Lady Elgin in a separate apartment, after which she returned to the Táj Mahal, her departure being as ceremonious as her arrival.

The same day, His Excellency received visits from the Chiefs of Rájgarh, Narsinghgarh, and other States of the Agency, and in the evening paid a return visit to Her Highness. He was accompanied by his Secretaries and Staff in full uniform, and was escorted from the Lál Kothi by the Minister, the chief Sirdars of the State, and a squadron of the Imperial Service Lancers. The State troops formed the guard of honour, and presented arms as His Excellency drove up to the outer gateway of the palace. A salute of thirty-one guns was again fired. Her Highness, supported by the Political Agent, received her visitors at the inner gateway and conducted them to the durbar hall. His Excellency sat on Her Highness's right, with the members of his Staff next to him. The Political Agent and the nobles of the State were seated on her left. The visit was a short one, and the usual formalities characterized the proceedings. His Excellency returned to the Lál Kothi at 4 p.m.

At 6 o'clock, Lady Elgin called on Her Highness, and, after taking tea with her, witnessed from the palace a display of fireworks. At night there was a State banquet. Her Highness was not present during dinner, but watched the proceedings from an adjoining apartment. When dessert was served, she joined her guests, and, after the royal toast had been honoured, proposed the health of Their Excellencies Lord and Lady Elgin. In reply His Excellency delivered the following speech:

"Your Highness, Ladies and Gentlemen,—I rise to respond to the cordial manner in which you have received the toast of our health, and to express my deep obligation to Her Highness, for the kind words in which she has proposed it. This is not the first time on which Her Highness the Begam has welcomed a Viceroy to Bhopál, and has proposed his health, and I think we may feel well assured that any one who comes in the name and as the representative of the Queen-Empress will always be certain to find a ready and friendly welcome from the Ruler of Bhopál. In saying this I wish to draw no invidious comparison, for I have met with too much kindness from other Princes and Chiefs of India, but it is well known that to none of them will the Rulers of Bhopál yield in the loyalty which they have shown to the British Ráj. I feel certain that that loyalty will not only be expressed, as it has been to-night, in eloquent terms by Her Highness, but will also be manifested in action, as it was in the time of her predecessor. I hope that in the circumstances of the present day we shall never see our friend Colonel Barr forced to quit Indore; but if he were, I have no doubt that, as a former Resident found, he also would find ready assistance from the Ruler of Bhopál. In the meantime, Ladies and Gentlemen, we are not surprised to find that Her Highness the Begam gave a ready assent to that movement which was instituted a few years back to give expression to the loyalty of the Princes and Chiefs of India to the Crown, and that she took advantage, as she has told us this evening, of the opportunity of establishing a regiment of Imperial Service Troops. I am already in a position, from having seen the regiment on escort duty, to congratulate

Her Highness on the excellent manner in which they are horsed and equipped, and I have no doubt that in the parade to-morrow they will give a satisfactory account of themselves, and show that they have profited by the supervision they have received from Colonel Melliss and his able Assistant, to whom this movement owes so much.

"Ladies and Gentlemen, there is another matter in which Her Highness the Begam has followed the traditions of her house. The Rulers of Bhopâl have ever been known for their charitable instincts, and Her Highness has devoted much time and money to the promotion of public works. I think that there is only one occasion, and that is one to which Her Highness has alluded, on which we regret the institution of public works, and that is when they are called for by deficiency of crops, and the consequent necessity of providing for the due employment of the people and the provision of the food which they require. I, therefore, sincerely join in the hope that Her Highness has expressed this evening, that the unsatisfactory seasons of the last two years may give way to a better prospect, and that the cultivators in this part of the country may reap the profits which justly accrue to them from the fertility of the soil. In other respects, I find it difficult to put a limit to the commendation which is due to a ruler of a State who devotes the revenue of the State to the promotion of works of public utility. There is only one proviso I should like to make in this matter, and that is, that works are undertaken with a prudent foresight and economy. There is a temptation to look to the immediate benefit which accrues from the opening up of a great country, the crops of which are unable to reach the markets readily; but I think it must be borne in mind that much of that benefit will be lost if the credit of the State is endangered: and the credit of the State is for the future as well as for to-day. It is from an earnest wish to see the highest possible honour associated with the name of Her Highness that I venture to refer to a point that is sometimes overlooked, but which most probably she has already considered and kept in view. Her Highness has alluded to one great work, the Ujjain Railway, in which she has taken a conspicuous interest, and over which I had hoped about this time to be travelling. I have no doubt that that work will be one of great benefit to the country, and that Her Highness will derive all the profit from it which instigated her in undertaking it.

"Ladies and Gentlemen, Her Highness has spoken this evening of the favours which she has received from Her Majesty the Queen-Empress. I hope that Her Highness will believe that Her Majesty, and the Government of India which represents Her Majesty, are ever willing to recognize the good work which is done by the rulers of States for the benefit of their subjects; and, therefore, in thanking her once again for the kindly welcome which she has given to us, for the splendid reception which she has provided for us, and for the magnificent spectacle which we have seen in our drive to the city this evening, I should like to express an earnest hope that she may have long life and happiness to enjoy the honours which have been so worthily conferred upon her. I ask you, Ladies and Gentlemen, to join with me in drinking to the health of Her Highness the Begam of Bhopál."

The next day, Lady Elgin, accompanied by Surgeon Lieutenant-Colonel Franklin, Honorary Secretary to the Central Committee of the Lady Dufferin Fund, inspected the Lady Lansdowne Hospital. Both Lady Elgin and Colonel Franklin spoke in high praise of the arrangements of the hospital, and recorded their approbation in the Visitors' Book. In the evening, Their Excellencies left Bhopál by special train, their departure being private.

Not long after the visit of Lord Elgin, the death took place of Munshi Imtiyáz Ali Khán. He had been one of the chief adherents of Sidik Hasan Khán, and, as my readers know, succeeded Colonel Ward as Minister of the State. Munshi Imtiyáz Ali Khán was a native of Kárkori, in the district of Lucknow, and his appointment to the office of Minister was engineered by Sidik Hasan Khán. He was the product of an ancient and narrow system of education, and had passed most of his life as a pleader. To maintain the administration in the same state of efficiency in which his predecessor had left it, required only ordinary ability and experience. But Imtiyáz Ali possessed neither of these qualifications, nor was he fitted by character or breeding for the post he occupied.

Colonel Ward had reformed every branch of the State service, and a substantial increase in the revenue was already testifying to the wisdom of his management. Imtiyáz Ali's

THE EARL OF ELGIN AND KINCARDINE.

THE COUNTESS OF ELGIN.

p. 172]

assumption of office was signalized by a complete reversal of the policy of the two previous years. One of his first acts was to discharge a number of able and trustworthy officers who had been appointed by Colonel Ward, and to fill their places with indigent friends and relatives of his own, who were incapable of earning a livelihood elsewhere, and who possessed not a single qualification for the work they were given to do. He then proceeded to make a radical change in the revenue department, abolishing the *mustájiri* system[1] of collecting land revenue, and introducing the *khám* system in its place. Hundreds of villages were made *khám*, and large advances in grain and money were made by the State. The ostensible object of this legislation was to improve the condition of the cultivator. Its actual result was that the cultivators became worse off than they had been for years, while many *mustájirs* were practically ruined, and the State treasury was seriously impoverished. This disastrous result was due, not so much to the new system, as to the iniquitous manner in which it was carried into effect. The cultivators, for whose benefit corn and money were advanced by the State, grew poorer and poorer, while those who were entrusted with the distribution fattened on their ill-gotten gains. To make matters worse, three bad seasons came in succession, the wheat crops failing almost entirely. The cultivators received no compensation, and the result of this accumulation of calamities was that the area of cultivated land decreased by a third, and the population of the State fell from 900,000 to 600,000.

But if the revenue administration was bad, judicial affairs were in an even worse case. Laws and courts of justice there certainly were, but any appeal to them which was not backed up by a full purse was made in vain. Civil suits were little more than bribery competitions, and criminals were acquitted or convicted according to the means at their disposal. The high officials of the State had their private agents in every district, whose business it was to line their patrons' pockets,

[1] Under the *mustájiri* system the cultivator holds his land under a *mustájir*, or middle man; under the *khám* system he deals directly with the State, or the proprietor of the land.

receiving, in return, protection whilst they lined their own. If a complaint against a subordinate officer was made to the Begam, she referred the matter to the Minister, and the person who lodged the complaint generally found it to his advantage to withdraw it. Complaints against the Minister himself were equally futile; for Imtiyáz Ali Khán had his full share of Lucknow eloquence, and he easily persuaded Her Highness to regard such attacks as gross and malicious libels on his spotless character. The consequences of his three years' administration are apparent to this day, and the State is still engaged in undoing the mischief which he wrought. Most of those who aided him in his progress of corruption were from Lucknow. They came, many of them, as Tahsildars on small pay, and in little more than two years returned to their native city wealthy men. It is little wonder, then, that there is keen competition in Lucknow for posts in the Bhopál State, which is evidently regarded there as a modern El Dorado.

Imtiyáz Ali Khán owed his powerful position in the State to the support he received from Sidik Hasan Khán, who not only helped him to grow rich, but shielded and defended him whenever there was danger of his conduct being called in question. On the death of the latter, however, it became necessary for the Begam to take a more active and personal part in the conduct of affairs, and Imtiyáz Ali's position at once became insecure. Complaint after complaint was brought against him, and at last the Begam's suspicions were thoroughly roused. A public investigation of his conduct was on the point of being held when he fell ill and died. Imtiyáz Ali Khán will not escape the investigation, but it will take place in a court where truth, and not gold, will determine the verdict.

The next Minister of the State was Khán Bahádur Maulavi Abdul Jabbar Khán, C.I.E., an account of whose administration will be given in a later chapter.

After the opening of the Bhopál State Railway, it soon became apparent that the construction of a line from Bhopál to Ujjain, besides being of great service to the travelling public, would add considerably to the commercial prosperity of Central India. After corresponding with the States of

Gwálior, Diwás, and Bhopál, the Government of India, in 1891, caused a survey of the route to be made. It was at first proposed to make a narrow-gauge line; but this did not meet with the approval of Her Highness, and, after a lengthy correspondence, she persuaded the Government to consent to the adoption of the broad gauge. The railway was built in five years, and in February, 1896, both goods and passenger traffic commenced. The construction of this line was much more rapid than that of the Bhopál State Railway. Moreover, the latter had been open for nine years before the State drew any income from it, whereas the new line commenced to pay from the very outset. The actual opening ceremony did not take place till January, 1897. It was performed by the Honourable Colonel Barr, Agent to the Governor-General for Central India. A large company witnessed the ceremony, the European guests including the chief officers of the railway with the ladies of their families. At the conclusion of the ceremony, all the arrangements for which were made by, and at the expense of, the Company, Her Highness, with the Agent to the Governor-General and her other guests, embarked on a special train, and were taken to Sehore, where they were entertained at a garden party. Before returning to Bhopál, Her Highness, with the consent of the Company, distributed presents to all the subordinate servants of the railway, and announced her intention of providing a library at the Bhopál Station for the use of the staff. Later in the evening, a large number of fakirs and poor people were fed at her expense at the Sehore Station. The total cost of the section of the line lying within the Bhopál territory was Rs. 18,890,68. 2. 11.

Amongst the speeches made on this occasion, the two following are worthy to be recorded:

Speech of Her Highness the Begam

"Colonel Barr, Ladies and Gentlemen,—I thank God for this happy day, on which, thirteen years after the completion of the Bhopál State Railway, we are able to open this new line from Bhopál to Ujjain. For the benefits that will result from it to the trade and the people of Central India, and especially to the inhabitants of Bhopál, we are indebted, firstly, to the grace and favour of Her Most Gracious Majesty, the Queen-Empress, and, secondly, to the good government which this small State has enjoyed through the kind patronage of His Excellency the Viceroy, and the sympathetic support of Colonel Barr, Agent to the Governor-General in Central India, and Major Meade, Political Agent in Bhopál. I am most grateful to Colonel Barr for the honour he has conferred upon us by coming here to-day to perform the opening ceremony. And I offer my congratulations to Mr. Sherman, Chief Engineer of the railway, on the able manner in which he has carried out the construction of this line, and on his having so skilfully combined speed with economy, that we are already enjoying our share of the profits, instead of having to wait nine years for them, as we had to do in the case of the Bhopál State Railway. I also desire to thank Major and Mrs. Meade, and all my other guests, for their kindness in coming to grace these proceedings. In conclusion, I pray for the continued prosperity of the British Empire, and for that of its Ruler, whom I shall ever regard as a Mother. May she never cease to bestow, upon my State and myself, the blessings of her royal favour."

Speech of the Honourable Colonel Barr

* "Nawáb Begam Sáhiba, Ladies and Gentlemen,—Before I fulfil Her Highness's desire and declare the Bhopál section of this railway open, I must briefly explain to you why it is that we are taking part in this ceremony to-day. The Bhopál-Ujjain Railway has actually been open to traffic since the month of April; but as it was then the hot season, and the journey to Bhopál would have been attended with a certain amount of discomfort, Her Highness, at my request, very kindly postponed the opening ceremony till the present more favourable occasion. It is a great pleasure to me that, on this my first official visit to Bhopál, I have been able to comply with Her Highness's wishes, and to accompany her in her first journey over this new line.

"Her Highness the Begam is among those Indian Chiefs who have been the first to recognize the advantage of railway extension. The Bhopál State Railway, from Itársi to Bhopál, was opened in 1884. It was a very costly undertaking; for not only had the Narbadda to be bridged at Hoshangábád, in itself a gigantic task, but the line had to be carried across the

SIR DAVID W. KEITH BARR.

p. 176]

Vindhia Hills, necessitating bridges and cuttings which involved great labour and heavy expense. Although it is true, as Her Highness has remarked, that for several years the line was worked without any pecuniary profit, yet its importance can hardly be over-estimated: for it was one of the foundations of the Indian Midland Railway system, which now traverses so large a portion of Central India, extending from Itársi through Bhopál, Jhánsi, and Gwálior, to Agra, with branches connecting Jhánsi with Cawnpore and Manikpur, and Bhopál with Ujjain. I am sure, ladies and gentlemen, that you will join me in congratulating Her Highness most cordially on the completion of this last section of the Indian Midland Railway, and in expressing the hope that she may enjoy the fruits of the liberality she has displayed in its construction. I trust that this line will not only prove a source of profit to Her Highness, but that it will increase both the trade of her State and the prosperity and comfort of her people, and, which is of even greater importance, that it will, by facilitating the transportation of grain, do much to mitigate the sufferings of the poor in years of scarcity like the present.

"Her Highness has acknowledged her indebtedness to Mr. Sherman, who has been the Chief Engineer of this railway from the day it was commenced till its completion. I, also, desire to offer my thanks and congratulations to Mr. Sherman, and to all those who have been associated with him in his labours. We are so accustomed in these days to travelling on railways that we seldom think of or appreciate the thousand difficulties and responsibilities that have to be faced by those who, like Mr. Sherman, undertake the planning, constructing, and organizing of these great works.

"Nawáb Begam Sáhiba, I assure you that I and all your guests have heard with real pleasure the words of loyalty you have spoken to-day, for we know that these words are the genuine expression of your personal feelings; and we look upon the zeal and energy with which you have supported this and other works of public utility as the natural outcome of your devotion to that Noble Lady who is not only the Queen of England, but the Mother of her people in all parts of the world.

"Ladies and gentlemen, I now declare this line open, and I ask you to join me in drinking to the health of Her Highness the Begam, and to the prosperity of the Bhopál-Ujjain Railway."

CHAPTER XVIII

THE LAST YEARS OF MY MOTHER'S REIGN

EARLY in June, 1897, the State Minister, Maulavi Abdul Jabbar Khán, C.I.E., received a letter from the Political Agent informing him that, in accordance with the orders of the Viceroy, the 21st and 22nd days of June would be observed as public holidays throughout British India, in honour of the completion by Her Majesty the Queen-Empress of sixty years of her reign. Her Highness at once directed that the same days should be observed as holidays in the State, and preparations were made to celebrate so memorable an event in a loyal and becoming manner.

On the appointed day, a grand durbar was held at the Shaukat Mahal and was attended by all the nobles and chief officers of the State. At its conclusion, presents were distributed to a large number of deserving officials, and twenty-four poor students of the Victoria School received each a new suit of clothes. Orders were given for the release of a number of prisoners from the jail, and for the reduction of the sentences of others. A parade of the State troops took place on the Jahángírábád parade ground, and a royal salute of a hundred and one guns was fired. In the evening, the public buildings, forts, and offices, as well as the chief private houses of the city, were illuminated, and corn and rice were distributed to the poor. The public offices remained closed on both the above-mentioned days, and corn was distributed in all the *tahsils* of the State. On July 8th, Her Highness gave a dinner to her European friends at the Lál Kothi. The health of the Queen was proposed by Her Highness in person, the Political Agent proposed the health of Her Highness, and the Minister that of the guests. Her Highness's speech was as follows:

"Ladies and Gentlemen,—I have asked you to meet me here to-night that we may rejoice together on the great and memorable occasion of the Diamond Jubilee of Her Majesty the Queen-Empress—an occasion that has filled every heart in India, and especially my own, with thankfulness and joy. I say 'especially my own,' for it was in Her Majesty's reign that I was born, it was in Her Majesty's reign that I became the Ruler of this State, and it was Her Majesty who bestowed upon me the order of the Crown of India, and who made me a Grand Commander of the Star of India. I rejoice, too. to think that my Sovereign is a woman, and, though I have never had the high privilege of paying my loyal respects to her in person, I yet regard her with all the affection of a daughter; indeed, she occupies the same place in my heart as did my Mother, Nawáb Sikandar Begam. The greatness of her virtues, and the blessings of her rule, are more than mere words can utter. The history of her reign is a record of progress in science, art, commerce, and all that makes for civilization and peace, such as the world has never known before.

"I did not arrange this dinner on the 21st of June, because I thought that on that day every one would prefer to rejoice in his own home. The celebration of the Jubilee in England has not yet come to an end, so there is nothing unbecoming in thus prolonging the period of our festivities in Bhopál.

"Ladies and Gentlemen, I ask you to join me in drinking to the health of Her Majesty the Queen-Empress, and I pray God to prolong her life for many years to come."

A ***kharíta***, containing an account of the celebrations that had taken place in Bhopál, was dispatched to His Excellency the Viceroy, and a sum of two thousand rupees was contributed to the fund which had been opened for the purpose of erecting a statue of Her Majesty the Queen in Calcutta.

Another interesting event that took place during the year 1897 was the introduction into the State of the coinage of British India. Previous to this time, the State had coined its own silver and copper money, which was stamped with the name of the ruler and the date of issue. My Mother, foreseeing that the financial administration of the State, and commercial transactions generally, would be greatly facilitated by the adoption of the coinage current in British India, had approached the Government of India on the subject as far back as the year 1892. After a great deal of correspondence, the Government of India agreed to take over the current money of the State at the rate of 124 Bhopál rupees for 100 British. The details having been settled, a circular containing the rules of exchange was published throughout the State, as well as in Narsinghgarh, Rájgarh, Maksudgarh, Sotiála, and other States of the Agency where Bhopál money was current. The period fixed for the exchange was from October 1st, 1897, to February 1st, 1898, after which Bhopál money ceased to be current, and represented nothing more than its market value as silver or copper. A 10-per-cent. reduction was made in the revenue demanded from *mustájirs* and cultivators as soon as the new system was established.

On all sums deposited as security by *mustájirs* as well as on money realized from attached *jágír* villages, exchange was calculated at government rates. That her subjects might not have to incur any loss, Her Highness agreed to accept all Bhopál money, that had not lost more than 2 per cent. in weight, in exchange for British coin, and to bear all expenses incidental to such transactions. The pay of all State servants drawing ten rupees a month, or less, remained unchanged, a reduction of 10 per cent. being made in the case of those who drew more than that amount. The new system being completely established, information to that effect was sent to the Government of India. A reply was received in which the Government expressed its gratification, and congratulated Her Highness on the able manner in which the exchange had been effected.

In September, 1898, Her Highness wrote to Lord Elgin, who was about to leave Simla, expressing her desire to bid him farewell before his departure for England, and asking permission to meet him at any point on his journey that might be convenient. A *kharíta* was received in reply, stating that it would give His Excellency great pleasure to see Her Highness again, and that Cawnpore would be the most convenient meeting-place. Accordingly, my Mother, accompanied by the Political Agent and the Minister, went to Cawnpore on November 8th. The meeting took place at the railway station, where suitable arrangements had been made by the State, and His Excellency remained in conversation with Her Highness until the departure of his train. Her Highness rested the night in Cawnpore, and returned to Bhopál the next day.

Lord Elgin, as my readers know, was succeeded in the Viceroyalty by Lord Curzon ; and in November of the following year, he, too, honoured my Mother by paying a visit to her Capital. The announcement was made to Her Highness three months beforehand by the Political Agent. It is unnecessary for me to describe the preparations that were made. Suffice to say that the welcome extended by the State to Lord and Lady Curzon was no less magnificent, and no less hearty, than those which had greeted his predecessors. Many English and Indian guests were invited to meet Their Excellencies, the latter including the Rájas of Narsinghgarh, Rájgarh, and Kilchipúr, and the Nawábs of Maksudgarh and Basoda. As usual, a programme of the visit was received beforehand, and it was announced that the arrival of Lady Curzon would take place ten minutes before that of the Viceroy.

In accordance with the programme, Her Highness reached the railway station shortly after 9 a.m. on the morning of the 25th. She was accompanied by the Minister and other State officers. Lady Curzon arrived at 9.45 a.m. by special train, and was welcomed by Her Highness, with whom she remained in conversation until the arrival of His Excellency's train at 10 o'clock. Her Highness, clad in a *burkha*, and wearing the orders of a Grand Commander of the Star of India, received His Excellency on the platform, and with great cordiality bade him welcome to her State. The chief officials present were then introduced, after which His Excellency inspected the Imperial Service troops and the State troops, which were drawn up outside the station, the latter carrying the *máhi marátib*, and the flag which had been presented to the State at the Delhi Durbar. The party then went in procession to the Lál Kothi, Lord and Lady Curzon, with Major Newmarch and Captain Wigram, occupying the first carriage, and Her Highness following in the second. A squadron of the Victoria Lancers formed the escort, and His Excellency was loudly cheered by the spectators, who had gathered in large numbers along the route. At noon the Ministers and two Sirdars called at the Lál Kothi to make the *mizáj pursi*, and at 3 p.m., Her Highness paid His Excellency a State visit. The visit was returned at 6 p.m. the same evening at the Táj Mahal, His Excellency expressing himself greatly pleased at the decorations and illuminations in honour of his visit. In the evening, Her Highness entertained her guests at a banquet at the Lál Kothi, and in the following words proposed the health of Lord and Lady Curzon:

"Your Excellencies, Ladies and Gentlemen,—I have no fear of being contradicted when I say that, at the present moment, there is no one in this vast Empire of India more fortunate or more honoured than I am, in that I have the privilege of counting among my guests the Viceroy of our beloved Queen—may her Empire last for ever!—and the noble Lady who shares the dignity of his high office. My gratitude for the honour done to me and to my State by their presence here to-day is more than I can express. His Excellency knows that my predecessors have ever been loyal to the British Throne, and, since I became the Ruler of Bhopál, I have had no dearer ambition than to follow the example they have set before me. My subjects, both Muhammadan and Hindu, are faithful supporters of Her Majesty's Government, and I trust that the regiment of Imperial Service Lancers, which the State now maintains, will enable many of them to give a practical proof of their desire to defend and advance its welfare. Since the visit of Lord Lansdowne, the most important events in the history of the State have been the introduction of the coinage of British India, and the passing of the Arms Act. The former, by abolishing the difficulties of exchange, has done much to facilitate commerce; and the latter, by making it impossible for persons of criminal disposition to go about armed, has added greatly to the security of the people. The

LADY CURZON.

p. 182]

most important public work has, of course, been the construction of the Ujjain Railway. Owing to a succession of bad seasons, there has, during the past two or three years, been much distress in the State; and, although better crops were raised last year, the cultivators are still feeling the effect of their heavy losses. This year the monsoon has again partially failed us; but if, by the Grace of God, rain falls in the cold season, we may hope to escape the misfortunes of a famine.

"I beg to express once more my deep sense of the honour Your Excellency has done me in visiting my Capital. Your Excellency will be entertained by many worthier hosts, but it will be long before I can again have the good fortune to welcome so distinguished a guest. May God long preserve Her Imperial Majesty Queen Victoria, and may He grant health and happiness to her Viceroy in India, and bless his rule with peace and prosperity.

"Ladies and Gentlemen, I ask you to drink the health of Their Excellencies Lord and Lady Curzon."

Lord Curzon replied as follows:

"Your Highness, Ladies and Gentlemen,—Her Highness the Begam, whose guests we have the pleasure of being to-night, has the gift of graceful speech no less than that of magnificent hospitality. She has proposed the health of Lady Curzon and myself in terms so felicitous that in our recollections they will always crown the memory of our first official visit to one of the principal Native States of India. It is a satisfaction to me to think that the particular State which thus receives us should be one the Ruler of which has during a period of more than thirty years won so honourable a reputation for enlightenment and public-spirited administration, besides sustaining the tradition, already rendered notable by the conduct of her mother, of devoted loyalty to the British Crown. That the sceptre need not pass into feeble or irresolute hands when, by the accident of fortune, it is wielded by a woman, is shown by the career of our beloved sovereign Her Majesty the Queen-Empress; nor may we fail on a smaller scale to find an illustration of the same phenomenon in the case of the two successive Begams who have now, for a combined period of more than half a century, presided over the fortunes of the State of Bhopál. Her Highness's mother was distinguished, not only, as I have said, for her fidelity to the British Ráj, but also for her ability as a ruler. Similarly the rule of Her Highness has been rendered memorable by many acts of administrative prudence and private generosity, while from the speech which has just been delivered I gather with pleasure that her active interest in the well-being of her subjects is far from being exhausted, and that she still continues to devise and carry out projects which testify to her practical wisdom and will conduce to the prosperity of the State.

"I shall on Monday morning have the pleasure of inspecting on the parade ground the regiment of cavalry which Her Highness has contributed to the defence of the Empire, and which she has designated with the name of Her Majesty the Queen-Empress. Her Highness has never failed to take as great an interest in these men as though she were herself their military commander, and I am pleased to hear that she has recently added to the attractions of the regiment by raising the scale of pay.

"I look with great interest on the conversion of the native currencies in the Feudatory States of India, and the substitution for them of the uniform and stable coinage of the British mints. In taking this step, as far back as 1897, Her Highness has acted as a pioneer in a movement in which I believe that she is destined to find many followers, and which must unquestionably tend to the commercial advantage of the entire community. Similarly, Her Highness has been well advised in keeping her eye upon the gangs of desperate and unruly men who from time to time raise their heads even in modern India, and who find in any season of distress an opportunity for reviving the discredited profession of predatory crime. The first test of an orderly State is the security which it gives to the life and property of its citizens, and dacoits are a public scourge to whom the State should show no mercy.

"It is a source of great gratification to me to find on coming into the Bhopál State that although, as Her Highness has said, the situation is not altogether free from anxiety as to the agricultural outlook, yet the circumstances of this part of India are much more favourable than many of those which I have lately been visiting. It is a trying experience to see pinched human faces and dying cattle. I echo Her Highness's prayer that in this State she may escape both calamities, and that Providence may be merciful to her people. In conclusion, it only remains for me to thank Her Highness the Begam for the friendly and auspicious wishes she has uttered on behalf of

BARON CURZON OF KEDLESTON.

p. 184]

Lady Curzon and myself, to assure her that we shall not forget our right royal welcome in this State, and to ask all the ladies and gentlemen seated at this table, and who, like ourselves, are recipients of her profuse hospitality, to join with me in drinking long life and prosperity to Her Highness the Begam of Bhopál."

His Excellency's speech met with loud applause, and Her Highness received the hearty good wishes of all her guests. The company then adjourned to the gardens, where a grand display of fireworks brought the evening's entertainment to a close. In the morning, His Excellency visited the Fort, and rested during the remainder of the day. Lady Curzon, in company with Her Highness, visited the Lady Lansdowne Hospital. Her Excellency went through all the wards, and spoke to many of the patients, inquiring minutely about their treatment. She was much pleased on being informed that nurses were trained in the Hospital, and sent out to attend cases in the city and district.

On the morning of the 27th, Lord Curzon reviewed the Imperial Service Troops. After the march past, he briefly addressed the Officers, complimenting them on the behaviour of their men on parade, and speaking in high terms of the good order and completeness of their accoutrements and the condition of their horses. After breakfast, a snipe-shooting expedition was organized, and resulted in the biggest bag ever made in Bhopál, His Excellency making the top score. Farewell visits occupied the afternoon, and in the evening, after dinner, Their Excellencies drove to the railway station, and spent the night on board their train, which left early in the morning for Sánchi. Here a halt of two hours was made, and a visit was paid to the Buddhist topes, after which the party re-embarked for Gwalior.

Lady Curzon, during her visit to Bhopál showed me the greatest kindness; and as long as she remained in India, I continued to receive tokens of her friendly feelings towards me. I shall never forget this kindness; and when, in the year 1906, the news of her untimely death reached me, I was filled with sorrow, for I felt that I had lost a true friend.

When my two sons, Sáhibzáda Obaidullah Khán and Nawáb Nasrullah Khán, reached the ages of 22 and 23 years respectively, I began to consider seriously the question of their nuptials. My Mother's anger had, so far, prevented any steps in this direction from being taken. Now, however, my sons had reached manhood, and since it is generally acknowledged that, in a hot country like India, late marriages are undesirable, I felt that the necessary negotiations could be no longer delayed. Proposals had already reached me from several of the Muhammadan States of India, and I had reviewed in my own mind the qualifications of the various marriageable daughters in the families of my husband and my father ; but I had come to no definite decision, for custom and the terms of my own marriage agreement alike demanded that the selection of my sons' brides should rest with Her Highness. I therefore made known my desire to her in the following letter, which I sent through the Minister of the State :

"Seeing that my two sons, Nawáb Nasrullah Khán and Sáhibzáda Obaidullah Khán, are now grown up, I desire to consult Your Highness on the subject of their marriages, which has been causing me anxiety for some time past. Pecuniary embarrassments, consequent upon the late famine, have prevented me from taking this step before. Even now I am hardly in a position to incur heavy expenditure ; but the ages at which my sons have arrived make it undesirable that there should be any further delay. In my opinion, there are only two families with which alliances would be acceptable, namely, those of my father and my husband. I have received proposals from Hyderabad, Jaora, and other States, to none of which I have, as yet, sent replies. I beg, therefore, that you will be good enough to favour me with your opinion and advice."

My Mother sent me no written reply to this letter, but she summoned the Minister, and said to him, "I have no objection to the Sáhibzádas' marrying into the family of their father, but alliances with the family of Sultán Jahán's father are out of the quest on, and would never receive my consent."

Her Highness's answer was communicated to me by the Minister, who concluded his letter with these words: "My own advice, if I may be allowed to offer it, is that the two daughters of your husband's sister should be chosen as brides for your sons. I do not think that any selection could be more suitable." This advice pleased both me and the Nawáb Sáhib: and, as the sister in question expressed her readiness to abide by her brother's decision, the matter was finally settled.

There are few events which afford greater joy to parents than the marriages of their sons. I felt that my happiness would be complete if only I could secure Her Highness's presence at the nuptial ceremony, and I resolved to make yet another attempt to win her forgiveness. My letter, and the reply I received to it, will acquaint my readers with the result of my appeal. With mingled feelings of hope and despair I wrote:

"Your Highness has, doubtless, read my letter of the 15th Zil Kádah, regarding the celebration of my sons' nuptials. Save Your Highness, I have no other patron, and to Your Highness my husband and I owe all that we possess—our property, our position, and our honour. It is my earnest wish that Your Highness should preside over this ceremony, for otherwise there can be no happiness for me in it. If I have offended, it has never been willingly or consciously; and my husband and I have no other desire than to consult in all things your will and pleasure. But man is prone to sin: we, therefore, beg for the forgiveness of our faults, to the better comfort of ourselves and of Your Highness in both the worlds. In spite of my own unworthiness, I am bold enough to rely upon Your Highness's generosity for a favourable reply."

The answer to this petition was forwarded to me by the Minister:

"My presence at the nuptials of Mián Nasrullah Khán and Mián Obaidullah Khán can do no good, nor can my absence cause any ill either to them or to their parents. To the parents the responsibility of arranging such matters belongs, and my presence, being a matter of no importance, should be neither desired nor expected.

"The forgiveness of sins rests with God alone. I, too, am a sinner, and to Him only I look for pardon.

"I trust that Sultán Jahán Begam will refrain from troubling me in future, and that the question of my attending the marriage will not again be referred to."

Simultaneously with the nuptials of my elder sons, it was my intention to celebrate the *khatna* ceremony of my youngest son, Sáhibzáda Hamidullah Khán, following the example of the Prophet, and of those who came before him since the days of Abraham, the Friend of God. In spite of the disappointment which filled our hearts on account of the rejection of our petition, we decided that these several rites could not be deferred, and they were, accordingly, performed at the Sadar Manzil at 5 p.m. on Saturday, the 15th of Rajab, 1318 A.H. I have always looked with disfavour on the superfluous ritual with which Muhammadans usually adorn their religious ceremonies, and I endeavour, as far as I can, to set an example of simplicity. On the present occasion, no ceremonial was observed which the laws of Islám do not strictly enjoin. The members of my household were the only people who witnessed the proceedings : my relations followed the example set by my Mother, and none of the State officials were present. The marriage *khatbah* was read by Kázi Abdul Hak, the State Kázi, and everything, including the *khatna* ceremony of Sáhibzáda Hamidullah Khán, was completed before the hour of evening prayer.

The *nikah*, or marriage proper, which had just been performed, is a purely religious ceremony, and is not the occasion for any great display of joy. The actual wedding festival, or *shádi*, takes place when the bride is welcomed to her new home. A considerable period of time often elapses between the *nikah* and the *shádi*, and in the present instance I determined that the latter should be postponed, for I had a lingering hope that my Mother might yet be induced to relent. Early the next month, however, we heard that Her Highness had fallen ill, and, as day by day the reports of her condition became more and more unfavourable, I decided to abandon all thoughts of the *shádi* until her recovery ; for while she lay on a bed of suffering, I felt that I had little heart for scenes of joy and mirth. In spite of all that had passed, my love for her had never diminished. She was still to me the mother I had known in my childhood; for I knew that her coldness towards me was no part of her real nature, but had been thrust upon her by those whom she had no power to resist. I earnestly hoped that her life might be a long one, for I coveted neither her position nor her wealth, and I felt that, sooner or later, the day must come when I should be restored to her affections, and, beyond this, I had no further ambition.

CHAPTER XIX

THE DEATH OF NAWAB SHAH JAHAN BEGAM

ABOUT the beginning of Rabi-ul-awwal, 1318 A.H., a small sore appeared on my Mother's left cheek. At first it was considered too trifling to need attention. After some days, however, it became large and painful, and native remedies were applied, but their only effect was to aggravate the sore. Skilled Indian doctors were then called in, but their treatment gave my Mother no relief, and it soon became apparent that she was suffering from cancer. Doctor Anderson, a physician of repute from Lucknow, was next summoned. He at once recognized the seriousness of the case, and said that the removal of the cancer was the only means of saving the patient's life. Doctor Dane, the Agency Surgeon, was of the same opinion, and my Mother expressed herself willing to be guided by their advice. A time was, accordingly, fixed upon, and the necessary arrangements were made. Instruments, bandages, antiseptics, all were laid out in readiness, when my Mother, for some unaccountable reason, changed her mind, and refused to undergo the operation.

There was nothing for it but to fall back upon ordinary remedies, and hope for the best. Unfortunately, many things were happening to disturb my Mother's peace of mind. In addition to her illness, the serious nature of which she fully understood, and the anxiety which her inability to attend to the business of the State naturally caused her, a new and heavy trouble came upon her; for she began to realize, for the first time, that those about her, whom she had been accustomed to regard as her faithful friends and retainers, were mere sycophants, indifferent alike to her sufferings and her commands, and intent only on turning to their advantage any opportunities which the adversity of their mistress might afford.

Nawâb Shah Jahân Begam was, by nature, tender-hearted and affectionate. She was my Mother; and it was plain to all who had access to her that her days were numbered. In such circumstances, no efforts should have been spared to banish from her mind the remembrance of all past misunderstandings, and to restore me again to her affection. But her "friends" thought otherwise, and did their best to turn her thoughts away from me and my family, and to foster her determination never to see me again. In addition to this, my Mother's private affairs were mismanaged in the most shameful manner. Realizing that her malady was incurable, one object seemed to animate the members of her household, and that was to lay hold of as much wealth as possible before the end came. Even her sickness was turned into a source of profit; and the major portion of the huge sums sanctioned for doctors' fees, and for daily distribution in alms to the poor, found its way into their hands. Information of these doings reached my Mother; indeed, they were a matter of common talk; and, though keenly grieved by the treachery and ingratitude of those for whom she had done so much, she could not bring herself to charge them openly with their malpractices, which continued unchecked till her death.

Among those who were in constant attendance at the palace was Ali Hasan Khân, the son of Sidik Hasan Khân. His daughter had recently been betrothed, and Her Highness had promised to bestow upon her a rich dowry. No one with any real affection for Her Highness could have considered the time suitable for marriage festivities. Nevertheless, Ali Hasan Khân begged her to permit his daughter's nuptials to be celebrated during her lifetime. The permission was given, and orders were issued for the payment of the dowry, though Her Highness saw plainly the motive for Ali Hasan Khân's indecent haste, and bitterly complained of his behaviour. "My daughter," she said, "whose two sons have just been married, will consent to no rejoicings whilst I am on a bed of sickness. But from these people, whom I have treated as my children

I receive neither consideration nor respect." Ali Hasan Khán's house was close to the Táj Mahal, and the sounds of revelry and merriment, which accompanied the celebration of the marriage, were plainly heard in the chamber where the ruler of the State lay awaiting the approach of death. It was a heartless and unseemly proceeding; but those who took part in it were strangers, noble neither by birth nor by nature: and it must have been a melancholy thought for my Mother that it was by such as these that she had allowed her own flesh and blood to be supplanted.

Soon after Her Highness had refused to submit to an operation, Mián Alamgír Muhammad Khán came to the palace to make inquiries. He was admitted to the sick-room, but instead of approaching the couch on which the patient lay, he seated himself as far away from it as possible. This behaviour, so different from that which Her Highness was accustomed to from him, wounded her deeply, and she said: "Alamgír, I know why you do not come near me. Now that I am sick, I am no longer worth consideration. I have put you in the place of my own child, I have lavished lákhs of rupees upon you, and this is my recompense." She said no more, but the bitterness of her feelings was plainly manifested in her face. Alamgír Muhammad Khán tried to make excuses. "It is not for that reason," he said, "that I do not approach you. It is because I cannot bear to see you so ill. Why do you remain obstinate? Why will you not undergo the treatment which is so necessary?" "The presence of Sultán Jahán alone can do me good," was Her Highness's reply. The words escaped her involuntarily, and she immediately added, "But because of Sultán Dula, I will never see her."

That my Mother's thoughts were constantly turning towards me there can be no doubt. Many of those in the palace expected that I should be sent for; and, believing that my restoration to favour was not far distant, their manner towards me underwent an entire change. Indifference gave way to obsequious respect: those who had ignored my existence before came to me hourly with reports of my Mother's condition, and of all that took place in the Táj Mahal. Whether the news they brought me was true or false, I had no means of telling, and my anxiety and agitation were increased rather than diminished by their behaviour.

Five months before her death, my Mother announced her intention of performing the *haj*. "My end is near," she said, "and in the Holy City I shall find comfort and peace. The administration of the State I will leave in the charge of Sultán Jahán." But this pious resolution was never accomplished, though full preparations for the journey were made. As soon as it became known that I was to be appointed regent, Alamgír Muhammad Khán, Ali Hasan Khán, Hámid Husein, Keeper of Her Highness's household, and others of their kindred, at once set to work to prevent the pilgrimage from taking place, for my assumption of authority would have meant to these men not only loss, but exposure, neither of which they were at all prepared to face. For some little time it appeared that their efforts would be unsuccessful. They of course pointed out the impropriety of handing over the reins of government to one as undutiful as I had shown myself to be; but Her Highness's only reply was, "For the advancement of your children, about which you have always been so solicitous, I have done more than enough, and you will therefore forgive me if I now refuse to do injustice to my own." At last, they determined to work upon her fears. She had an instinctive dread of the sea, and the prospect of an ocean voyage was for her full of terrors. It so happened that a shipwreck, involving the loss of many lives, had recently taken place. On a suitable occasion, therefore, the subject was mentioned in her presence, and this led naturally to a detailed account of the whole tragedy, the horrors of which made such an impression on her mind that she there and then abandoned her project. And thus, by those who owed everything to her favour and generosity, the highest purpose of her life was defeated.

Days passed, and my Mother's condition grew steadily worse. A few days before her death, she caused the following pathetic notice to be published:

"If there are any among my subjects who, during the

thirty-three years of my reign, have received unmerited punishment at my hands, I ask them, in the name of God, to forgive me."

The people of Bhopál received this last message from their dying ruler with sorrow and sympathy, and there was not one amongst them who did not pray to God that the burden of her afflictions might be lightened. My own emotion as I read the words I will not attempt to describe. I longed for only one sentence more, "I too forgive the faults of others," and I read and re-read the message in the vain hope that I had overlooked it. With such words to support me I could have gone to my Mother, and, having won the forgiveness which she could no longer have withheld, I could have cheered the last moments of her life with the pent-up love of twenty-seven long years. I prayed for her recovery night and day, and the thought of her sufferings filled my mind.

The last stage of the disease was very rapid, if we can call that disease which is almost a living death. Disease has many forms, some of which inspire terror in a greater degree, others in a less. But, when all has been said, it is Death, and not disease, who baffles human skill. Death's approach may be announced by disease, or he may greet us suddenly—in our sleep, our work, or our play. Whatever the manner of his coming, his hour is fixed, and he neither hastens nor delays. With each one of us Death has an appointment, and whether we go down into the deepest dungeons, or barricade ourselves in fortresses of iron, whether we climb to the tops of the mountains, or fly to the heart of the desert, not by the smallest fraction of time can we postpone the interview.

Ainama takunu yúdrik kumulmauto walla'ho kúntúm fi burújim mushayyadah.[1]

Her Highness passed away at fifteen minutes past 12 o'clock on the 28th day of Safar, in the year 1319 A.H. (June 16th, 1901). In the presence of Captain Lang, the Political Agent, and Maulavi Abdul Jabbar Khán Sáhib, the First Minister of

1 "Wheresoever ye be, death will overtake you, although ye be in lofty towers" (Sale's translation of the Korán).

ENTRANCE TO THE TAJ MAHAL.

p. 194]

the State, my Mother's private apartments were locked and sealed, and guards were placed at the doors. The melancholy news was conveyed to me by the Minister. From early morning I had been unusually depressed, and the news came to me as the fulfilment of the gloomy forebodings which had taken possession of my mind. Weeping bitterly, I set out for the Táj Mahal. As I drove along, I seemed to be in a trance. I saw the days of my childhood as in a beautiful picture. My Mother was smiling down upon me, and there was no cloud in the sky. Then the picture faded, and another took its place; but it was dark, and there was no sky: and I seemed to see all the trials and sorrows of the succeeding years of my life moving to and fro in it like gloomy spectres. Then it, too, faded, like the circles on a pool of water; and, almost before it had gone, I seemed to be gazing on the World itself; and whilst I looked, a mighty whirlwind, with a sound like the roaring of oceans, swept over it, and the earth and sky were shattered, and out of the darkness which followed came a voice:

Kullo sha'ín halikúm illa wajha lahul' hukmo wa' allaihe turja'ún.[1]

In the silent palace, everything seemed to be proclaiming the instability of the world, and the vanity of human ambition. At sunrise, this palace was the abode of a powerful Chief, whose sway extended over eight thousand square miles of territory. Thousands were ready to obey her slightest command. Her smallest word could make a beggar rich. The reins of justice and mercy were in her hands, and upon her will depended the welfare of near a million human souls. A few short hours, and the sun has crossed the meridian. The palace stands unchanged, and the Ruler—is less than the dust of the ground.

Inna fi zálika la'ibratal le'úlil absar.[2]

I entered the room where my Mother, having laid aside all earthly power, was peacefully sleeping. I stooped and kissed

[1] "Everything shall perish, except Himself: unto Him belongeth judgment: and before Him shall ye be assembled at the last day" (Sale's translation of the Korán).

[2] "Verily, herein is an instruction to men of understanding" (Sale's translation of the Korán).

the feet from whose path I had so long been banished, and beneath which the rivers of Paradise were then flowing, and I gazed long and sorrowfully on the face I had so often yearned, with tears, to see, and which I should not look upon again till the Day of Judgment. With an effort, I controlled my emotions, and set myself to perform the last services my Mother would ever require from me. I told those who were weeping to dry their tears, and bade them read the *Súrat-i-bakra*[1] and the holy *Kalima*,[2] while, with my own hands, I prepared the body for burial. In accordance with the requirements of the Musalman faith, the *Súrat-i-bakra* was read through seven times, and the *Kalima* was repeated one hundred and twenty-five thousand times.

At five minutes past four, the body was carried from the Táj Mahal to the Nishát Afzah garden. The funeral took place with full Islamic rites. It was an impressive ceremony, void of all outward display, and dignified by reason of its simplicity. It was attended by Nawáb Ihtishám-ul-mulk with my two elder sons, the Agent to the Governor-General, the Political Agent, and the chief officers and Sirdars of the State. A funeral prayer was said in the Id-gah, and the burial took place at sunset. All the offices and bazaars were closed, and, for forty days, grain and money were distributed in alms amongst the poor. Telegrams of condolence were received from His Majesty the King, and from the Viceroy, and in a *Gazette Extraordinary*, published by the Government of India, the following obituary notice appeared:

"His Excellency the Viceroy and Governor-General in Council has received with profound regret intelligence of the death, on the 16th of June, of Her Highness the Nawáb Shah Jahán Begam of Bhopál, Knight Grand Commander of the Most Exalted Order of the Star of India, and Member of the Imperial Order of the Crown of India. During the thirty-three years for which Her Highness ruled her State, she followed worthily in the footsteps of her predecessor, Her Highness the

[1] The *Súrat-i-bakra* is the second *súrat*, or chapter, of the Holy Korán.

[2] The *Kalima* is the Muhammadan confession of faith, "Lá illah, illilah, Muhammad ar rasúl allah."

Sikandar Begam of Bhopál. She administered her country with marked ability and success. She was distinguished for her liberality and benevolence, and she maintained undimmed the loyal traditions of her house, which has always been conspicuous for its zeal and fidelity to the interests of the paramount Power. By Her Highness's death her people have lost a just and considerate Ruler, and the British Crown one of its most faithful feudatories."

Her Highness Nawáb Shah Jahán Begam Sáhiba, G.C.S.I., was born at Islámnagar on the 6th of the month Jamádi-ul-awwal, 1254 A.H. (June 20th, 1838), and on the 15th of Muharram, 1263 A.H., at the age of 9 years, was installed as ruler of the Bhopál State. On the 11th of Zil Kádah, 1271 A.H., she was married to Bakshi Báki Muhammad Khán, Nasrat Jang, Commander-in-Chief of the Bhopál Army. On the 9th of Shawwal, 1276 A.H., she voluntarily resigned the title and powers of ruler to Nawáb Sikandar Begam, herself becoming the heir-apparent; and, on the former's death in 1285 A.H., she again took her seat on the *masnad* of the State. In 1872, Her Majesty the Queen conferred upon her the title, Grand Commander of the Star of India, and in the year 1878, the medal and Order of the Crown of India. In 1892, she received the Order of the Medjidie, of the first class, from His Majesty the Sultan of Turkey. Her first husband having died, she married, in 1288 A.H., Nawáb Sidik Hasan Khán, and again became a widow in 1307 A.H.

Nawáb Shah Jahán Begam was both a scholar and an author, with a wide knowledge of Oriental literature. Her best-known works are *Tájul Ikbál*, or *History of Bhopál*, *Diwáni Shírín*, *Kházinátul Loghat*, *Tahzibun Niswán*, and *Loghat Shahjaháni*. Her court was frequented by men of learning from all parts of India, and she founded many schools for the study of Arabic and Persian. To popularize these schools, many scholarships were given; but, in the majority of cases, the recipients looked upon the money they received as a means of living in idleness rather than of acquiring knowledge, and the schools, in consequence, never achieved the object for which they were opened. Education on modern lines was in an equally backward state, and the only High School that existed was ill-managed and ill-attended. Prejudice against new learning and new methods dies hard: and we have to thank those who kept it alive that, to this day, it is not possible to find, amongst the people of Bhopál, men qualified to hold positions of responsibility in the service of the State. Nawáb Shah Jahán Begam is not to be included among such people. She was an enlightened ruler, and fully alive to the necessity of progressing with the times. But she was served by men of the old school, who looked askance at progress, and were inclined to eye with suspicion any form of education which went beyond teaching lads to learn by rote the oldest and mouldiest books which their ignorant and narrow-minded instructors could supply.

But if the needs of education were neglected, it may safely be said that, in all other respects, the reign of Nawáb Shah Jahán was a period of continued progress—a progress testifying to the hand of an enlightened and far-seeing ruler. But my Mother was not only enlightened in a manner rarely to be met with amongst Musalman ladies in India; she was, at the same time, generous, charitable, gentle in disposition, refined in manner, and faithful to her word. No one, from the Viceroys of India down to the lowest of her subjects, has ever denied her the possession of these qualities. During the famine of 1899, hundreds of human beings owed their lives to her liberality; and even strangers, who sought refuge in the State during that terrible time, were fed and cared for. She established a special fund for the relief of the poor, from which hundreds of people, daily, received money sufficient for their subsistence. In her passion for building, she rivalled her namesake the Emperor of Delhi. The Táj Mahal and the Ali Manzil and Benazír palaces bear eloquent testimony to the elegance of her taste. The Táj-ul-masájid, though still incomplete, is a remarkable memorial of her piety. Over sixteen lákhs of rupees have already been spent on its construction. The crystal slabs, designed for the floor, were prepared in England at a cost of seven lákhs of rupees; but as their polished surfaces would have reflected the

NAWAB SHAH JAHAN BEGAM.

p. 198]

forms of the worshippers, their use in the mosque was forbidden. When finished, the Táj-ul-masájid will rank amongst the finest buildings in the world. But besides mosques and palaces, Her Highness constructed many public works of permanent benefit to the State. Among these are the Lady Lansdowne Hospital, the Prince of Wales's Hospital, the Shah Jahán Bridge, the Kaisar Embankment, and the Post Office. The most distant parts of the State were connected with the city of Bhopál by metalled roads, while the sinking of wells, and the making of tanks for the storage of water, conferred a lasting boon on the rural population.

True to the instincts of her race, Nawáb Shah Jahán Begam displayed the greatest interest in military matters, and did much to increase the strength and efficiency of the forces of the State. Besides the establishment of the Imperial Service Lancers, referred to in a previous chapter, she reorganized the State artillery and the Body-Guard, built lines for the State cavalry and infantry in Jahángírábád, and raised the pay of both officers and men. In other directions, also, her reforms were numerous. The judicial department was reorganized, and the legal codes revised and amplified. The postal system was reformed and new stamps issued, a printing-press was set up, a steam factory built, and, last but not least, the State was connected with the outside world by a railway of its own, and telegraphic communication.

During Her Highness's reign, three Viceroys visited the State, and on each occasion the loyalty of the ruler and her people was abundantly manifested. The Government of India frequently acknowledged Her Highness's excellent qualities and high administrative ability: and if further proof of her faithfulness to the British Throne is needed it can be found in the letters which, from time to time, she received from Her Majesty Queen Victoria, which show the high place she occupied in Her Majesty's affection and esteem. In his *Life of Lord Mayo*, Sir William Hunter, after referring to the services of Nawáb Sikandar Begam during the Mutiny, tells how this famous Begam died, and "left her territory to a daughter worthy of her blood."

"This Princess," he continues, "at the time of her accession in 1868 was a widow of 31 years of age. She inherited her mother's firmness and good sense, with a rare aptitude for the duties of administration. During Lord Mayo's Viceroyalty, she devoted herself to the measures of progress which the Viceroy pressed on every Feudatory Chief who came under his influence. She opened out roads, organized a system of public instruction, executed a survey of her State, reformed the police, suppressed the abominable but deep-rooted trade of kidnapping minors for immoral purposes, and improved the jails. Lord Mayo received her in his capital with marks of distinction, and on the occasion of the visit of the Duke of Edinburgh presented her with honour to His Royal Highness. The Princess carried back to her State the liveliest recollections of his hospitality and kindness,[1] and the next few years of her rule became conspicuous for good government and prudent administrative reforms.

"Her Highness was created a Grand Commander of the Star of India, as the Ruler of a model State."[2]

When we consider my Mother's eminent virtues, and the wisdom and ability she displayed as a ruler, we feel all the more at a loss to comprehend those unfortunate episodes which marred her otherwise meritorious reign. The treatment to which I and my family were subjected, the evil acts of Sidik Hasan Khán, and the corrupt administration of Munshi Imtiyáz Ali Khán, sort so ill with her character and capacity that it is difficult to believe that they form part of the history of her life. I think, however, that enough has been said in the previous pages to show that it would be altogether unjust to estimate my Mother's character in the light of these events. From a nature such as hers, endowed as it was with all the nobler qualities of womanhood, it was impossible that injustice and oppression could proceed.

Perhaps the worst fault that can be laid to her charge is that, like the large majority of her sex, she was wilful and obstinate. It was rarely that she could be induced to change her opinion, or to deviate from a course of action she had once

[1] See Appendix E.

[2] *The Earl of Mayo*, p. 112 (*Rulers of India* series).

THE EARL OF MAYO.

p. 200]

determined to follow. This trait is especially noticeable in her relations with Sidik Hasan Khán, and it doubtless contributed, in no small degree, to the prolongation of her displeasure against me. For years after her marriage, her belief in the Nawáb Sáhib was complete and unshakable, and it necessarily followed that she believed every charge brought by him against my husband and myself. That these charges were untrue she had no means of knowing, for no friend of mine was ever allowed access to her, and certain punishment awaited any attempt to speak in our favour. The treatment I met with never lessened my affection for her, for I knew that her anger was directed, not against me, but against the false image of me that was unceasingly presented before her. I knew, too, that her love for me, though it was withheld, was not destroyed ; and I rejoiced, and I still rejoice, to think that, however dark my earthly abode, the light of that love will shine upon me with tenfold brightness in the gardens of Paradise, where there will be none to intercept its rays.

The acts of oppression, and the mischievous writings of Sidik Hasan Khán, were equally outside my Mother's control. So skilfully were his methods concealed, and his political opinions masked, that for years she was in ignorance of both. That he was engaged in propagating disaffection towards British rule she had no knowledge whatever until the matter was brought to her notice by the Government of India. Her anger that anything in the nature of disloyalty should have had its origin in the State of Bhopál was almost beyond expression, and she did her very utmost to turn her husband from his evil courses. But Sidik Hasan Khán was impervious alike to threats and entreaties. Whenever my Mother's opposition seriously alarmed him, he used the counter-threat of divorce, and against a Muhammadan lady of high rank he could wield no weapon more powerful. The Government of India clearly saw how she was situated, and never, for a single moment, associated her with the evil doings for which her husband was punished ; nor did she forfeit, in the smallest degree, the respect in which she had previously been held. After the degradation of the Nawáb Sáhib, she received expressions of the sincerest sympathy, not only from Colonel Kincaid and Sir Lepel Griffin, but from the Foreign Secretary, the Viceroy, and the Secretary of State for India.

For the corrupt administration of Munshi Imtiyáz Ali Khán, Sidik Hasan Khán alone is to be held responsible. Until the latter's death, it was practically impossible for any report of the Minister's doings to reach Her Highness's ears. With the support of his patron, he grew rich and powerful enough to silence the tongue of every one who was opposed to him, and it was not until he attempted to stand alone that my Mother had any conception of the havoc he was creating.

Imperfection is inseparable from human nature, and the history of a faultless ruler never has been and never will be written. When we contemplate the lives of good men and women, it is not on their mistakes that we fix our attention, though it is often through their mistakes that their goodness is rendered more plain to us. For sixty-seven years my Mother lived a life worthy of all honour and respect. She will be remembered not only as an able and successful ruler, but as an accomplished, loyal, and virtuous lady. When we realize the difficulties of the position she was called upon to fill, remembering at the same time the limitations by which in Eastern society ladies of noble birth are surrounded, we cannot but be amazed that her success was so great and her mistakes so few.

But one occurrence belonging to the period of my Mother's reign remains to be told. When Nawáb Shah Jahán Begam died, the world was still mourning the loss of the greatest and noblest Queen that ever occupied a throne. A brief reference to this sad event seems to me the fittest manner of bringing this, the first part of my task, to a close.

On the 29th day of Ramazán, 1318 A.H. (January 21st, 1901), a telegram was received from His Excellency the Viceroy, containing the following mournful intelligence:

"Her Majesty is sinking fast. All the members of the Royal Family have been summoned to her bedside."

Her Highness received the news with the deepest sorrow,

and the Kotwál was ordered to stop all music and beating of drums in the city. The next day was the festival of the *Id-ul-fit'r*, a time for general rejoicing among Muhammadans; but, on this occasion, gloom and sadness prevailed everywhere. After the *Id* prayers had been said, all the Muhammadans assembled in the *Id-gah*, and in the mosques of the city prayed humbly and fervently that their beloved Sovereign might be restored to health. At 10 o'clock in the morning, a second telegram was received, stating that a slight improvement had taken place in Her Majesty's condition. Her Majesty had slept, and had taken nourishment. Hope was rekindled by this news; but scarcely had there been time to make it public when a third telegram arrived, containing these words:

"Her Majesty the Queen is dead."

By the directions of Her Highness, the Minister at once dispatched the following message to the Private Secretary to the Viceroy:

"Her Highness is greatly shocked at the terrible calamity which has befallen the Empire. Her Highness feels that she has lost a Mother, and is in great grief."

A second message was sent on behalf of the State, and the Political Agent was requested to telegraph Her Highness's sympathy to the Viceroy. A proclamation was made that all the bazars in the city should remain closed for a period of three days, and all public offices in the city and districts for seven days. The flag on the Fatehgarh fort was lowered to half-mast, and the Commandant received orders to fire, on the day of the funeral, eighty-one minute guns, the number corresponding with the years of her late Majesty's life.

The official announcement of the death of the Queen, and of the accession of King Edward, was received from the Political Agent, who also sent instructions that, immediately after the funeral salute, a royal salute of a hundred and one guns was to be fired in honour of the latter event, and the flag was again to be hoisted. On February 2nd, the day of the funeral, these instructions were carried out. Telegrams of condolence were sent to the members of the Royal Family, and another to the Government of India, containing Her Highness's congratulations on the accession of King Edward VII.

There are some things which it is better that the pen should not attempt to describe. The great Queen was dead, and the grief that shook India, as the distressing news flew from district to district and from village to village, is not for words. Nor is it for my humble pen to recount the virtues of her whom, not the Empire, but the world, has acknowledged a peerless woman and a peerless Queen. Great writers have told, and will tell again, the story of her life, and its example will be an heritage to mankind for all time.

PART II

CHAPTER I

THE FIRST DAYS OF MY REIGN

ALTHOUGH I had been formally recognized as heir-apparent by my Mother, yet, as soon as it became known that her illness must terminate fatally, the Political Officers, being fully aware of the estrangement that had sprung up between us, and of the circumstances that had led to it, took immediate steps to secure my undisturbed accession to the *masnad*. On being informed that the end had come, Mr. Lang, the Political Agent, wrote at once to Maulavi Abdul Jabbar Khán, the Minister of the State, informing him that the Government of India had "recognized the right of Nawáb Sultán Jahán Begam to become the Ruler of Bhopál," and directed him to break the news of Her Highness's death to me, and afterwards to conduct me to the Táj Mahal, and bid me assume control of the affairs of the State. On receipt of these instructions, the Maulavi Sáhib hastened to my palace, and communicated his melancholy tidings first to me, and then to my husband, after which we all went together to the Táj Mahal. To the sad duties which there awaited me I will not again refer: these, as well as the events connected with my Mother's funeral, and all else that occurred on that unhappy day, have been fully described in the previous chapter.

At noon, on the 28th of Safar, 1319 A.H., my reign may be said to have commenced; but, for the remainder of that day, I gave little thought either to the powers or to the position to which I had succeeded. One by one, the past twenty-seven years, each with its burden of sorrows, took possession of my mind, and scenes and events long forgotten came back to me with such vividness that I seemed to be living through them again. All the bright hopes, which but a short time before had filled my heart, were lost behind clouds of despondency, and the palace itself, in spite of the crowds that thronged it, filled me with a sense of loneliness and desolation. Since the Táj Mahal had been built, I had never, save on one occasion, stayed long within its walls. That occasion was the *nashra* ceremony of my daughter Bilkis Jahán Begam, an event which is among my happiest memories. The palace was thronged with guests from far and near, and my Mother seemed to have no thought except for the comfort and enjoyment of those about her. Every one and everything was gay, and a tumult of merry noises filled the air. My husband and I presented *jora* to our daughter, and we, in turn, received robes of honour from Her Highness, which she placed upon us with her own hands, and with every sign of goodwill. How proud was little Bilkis as she displayed her trinkets and finery, first to her grandmother, then to me! How full of hope and promise did the future seem, as we watched her childish face dimpled all over with smiles! Attendants and servants shared in the general joy, for all had been rendered happy with presents and favours. Indeed, only those who have witnessed such celebrations in the houses of Indian nobles can picture to themselves the scene of unmixed happiness which the Táj Mahal presented at that time. But on this 28th day of Safar, the scene is changed—changed as only time can change things. Gone are laughter and mirth, and in their places, tears and cries of lamentation. My Mother, my little Bilkis, they too are gone, vanished with all the merry pageant "into yesterday's seven thousand years."

In some respects, the Táj Mahal resembles the palaces of Delhi, being built in the form of a square with a large open courtyard in the centre. The interior, however, is not attractive. The rooms, of which there are a vast number, are small, dark, and ill-ventilated. My Mother had lived from childhood in old-fashioned houses, and had grown so accustomed to an atmosphere of confinement, that she would probably have been ill at ease in a building of any other

COURTYARD OF THE TAJ MAHAL.

[p. 206]

description. The Táj Mahal was, accordingly, designed on old-time lines, without any regard to modern requirements. At the time of which I am writing, the rains had just set in, and the palace, dark even on the brightest days, appeared to me the gloomiest abode I had ever entered. To grow accustomed to a new home is never an easy process ; and for me the Táj Mahal, setting aside its uncongenial surroundings, could have but few attractions. I longed for more light and fresh air ; but I longed still more to escape the sad thoughts which crowded in upon me, for it seemed to me that all the troubles of my previous life had emanated from its dismal apartments and gloomy corridors.

The first night I slept little. One after another, the scenes and events in my Mother's life passed before me like the pictures of a cinematograph. I saw again the kind, indulgent mother of my childhood, I heard the warnings and reproaches which saddened the early years of my married life, and I felt once more the pangs of separation, and all the heartache and sorrow of the succeeding twenty-seven years. In the morning, I rose early, and prayed to God—first that my sins might be forgiven me, then that my Mother might be received into Paradise, and, lastly, that strength might be given me to bear the great responsibilities which He had seen fit to lay upon me. Thus, in some measure comforted, I went forth and gave the orders for the day.

In the course of the morning, the Minister of the State came to the Táj Mahal to offer his condolences. Soon after his departure the lady doctor came. She had been in Bhopál for more than a year, but this was the first time that she had ever visited me. At three o'clock in the afternoon, I received Colonel Malcolm Meade, the Agent to the Governor-General, and Mr. Lang, the Political Agent. As had been the custom during my Mother's reign, they were met at the entrance to the palace by Mián Alamgír Muhammad Khán, Mián Núr-ul-hasan Khán, and Mián Ali Hasan Khán. Within, they were received by Nawáb Sultán Dula and the Minister of the State, and were conducted to the visiting-room where I was seated. After the usual greetings, Colonel Meade told me how shocked he had been to hear of Her Highness's death. He talked long of her life and reign, and gave me much comfort. He then informed me that the Government of India recognized me as the ruler of Bhopâl, and proposed that my installation should take place in three days' time. On account, however, of the general mourning throughout the State, I requested that a later date might be selected. Colonel Meade at once expressed his approval, and it was decided that the ceremony should take place on the 27th of Rabi-ul-awwal.

It is customary in India, on the death of any distinguished person, for the relatives, dependents, and servants of the deceased to send their women to mourn with the bereaved family. Owing to my long separation from my Mother, I was practically a stranger to the large numbers who, in accordance with this custom, now came to visit me. Nevertheless, I did my best to talk with them, and to treat them in as friendly a manner as possible, while, every day, arrangements were made by the State for their entertainment. When a death occurs in a Muhammadan family, three days are usually allowed to elapse before any meals are prepared in the house of mourning. During this time, it is customary for relatives and near friends of the deceased to send or bring dishes of elaborately prepared food for the mourners. Food thus presented is a mark of the sender's sympathy; but the custom is not enjoined by Muhammadan law, and often leads to extravagant excesses. For it is not only the mourners who have to be taken into consideration—every person who can claim even the most distant connection with the family of the departed comes to offer his condolences, and, as custom demands that all should partake of the food thus provided, the expense incurred by the senders is often extremely heavy.

A large number of people were anxious to show their sympathy with me in the manner I have just described. But, wherever it was possible to do so, I firmly but courteously declined to accept presents of food from them; for it has always been my desire to discourage the expenditure of large sums of money on ceremonial observances which are not actually necessary, and particularly in the case of weddings and funerals; and I have myself always endeavoured to set an example in this respect. In doing so, I have followed in the steps of my Mother and Nawáb Sikandar Begam. The latter observed the strictest economy in such matters; indeed, she used simplicity in all things, and especially in the management of her household. Before her death, she gave orders that her funeral was to be devoid of all outward display, and that no ceremonial was to be observed which the laws of Islám did not sanction. My Mother, although she displayed great liberality both in the performance of essential ceremonies, and in the celebration of the great Muhammadan festivals, discountenanced heavy expenditure in connection with any custom that could be set aside without a breach of orthodoxy. I am thankful to be able to say that the example of their rulers has had, and continues to have, a wholesome effect on the people of Bhopál, who are much less addicted to extravagances of this nature than is the case in most parts of India.

On the 29th and following days, enormous numbers of State papers were brought to me for signature. These were all papers on which my Mother had passed orders, but which she had been too ill to sign. In addition, long arrears of accounts had to be checked, and bills of expenditure and revenue returns, which had been accumulating during Her Highness's illness, had each to be examined and signed. I also devoted considerable time to the current affairs of the State, and, daily, in consultation with the Minister, issued such orders as were necessary. As I did this work, I refrained from either comment or criticism. I knew, of course, that many corrupt practices had crept into the administration, while the names of those officials who had abused my Mother's confidence and traded upon her generosity were well known to me. But I determined to introduce no radical reforms, to dismiss no one from his office, nor make any new appointments, until I had had time to feel my way, and make myself acquainted with the manner in which the various branches of the administration were being conducted.

CHAPTER II

MY INSTALLATION

As has already been stated, the date fixed for my installation was the 17th of Rabi-ul-awwal, 1319 A.H. (July 4th, 1901). The Chiefs of the Bhopál Agency, and many European guests, were invited to be present. Mr. Lang, from whom I always experienced the greatest kindness, arrived some days beforehand to assist me in my preparations. On the morning of the 16th, he personally superintended a rehearsal of the whole ceremony. The Agent to the Governor-General arrived at 3 p.m. the same afternoon, and was accorded a public reception. The State troops with the *máhi marátib*, and the Imperial Service cavalry, occupied the yard of the station, and the principal Sirdars of the State were also present. The entire platform was covered with scarlet cloth, and the station buildings were gaily decorated. On the arrival of the train, I came out from my waiting-room, and met Colonel and Mrs. Meade as they alighted from their saloon. I wore a *burkha*, and was accompanied by my three sons. Most cordial greetings were exchanged; and, as we drove from the railway station, Mrs. Meade seated in my carriage, and Colonel Meade in that of the Nawáb Sáhib, a salute of seventeen guns was fired from the Fatehgarh fort. According to the usual custom, I accompanied my guests as far as the Pukhta Pul, whence they proceeded to the new Kothi, whilst I, with the Nawáb Sáhib and my sons, returned to the palace.

By the morning of the 17th, all the guests, European and Indian, had arrived. The former were accommodated in a camp adjoining the Purána Kothi, and the latter in various houses in the city. The ceremony was to take the form of a durbar at the Sadar Manzil palace. The building, within and without, was profusely decorated. The entire courtyard was carpeted, as were also the verandahs and terraces, while the floor of the durbar hall was covered with rich velvet cloths heavily embroidered in gold and silver. A gilded dais occupied the centre of the hall, on which were placed two massive gilt chairs, upholstered in purple velvet. These were for the Agent to the Governor-General and myself. On the left of the dais were the seats of the Political Agent, the Nawáb Sáhib, and the chief officials of the State, the right being occupied by the staff of the Agent to the Governor-General and other English officers. In the verandah in front of the durbar hall, which is in reality an extension of the hall itself, the *jágírdárs* and minor officials of the State were seated.

The whole length of the route from the Pukhta Pul to the Sadar Manzil was lined with troops, punctuated, as it were, at every bend of the road by elephants or camels, majestic in housings of scarlet and silver. The people of the city, as is their habit on such occasions, abandoned themselves to enjoyment, and multicoloured crowds filled the streets and housetops. At ten o'clock, the Superintendent of the Daftar Huzúr and the Naib Bakshi of the State army proceeded to the new Kothi to conduct the Agent to the Governor-General to the durbar. The Nawáb Sáhib, the Minister of the State, and the Mír Bakshi met the procession as it reached the Pukhta Pul, and the Nawáb Sáhib entered the carriage in which Colonel Meade was seated. The procession was led by the Body-guard and a squadron of the Imperial Service Lancers. Behind these came a band of pipers, followed by an elephant bearing the coronation *khilát*. The Mír Munshi of the Agency, who had charge of the *khilát*, rode on the same elephant. A number of horses richly caparisoned in harness of silver and gold came next, and after these the carriage containing the Agent to the Governor-General and the Nawáb Sáhib, on either side of which, with drawn swords in their hands, rode the Mír Bakshi and the chief of the State police. Other carriages containing the Political Agent and the principal European and Indian guests completed the procession. On reaching the entrance to the Sadar Manzil, Colonel Meade was received by Sáhibzáda Obaidullah Khán and Sáhibzáda Hamidullah Khán. The troops occupying the palace square presented arms as he descended from his carriage, and the band played the National Anthem. On mounting the steps which lead to the inner court, he was met by Nawáb Nasrullah Khán, by whom he was conducted to the durbar hall. I myself awaited him in an inner apartment, and as soon as he reached the entrance to the hall, I advanced to meet him, and led him to his seat on the dais. The whole assembly remained standing until we had taken our places, when a salute of guns from the Fatehgarh fort announced that the durbar had commenced.

As soon as all the guests were seated, Mr. Wyndham, First Assistant to the Agent to the Governor-General, read the following *kharíta* from His Excellency the Viceroy:

"To Her Highness Nawáb Sultán Jahán Begam of Bhopál.

"My Esteemed Friend,

"As my Agent, Colonel Meade, has already informed you, I received with profound regret the news of the death of your distinguished mother, Her Highness the Nawáb Shah Jahán Begam, G.C.S.I., C.I. In her the British Government has lost a most loyal feudatory and a faithful friend, and I take this opportunity to express again to Your Highness my sorrow at the sad event which has occurred, and my condolence with yourself and your family. I have caused to be forwarded to Your Highness, through my Agent in Central India, a copy of the notification which was published by the Government of India on the receipt of the melancholy intelligence; and I have since transmitted to Your Highness a telegram conveying to yourself and your family an expression of the regret and sympathy of His Majesty the King, Emperor of India.

"I have now to offer you my congratulations on your accession to the *masnad* of Bhopál. I have learnt with much satisfaction that Your Highness has announced your intention of following in the footsteps of your distinguished predecessors, whose traditional loyalty to the British Crown is so well known throughout India. Rest assured that in His Majesty's Viceroy you will always have a firm friend, and that, so long as the Bhopál State maintains under your rule its ancient reputation, the favour hitherto shown to your illustrious family by the British Government will be extended without diminution to yourself.

"I remain, with much consideration,
"Your Highness's Sincere Friend,
(*Signed*) "CURZON,
"*Viceroy and Governor-General of India.*

"SIMLA, *June 28th*, 1901."

The ***kharíta*** having been read, Colonel Meade rose and made the following speech, an Urdu translation of which was afterwards read by the Mír Munshi :

"Your Highness,—His Excellency the Viceroy, representing His Most Gracious Majesty the King-Emperor, has this day been graciously pleased to publicly acknowledge Your Highness's succession to your lamented mother, the late Nawáb Shah Jahán Begam Sáhiba, G.C.S.I., C.I., of Bhopál. I know that His Excellency Lord Curzon would have liked to invest Your Highness himself, but, unfortunately, this was not possible. It is also a matter of regret that neither Colonel Barr, who was for so many years Agent to the Governor-General in Central India, nor Mr. Bayley, has been able to be present ; but while regretting the absence of these high officials, I am bound to tell Your Highness that I feel it a great honour and satisfaction that it has fallen to me to represent the Government of India on this auspicious occasion. It is doubly pleasant to me to be here to-day : first, because Your Highness's mother, Her Highness the Nawáb Shah Jahán Begam, was similarly installed as Ruler of Bhopál by my father nearly thirty-three years ago ; and, secondly, because I was for so many years Political Agent in Bhopál, and am personally acquainted with Your Highness and Your Highness's family. Your Highness is now installed upon the *masnad* of your ancestors ; and though you will not, I hope, have to act the part which fell to the lot of some of them to repel the invader at the gates of Bhopál, like Wazír Muhammad, or to go down yourself among your troops as your grandmother, the illustrious Sikandar Begam, did in 1857, there will be for you in the administration of your country an ample field for those talents which, I believe, you have inherited from the rulers who have preceded you. Your State has suffered terribly of late years from famine and pestilence, and I believe that the present census will show that nearly twenty-nine *per cent.* of its inhabitants have gone, and nearly a third of its land lies fallow. This, if correct, must entail, among other difficulties, a considerable loss of revenue, and it will be for Your Highness by wise measures to restore the population and revive the finances of your State. You have an experienced Minister in Khán Bahadur Maulavi Abdul Jabbar Khán, and my friend Mr. Lang, the Political Agent, will always give you his advice and assistance. But above all I am glad to think that in the Nawáb Consort, Ihtishám-ul-mulk Alijah, Ahmad Ali Khán, to whom I offer my congratulations, Your Highness has an adviser and helper, in close communion with yourself, whose tried experience will assist and guide you in governing your State. It is unnecessary to say much to a ruler of Bhopál about her relations with the Paramount Power. Since the days that we first came in contact with the Chiefs of Central India, the Nawábs and Begams of this State have always been famous for the loyal fidelity with which they have adhered to their engagements with the British Government, and I am absolutely confident Your Highness will maintain and hand on untarnished the high traditions of good faith and loyalty which you have yourself inherited. I will only add that I congratulate you most heartily on behalf of the English ladies and gentlemen present, as well as on behalf of myself, on your having ascended the *masnad* of Bhopál, and we wish you a happy and prosperous future as Ruler of your State. May Your Highness's age be prolonged like that of your great-grandmother the Kudsia Begam, and may you be illustrious and honoured as your grandmother and mother, the Sikandar and Shah Jahán Begams."

My reply to this speech was as follows:

"Colonel Meade, Ladies and Gentlemen,—I cannot commence my speech without making reference to the deep sorrow which has fallen, not only upon me, but upon all the people of Bhopál, by the death of my august Mother. Her name will go down to posterity as that of a beneficent ruler and a faithful servant of the British Government. May God give patience to us in our affliction, and to her a place in Paradise.

"From the bottom of my heart I thank His Majesty the King-Emperor and his Viceroy in India, who, in recognition of my rights, have advanced me to the high position which I now hold as ruler of this State. No one in this durbar hall will deny that the blood which flows in my veins is the blood of those who earned honour and fame by serving the British Government with loyalty and self-sacrifice; and since this is so, it is impossible that I should have any dearer ambition than to follow in their footsteps. Colonel Meade, I thank you sincerely for your good advice, and I cannot but regard it as a happy omen that the powers of a ruler have been conferred upon me by the son of Sir Richard Meade, who himself conferred the same powers upon my Mother. I am very grateful to you for the manner in which you have referred to Nawáb Ihtishám-ul-mulk Alijah. For twenty-seven years I have experienced his constant sympathy. I am confident that in all State affairs I may count upon his assistance and advice, as also upon the loyal services of the Minister of the State.

"Owing to various causes, the financial condition of the State is far from satisfactory, and demands serious attention. Many cultivators have been reduced to insolvency, the population has decreased by nearly thirty *per cent.*, and large tracts of fertile land have fallen out of cultivation. I know that a long and difficult task lies before me; but God, who has thought fit to place so large a responsibility on my shoulders, will help me in my hour of need.

"Once more I thank the Viceroy of India for the honour he has conferred on me. And I thank you, Colonel Meade, and my friend Mr. Lang—to whom I shall always look for help and guidance—and Mrs. Meade, as well as all my other friends, for so kindly coming here to-day to take part in this ceremony, and I pray that the Almighty will keep me and my children steadfast in our loyalty to the British throne, and that He will aid me in gaining and keeping the affectionate regard of all classes of my subjects."

At the close of my speech, a salute of twenty-one guns was fired by the State artillery, after which the Mír Munshi stepped forward, and placed the trays containing the *khilát* before Colonel Meade, who at once rose, and taking up a necklace of pearls, placed it round my neck. The trays containing the remainder of the *khilát*[1] were then placed in front of me, and Colonel Meade, taking up another necklace, fastened it round

[1] The *khilát* which was presented to me on this occasion consisted of a pearl necklace, a *sarpech* or jewelled ornament worn on the front of the head-dress, a robe of honour, a gun, and a sword. The Nawáb Sáhib received a necklace, a *sarpech*, a robe of honour, and a sword.

the neck of the Nawáb Sáhib, to whom he also presented a handsome sword. The Nawáb Sáhib, in a brief speech, expressed his gratitude to the Government of India for the favours bestowed upon him, and to Colonel Meade and Mr. Lang for the many kindnesses he had received at their hands. He then presented to Colonel Meade, as representing the Government of India, a *nazar* of a hundred and one gold mohurs. *Nazarána* were also presented by my three sons, and by the Mír Bakshi. The durbar terminated with the customary distribution of *'itr* and *pán* and garlands. I myself presented these to Colonel Meade and Mr. Lang, the other European officers receiving them from the Minister, and the remaining guests from Munshi Ahmad Hasan Khán, Mír Munshi of the State. My sons escorted Colonel and Mrs. Meade to their carriage, and the assembly dispersed.

Colonel John Malcolm Meade, besides being Agent to the Governor-General for Central India, was an old and valued friend of my family. He could hardly have treated us with more kindness had we been his own relations. I believe his presence at my accession was as great a pleasure to himself as it was to me. As he had been Political Agent at Bhopál for more than five years, he was intimately acquainted with all the affairs of the State, as well as with the circumstances that had led to the breach between my Mother and myself. During Her Highness's reign, I attended scarcely any durbars, and I had had no experience in administration beyond what had been afforded me in the management of my own *jágír*. Previous to her accession, my Mother had had no actual share in the government of the State ; but though she had not done things herself, she had had the great advantage of seeing them done by others. She was constantly at the side of Nawáb Sikandar Begam, attended all durbars and interviews with political officers, and was kept informed of everything that took place in the State, so that, when she assumed ruling powers, she was no stranger to the duties that lay before her.

Knowledge is, no doubt, a most excellent thing, but without practical experience it can benefit us but little. This is especially true in the case of those who are destined to become

COLONEL MALCOLM J. MEADE.

p. 216]

rulers of States. The training of a young chief can never be adequate if it is confined to the study of books and to such experience as he can gain from intercourse with his teachers. As I have already said, my own experience of the work of a ruler was, at the time of which I am writing, practically *nil*. When, on the death of Nawáb Sikandar Begam, my Mother took in hand my education, it was her custom to send to me daily a certain number of official papers, which I was directed to read and sign. These were papers on which Nawáb Sidik Hasan Khán had already passed orders, and were connected with matters of no interest or importance. I read and signed them in obedience to my Mother's orders, but by doing so I gained neither experience nor information. After my marriage, no more papers were sent to me, and I was left to fit myself as best I could for the position which I knew that, if I lived long enough, I should one day have to occupy. I studied hard to increase my knowledge of men and things, and made the most of such opportunities of getting experience as chance threw in my way; so that, on the very day after my accession, although difficulties began to thicken around me, I did not lose heart, and I gradually found out that there are few obstacles which determination and perseverance cannot overcome.

Colonel Meade was greatly pleased with my speech at the durbar. No one understood my difficulties better than he; and it was a complete surprise to him that, in spite of my being obliged to speak in a *burkha*, and that, too, before a large and critical audience, I was yet able to go through the ordeal without betraying any signs of nervousness. When I had finished speaking, the words "*Shábásh! shábásh!*" escaped from his lips, and my readers can well understand how this expression of his approval pleased me.

In previous chapters, I have frequently referred to my husband as the Nawáb Ihtishám-ul-mulk Alijah, but, as a matter of fact, it was not until the day of my accession that this title was conferred on him, and it was used for the first time in Colonel Meade's speech. My husband and I received intimation of this honour only a few minutes before the durbar commenced. The title is one worthy of the consort of a ruler, and I was greatly pleased that His Excellency had chosen such a happy occasion for bestowing it. Eighty-four years had elapsed since the first Begam occupied the throne of Bhopál, but the title had never been conferred on any previous Nawáb Consort.

One other incident in connection with this durbar is worth recounting. As soon as the Agent to the Governor-General had departed, a very aged man, Munshi Kudrat Ullah by name, who had spent many years in the service of the State, and had witnessed durbars not only in my Mother's reign, but in that of Nawáb Sikandar Begam also, forced his way into my presence in spite of the opposition of the palace attendants, and addressed me thus: "Your faithful servant, Kudrat Ullah, who held you on his knee, and carried you in his arms, offers his humble congratulations, and prays God that you may live to celebrate your silver, golden, and diamond jubilees." I was greatly touched by the sincerity of the old man's good wishes. He had been Mír Munshi to Mr. (afterwards Sir Robert) Hamilton, a former Resident at Indore, by whom he was recommended, on account of his faithful services, to Captain Hutchinson, who was Political Agent in Bhopál in the year 1859. Captain Hutchinson, in turn, recommended him to my grandmother, Nawáb Sikandar Begam. At the time of my accession, he was still in the service of the State, but has since been pensioned.

After the durbar, a telegram was sent to Colonel Barr, the Resident at Hyderabad, informing him that my installation as ruler of Bhopál had taken place. Colonel Barr had long been intimately acquainted with me and my family, and I knew that the intelligence would give him pleasure. The occasion was also marked by the liberation of twenty prisoners from the State jail. In the afternoon, the Imperial Service Troops gave an assault-at-arms on the Jahángírábád parade ground, which was witnessed by all the guests. At night, a banquet took place at the new Kothi, at the conclusion of which it was arranged that all my guests should repair to the Sadar Manzil, and witness a display of fireworks. The new Kothi was tastefully decorated, and the gardens were illuminated with torches and Chinese lanterns. According to custom, I joined the party at dessert, the Nawáb Sáhib, my sons, and the Minister accompanying me. As soon as I had arrived, Colonel Meade proposed the health of His Majesty the King-Emperor, which was drunk with loyal enthusiasm. I then rose and said :

"Colonel Meade, Ladies and Gentlemen,—

"'To heaven let our grateful praise ascend,
When at our board we entertain a friend.'

"I am very pleased and proud to have the honour of entertaining Colonel and Mrs. Meade and so many other friends this evening. To be able to show hospitality to friends is indeed a privilege. To me it is more than a privilege—it is a sacred duty, enjoined both by my religion and by the traditions of my race. At this time, when I am mourning the loss of my revered Mother, the presence of friends is especially welcome to me, and I beg to offer you, ladies and gentlemen, my sincere thanks for your kindness in accepting my invitation. I am very grateful to the officers of the Government for the kindness which they have shown to me. The head that wears a crown can expect, as you know, to escape neither anxieties nor difficulties ; but the assurance that I can rely upon the support and assistance of the British Government fills me with strength and courage.

"Ladies and Gentlemen, it is not my intention to weary you with a long speech, for I should like you all, if it will not be putting you to too much inconvenience, to come and see the illuminations at my palace, and a display of fireworks. In conclusion, I have one toast to propose—the very good health of my friends, Colonel and Mrs. Meade."

The Minister of the State proposed the health of the Political Agent, who, in the course of his reply, proposed that of the Minister, after which an adjournment was made to the Sadar Manzil. This building, the Shaukat Mahal, and the Moti Mahal were all brilliantly illuminated with coloured lights, which, in spite of a high wind, remained burning till one o'clock in the morning. The display of fireworks took place in front of the Sadar Manzil. At its conclusion, *'itr* and *pán* were distributed, and it was past midnight before my guests had departed.

On the morning of the 18th, the Agent to the Governor-General inspected the new jail which had been built by my Mother; and on the following morning, he visited the lines and inspected the horses of the Imperial Service Lancers. Accompanied by Mrs. Meade, he then drove to the Nishát Afzah garden to see my Mother's grave. Here he again spoke of the many good acts of Her Highness's reign, and of the sorrow which he felt at her death. On the way back to the new Kothi, Mrs. Meade stopped at the Lady Lansdowne Hospital, where she inspected the various wards, and recorded her remarks in the visitors' book. Later in the day, I paid a farewell visit to the new Kothi. As this was a State visit, the usual salute was fired from the Fatehgarh fort. Before I left, two photographs were taken: one of Colonel Meade, Mr. Lang, and my three sons, and the other of Mrs. Meade and myself. At nine o'clock, Colonel and Mrs. Meade left by train for Indore. Their departure was private, and as it took place after sunset, the salute announcing it was fired on the following day. By the evening of the 20th, all my other guests had departed. The Rájah Sáhib of Rájgarh, on account of his ancient connection with the State, sent me a rich dress and two horses, which I accepted, and gave orders that a *khilát* and other presents should be given to the Rájah's messengers. Suitable answers were sent to all the congratulatory letters that I had received, and presents were distributed amongst those servants of the State to whom the general arrangements in connection with my accession ceremony had been entrusted.

It was not until the 9th of October that my eldest son, Nawáb Nasrullah Khán, was formally appointed heir-apparent in Bhopál. Grief on account of my Mother's death, combined with pressure of work, had prevented me from pushing the matter forward, and I felt, too, that there was no real necessity for haste. A few days before my accession, the draft of an agreement[1] was, according to the custom of the State, sent to

[1] This custom is one of long standing in the State. Nawáb Shah Jahán

my son, which was duly executed by him. The clauses, which were ten in number, were as follows:

"(1) I hereby promise and declare that I will always remain loyal to the State, and that I will be bound by all the conditions set forth in this agreement. Should I at any time act contrary to the conditions herein stated, it shall be within the power of Her Highness, or of the officers of the Government, to call me to account for the same, and to restrain me from such actions in the future.

"(2) I promise to hold no intercourse with persons of evil character, enemies to the State, or any person of whom Her Highness does not approve, and that I will not give employment to any one who has been dismissed from the service of the State, or of the *deorhi kháss*.

"(3) I, being a Muhammadan of the Sunni sect, promise that I will never, either for private motives, or at the instigation of others, change my religion.

"(4) I acknowledge that my Mother has full power to arrange the marriages of my children, and to decide all matters connected with their education, training, and place of residence. I promise to treat the members of my family with courtesy and affection, and to abstain from violence and oppression, and all else unbecoming the character of a gentleman. I also promise that I will never make a second marriage without the permission of my Mother.

"(5) Whatever *jágír* Her Highness shall set apart for my maintenance, I agree to accept, and I promise that I will keep the expenditure of my household within the income I derive from such *jágír*, and that I will not incur debts by extravagant living.

"(6) I promise that I will make no complaints about my parents, either verbally or in writing, to any officer of the British Government, and that I will never hold direct communication with such officers. I promise to place before Her Highness any matter of which I may have cause to complain.

"(7) I promise that I will manage my *deorhi* in accordance with the laws of the State, and with such instructions as Her Highness may, from time to time, think fit to give me. I

Begam executed a similar agreement when she was declared heir-apparent and though I was too young when my grandmother died to understand what an agreement signified, I was made to sign one as soon as I reached years of discretion.

also promise, on receipt of Her Highness's instructions, to dismiss from my service any person, male or female, who has been guilty of intrigue, or other misconduct.

"(8) I promise that I will engage in no pursuits that are inconsistent with the character of a gentleman, or such as may lead to bad practices, or otherwise endanger my reputation.

"(9) I promise that, in accordance with the custom of Bhopál, I will never leave the State without Her Highness's permission.

"(10) I promise to treat every member of my family, and every servant of the State, with the respect due to the rank or position which he may hold, whether at public durbars or elsewhere, so that none may take offence, or have cause of complaint against me. I promise that I will be specially careful in this respect in my intercourse with my two brothers."

The agreement having been executed, I directed the Minister to forward it, on my behalf, through the Political Agent, to the Government of India, with the request that my son's appointment as heir-apparent might be sanctioned. A considerable time having elapsed without any answer being received, I wrote a second time to the Political Agent, and, at last, on the 9th of October, a letter came informing me that my request had been granted. Accordingly, on the 1st of Rajab, 1320 A.H., a notice was circulated to the head of every department, as well as to all officers in the *mufassal*, that, with the approval of the Government of India, Nawáb Nasrullah Khán was appointed heir-apparent in Bhopál.

NAWAB NASRULLAH KHAN, HEIR-APPARENT IN BHOPAL.

[p. 222]

CHAPTER III

THE DEATH OF NAWAB I-HTISHAM-UL-MULK

THE difficulties which surrounded me at the commencement of my reign may be traced to certain definite causes. Nawáb Shah Jahán Begam ascended the *masnad* in the year 1285 A.H., and the vigour and assiduity with which she carried on her administration won the praise not only of the Government of India and her own subjects, but of the world in general. The speeches and correspondence of contemporary Viceroys and other high officers of the Government, as well as the pages of the *Táj-ul-Ikbál*, bear clear testimony to her devotion to the interests of the State. Combined with many natural abilities, she possessed a large capacity for work, and an unusual amount of shrewdness, so that it was seldom that any administrative knot remained unravelled in her hands. Every department had its own responsible head, yet she regarded herself as responsible for any measure, great or small, that came into operation. The result was that each day was marked by progress and reform: the people were contented, and the State prosperous.

In the year 1288 A.H., my Mother performed, as her religion permitted her to do, a second marriage. Nawáb Sidik Hasan Khán was a man of learning and ability, and Her Highness reposed great confidence in him. In these days, he, no doubt, rendered her valuable assistance. In course of time, however, having effected many judicious reforms, and seeing that the State was being administered efficiently, and in accordance with her wishes, her reliance on the Nawáb Sáhib increased to such an extent that it passed all due bounds. I cannot blame my Mother greatly on this account; for, without mutual trust, there can be no real happiness in married life. Had,

Sidik Hasan Khán possessed no children by his former wife, I think it quite possible that her confidence would have been justified, and that his abilities would have been devoted to the true interests of the State.

But Sidik Hasan Khán had other ends in view. Having gained my Mother's trust to such an extent that she allowed him to become the virtual ruler of Bhopál, he filled, one after another, all the high posts in the State with his own adherents—men who possessed no qualifications for the offices they held, and who could never, under any possible circumstances, abstain from mischief and intrigue. I have previously told my readers of the machinations and evil designs of which I and my family became the victims, how the whole policy of the State was changed, and how all the good that my Mother's wise management had achieved was undone, so that the administration of Bhopál became a by-word in the land. The end of it all was that a Minister with full powers was appointed by the British Government. Colonel Ward, the first to hold the office, was a man of noble character and of great administrative ability. He restored the government of the State to order and efficiency, and my Mother began once again to take some part and interest in its affairs; but she had lost heart for the work. The result of Sir Lepel Griffin's investigation into the conduct of her husband had had a very depressing effect upon her, and I doubt if she ever recovered her former happiness of mind. And now, having been given to understand that the Minister was free to govern according to his own will, she remained silent in regard to all matters on which her opinion differed from his, leaving him to take whatever action he chose, which, after all, was the only course open to her.

In a native State, the appointment of an absolute Minister can seldom be productive of good results. It is only in accordance with the natural order of things that a person so appointed should be jealous of his authority, and should endeavour to make his will the law of the land. He would need to be a man of very exceptional loyalty who could, in such a situation, patiently defer to the wishes of the Chief when they happened to be in conflict with his own. Such persons are, no doubt, to be found in the world, but they are rare; and let a Minister be never so loyal, it is impossible that he can be in sympathy with the people and their interests to the same extent as the natural ruler of the State. Nothing can compensate for the loss of the personal interest of a Chief in the government of his subjects.

Until the end of my Mother's life, the affairs of the State were in the hands of a Minister with full powers, and all the difficulties which I had to face at the commencement of my reign were the direct outcome of this system. Colonel Ward's ministry was, as I have already said, a period of progress and reform, but he held his office for only two years. He was succeeded by Munshi Imtiyáz Ali Khán, and of the calamities which befell the State and the people of Bhopál during his *régime*, there is no need for me to write again. My Mother's last Minister was Maulavi Abdul Jabbar Khán, C.I.E., who wielded the same independent powers as his predecessors. He was a worthy and upright man; but, partly on account of advancing years, which had rendered him unfit for hard work, and partly through inexperience of revenue administration, he was unable to make any head against the evil practices that went on around him.

During Her Highness's long illness, things went from bad to worse, and wholesale frauds were committed in every department. When, on assuming control of affairs, I examined the State accounts, I found that there was a sum of only Rs. 40,000 in the treasury, and less than two lákhs in the *deorhi kháss*. A sum of five lákhs of rupees, which should have been in the custody of Chunni Lál, the officer in charge of the treasury, had disappeared. Chunni Lál stated that it had been handed over to Munshi Abdul Husein; but the latter denied having received it, and no trace of this large sum was ever found. Abdul Husein was superintendent of the *deorhi kháss*, and his accounts, when produced, were an inextricable mass of erasures and corrections. At the *tosha khána*, which was in the charge of Gul Chaman Husein, things were no better. The registers were in a state of hopeless confusion. No accounts had been kept of the large amount of jewellery that had been given away, nor was there any means of checking what remained. Articles were there which had never been entered in the registers at all, and many others of which entries existed were not forthcoming, nor could their absence be accounted for.

Almost daily throughout her illness, my Mother had given away large sums of money. These presents were partly the outcome of her natural generosity, and partly the result of the cajolery of her adherents, who, as I have said before, never lost an opportunity of trading upon her good nature, and abusing the confidence which she placed in them; while the knowledge that she was too ill to look after the management of her affairs only served to increase the boldness with which their nefarious schemes were conducted. The accounts which had been kept of money spent in this manner were as disorderly as they were untrustworthy. Those who had been implicated in these transactions were well known; indeed, guilt was written on their faces; but the most informal questions failed to elicit from them a straightforward answer. The accounts of the current expenses of the household, kept by Nastúran Farídan Khán and Mahmúd Khán, were even less trustworthy; but these two persons were both dead, and no one could be held responsible for their misdeeds. All these accounts were kept on what is known as the *kayáth* system—an extremely intricate system, and one which lends itself in a peculiar degree to fraudulent practices. Owing to the enormous masses of papers to be gone through, I determined to postpone a complete investigation of these matters to some future period, and to content myself for the time being with ascertaining the actual financial position of the State and the amount of the funds available for carrying on the work of the administration.

My Mother had long watched, with increasing alarm, the gradual exhaustion of the State treasury. From the time her illness began, all kinds of irregularities had taken place in the payment of monthly salaries. Month by month, too, the revenue of the State had decreased, while *názims* and *tahsíldárs* responsible for its collection grew richer and richer. When I came to examine the account of receipts and expenditure for the previous year, I found that the income of the State had falled to eighteen lákhs of rupees. And, worse than this, salaries for the month of Rabi-ul-awwal, amounting to two lákhs of rupees, were due in fifteen days' time, and there was only Rs. 14,000 in the treasury, and, so far as I could see, no possible means of raising more. My readers can easily imagine my anxiety. To tide over the immediate emergency, I caused a lákh of rupees to be transferred from the *deorhi kháss* to the State treasury, and by one means or another, when the end of the month came, the State was able to meet its liabilities. But the future outlook filled me with apprehension. Fortunately, the *asarh* payments were now due, and urgent instructions were sent to all *názims* and *tahsíldárs* to expedite their collection. The Minister was ordered to draw from the State Railway any balance that might be standing to the credit of the State, and in the course of a few days, money slowly began to come in.

I found the records and accounts of the revenue department in great disorder. A land settlement was at this time being introduced, which threatened grave dangers in the future. Originally, the settlement had been for a period of twenty years. This had been followed by a ten years' settlement. But before the results of this latter system had begun to be apparent, it, too, was abolished, and the Minister was now engaged in making a settlement which was to extend over a period of thirty years. But assessments and boundaries were being fixed in a most arbitrary fashion, and the documents in which the scheme was embodied were full of contradictory statements. I, therefore, decided not to take any definite action until I had had time to reconsider the whole question. I did not myself believe in long-term settlements, and whilst the matter was still under discussion, I happened to read the resolution of Lord Curzon, published in the *Government Gazette* of January, 1902, dealing with the question of revenue administration in British India. Amongst other things, the resolution set forth the principles on which the term of a land settlement should depend, and the views expressed were by no means favourable to long settlements. This confirmed me in the opinion I had already formed, but I determined to give the matter yet further consideration before coming to a final decision.

From the first, my husband was ever ready to advise me, and to render me all the assistance in his power. Such assistance as he gave me I could have looked for from no other, for he alone shared my anxieties and sympathized with my ambitions. My misfortunes were his, and he always looked upon the protection of my honour and reputation as equivalent to the protection of his own. The Minister of the State was, I regret to say, far too jealous of his prerogatives to afford me any real support, regarding the smallest opposition to his wishes or views as an attempt to undermine his authority and influence. It is, of course, perfectly true that a ruler cannot, and should not, attempt to do everything himself; but it is unquestionably his duty, not merely to entertain able officers in his service, but to superintend personally the working of every department of his government.

The importance I attached to my husband's advice may be demonstrated by the following circumstance. Finding that I had succeeded to an almost empty exchequer, it seemed to me that the curtailment of expenses was a matter which, before all others, demanded my attention; and I came to the conclusion that the only way of dealing with it effectively was to reduce the establishments of the various offices. Measures of this nature are better calculated than any others to stir up opposition and resentment. My old enemies were already busy sowing seeds of discontent and suspicion, and all kinds of slanderous reports about me were being circulated. I was branded as cruel and avaricious, and my smallest actions were misrepresented and misjudged. I nevertheless, after a careful examination of the budget estimates, drew up my scheme of reductions; but the Nawáb Sáhib, when I placed it before him, did not regard it with favour. He agreed with me as to its necessity, but he did not think the time suitable for carrying it into effect, and advised me to postpone it. I knew that his opinion had not been formed without careful consideration, and I accordingly decided, at any rate for the time being, to abolish no existing appointments, and to content myself with curtailing expenses in the *kár-khána*, and wherever else waste or extravagance was apparent.

Whilst we were engaged in these affairs, my husband and I determined that the time had come for celebrating the *shádi*, or marriage festival, of my two sons, the causes which had led to its postponement having ceased to exist; and we arranged that it should take place on the 6th of Shawwál. The celebration was to be conducted on a grand scale, and in a manner befitting the family of a ruling chief. All classes of the people were to participate in its pleasures, while, at the same time, every effort was to be made to keep the attendant expenses within due limits. From the first week in Ramazán, or nearly a month before the date fixed for the festival, the presentation of *jora* commenced, and every evening relatives and friends assembled at the Sadar Manzil to break their fast. A band was always in attendance, and night after night, the Nawáb Sáhib, in the best of spirits, was to be seen distributing *'itr* and *pán* amongst his guests.

But it was not only the approaching *shádi* which made these days so happy. Those of my readers who have read the first part of this story of my life, may remember my description of a former Ramazán, when my second son, Sáhibzáda Obaidullah Khán, attained the rank of a *háfiz*. The Nawáb Sáhib was very proud of his son on this account, but it had always been a matter of regret to him that, owing to my Mother's displeasure, so few besides the members of our household had attended the recitation given on that occasion. He therefore arranged a repetition of the performance, to which not only the members of our household, but all the officials of the State and the chief residents of Bhopál were invited. It took place beneath a huge *shamiána* erected for the purpose in the open square facing the Moti Mahal. The evening meal was provided for the entire audience, at the conclusion of which my son, nightly, recited a fixed portion of the Holy Book.

During this month, the Nawáb Sáhib had much to occupy

him. Amongst other things, he undertook the reorganization of the Body-guard, for he was keenly interested in military matters. He took great trouble in designing a new uniform for the troop, and with a view to improving its discipline and efficiency, asked my permission to utilize the services of Captain Abdul Kayúm, of the Imperial Service Lancers—a request with which I was only too glad to comply. Preparations for the *Id* festival, which was now close upon us, also engaged his attention. It was necessary that I should attend the prayer at the *Idgah* on that day, and the Nawáb Sáhib himself went there to see that the necessary preparations were made. The same evening he worked till a very late hour, being engaged with Munshi Kushi Lál, head *munshi* of the *rúbkári*, in dispatching invitations in connection with the coming festival. I happened to be working late myself, and about midnight I sent an attendant to inquire if the Nawáb Sáhib was yet at leisure, as I wished to consult him about the list of guests. The attendant returned saying that the Nawáb Sáhib was still working; so, as I was tired, I went to my room and slept. At two o'clock in the morning, I was aroused and informed that the morning meal was prepared, but that the Nawáb Sáhib was not yet awake. I therefore went myself to inform him of the hour. Approaching his couch, I called him by name, but he did not awake. I called him a second time, and yet a third time, but still he lay motionless. A sudden and nameless dread took possession of me. I approached closer, and placed my hand on his wrist; but I could feel no pulse, and he seemed not to breathe. Without losing a moment, I summoned my two elder sons, who hastened to my side. Sáhibzáda Obaidullah Khán was the first to enter the room. He asked me what was the matter. "Your father!" I said. "His pulse has stopped, and he does not breathe!" The same moment, Nawáb Nasrullah Khán entered. He put the same question, and I answered him as I had answered his brother. My words seemed to render them incapable of speech or action. Begging Nasrullah Khán to control himself, I told him to go at once and call Hakím Núr-ul-hasan and doctor Walli Muhammad, and bade him also summon the Minister. At the same time, I sent an attendant with a message to the Nawáb Sáhib's sister. The two doctors were the first to arrive. Though I did not for a moment doubt that my husband was dead, yet, as they made their examination, I still clung to the hope that I should hear them say "He breathes," or "His pulse yet beats." But the words which after a brief space fell upon my ears bore a meaning all too different: "According to the will of God," they said, "so has it fallen." With this sentence, my last flickering hope went out. The shock which I felt it would be useless to try to describe. The pen may write the word "shock" or the lips may utter it; but that for which it stands neither pen nor tongue can depict. At this moment, the report of the morning gun broke the stillness, and the day began to dawn.

To be deprived in a moment of one who for twenty-seven years had been my constant and loving companion, the only being in the world on whose loyal assistance and wise judgment I knew that I could rely; whose actions, whether in public life or private, were always characterized by the same high motives and the same unswerving devotion to duty; whose sympathy was as strong as it was unfailing—how strong and unfailing I alone knew—to lose such a one, and at a time when I was in the sorest need of a faithful friend and wise counsellor, was, as my readers can well imagine, not only an unspeakable grief, but a dire calamity. If we were to study a record of the trials and sorrows that have come into the world, we should find that in many cases God has allowed them to fall on the just and the pious, for it is thus that He makes proof of their faith and patience. And to those who fail not under the test, He sends this blessed message of compassion and love:

"We will surely prove you by afflicting you in some measure with fear, and hunger, and decrease of wealth, and scarcity of fruits; but bear good tidings unto the patient, who, when a misfortune befalleth them, say, We are God's, and unto Him shall we surely return. Upon them shall be blessings from their Lord and mercy, and they are the rightly directed."[1]

[1] Sale's translation of the Korán.

The trial which I was called upon to face was, indeed, a severe one. But I prayed for patience, and bowed my head in submission to His will. I continually repeated to myself the words,

"Sufficient is God as a help,"

and I derived much comfort therefrom, for in the Holy Book it is written,

"Shall not men's hearts rest securely in the meditation of God?"[1]

Ere the doctors had finished their examination, the whole household was collected round the door of my husband's room. The Minister, too, came. He was greatly agitated, and, as his eye fell upon the Nawáb Sáhib's lifeless form, a heavy sigh betrayed his emotion. My two sons, with grief-stricken countenances and eyes wet with tears, sat beside their father's couch. My youngest son, Hamidullah Khán, as yet knew nothing. He was still asleep, and I refused to have him awakened; for he was but little more than seven years old, and I feared the effect a sudden shock might have upon him. It was, therefore, not until the morning was well advanced that he knew that he was fatherless. He wept piteously when he realized what had happened, and as his father's kind deeds came one by one into his memory, his grief became past control. His elder brothers tried to comfort him, but sorrow overcame them too, and they wept with him.

Had I been able to tend my husband at the last, or to try even a single remedy, I think my burden would have been less hard to bear. He had been, in every sense, a good man; and yet, apart from the happiness he found in his home and his family, life had afforded him but scanty pleasures. The kindly affection of Nawáb Sikandar Begam had, indeed, cheered his early years; and, for a brief period, too, he was happy under my Mother's care. But from the day when the shadow of Sidik Hasan Khán fell across his path, all was changed. My Mother's loving care was replaced by the Nawáb Sáhib's implacable enmity, and his peace of mind was destroyed by the

[1] Sale's translation of the Korán.

malice and intrigue by which, from that day forth, he was surrounded. My accession opened out a new life to him—a life which promised, not only happiness, but, what he valued far higher, scope for his talents and ambitions. But, on its threshold, death claimed him, and he was summoned from the world when its treasures were in his very grasp.

Before the day was well advanced, news of the calamity which had befallen the State had spread throughout the city. At first, it was hardly credited, and people came in crowds to the Sadar Manzil. On learning the truth, many wept, and, within the building and without, nothing was to be heard save the noise of mourning. The Political Agent arrived in Bhopál at eleven o'clock, and drove straight to the palace. He was accompanied by Miss Blong, the lady doctor. The latter, after a brief examination of the body, attributed death to the bursting of a blood-vessel, and the consequent accumulation of blood on the brain. At four o'clock, Doctor Dane, the Agency Surgeon, came, and his opinion confirmed that of the other doctors. The breaking of a blood-vessel had, he said, proved too great a strain for an already weakened heart. A half-smoked cheroot and the remains of a glass of drinking water, found by the Nawáb Sáhib's side, had been carefully preserved, and these were now handed over to Doctor Dane, by whom they were dispatched to Bombay for chemical examination.[1]

For nearly seven years, my husband had complained of slight pains in the region of the heart. These pains were generally more distinct after riding, walking up hill, or other forms of hard exercise. He had, on more than one occasion, consulted Doctor Dane, who always assured him that there were no signs of disease, and that there was no need for him to be in any alarm. Nevertheless, he continued to lose both weight and strength. During the illnesses of my two daughters, Bilkis Jahán Begam and Asíf Jahán Begam, he had many opportunities of discussing his symptoms with well-known medical men, and he used also to read books treating of the heart and its diseases. As a result he had long

[1] The Chemical Examiner's report showed that no properties of a suspicious nature had been discovered.

taken a serious view of his condition, and he often used to say that his disease would one day kill him. At such times, we used to tell him that his fears were imaginary, and made light of his symptoms as indicating nothing more than a disordered digestion. About three years before his death, his health greatly improved. The pain almost disappeared, and his weight and strength increased. After my accession, notwithstanding heavy work, his health continued good, and only five days before his death, he said to me, " I suffer much less pain than formerly; I expect it will gradually disappear altogether." On the 20th of Ramazán, I saw him raise and throw a weight of twenty seers. I was standing near him at the time, and I noticed a sudden change in his colour, and beads of perspiration stood on his forehead. I said nothing, however, for when performing feats of strength, he always resented any attempt made to restrain him. On the day of his death, he was quite free from pain, and apparently in the best of health. After sunset, having broken his fast, he sat some time with me, telling me about a certain horse that an Arab dealer had brought for his inspection. I myself was feeling somewhat indisposed, and noticing this he said, " You look tired: your long fast is beginning to tell upon you." He then left me and seated himself in a chair in an open verandah. It was the winter season, and the cold was very severe. For an hour he sat there, absorbed in a conversation about horses, of which he was passionately fond; and though I went to him two or three times, I could not persuade him to move. At last, as it was growing late, and I had work to do, I retired to my room. He sat on for another hour, and then went to the residence of my second son, where he, too, had work to do. It was not until one o'clock that he lay down to take a brief rest. In an hour's time he must arise for the morning meal. But, alas! ere that one brief hour has ended, his soul is far sped on its lonely flight.

After the Political Agent had gone, I set myself to perform for my husband the same sad offices that, but six months before, I had performed for my Mother. Shortly before three o'clock, the body was placed on its bier, and at four o'clock, it was carried from the Sadar Manzil to the Hayát Afzah garden. The funeral ceremony was attended by the Political Agent, all the officials of the State, and by a large number of the general public. The Nawáb Sáhib was laid to rest by the side of his two daughters. The forces of Grief are Death's body-guard; but seldom, surely, has his gloomy escort been mustered in more formidable array.

All the preparations which had been made for the *shádi* at onces fell to pieces, and every thought of pleasure was abandoned. Those who now came to condole with us in our sorrow were accommodated in the same pavilion in which, but the day before, those who had come to congratulate us had made merry; and the day on which they assembled there, was the very day on which my son was to have completed his recitation of the Holy Korán. Some trifling accident had caused a delay of one day in the recitation, and, but for this, my husband would have been present at its close, and one of his dearest wishes would have been fulfilled. The repetition of the Holy Korán is a duty which, once undertaken, should not be left unfinished. My son, therefore, brought his recitation to an end on the day following the Nawáb Sáhib's death; but instead of illuminations and rejoicing, only gloom and sadness signalized the event. His task closed in affliction, but its merit was was not lessened, and it carried peace and joy to his father's spirit.

Out of respect to my husband, all the State offices remained closed for three days. On the 27th of Ramazán, the Political Agent, accompanied by Mrs. Lang, paid me a formal visit of condolence. On account of mourning, no public reception took place, and no salute was fired. Mr. Lang spoke for some time of the Nawáb Sáhib's many high qualities, and his words gave me no little comfort. His Excellency the Viceroy expressed his sympathy with me through the Political Agent,[1] and I received a large number of letters and telegrams

[1] The letter was as follows: "My dear Friend,—His Excellency the Viceroy has heard with deep regret of the sudden death of the Nawáb Sáhib, and has instructed me to convey to Your Highness, and to Your Highness's family, his sincere sympathy. (*Signed*) JOHN LANG, *Political Agent in Bhopál*."

from my European and other friends. Amongst the former were Colonel Malcolm Meade, Resident at Baroda, Mr. Warburton, Resident at Mysore, and Colonel Barr, Resident at Hyderabad, who had been intimately acquainted with my husband, and had held him in high estimation. I also received a telegram of condolence from the Society of Friends in Sehore, and at Aligarh, a meeting of the members of the staff and the students of the M.A.O. College was held in the Strachey Hall, to give expression to the sympathy which was felt for me and for the State, and a telegram of condolence was sent to me by Nawáb Mushhín-ul-mulk, the Honorary Secretary of the college.

That my husband's spirit might not lack the reward of the faithful, I caused his *haj badal* [1] to be performed, and, at the same time, that of my Mother [2] and of my daughter Asíf Jahán Begam. I also distributed large sums of money in charity. A chronogram,[3] signifying the date of the Nawáb Sáhib's death, was composed in Persian by Munshi Jamíl Ahmad. It may be rendered into English as follows:

"Our loved Nawáb, good Ahmad Ali Khán,
From earth has passed away:
His servant Jamíl breathes a heavy sigh,
And thus his verse records the melancholy day."

"The souls of the good arise,
And tread in peace the paths of Paradise."

The Nawáb Sáhib's *jágír* reverted to the State, and his transferable property was divided between his three sons. Only the Sadar Manzil, which is my residence, and which was built at my husband's expense, together with a certain sum of money deposited in the State treasury, yet remain to be apportioned. This property will also go to the three Sáhibzádas, who, according to Muhammadan law, inherit all their

[1] The *haj badal* is a vicarious pilgrimage undertaken for the spiritual benefit of a person who has died without having himself performed the *haj*.

[2] I caused the *haj badal* to be performed for my Mother because when, at the age of seven, I fell dangerously ill, the same service was undertaken at her command for my recovery. The three persons whom I now dispatched to Mecca were Maulavi Abdul Hak, the late Nawáb Sahib's *hámdár*, Maulavi Azam Husein, and Maulavi Abdur Rahman.

[3] See chap. xii., p. 146, footnote.

NAWAB IHTISHAM-UL-MULK WITH SAHIBZADA HAMIDULLAH KHAN.

p. 236]

parents' possessions. There was a certain amount of land at Jalálábád, my husband's native place, and to the whole of this Sáhibzáda Hamidullah Khán succeeded, his two elder brothers voluntarily resigning their shares. The Nawáb Sáhib's personal effects went to his sons. I had renounced all claim to my *mahar* [1] during his lifetime.

[1] The *mahar* is a marriage portion settled by the husband on the wife before marriage. In Muhammadan families of position, the amount thus settled is often very large. Not infrequently, the wife gives up her claim to the *mahar* on the death of her husband, and, occasionally, as in the above case, during his lifetime.

CHAPTER IV

THE DAYS OF MOURNING

NOTHING is more necessary for effective administration than an intimate acquaintance, on the part of the ruler, with the state of affairs prevailing in each division of his territory. I had made up my mind to visit the various districts of the State at an early date ; but, after my installation, as so many urgent matters claimed my attention, I decided that the Nawáb Sáhib should go in my place, and inspect and report on the condition of the people, and the work of the district officials. This purpose was never accomplished. Many matters, which I could only deal with in consultation with him, delayed his departure, and he died before the final arrangements for his tour had been made.

Islám imposes very strict rules on widows during the period of their mourning. The period is four months and ten days, and during this time no new garments, ornaments, or bright colours should be worn. A widow is even forbidden the use of oil for the hair. Except in cases of the most urgent necessity, she is prohibited from leaving the house in which her husband's death has taken place, and from holding communication with any but her closest relations. From this last rule, owing to my duties and position as a ruler, I was obliged to consider myself exempt ; but all the others I faithfully observed.

The confusion and disorder which prevailed in the administration, combined with the untimely death of the Nawáb Sáhib, filled me with indescribable anxiety, and, at times, during these months of mourning, my mind was almost distracted by the gloomy pictures that rose before it. In the whole State of Bhopál, there seemed none to whom I could look for help. My sons were too young and inexperienced in the ways of the world to be my counsellors. The older members of my family possessed, for the most part, neither education nor ability, while, owing to the family feuds of my Mother's reign, I was practically a stranger to the few amongst them who might otherwise have been some support to me. Nearly all the officers of the State were new men ; and if I wanted information in regard to previous administrative methods and policy, there was no one who could give me the smallest assistance. Two old servants of the State did, indeed, survive, in the persons of Díwán Thákur Parshád and Sheikh Muhammad Hasan, auditors of accounts in the *deorhi kháss*, but of past events unconnected with their own department they knew practically nothing. I had hoped to be able to rely upon the support of the Minister, seeing that he was a man of experience and had spent many years in the service of the British Government ; but he took a different view of our respective positions. In his eyes, I was a child that must be taught to say its lessons and to do only those things which its master deemed proper for it to do. I had, consequently, little to hope for in that quarter. Indeed, during those early days, the only person who was of real help to me was Mr. Lang, the Political Agent, to whom, in times of special difficulty, I was forced to turn for advice and support.

So great were the troubles that beset me during my Mother's reign, that I had, at one time, made up my mind that I would quit Bhopál and seek a residence elsewhere, and I set forth my desire in a petition to Her Highness. It seemed to me that, outside my native country, no place in the world could offer me a more peaceful retreat than the holy city of Mecca, which the Almighty God has Himself appointed to be a city of refuge for His servants, and which offers to the weary pilgrim, not only shelter from the ills of this world, but a sure hope of happiness in the world to come.

When my daughter Asíf Jahán Begam was sick, I had arranged to take her to Bombay for the sake of the change of climate, and my intention had been to write to my Mother from that place, and ask her permission to proceed thence to Mecca. It is almost a law of nature that man, in times of trouble and misfortune, when he sees his undertakings fail and his hopes come to naught, turns to Him Who alone knows the longings and the afflictions of the human heart. For God is ever close at hand. "I am nearer to him," He has said in His Holy Word, "than his jugular vein." By His infinite wisdom and power, He can, in a moment of time, change all things according as it seems good to Him.

"His command, when He willeth a thing, is only that He sayeth unto it, Be; and it is."

Situated as I was at that time, I felt that a pilgrimage to Mecca and to the tomb of the Prophet—on whom and on his descendants may the peace of God rest for ever—would both heal the affliction of my heart and secure for me the spiritual comfort which belongs to those who fulfil the high command,

"Having made preparation for thy pilgrimage, let thy steps be turned to the House of the Caába, to Jerusalem, and to Medina which is my abode."

Unfortunately, I was forced to abandon my proposed journey to Bombay, and my pious resolve, which, up to that time, I had made known to no one, had to be laid aside.

"Every event has its appointed time. Its happening can neither be hastened nor delayed."

Subsequently, I spoke often to my husband of my desire to perform the *haj*, for to neglect this duty when God has provided the means of accomplishing it is a heavy sin.

"And it is a duty towards God, incumbent on those who are able to go thither, to visit this house."

Amongst the duties of an orthodox Musalman, there are five of such paramount importance that to neglect them is to merit everlasting punishment. They are the following:

(1) Belief in the unity of God, and in Muhammad the Prophet of God.

(2) The performance of prayers.
(3) The giving of alms.
(4) The observance of the fast of Ramazán.
(5) The performance of the *haj*.

By the grace of God, I had, up to the time of which I am writing, obeyed to the best of my power the first four of these commands. The last, through circumstances over which I had no control, was still unfulfilled. But now all was changed. My life was free from restrictions, and the desire to perform the *haj* and to make the pilgrimage to the tomb of Muhammad, the holy one and chosen of God, took complete possession of my mind. I had neither husband to restrain me, nor mother to withhold her permission. All I needed was the consent of the Government of India, and this I had little doubt of obtaining, for under British rule religious freedom belongs to all. Accordingly, when after my husband's death the Political Agent called upon me to express his sympathy, I told him that, as soon as I had celebrated my sons' marriage festival, it was my intention to undertake this sacred duty, for, as time went on, my administrative work was likely to become heavier and heavier, and I might never find another opportunity.

Shortly afterwards, I dispatched the following *kharíta* to His Excellency the Viceroy:

" *Zikád 22nd*, 1319 A.H. [*3rd March*, 1902.]

" With due respect, I make my humble petition: It is the duty of every Muhammadan who is in possession of sufficient means, to visit the holy city of Mecca, and perform there the sacred duties which his religion enjoins. I have long desired to make this pilgrimage, but, up to the present time, various circumstances have stood in my way. The sudden death of my husband, Nawáb Ihtishám-ul-mulk, Sultán Dula, has been a great shock to me, and, in consequence, I have lost both health and strength. It seems to me, therefore, that no time could be more suitable than the present for the performance of this journey; for in addition to discharging a sacred duty, I shall, I have no doubt, derive considerable benefit from the sea voyage and change of climate. I therefore beg that the supreme Government will be pleased to sanction my absence from India for a period of seven or eight months from October next. If I return in safety, I shall devote myself with renewed vigour to the welfare of the people whom Almighty God has placed in my charge. I propose to take with me my two younger sons, Sáhibzáda Muhammad Obaidullah Khán and Sáhibzáda Muhammad Hamidullah Khán, and I shall require a European officer to accompany me as far as the port of Jeddah, just as, on a like occasion, Doctor Thomson accompanied my grandmother, Nawáb Sikandar Begam. The Minister of the State will, in consultation with the heads of the various departments, continue to discharge his present duties. I have not yet arranged for the disposal of my own work, for there is still ample time before me. During my absence, I shall have abundant opportunities of testing the capabilities of my successor ; for my eldest son, Nawáb Nasrullah Khán, will not accompany me on my pilgrimage. Before leaving Bhopál, I shall make arrangements for the discharge of my personal duties as circumstances shall seem to require, and I trust that, by the grace of God, the administration of the State will not suffer during my absence. I beg that I may be honoured with an early and favourable reply."

In reply, I received a *kharíta* from His Excellency the Viceroy approving of my desire to perform the *haj*, but expressing the hope that I would defer its fulfilment until after the durbar which was to be held in the ensuing January in honour of the coronation of His Majesty the King-Emperor. Owing to the unique character and great importance of the event referred to in His Excellency's *kharíta*, and since it was not necessary on religious grounds that I should perform my pilgrimage immediately, I resolved to defer its accomplishment till the following year.

At this time, Mr. Lang, who had held the post of Political Agent for the last three years, was transferred, and his place was taken by Major L. Impey. Previous to this, Major Impey had been on special duty in the Bhopál Agency, and I had experienced great kindness at his hands. I had, therefore, no hesitation in acquainting him with all my difficulties, and he gave me, in return, both sympathy and encouragement. Whenever I spoke to him of the anxieties and apprehensions with which I looked forward to the future, he used to say to me, "Remember, Begam Sáhiba, that Rome was not built in a day. With patience and calm deliberation everything will gradually come right, and God will help you to overcome your difficulties." I, accordingly, devoted all my energies to the duties that lay before me, and I soon discovered that, for an afflicted mind, there is no better medicine than hard work.

The question of the land settlement I had been obliged, as I have already told, to postpone; but it was one of too great importance to admit of long delay. I had every hope that, as soon as the new scheme could be carried into effect, the existing confusion in the revenue department would be materially reduced. The first step I took was to write to Colonel Barr and ask him if he could recommend me a thoroughly experienced and qualified man to take up the duties of settlement officer. Colonel Barr had, at one time, held the appointment of Boundary Officer in Sehore, and had subsequently risen step by step until he became Agent to the Governor-General in Central India. He therefore possessed great experience, and he was, in addition, closely acquainted with the affairs of the Bhopál State. In replying to my letter, he recommended me to engage the services of one Maulavi Syad Hasan Khán. This gentleman, accordingly, came to Bhopál, and after an interview with the Minister, was brought to see me. He declined, however, to accept the pay which the durbar had fixed for the post; and, as the State was not at that time in a position to offer more, and as the Minister did not approve of the proposed appointment, the negotiations came to nothing, and the Maulavi Sáhib took his departure.

During the days of mourning, I made a thorough examination of the land records. In each and every part of India, whatever the prevailing system of land revenue administration may be, the relations existing between the cultivator and the ruling power are based upon the records of the *patwáris*[1] and *kánúngos*. It is, in fact, these men who constitute the revenue department. My Mother, at one time, established a school for the training of *patwáris*; but the then Minister,

[1] A *patwári* is a village registrar and accounts-keeper. A *kánúngo* is a higher revenue official who supervises the work of the *patwáris*.

who was responsible for its management, placed two of his own relatives in immediate charge, and the only result of the school was that these men grew rich, while the *patwáris* remained as ignorant as they had been before.

It is not to be wondered at, therefore, that I found the records of the revenue office in the direst disorder; indeed, ten years have barely sufficed to repair the confusion. *Patwáris* and *kánúngos* had come to regard their posts as hereditary, and son succeeded father without the smallest regard being paid to his qualifications; and to such lengths was this principle carried that five-year-old children were allowed to succeed to their fathers' posts, and substitutes, who usually considered themselves free from all responsibility, were appointed to carry on the work. These things took place under the very eyes of the Minister and other high officers of the State, although all such appointments were entirely under their control. A single instance will give some idea of the loss which the State sustained in these days. The records in the revenue office showed the revenue due from a certain village to be Rs. 2,000. According to the *patwári* records, the amount due from the same village was Rs. 1,500. An examination of the revenue returns showed that the actual amount collected was Rs. 100; and this, in spite of the fact that the State maintained a highly paid settlement officer with an expensive establishment!

Among the oldest servants of the State were Díwán Thákur Parshád, Bakshi Muhammad Hasan, and Munshi Syad Kudrat Ali Khán, and these officers, together with Munshi Ináyat Husein Khán and Munshi Badar-ul-hasan, who had also worked a number of years under my Mother, I consulted in regard to the period to be fixed for the new settlement; and all of them were of opinion that, in the present state of affairs, a long term settlement was inadvisable. I also took counsel with Munshi Isrár Hasan Khán (now *Nasír-ul-muhám*, or Judicial Minister), who had recently had experience in British India of the working of the short-term system, and was, in addition, well acquainted with the conditions prevailing in Bhopál. He, too, considered that, for the present, a short settlement should be carried out, during which the accounts and records could be thoroughly revised and corrected so as to form a reliable basis for a longer settlement at some future time.

It had always been my grandmother's practice to take into her counsel on matters of importance, not only the chief officers of the State, but such of her nobles as were capable of understanding and taking an intelligent view of administrative questions. Following this principle, I consulted, in addition to the officers above mentioned, my two sons Nawáb Nasrullah Khán and Sáhibzáda Obaidullah Khán, who, although they had as yet had little experience of public business, had nevertheless been well educated, and I considered it time they should take some part and interest in the affairs of the administration. They expressed their opinions at considerable length, but with clearness and decision, agreeing on nearly all points with the views of the State officials. I caused the statements of all those whom I had consulted to be filed in my office, and I constantly referred to them whilst drawing up the new scheme.

Being seriously hampered for want of funds, I determined to take immediate steps for the collection of arrears of revenue. Munshi Isrár Hasan Khán had come to Bhopál at this time to condole with me on my husband's death. As my readers are aware, he had formerly been in the service of the State; and on account of what I had heard of his work at that time, and because he had stood high in the estimation of Nawáb Ihtishám-ul-mulk, I considered him eminently qualified for work of this kind, requiring as it did both ability and integrity. I therefore spoke to him on the subject, and he replied that, if the Government of India would consent to the transfer of his services, he would gladly undertake the duties I had mentioned. Before finally deciding the matter, I thought it better to take the opinion of Colonel Ward, under whom Isrár Hasan Khán had worked during his former service in Bhopál. Colonel Ward's reply to my letter was entirely satisfactory, and as Mr. Bayley, Agent to the Governor-General in Central India, also expressed his approval of my intention,

I wrote, through the Political Agent, to the Government of India, requesting that the services of Isrár Hasan Khán might be lent to the State. My request was granted, and in Rabi-us-sáni, 1320 A.H., he took charge of his new appointment, and the collection of arrears of revenue commenced.

Amongst other matters that claimed my attention at this time was the Educational Department, which, like practically every other branch of the administration, I found to be in an extremely unsatisfactory condition. My Mother had made vigorous attempts to place instruction within the reach of the better as well as the poorer classes of her subjects. For the former, she opened, early in her reign, the Shahjaháni School, in which instruction was given in English. But in those days, few people understood the value of an English education, and still fewer were inclined to spend money in acquiring it. A certain number of students did, indeed, join the school, but in a short time, they began to beg for exemption from the small fees that were demanded of them, and the attendance gradually dwindled down until at last the school had to be closed. For the poorer classes, an institution called the Sulaimánia School was established, and some fifty or sixty elementary schools were opened in various parts of the State; but, for the most part, the people refused to take advantage of the facilities afforded them, and out of a population of nearly a million, less than three thousand people were receiving instruction, while as much as Rs.16,000 was given away yearly in free scholarships. Towards the end of her reign, my Mother took a great personal interest in educational matters; she appointed a permanent staff of inspectors, and established a Board of Education to direct the general policy of the department. Unhappily, she died before the benefit of these measures had begun to be felt.

My two elder sons were now come of age, and custom demanded that they should leave my roof and commence to live in homes of their own. It was, therefore, necessary that *jágírs* should be granted to them for their maintenance. Shortly after my accession, my own *jágír* of Rs. 90,000, and that of my husband of Rs. 40,000, had reverted to the State, and in view of the financial position, I was anxious that my sons' *jágírs* should be as small a burden as possible on the exchequer, though I, of course, desired that they should be able to maintain themselves in comfort and in accordance with their respective positions. After careful consideration, I decided that a grant of Rs. 146,000, or Rs. 17,000 more than the combined *jágírs* of myself and my husband, should suffice, and *jágírs* were, accordingly, granted as follows:

To Nawáb Nasrullah Khán	Rs. 62,661	0	3
To Sáhibzáda Obaidullah Khán	Rs. 53,500	0	9
To Sáhibzáda Hamidullah Khán	Rs. 30,807	0	0

The Nawáb Sahib had entered into an agreement with the State on being declared heir-apparent, and no further assurances from him were considered necessary. Sáhibzáda Hamidullah Khán was still a child, and his *jágír* continued under my control. My second son entered into an agreement similar to that signed by his brother, the only difference being the addition of the two following clauses:

(1) I promise that I will respect and obey my elder brother as long as he continues to treat me with kindness, and that I will always love and cherish my younger brother.

(2) I promise that, in obedience to my religion, and to the will of my parents, I will always keep the Holy Korán fresh in my memory.

From petitions that were constantly reaching me from cultivators in various districts of the State, and from other sources of information, it was well known to me that the *mufassal* administration was being carried on in a highly unsatisfactory manner, and that corruption was widely spread amongst the district officials. It was essential that a tour of inspection should be made, and as I was unable to go myself, the period of my mourning not yet being completed, I could think of no better plan than to send my two elder sons in my place. The hot season had just set in, but I decided that the tours should take place without delay, for the condition of the cultivators was causing me much anxiety, and I was determined to possess myself of reliable information. Accordingly, I dispatched Nawáb Nasrullah Khán to the eastern and northern districts, and Sáhibzáda Obaidullah Khán to those in the south and west. The Minister disapproved of the whole scheme, but I declined to change it, for, apart from the useful results which I anticipated from their tours, I believed that my sons themselves would be greatly benefited by the knowledge and experience which their work amongst the people would provide.

Before their departure, I caused a notice to be printed and circulated in all the villages of the State to the effect that the people were to lay their complaints before my sons without fear or hesitation. I personally arranged the details of their tours, and as the eastern district alone was traversed by metalled highways, and much time would have been required to render the country roads of other districts fit for carriages to pass over, I put my sons' convenience out of the question, and told them that they must perform their marches on horseback. I also instructed them to remain as short a time as possible at each halting-place, partly because the date fixed for their marriage festival was not far distant, and partly because harvest operations had already begun, and it would fall hard upon the ryots if they were kept long from their fields at such a time. They set out on their respective tours on April the 25th, 1902. Wherever they halted, they inspected the crops, the offices of the *tahsíl* and the *thána*, the schools, and the dispensaries, and they sent detailed reports to me of everything that came under their notice. Between them they heard two thousand three hundred petitions, all of which they investigated and sent on to me for orders.

Sáhibzáda Obaidullah Khán returned on the 12th of Safar. He reached Bhopál by rail, having taken the train at Budhni. To mark the completion of his first tour, he was accorded a public reception. The Body-guard and a detachment of the State troops occupied the station yard, and Sáhibzáda Hamidullah Khán, the Mír Bakshi, the Kámdár of the *deorhi khláss*, and the Military Secretary were present on the platform. The band of the State troops was also present, and a salute of five guns was fired from the Fatehgarh fort. Nawáb Nasrullah Khán returned a week later. His reception was equally ceremonious, and took place at Chaurimli, a place about three miles from the city. He was met by his two brothers and the officers mentioned above. His arrival was announced by a salute of seven guns.[1]

The result of these tours more than justified my expectations. An excellent effect was produced on the cultivating classes, for they found themselves treated with consideration and their petitions heard with patience and sympathy. The detailed reports which my sons sent me almost daily, put me in possession of much useful information, so that I was able to deal satisfactorily with nearly all the petitions that were forwarded to me. I was able also to detect a large number of corrupt practices, the perpetrators of which I promptly dismissed, whilst other officials, whose work was proved to have been satisfactory, were promoted or otherwise rewarded.

[1] I increased Nawáb Nasrullah Khán's salute by two guns on his being proclaimed heir-apparent.

CHAPTER V

A MARRIAGE FESTIVAL

Of all the affairs that claimed my attention after my accession, there was none that I was more anxious to see accomplished than my sons' marriage festival. The 8th of Shawwál was the date originally fixed for the celebration, and early in the month of Ramazán, my husband had commenced to issue invitations. His death on the 22nd of the month put a sudden end to all our plans and preparations, so that everything had now to be arranged afresh, and a new date fixed. The performance of this ceremony was a duty which I was determined should not be postponed longer than was absolutely necessary, and the date I selected was the 29th of Safar, the first day available after the period of mourning and the completion of my sons' tours.

It had been my husband's intention that this *shádi* should be celebrated on a large and magnificent scale, one of the chief features being the marriage procession which was to start from the Hayát Afzah garden, and make its way to the house of the brides, and thence to the Sadar Manzil palace. He had also made elaborate plans for the illumination of the city at night, and the decoration of the streets. I determined to carry out all my husband's plans, for I wished to do nothing that could in any way interfere with my sons' happiness. They, however, on learning my intentions, came to me together, and, with a due display of respect, begged me to curtail as far as possible all public display and demonstrations of joy. "A year has not yet elapsed," they said, "since our father's death, and grief is still fresh in our minds. It will please us both, therefore, if our marriages are celebrated with as much simplicity as circumstances will permit." I readily granted my sons' request, for my bereavement had left me little heart for scenes of pomp and gaiety, and I was glad, too, of the opportunity of curtailing, to some extent, the heavy expense the *shádi* necessarily involved. "Your wishes," I said, "are mine; and that which gives no pleasure to you, can give none to me."

Preparations for the festival had commenced nearly two and a half years ago at the time of the betrothal, and everything necessary for the various ceremonies and entertainments was ready in my *deorhi*. In accordance with my sons' wishes, I decided that there should be no marriage procession, and all preparations for it were at once discontinued. I thought it right, however, that the entertainment of guests and the distribution of presents should take place in the manner in which my husband and I had arranged; for the occasion was one to which all classes of the people had long been looking forward, and there seemed to be no reason why they should be deprived of their enjoyment. A number of European ladies and gentlemen, including the Agent to the Governor-General in Central India and the Political Agent in Bhopál, were invited to take part in the festivities. Invitations were also sent to the members of the late Nawáb Sáhib's family in Jalálábád, as well as to the chiefs and nobles of various States with which Bhopál had friendly connections.

On the 22nd of Safar, an entertainment was given to the servants of the *kárkhána* and gardens attached to my *deorhi*. On this occasion, my youngest son, Sáhibzáda Hamidullah Khán, who took the liveliest interest in all the proceedings connected with his brothers' *shádi*, distributed *jora* and other gifts to those who were present. On the 27th of the month, the Sirdars, *jágirdárs*, and chief officers of the State were invited to a durbar held in the hall of the Sadar Manzil, at which every one present received a *khilát*. The distribution was performed by Nawáb Nasrullah Khán and Sáhibzáda Obaidullah Khán, after which I presented each of the latter with a *khilát* consisting of a robe of honour, a sword, and a pearl necklace, in recognition of the excellent work they had accomplished during their recent tours. When all the gifts had been presented, I rose and made the following speech:

"The meeting in which we are to-day taking part is one that I have long been intending to hold; but every event has its appointed time, and only when God wills can it come to pass. Who could have foretold that this durbar would take place without the presence of Ihtishám-ul-mulk Alijah Nazír-ud-daulah Sultán Dula Nawáb Ahmad Ali Khán, may God give rest to his soul! In all things and at all times he was my counsellor and helper, and it was only the knowledge that I could rely upon his wisdom and guidance that enabled me to look forward with confidence to the restoration of order in the administration of my State.

"All that has hitherto taken place in connection with this marriage ceremony, as well as all that is to follow, was planned and thought of by the late Nawáb during the days when I was still heir-apparent. It is in consequence of the decision that we together formed, that the entire cost of the celebration is to be borne by the *deorhi kháss* and not, as has previously been the custom on such occasions, by the State.

"The present financial situation is known to you all. You know that in the second month of my reign I was obliged to pay the salaries of the servants of the State from my private exchequer. In such circumstances, there is no other course open to me but to reduce, as far as I am able, the cost of the administration. For some time past, the State has been spending more than its income, and the condition of the cultivators has been going from bad to worse. I do not say this for the purpose of bringing discredit on the financial policy of my predecessors, but at the same time it is not possible to ignore the losses which the State has suffered. Since the reins of government have been in my hands, anxiety for the welfare of my ryots has filled my mind day and night. The difficulties that beset me in this connection are too many and too great to be described at a time like the present. With a view to overcoming some of them, it was my intention to make a tour throughout my State; but, as you all know, God willed otherwise, and I therefore sent my sons, Nawáb Nasrullah Khán and Sáhibzáda Obaidullah Khán, in my stead, that they might see and report to me on the condition of my subjects in every part of my territory. Setting out in the very heart of the hot season, they yet worked so zealously that, in the space of a month, they visited nearly every district of the State, and collected for me a large amount of valuable information. Their reports of the corruption and mismanagement of *mustájirs* and other officials, which they saw with their own eyes, will greatly assist me in devising means to check such evil practices in the future.

"I look to the officers in every branch of my service to remain steadfast in the performance of their duties, and in this way to win my approbation and contribute to the well-being of the State. I trust that my Minister will give me, at all times, the full benefit of his wisdom and practical experience. I have chosen this occasion for rewarding my sons so as to be able to express publicly my appreciation of the work they have accomplished."

On the morning of the 28th, the officers and men of the Body-guard assembled in full-dress uniform at the Sadar Manzil. I received them in person, and in a brief address informed them that their troop, in memory of the interest which the late Nawáb had taken in its reorganization, was from that time forward to bear the name *Risálah Ihtishámia*, or the Ihtishámia Horse. I then presented each man with a *kalgi*, or badge, to be worn on the front of the turban, on which the name of the troop was engraved. The words of my address were as follows:

"Mír Bakshi Sáhib Bahádur, Major Karím Beg, Commandant of the Victoria Lancers, and officers of the Bhopál Forces:—There is no need for me to describe to you the heaviness of the sorrow which has fallen upon me and upon the State by the untimely death of Ihtishám-ul-mulk Alijah Nazír-ud-daulah Sultán Dula Nawáb Ahmad Ali Khán Bahádur. We have lost one whose heart was like a mine of precious gems, so richly was it endowed with courtesy, manliness, firmness, sympathy, and the love of justice. Possessing talents which might have won him distinction in any walk of life, there was no career for which he was more pre-eminently fitted, both by his abilities and his natural inclinations, than that of a soldier. From the day of my accession, he had no dearer wish than to see the ill-regulated and ill-equipped forces of the State converted into a disciplined and efficient army. And in spite of the large amount of administrative work which, at the commencement of my reign, necessarily fell to his share, he never allowed a single day to pass by without some new effort towards the realization of his desire. The reorganization of my Body-guard was but the first step in his scheme of reform, and barely was this accomplished when God willed that his labours should cease. Brief as was his public career, his earnest and practical endeavours for the good of the State and the prosperity of its people will never be forgotten. Men and officers of my Body-guard, the smart appearance and soldierly bearing for which you are conspicuous to-day is due to him, and to him alone. It is meet, therefore, that your troop should bear a name that shall remind his children, and his children's children, of the honour which is due to his memory. From this day forward, you will bear the name Risálah Ihtishámia, and I now present to you these *kalgi*, engraved with the name I have conferred upon you, in memory of him to whom your troop is so deeply indebted. It is my earnest hope that my three sons, and especially Sáhibzáda Obaidullah Khán, whose military training has already commenced, will, like their father before them, take a practical interest in everything that concerns the State army. In military reforms, I shall look to the Mír Bakshi Sáhib, who has always been a faithful servant of the State, to assist me with his knowledge and experience. It is my ambition to see all the forces of the State raised to a standard of efficiency equal to that of the Victoria Lancers, so that they may be equally qualified in times of emergency to support the supreme Government, and maintain the loyal traditions of Bhopál.

"It gives me great pleasure to present to Captain Abdul Kayúm this pearl necklace, together with the Ihtishámia badge, in recognition of the good work he has done in connection with the State cavalry. This regiment has shown very marked improvement during the short time that Captain Abdul Kayúm has had charge of it. If every officer were to display equal zeal in the performance of his duties, the State army would, in a very short space of time, be converted into a strong and effective force. Finally, in all the affairs of the State, whether civil or military, I pray God to help me, and to fill the hearts of those that serve me with steadfastness and good faith."

On the 29th, Mr. Bayley, accompanied by Mrs. Bayley and his First Assistant, arrived, with other European ladies and gentlemen, from Indore. As it was the hot season, and I was anxious that my guests should suffer as little inconvenience as possible on their journey, I dispatched my own saloon to bring them from Ujjain to Bhopál. The visit of the Agent to the Governor-General was of a purely private nature, so I did not go myself to the railway station. The party was met by the Minister, and a guard of honour was present composed of the State cavalry.

The marriage party took place on the same evening at the Gohur Mahal. There was no procession, but troops, with the *máhi marátib* and other emblems of the State, occupied the palace courtyard, which was illuminated on all four sides with coloured lights. The bridegrooms came from their respective palaces mounted on elephants. I myself reached the Gohur Mahal a few minutes before their arrival, as did also my European guests, who watched this and the various other features of the ceremony with much interest. Their seats, with those of the other spectators, were arranged on the tops of the four main gateways—the Shahjaháni, the Kudsi, the Sultáni, and the Sikandri. The day had been overcast and very hot, but by the favour of God, a downpour of rain made the evening cool and pleasant.

The usual ceremonies took place at the houses of the brides, to whom I presented the same robes that I had received from my Mother at my own marriage. These robes had originally been a wedding gift to my grandmother, Nawáb Sikandar Begam. My grandmother presented them as a wedding gift to my Mother, who, in turn, bestowed them upon me. It is customary, both amongst Muhammadans and Hindus, for the parents of a bridegroom to present a gift of this kind to the bride. The robes are often very costly and handsome, and must never be less than two in number.

On the 1st of Rabi-ul-awwal, a feast was provided for the Sirdars, *vakíls*, office clerks, and students of the principal schools. On this occasion, I did not forget those who had lost their appointments in consequence of the recent reductions; for though economic reasons had obliged me to dispense with their services, they had done nothing to forfeit my favour or goodwill. In the evening, I gave a tea-party at the Sadar Manzil palace. Following the wishes of my sons, there was no display of fireworks, and the illuminations were on a much smaller scale than had been originally intended; but in other respects I did everything I could think of to add to the enjoyment and comfort of my guests: and, indeed, I could do no less; for they had one and all put themselves to much trouble on my behalf. The Agent to the Governor-General had come to Bhopál in spite of very heavy work, and all had faced the discomfort of travelling in the hot season rather than cause me disappointment. It is not too much to say that it was the presence of my European friends that made my sons' *shádi* a success; for the spirit of mirth which they brought with them, and with which they infected others, was the one essential accompaniment of a wedding festival which, at that time, the people of Bhopál were altogether incapable of supplying. As soon as the sun had set, the road from the guest-house to the Sadar Manzil was lit with torches and fairy lights. The palace itself was more richly illuminated than it had ever been before. A guard of honour was stationed before the entrance, and presented arms as the guests drove up. The State band was also present, and played a selection of music which was by no means the least enjoyable feature of the entertainment. Refreshments, in the shape of sweetmeats and choice fruits, were handed round before the guests departed, which they did shortly before eight o'clock.

Early the following morning, my European friends again came to the Sadar Manzil, where, after tea had been partaken of, a number of groups were photographed by the State photographer. In the afternoon, military sports were held on the Jahángírábád parade ground, in which both the Imperial Service Cavalry and the Ihtishámia Horse took part. The banquet which took place the same evening at the Lál Kothi was the last of the marriage festivities. Accompanied by my three sons, I joined the party at nine o'clock, and in the following speech, after thanking my guests for their kindness in coming to Bhopál, proposed the health of Mr. and Mrs. Bayley:

"Mr. Bayley, Ladies and Gentlemen,—My first duty is to render thanks to Almighty God for having permitted me to take charge of the administration of this State during the reign of our great and benign Sovereign, King Edward VII., and to share the prosperity and peace which belong to all who live in the shadow of his protection. I also desire to thank the Agent to the Governor-General and my other guests for their kindness in coming to Bhopál to take part in this ceremony, notwithstanding the inconveniences and discomforts of travelling at this very trying season of the year. I desire to express my special thanks to the Political Agent for the help he has given me in arranging the details of this festival. More than two years have elapsed since the date originally fixed for its celebration—in fact, it was during my heir-apparency that my husband, Nawáb Ihtishám-ul-mulk, planned, with so much interest, the scenes and ceremonies in which we have been taking part. He was never so happy as when preparing for, or performing the duties of a host; and, had God so willed it, nothing would have delighted him more than to have borne his part in entertaining you here this evening. You will be glad to hear that the entire cost of this marriage festival, though a legitimate charge on the State, has been borne by my *deorhi*, the State treasury being in too impoverished a condition to bear any but the most urgent expenses.

"To welcome to Bhopál Mr. and Mrs. Bayley and so many other friends, has been a great pleasure to me, and has enabled me to be joyful even in the midst of my grief. I rejoice, too, to think that this same month has witnessed both the conquest of the Transvaal and the Coronation of His Majesty the King-Emperor. I cannot but regard it as a happy omen that my sons' marriage ceremony should be celebrated at such an auspicious time. I pray God to grant to His Majesty length of days, health, and prosperity, and to maintain me and my children steadfast in our obedience and loyalty to the British throne. Ladies and gentlemen, I close my speech by calling upon you to drink to the very good health of the Honourable Mr. Bayley and Mrs. Bayley."

After the toast had been drunk, Mr. Bayley rose and said:

"Your Highness,—Your Highness understands English so well that I trust that you will allow me to reply in my own language to the very kind words in which you have been good enough to propose my health and that of Mrs. Bayley. You have thanked us and Your Highness's other guests for coming here at this season of the year, but I am sure that all present will feel with me that the thanks are due not from, but to Your Highness for your most friendly invitations and for the bounteous hospitality which you have extended to us all. I feared at first that, owing to pressure of other duties, I should not be able to come to Bhopál; but when Your Highness's wishes were repeated in terms of such unmistakable cordiality and sincerity, I felt that other considerations must give way, and that my duty, as well as my inclinations, would be best fulfilled by joining in the festivities with which you are celebrating the marriages of your two eldest sons. I should like to express in fitting terms the sorrow which we all feel that the Nawáb Consort has, by the inscrutable decree of Providence, to which all must bow, not been spared to rejoice with us over the completion of the marriages which it gave him and Your Highness so much pleasure to arrange. But I will not dwell on this sad subject now, and will only say that I am sure that in all Your Highness has done you have merely followed his wishes. This is specially true of the wise and generous decision by which you have determined that no portion of the expense of the ceremonies shall fall on the revenues of the Bhopál State, which have suffered severely of late years. Your Highness has said with perfect truth that these weddings have taken place at a particularly auspicious time, falling, as they do, between the conclusion of the war in which the British Empire has been so long engaged, and the Coronation of our Most Gracious Sovereign, King Edward VII. We all trust that the Empire will be blessed with peace and prosperity throughout His Majesty's reign, and that these blessings may be enjoyed to the full by the Bhopál State, which stands second to none in India in loyalty and devotion to the Crown. It is our fervent hope that Your Highness may live long to govern your territories with wisdom and justice, and that, from the unions which have now been celebrated, there may spring a long line of chiefs no less distinguished for loyalty and good government than those who have preceded them.

"Ladies and Gentlemen, I thank you most heartily on behalf of Mrs. Bayley and myself for the cordial manner in which you have received the toast which the Begam has proposed, and I ask you to join with me in drinking Her Highness's health, and I hope she will allow me to couple with hers

THE SADAR MANZIL PALACE.

p. 256]

the names of her sons, Nawáb Nasrullah Khán and Sáhibzáda Obaidullah Khán."

In the morning, I returned Mr. Bayley's visit at the Lál Kothi, and he left for Indore the same day.

Jora and other souvenirs were presented to the various newspaper correspondents who came to Bhopál on this occasion. They were lodged, with other Indian guests, in different palaces in the city and gardens, where every arrangement had been made for their comfort.

If the parents of a bride are in good circumstances, they usually present to their daughter, at the time of her departure to her husband's house, such furniture and articles of household use as they consider to be sufficient for her needs. My sons' requirements, however, were not of the ordinary kind; and that they might be able to live in a style compatible with their social positions, I decided that their palaces should be supplied with furniture and other requisites by the State and the *deorhi khάss*. Previous to my sons' nuptials, no marriage of a male representative of my family had been celebrated for a period of a hundred years. In the absence of all precedents, therefore, I decided to do as had been done in the case of my husband, and I, accordingly, on the day of the first *juma* ceremony, presented to my sons, in equal portions, the household goods which I had selected for them. The value of all the articles supplied by the State was Rs. 3,49,275. 4. 11, and from the *deorhi khάss*, Rs. 1,64,045. 1. 1, making a total of Rs. 5,13,320. 6. 0.

CHAPTER VI

MINISTERIAL CHANGES

In carrying out my administrative duties, I had expected the fullest assistance from my Minister, Maulavi Abdul Jabbar Khán, C.I.E., and the more so on account of his ripe age and experience; but in this I was doomed to disappointment. It is the duty of a ruler to become acquainted with everything that takes place in the State over which he or she presides, and to scrutinize the work and direct the policy of every branch of its administration. From the first day of my reign, I determined to act upon this principle; but the Minister, who, for nearly five years, had been practically independent, by no means appreciated the attitude I adopted, and his disapproval manifested itself in a policy of steady opposition to all my plans. At last, seeing that I was in earnest, and that I had no intention of being over-ridden, he signified his desire to resign his office. The letter which he addressed to me was as follows:

"*8th Rabi-ul-awwal,* 1320 A. H.

"Owing to advancing years, I find my duties are heavier than I can undertake, and I therefore feel that the time for my retirement from office has come. I most respectfully request that the resignation of Your Highness's humble servant may be accepted, so that he may devote the remainder of his days to praying for the prosperity of Your Highness and of Your Highness's children."

Maulavi Abdul Jabbar Khán had served the British Government for many years, and for this reason, although he was getting an old man, I knew that his experience would be valuable, and I believed that if only I could get him to work in harmony with me, we could soon put an end to the irregularities which existed in the State. I was unable, however, to persuade him to change his mind; and though I detained him till after the completion of my sons' marriage festival, so as to give him time to reconsider his determination, he remained obdurate, and there was no other course for me but to accept his resignation.

After his departure, I was for a time uncertain as to the best course to adopt. There seemed to be two alternatives: either to take the management of affairs altogether into my own hands and rule without a Minister, or to reconstruct the ministry on an entirely new basis. I knew that if I endeavoured to carry on the administration single-handed, I should sacrifice my own peace and comfort, and add largely to the difficulties of my position. At the same time, I saw that I should gain a knowledge of administrative detail which would be of the greatest service to me in after life. I determined, therefore, to try the first alternative, and for a year and a half I actually ruled the State unaided. During this time, I thoroughly mastered the working of every department, and I was able to get to the root of many of the disorders with which they abounded.

The Judicial Department alone gave me no cause for anxiety. It is true that the officers serving in it possessed but a rudimentary knowledge of law, and the legal codes themselves were badly in need of revision and amplification; but in spite of these drawbacks the department did satisfactory work, the courts were conducted with order and decency, and, on the whole, justice was dispensed. The police, on whom the people depend for security of life and property, were ill-organized and without discipline. My grandmother, Nawáb Sikandar Begam, had established police stations throughout the *mufassal*, to the great advantage of the country people. But Maulavi Abdul Jabbar Khán abolished all these stations, and instituted a kind of reserve police force to preserve order in the districts. The change had not operated successfully, and since it had been effected, crime had been steadily increasing. The condition of the Revenue Department was such that I could hardly contemplate it without despair. The settlement had been conducted on no fixed principle, and the officials who collected the revenue were incompetent and corrupt. For several years in succession the country had been on the verge of famine, and, while the people suffered, *tahsíldárs* and other revenue officials had looked on with careless apathy. As a natural result, cultivators and *mustájirs* were sinking deeper and deeper into ruin : many left the State ; and it was not an uncommon sight to see whole villages abandoned, and the fields around them lying uncultivated.

To cope with the calamities I have just been describing, I now determined to set up a joint ministry ; that is to say, instead of appointing one Minister, to appoint two, and to divide the work between them. The senior of the two was to be known as the Moin-ul-muhám and to be given charge of the revenue administration, and the other as the Nasír-ul-muhám, who was to control the judicial administration and the police. I thought that, by thus dividing labour and responsibility, I should give to each Minister a more effective and personal control, while I should, at the same time, have the advantage of being able to consult two people instead of one, to summon a miniature council, in fact, whenever matters of importance had to be decided.

It only remained to find two men suitable for my purpose. The qualifications I looked for were long experience, sound judgment, and the special knowledge necessary to inspire respect and ensure effective supervision and control. I lost no time in searching for the men I wanted, and I wrote to several of my European friends for assistance. Colonel Barr, in reply to the letter which I wrote to him, recommended to my notice Maulavi Nizám-ud-dín Hasan Sáhib, B.A., B.L., as likely to prove an able and trustworthy officer. At the same time, I heard very favourable accounts of one Munshi Mumtáz Ali Khán, a servant of the United Provinces Government, and from inquiries made through Mr. Bayley and the Political Agent, I found out that he was looked upon as a very capable revenue officer. Being anxious to settle the appointments with as little delay as possible, I entered into correspondence with a view to obtaining the transfer of his services. He was at that time employed as Superintendent of the Berhanpúr estate; but, as his appointment there was about to terminate, he expressed his willingness to undertake work in Bhopál, and as the Government approved of the proposal, his services were transferred to the State for a period of two years. His salary was fixed at Rs. 1,000 a month, in addition to which the State was to contribute towards his pension. On the first of Ramazán, Munshi Mumtáz Ali Khán took charge of his office from Syad Muhammad Kudrat Ali, who, since the departure of the Minister, had been acting as head of the Revenue Department.

The head of the Judicial Department was Khán Bahádur Ináyat Husein. He was an old man, and unable to undertake heavy work, so I did not propose to raise him to the position of Nasír-ul-muhám. Shortly after the appointment of Munshi Mumtáz Ali Khán, Maulavi Nizám-ud-dín came to visit me. I was on tour at the time of his arrival, so I sent Munshi Mansab Ali, an officer of my Secretariat, to receive him, and to conduct him to my camp at Samarda. As the Revenue Minister's post was already filled, I suggested that he should take the post of Judicial Minister, which was still vacant. This he declined to do unless I would make his position higher than that of the Revenue Minister. For various reasons, however, I deemed it inadvisable to accede to his request, so he definitely declined my offer. I now wrote a second time to Mr. Bayley, and having explained to him how it was that I had been unable to appoint Maulavi Nizám-ud-dín to the post of Nasír-ul-muhám, I concluded my letter thus: "I am anxious that both these appointments should be held by men who have earned distinction in the service of the British Government. I am sending you the names of three persons who have been recommended to me, and I shall be grateful if you will be kind enough to make inquiries about them from His Honour the Lieutenant-Governor of Bengal."

I can never sufficiently thank Mr. Bayley and Major Impey for the assistance they rendered me in these early days of my reign. Sir J. Woodburn, Lieutenant-Governor of Bengal, very kindly supplied the information I needed. His letter, which Mr. Bayley sent for me to read, strongly recommended Maulavi Nasír-ud-dín Ahmad Sáhib as suited to my requirements. The Maulavi Sáhib was described, amongst other things, as being a rapid worker, and as this was a qualification which appealed to me very strongly, I immediately applied for the transfer of his services. My request was granted, and Maulavi Nasír-ud-dín Ahmad was lent to the State for a period of two years. He joined his appointment on the 1st Rajab, 1321 A.H. I started on my pilgrimage to Mecca almost immediately after his arrival, so it was some months before I had any real opportunity of judging his work.

CHAPTER VII

THE CORONATION DURBAR

It had long been rumoured that a durbar in honour of the coronation of King Edward VII. was to be held in India. But it was not until the 7th of March, 1902 (28th Zil Kádah, 1319 A.H.), that a notification, published in the *Gazette of India,* stated that it had been definitely decided to hold such a durbar, and that it would take place at Delhi on the 1st of January, 1903. Not long afterwards, a *kharíta* was received from His Excellency the Viceroy containing a formal invitation to the durbar,[1] and forwarding a copy of the notification above

[1] The *kharíta* and notification were as follows:

Dated Calcutta, the 19th March 1902.

"My Esteemed Friend,

"I have the pleasure to inform Your Highness that it is my intention to hold an Imperial Darbar at Delhi on the 1st January 1903, for the purpose of celebrating in a befitting manner the solemn event of the Coronation of His Imperial Majesty King Edward VII., Emperor of India, and of his dearly beloved Consort the Queen.

"In instructing me to hold this Darbar, His Majesty has desired it to be made known that he is anxious to afford to all the Princes and Chiefs of India the opportunity of testifying their loyalty to his throne and person, and that attendance thereat will be regarded by His Majesty as equivalent to presence at his Coronation in England.

"I enclose, for Your Highness's information, a copy of the announcement which I have caused to be published in the 'Gazette of India,' and I request the honour of Your Highness's presence on that auspicious occasion.

"Due notice will be given through the usual channel of the particular date at which Your Highness will be expected at Delhi.

"I remain, with much consideration,

"Your Highness's sincere Friend,

(*Signed*) "Curzon.

"*Viceroy and Governor-General of India.*

"*To* Her Highness Nawab Sultan Jahan Begam of Bhopal."

NOTIFICATION

"Whereas by His Royal Proclamations bearing date the twenty-sixth day of June and the tenth day of December 1901, His Imperial Majesty King

mentioned. In reply, a *kharita*[1] was dispatched accepting the invitation, and the necessary preparations were commenced forthwith, and were carried out in accordance with instructions received from time to time from the supreme Government.

Mr. Cook, the State Engineer, was sent to Delhi to superintend the pitching of the Bhopál camp, a plan of which had been made beforehand, and tents, *shamiánas*, and furniture were dispatched by rail. The military contingent proceeded to Delhi by road; it included the Imperial Service Troops, half of the Ihtishámia Horse, detachments of the State cavalry and infantry, the band of the State troops, and a number of riding elephants. As soon as the camp equipment had arrived, and the tents had been pitched, Muhammad Kudrat Ali, Assistant Revenue Minister, Syad Muhammad Mansab Ali, my Secretary, Munshi Ináyat Ali, *kámdár* of my sons' *deorhi*,

Edward VII., Emperor of India, has declared His Royal intention to celebrate the Solemnity of His Royal Coronation and that of his dearly beloved Consort the Queen upon the twenty-sixth day of June 1902, I now hereby publicly notify under this my hand and seal, as Viceroy and Governor-General of India, that it is my intention to hold at Delhi, on the first day of January 1903, an Imperial Darbar for the purpose of celebrating in His Majesty's Indian dominions this solemn and auspicious event.

"To this Darbar I propose to invite the Governors, Lieutenant-Governors, and Heads of Administrations, from all parts of His Majesty's Indian dominions; the Princes, Chiefs, and Nobles of the Native States under His Majesty's protection; and representatives, both European and Native, of all the Provinces of this great Empire.

"I also hereby notify that I shall forthwith issue such orders in Council as may be suitable to the occasion, and in conformity with the desire that will be felt by all classes of His Majesty's subjects to demonstrate their loyalty by appropriate public ceremonies and rejoicings.

"Dated Calcutta, this fourteenth day of February 1902.

(*Signed*) "CURZON.

"*Viceroy and Governor-General of India.*"

[1] The *kharita* was as follows:

"I have received with the greatest pleasure Your Excellency's *kharita* of the 19th of March, together with a copy of the notification of the Government of India, informing me that a durbar will be held at Delhi on the 1st of January 1903, to commemorate the coronation of His Imperial Majesty Edward VII., Emperor of India, and his beloved Consort, the Queen-Empress. In compliance with His Majesty's wish, I shall gladly avail myself of the honour of attending the said durbar, and of manifesting the loyalty of my house to the British throne."

and Munshi Imám Khán, treasurer of the same *deorhi*, proceeded to Delhi to superintend the decoration and furnishing of the camp. When this had been done, and the above-mentioned officers had returned to Bhopál, I dispatched Munshi Israr Hasan Khán to make the many other arrangements necessary for the accommodation and provisioning of so large a party—a task which he accomplished in a most able manner.

I left Bhopál by special train on December the 24th, and 142 persons accompanied me. My whole retinue consisted of 568 people, but of these, 426 had been sent in advance. Before setting out, I placed the city in the charge of Khán Bahádur Ináyat Husein Khán, and my palaces I left in the hands of the *kámdár* of the *deorhi khάss*. Munshi Syad Kudrat Ali Khán was authorized to carry on the daily business of the administration, and to deal with any urgent matters that might require attention. The written instructions that I left for his guidance are given below.[1] My train left Bhopál at 10.20 a.m., and reached Delhi at eight o'clock the following morning. As it was necessary to walk from the platform to the place where our carriages awaited us, *kanáts* had been erected to screen us from the public gaze. Major Younghusband was present to welcome us, and a guard of honour was drawn up outside the station. We were escorted to the Central India camping ground by a troop of British cavalry, and our arrival was announced by a salute of guns.

[1] "It is my intention, God willing, to proceed to the durbar at Delhi on the *22nd* of Ramazán, 1320 A.H., and my Revenue Minister will accompany me. Until my return, you are, on my behalf, to pass orders on and sign all ordinary and urgent papers that are sent to you by my Secretariat. Papers awaiting my final orders, and such others as do not seem to call for immediate disposal, may be allowed to stand over till my return. Should difficulties arise in regard to any matters of importance, you are to consult with Sheikh Muhammad Khán and Díwán Thákur Parshád, auditors of my Secretariat, before passing orders. Urgent papers requiring my personal attention should be forwarded to me at Delhi, and in cases of special emergency you are to communicate with me by telegram. The appointment or dismissal of *nákiddrs*, sepoys, and other menial servants cannot be regarded as final until my sanction has been obtained. But, to prevent inconvenience, you may make such temporary appointments as you think necessary, pending my approval. On receiving my instructions by mail from Delhi, you are to have my orders written and issued in your presence by the clerks in my Secretariat. Dated 16th Ramazán, 1320 A.H."

The Bhopál camp, which was surrounded by those of other Central India Chiefs, was situated some four miles from the centre of the city; but such excellent arrangements had been made by Munshi Isrár Hasan Khán for the supply of food and other necessaries, that neither I nor any of my retinue suffered the smallest inconvenience. In accordance with instructions received from the supreme Government, all measures necessary for guarding the camp were taken by the State.

On the day of His Excellency's arrival, the Chiefs assembled at the railway station to give him welcome. There is no reason why a Muhammadan lady should not go abroad veiled, if she wishes to do so; yet, up to this time, such had not been my practice; and whenever political officers or other gentlemen came to visit me, I invariably conversed with them from behind a screen. But on this occasion, I had fully made up my mind to don my *burkha*, and join the other Chiefs on the platform. His Excellency, however, foreseeing that I might be exposed to a certain amount of inconvenience, had caused a screened dais to be erected on the right of the seats of the other Chiefs for my accommodation, from which I might witness the arrival without being myself seen. When I reached the station, I was carried to my place in a *palki*. My sons were with me, and when I had taken my seat, they remained on either side of the dais.

At the hour appointed, the special train containing the Viceroy and the Duke of Connaught entered the station. The arrival was announced by a salute of guns, and the military band present played the National Anthem. With great condescension, the Duke and Duchess of Connaught and Lord and Lady Curzon approached my dais, and shook hands with me, and after them, Mr. Bayley and other European officers and ladies came to talk to me. Major Impey introduced a Japanese lady to me, but, as neither of us was able to speak the other's language, we were unable to carry on any conversation. It is at such times as these, that one realizes the loss which inability to converse in other tongues entails. His Excellency drove in procession from the railway station to the camp. I was excused from joining the procession, but the State was represented by two elephants on which Khán Bahádur Munshi Mumtáz Ali Khán and other officials of the State were mounted.

On December the 30th, His Excellency opened the Industrial Exhibition, which formed one of the chief attractions of the durbar week, and which, in the manner of its organization and in its beneficial results, surpassed everything of the kind that had previously been seen in India. My three sons attended the opening ceremony, and the other cards of admission which the Government had sent I gave to the Revenue Minister, Munshi Isrár Hasan Khán, Munshi Ahmad Hasan Khán, and Munshi Ináyat Husein Khán, Muhtamim of the *daftar huzúr*.

The durbar itself took place on the 1st of January. This date happened to coincide with the first of the month Shawwál, on which day the *Id-ul-fitr*, the most important of Islamic festivals, takes place. The Viceroy, therefore, arranged that the durbar should not commence until midday, so that the many Muhammadans who wished to take part in it might have no difficulty in attending the *Id* prayer in the morning. That two events of such happy significance should fall upon one and the same day was indeed a cause for rejoicing. At every *Id* festival the Muhammadan's joy is great, but on this occasion it was well-nigh unbounded, and it emphasized to a peculiar degree the religious aspect of his loyalty to his earthly ruler. My own people said their prayers in the camp mosque. The attendance of women at such services is not obligatory, so I performed my devotions in my own tent.

At a durbar which my Mother attended in Bombay, the question as to whether or not she should be seated behind a *purdah* had given rise to a somewhat lengthy correspondence. Remembering this, the Government now wrote to me suggesting that, if I felt diffident about sitting amongst the other Chiefs, a seat could be arranged for me in a screened portion of the amphitheatre from which other Indian ladies were to watch the proceedings. But this was not my desire; and in my reply, while thanking the Government for their kind suggestion, I stated that, as custom did not oblige me to remain *purdah*, it was my intention to be present in the assembly wearing a *burkha*.

I drove to the durbar accompanied by my two eldest sons, our way taking us past the Mysore and Baroda camps and through Azádpur. My retinue consisted of the State Minister, Bakshi Háfiz Muhammad Khán, C.I.E., Rao Bahádur Thákur Satr-o-sál, Munshi Isrár Hasan Khán, and the State Vakíl, who followed in their respective carriages. Sáhibzáda Hamidullah Khán was considered too young to be present at the durbar, so he did not accompany me.

On entering the amphitheatre, we were received by the Foreign Secretary and the Military Secretary to the Government of India. The seats of the Central India Chiefs were on the left of the viceregal dais, and my own was next to that of the Mahárájah of Orcha. The higher the rank of the chief, the farther he was placed from the dais. Thus, the Mahárájah of Orcha came first, myself next, and then the Mahárájah of Gwálior. On the dais itself, beneath a magnificent canopy, were two massive silver chairs, the seats of the Viceroy and the Duke of Connaught, and in the centre of the amphitheatre waved the Union Jack, the banner of England.

When the Chiefs and other dignitaries, European and Indian, had taken their places, Their Royal Highnesses the Duke and Duchess of Connaught arrived, the former in the uniform of a Field-Marshal, and wearing the orders of the Garter, the Star of India, and the Indian Empire. The whole assembly rose as they entered the amphitheatre. A few minutes later His Excellency the Viceroy arrived, escorted by the Imperial Cadet Corps. He was accompanied by Lady Curzon, and was received with profound demonstrations of respect.

When the assembly was seated, the Foreign Secretary, with His Excellency's permission, declared the durbar open, whereupon Major Maxwell, the chief Herald, read, in a loud voice, the proclamation in accordance with which the durbar had been convened. The band then played the National Anthem, and a salute of a hundred and one guns was fired. After the salute, His Excellency briefly addressed the assembly. His speech, characterized as it was by the eloquence which invariably distinguished his public utterances,

THE CORONATION DURBAR:
A portion of the Amphitheatre.

p. 270]

is too well known to need reproduction. At its conclusion, the Chiefs, rising from their places, approached, one by one, the viceregal dais, and were formally presented to His Excellency. His Highness the Nizám of the Deccan, and the Mahárájah of Baroda, as His Excellency greeted them, offered their congratulations and testified their loyalty.

I, too, left my seat and made my way to the dais, and my two sons were permitted to accompany me. The younger of them, Sáhibzáda Obaidullah Khán, carried a casket containing an address which I desired to present through His Excellency to His Majesty the King. On nearing the dais, I took the casket into my own hands, and then, observing that it was His Excellency's intention to shake hands with me, I turned to give it to the Secretary who had met me, but he had already gone back to bring up the Chief who was following me, so I placed the casket on the dais, and taking His Excellency's hand, offered my humble congratulations. His Excellency, observing the casket, inquired what it was. I replied that it was an address offering, on behalf of myself and of all the Musalmans of India, heartfelt congratulations to His Majesty the King-Emperor on his Coronation, and that I hoped that he would be kind enough to forward it to His Majesty with the fullest assurances of my loyalty and good wishes. My hand remained in His Excellency's the whole time that I was speaking, and when I had finished, Sáhibzáda Obaidalluh took up the casket and presented it. I was then greeted by the Duke of Connaught, and, as I passed on, both the Duchess of Connaught and Lady Curzon leaned forward and shook me by the hand. The address which I presented was as follows:

"I give thanks to Almighty God that, of His great goodness, He has seen fit to place the Indian Empire under the sway of a Power foremost throughout the world for the benevolence and justice of its administration. I give Him thanks also that He has enabled us to celebrate the happy event of Your Majesty's coronation on this the holiest day in our year. In this durbar to-day, the descendants of the warlike and high-spirited Chiefs of India, whose names are famous in the history of their country, are met together to manifest their fealty and submission to the English Throne. I, the Chief of Bhopál, am proud to be amongst them, and to be able thereby to uphold the loyalty which my family has never failed to display towards that Throne, in the service of which my State is ready now, as it has been in the past, to expend its utmost means. On this long-to-be-remembered day, I desire to assure Your Majesty of the loyalty not only of myself, my children, and of every man and woman in my State, but of every Musalman in India, for loyalty and submission to the King who rules over him is one of the strictest duties that his religion enjoins. Lastly, I pray the Almighty God to advance the strength, the dignity, and the dominion of the British Government, and to add many bright jewels to the crown of our beloved Sovereign whose coronation we are celebrating to-day. I pray that his Empire may be long-enduring and prosperous, and that his reign may equal in honour and glory that of the revered and illustrious Queen whom he has succeeded."

When all the Chiefs, of whom there were no less than ninety, had passed before the dais, the durbar terminated.

On the 2nd of January, there was a garden party, followed in the evening by fireworks. The latter had been made in England, and consisted of eighty-one different kinds. I did not go to see the display myself on account of the extreme cold. My sons witnessed it from the Jáma Masjid, and described the scene to me on their return. On the third morning, there was a review of the English troops, and later in the day, in the *diwán-i-ám* of the Delhi fort, a Chapter of the Order of the Star of India was held. According to rule, none were permitted to take part in the Chapter except knights. Many Chiefs were present as spectators ; but as I had not yet received the order of knighthood, and as I had been a ruler for little more than a year, I did not care to be present, although an invitation had been sent to me. On this occasion, Sáhibzáda Hamidullah Khán and the son of the Mahárájah of Cashmere acted as pages to His Excellency.

On January the 7th, a procession took place in the amphitheatre of the troops and retainers of the various Chiefs. It was witnessed by the Viceroy and the Duke of Connaught, as well as by the Chiefs themselves, and all the distinguished

English and Indian officials and visitors who had taken part in the coronation durbar. Mián Afzah Muhammad Khán and Mián Ráof Muhammad Khán, sons of my step-brother, took part in the procession, in the garb of warriors of olden times. They wore steel helmets and complete suits of chain armour, and being both tall and powerful men, they formed a striking feature of the show. The Victoria Lancers were commanded by Major Karím Beg, and the State troops by Bakshi Háfiz Muhammad Hasan Khán, C.I.E. The order of the procession was arranged by the Foreign Office.

On Friday, the 8th of January, a review took place of all the troops present in Delhi, His Excellency Lord Kitchener. Commander-in-Chief of the Indian Forces, being in command. I was unable to attend the review owing to indisposition, and my seat was occupied by Sáhibzáda Hamidullah Khán, who went in the company of the Political Agent. One half of the Bhopál force was commanded by Nawáb Nasrullah Khán, and the other by Sáhibzáda Obaidullah Khán. The total number of troops, British, Indian, and Imperial Service, which took part in this review, exceeded twenty thousand.

On the 9th of January, the Chiefs were entertained at dinner in the viceregal camp, at the close of which the Nizám of the Deccan was presented with the badge of the Order of the Bath. The following day, His Excellency the Viceroy and His Royal Highness the Duke of Connaught left Delhi, and this famous durbar passed into the annals of History.

I and my party left by special train on the 1st of the month Shawwál, and reached Bhopál in safety on the following day. Our arrival was public, and Bakshi Muhammad Faríd Khán, second in command of the State troops, with other officers and sirdars, met us at the station.

In England the date originally fixed for the coronation was the 26th of June, and I had given orders that the event should be celebrated on the same day in Bhopál. A short time beforehand a telegram from the Political Agent announced His Majesty's illness. All our festal plans were, for the time being, abandoned, and, on the 27th of June, the Muhammadans of the city assembled in the Jáma Masjid to pray for their beloved sovereign's recovery. After the lapse of a few weeks, His Majesty, by the grace of God, was restored to health, and it was announced that the postponed ceremony would take place on the 9th of August.

This day was observed as a holiday throughout the State. In the morning, a royal salute of a hundred and one guns was fired from the Fatehgarh fort, and fifteen prisoners, six of whom were under life sentences, were released from jail. In addition, I held a review of the Imperial Service Lancers, the Ihtishámia Horse, and the State army. All the troops wore full-dress uniform and the review terminated with a march past. It was witnessed by my three sons and the leading officers and sirdars of the State. Besides such customary demonstrations, that my poorer subjects might remember the day with gladness, I cancelled a mass of outstanding debts amounting to more than two lákhs of rupees.

On January 1st, in accordance with the instructions I had left before setting out for Delhi, the nobles, *jágírdárs*, and leading officials of the State, assembled in a large tent which had been erected for the purpose in front of the Sadar Manzil. His Majesty's proclamation was read to the audience standing, after which a salute of a hundred and one guns was fired. The proceedings closed with a speech by Munshi Kudrat Ali, setting forth the benefits which the country had enjoyed under British rule. He referred to the friendly connection that had always existed between the State and the English Throne, to which, on behalf of himself and his fellow subjects, he expressed loyal devotion. On this occasion, the offices of the State remained closed for a period of four days, and six prisoners were set at liberty.

CHAPTER VIII

MY FIRST TOUR

After my return from the coronation durbar, I made a tour through the eastern and southern districts of my territory. I took with me the chief officers of my government, so that I might continue without interruption the daily business of the State. Before setting out, I gave instructions that all the roads over which I and my company were to pass should be put into as good order as possible; for, as I mentioned in connection with my sons' tours, the eastern district alone possessed metalled highways, the other portions of the State being traversed by mere cart-tracks, unsuited to any vehicle of a lighter description than a bullock-waggon.

Up to this time, the system by which supplies were obtained during such tours was one that gave to district officials unlimited opportunities for oppressing the villagers. With a view to checking this evil, my Mother issued instructions that her camp should always be accompanied by a bazar maintained by shopkeepers from the city. But this measure proved ineffective, for the major portion of the supplies required by a camp consists necessarily of such articles as can only be procured locally, and through the agency of *tahsíldárs* and other local officials. The price of provisions of this kind the people of the camp never paid, and *tahsíldárs* were too discreet to make any vigorous efforts to recover it. The result was that the unfortunate ryot, who had been forced to produce the supplies in question, and who was too timid to open his lips in protest, sustained a loss, which he, of all men, could ill afford. Loss came to him also from another source. These tours usually took place shortly before the *rabi* harvest; and it can easily be imagined that, at such a time, the passage through the district of a large body of people, with all the *impedimenta* of a camp the size of a small town, is likely, unless the strictest precautions are taken, to result in considerable damage to standing crops. Before I had forfeited my Mother's favour, I used to accompany her on her tours, so that I knew from personal experience, as well as from the complaints that I had so often heard since, that these hardships were not exaggerated, and I determined to do all I could to mitigate them. I gave the matter a great deal of thought, and before I commenced my tour, I caused the following stringent order to be issued:

"By the favour of God, it is my intention to make a tour, during the month of Shawwál, through the eastern and southern portions of my territory, and the chief officers of my government, with their subordinate staffs, will accompany me. These officers are to give strict injunctions to their subordinates and servants that, in the course of this tour, no person is to obtain supplies, either from the camp bazar or locally, without making due payment for the same. Clerks, *chobdárs*, *chuprássis*, and all other servants, are expressly forbidden to receive presents of any kind from *názims*, *tahsíldárs*, *thánadárs*, *mustájirs*, or cultivators, and they are likewise forbidden to gather grain or any other produce from, or to damage in any manner, the fields of the cultivators. Any person wilfully disobeying these orders will be punished with dismissal, and will never again be admitted into the service of the State."

In addition to this order, I gave instructions that all supplies obtained through the agency of *mustájirs*, or other local officials, were to be purchased by the shopkeepers belonging to the camp bazar, by whom alone they were to be sold. The shopkeepers, in the presence of Munshi Isrár Hasan Khán and the head official of the district, were to pay the *mustájirs* for the goods supplied, and to return any surplus that might remain unsold. Any shopkeeper refusing payment, or keeping back surplus supplies, would be very severely dealt with.

During this tour, my main work was connected with the settlement, that is, in determining and granting leases. Khán Bahádur Munshi Mumtáz Ali Khán and Munshi Isrár Hasan

Khán were engaged in the collection of arrears of revenue, and in connection with this also I had to spend a considerable amount of time daily. I deputed my son Nawáb Nasrullah Khán to inspect the offices and buildings of the *táhsíls* and *thánas*, and to submit detailed reports for my information. Such inspection work was very important, but, owing to the duties I have already mentioned, I had not time to carry it out myself. In consequence of the Delhi durbar, my tour had commenced late. The hot weather was fast approaching, and I had determined to complete the inspection of eighteen *mahals* before my return to headquarters. Even after lengthening the ordinary office hours, it was impossible to get through the work of a single *mahal* in less than eight days. My own work occupied me eighteen hours daily. From seven o'clock in the morning till ten o'clock, I received in durbar the officers of the local *táhsíl* and *thána*, and received visits from *jágírdárs*, *mustájirs*, and *muáfidárs*, with whom I discussed all the affairs of the surrounding *mahals*. At ten oclock, I took my morning meal, after which I disposed of the petitions that had been presented to me at the previous durbar. This done, the Revenue Minister came to submit papers dealing with rents and assessments. These papers were endorsed with his own suggestions and opinions, and it remained for me to settle finally the amounts to be demanded, in accordance with which leases were then granted. At two o'clock Díwán Thákur Parshád, whose experience of settlement work dated from the fifteen years' settlement established in the reign of my grandmother, brought me the leases which he had drafted, and in my presence they were delivered to the *mustájirs* concerned. This occupied me till six o'clock; and then Sheikh Muhammad Hasan and Munshi Isrár Hasan Khán came with papers and accounts connected with the collection of arrears. I have spoken in a previous chapter of the state of confusion which these accounts presented when I took charge of the administration. I had now ordered statements to be prepared showing the amounts for which the *mustájirs* themselves acknowledged their liability, and I spent two hours every evening, from six till eight o'clock, in examining these statements. At eight o'clock I took my evening meal, after which, until eleven o'clock, and sometimes until past midnight, I was occupied with correspondence on various State matters, and in devising and directing measures for the suppression of plague, which had, at that time, begun to make its appearance in Bhopál.

When I am on tour, it is always my practice to hold friendly and informal intercourse with the wives and daughters of *mustájirs* and ryots; for in this way I not only give a great deal of pleasure, but I often glean much useful information. As soon as the people of a village become aware of my approach, the women come out in crowds to meet me, with their little ones in their arms, and carrying tiny bowls of water, the sprinkling of which, as they firmly believe, is to bring good fortune to their Chief and protector. As my carriage draws near, they all join together in a song of welcome, which I acknowledge by dropping *bakshish* into their little water vessels. At each new camping ground, the gaily coloured throngs of women, matrons, and maidens, who greet my arrival, rendered glad with *bakshish*, and making the air resound with their happy songs, make a sight well worth the seeing. I have always considered that to give pleasure to these people, and to sympathize with them in their griefs and difficulties, are among my most important duties. To entertain them in my own tents, and to watch their enjoyment, is to me a very real pleasure, and I usually spend the hour of the midday siesta in their company. At such times, they talk to me freely of their families and their circumstances, and their chatter throws many interesting side-lights on the general condition of the district.

On the 14th of Zil-kádah, I halted at Deori for the *Id-uz-zuha*, and proceeded thence to Raisen, where I considerably reduced the size of my camp. My son, Sáhibzáda Obaidullah Khán, met me on my arrival at this place. He spent some hours with me, and then returned to Bhopál, taking Sáhibzáda Hamidullah Khán with him. This was the first time that the latter had ever been separated from me for more than a single day. My other sons had, from time to time, accompanied their father on his shooting expeditions to Samarda and other places, but even they had seldom left me for more than a week at a time. Sáhibzáda Obaidullah Khán had, as yet, no special duties to perform, and being lonely in Bhopál, he had visited me several times during the tour. Between my two younger sons a very strong affection has always existed. The birth of Hamidullah Khán took place fifteen years after that of my next youngest child, Asíf Jahán Begam, and no one took more pleasure in the new arrival than Obaidullah Khán. He was overjoyed to have a baby brother to play with, and from the very first became deeply attached to him.

One night, shortly after their return to Bhopál, they formed the plan of coming to Raisen the next day to pay me another visit. They set out by rail at three o'clock in the afternoon, and, alighting at Guláb-gang station, started in the evening to drive to Raisen. The Mír Munshi, who had been into Bhopál on business, and an old servant of my *deorhi*, by name Akil Khán, were with them. Before reaching Raisen the road crosses the Kori river. The banks of the river are steep, and, at the time of which I am writing, the bridge by which it was crossed had no parapet. The road slopes down to the bridge somewhat sharply, and on reaching this spot the coachman, who was not an experienced driver, lost control of his horses. The night was pitch dark, and as he drove on to the bridge, which was a very narrow one, he lost his direction, and a moment later the entire equipage was precipitated into the river bed thirty feet below. The coachman and both horses were killed on the spot, and the *syce* was too severely injured to be able to render any assistance to the occupants of the carriage, which lay upside down in the dry river bed. The vehicle was a landau, and as the night was cold, both windows had been closed at the commencement of the drive. Sáhibzáda Obaidullah Khán's first thought was for his brother, and in agitated accents, he called out "Hamíd! Hamíd!" The latter was lying unhurt, but too frightened to speak, in the hood of the carriage, where, in the darkness, it was impossible to see him. Still more agitated at getting no reply, Obaidullah Khán forced the glass from the broken window, and, with difficulty extricating himself from the débris, called again, "Hamíd! Hamíd!" By this time Hamidullah had recovered from the first effects of his fright, and he too began to cry out lustily to his brother. In a very few seconds, Obaidullah Khán had taken him in his arms, and, to his unspeakable relief, found that he had escaped uninjured. He now discovered that he himself was bleeding freely from a severe wound in the head, which, in his anxiety for his brother, he had not before been aware of, but which now began to cause him great pain. Having soothed Hamidullah, who wept loudly on finding that his brother was hurt, Obaidullah Khán washed his wound in an adjacent pool of water, and having tied it up as well as he was able, he dispatched a *sowár*, who happened to be passing at the time, to Raisen for assistance. On reaching the camp, the *sowár* roused Nawáb Nasrullah Khán and told him what had happened, and in a few minutes a carriage containing Doctor Wali Muhammad and the Nawáb Sáhib himself was on its way to the scene of the accident. In the meantime, however, another carriage, on its way from the railway station, reached the spot; and in this my two sons set out for the camp. On the way, they met the Nawáb Sáhib, who returned in advance of the others to communicate the news of the accident to me. I had scarcely had time to grasp what had happened when my sons arrived. I was greatly distressed on account of Obaidullah Khán's injury; but I thanked God that it had been no worse, and that Hamidullah was restored to me safe and unhurt.

The Sáhibzáda's wound was dressed by Doctor Wali Muhammad, and a telegram was dispatched to Bhopál to summon Doctor Joshi, the State surgeon. The pain of the wound, which the cold air seemed to increase, was very severe throughout the night. A large fire was kept up in the patient's tent, and towards morning a sleeping draught was administered. When he awoke, he was still in great pain, and it was decided, on account of the cold, to remove him to Bhopál, whither we set out at 10 a.m. on the following day.

I remained in Bhopál four days, and then, seeing that my son was progressing favourably, I returned once more to Raisen, where the Minister and Nawáb Nasrullah Khán had been carrying on the work in my absence. We had been labouring night and day, and only four *mahals* remained to be dealt with, when news came that plague had broken out in the city. The people were in a state of great alarm, on account, not only of the disease, but of the measures that were being taken to stay its progress. This new trouble, and the additional labour involved, combined with the daily increasing heat, began to tell upon my health, and, seeing that the time of the harvest was at hand, I decided to break up my camp, and retire for a month to Samarda, where, in accordance with my instructions, Sáhibzáda Obaidullah Khán had already taken up his quarters. On the same day that I left Raisen, Nawáb Nasrullah Khán departed to Ghairatganj, the headquarters of his own *jágír*, and the Minister returned to Bhopál to direct operations against the plague. After my arrival at Samarda, my son's wound began to heal rapidly, and in twenty-one days from the time of his accident he was entirely recovered. My own health also improved, so that I was able to complete the work connected with the four remaining *mahals* before I left Samarda.

I reached Bhopál on the 17th of Safar, 1321 A.H. Following my instructions, Khán Bahádur Ináyat Husein Khán and the Moin-ul-muhám had carried out the inspection of the remaining *táhsíls* and *thánas*, and their reports were already in my hands. The same officers had, before leaving Raisen, seen to the carrying out of my orders in connection with camp supplies. I was now more than ever convinced of the necessity of touring personally in the various districts of my State. The affairs of every *mahal* that I visited stood in urgent need of reform, and of the personal attention of the ruler. Four thousand six hundred and ninety-nine petitions were presented to me during this tour, and one hundred and two others were received by the Minister. Amongst these there were very few which were undeserving of attention, and on which orders were not passed.

CHAPTER IX

TWO YEARS' ADMINISTRATION

I DO not propose to describe in these pages every detail connected with my administrative duties. I have thought it necessary to write fully of my accession and matters connected therewith, but of my work during the two following years, and of such minor events belonging to that period as appear worth recording, I shall give but a brief summary. For a considerable portion of this period I had to bear alone and unaided the entire burden of the administration. It was the will of the Almighty that this should be so, and that I should, thereby, learn to regard Him as my only helper. For it is written:

"And God suffices as a patron, and sufficient is God as a help."[1]

I had, fortunately, the great advantage of being accustomed to hard work. During my heir-apparency, and all through the years of my Mother's displeasure, I had never allowed myself to fall into habits of idleness. In addition to the management of my own *jágír*, I had devoted my time to reading, needlework, the training of my children, and the general management of my household. No one will deny that moderation is a virtue; but though to do too much may be a vice, it is unquestionably a very much smaller one than to do too little.

If I was no stranger to work, still less was I a stranger to care and anxiety. For twenty-seven years, my mind had never known freedom from trouble, softened though that trouble had been by the affection and sympathy of him who shared it with me. Hence it was that, when I took charge of my new duties, I was neither discouraged nor appalled, as I

[1] Sale's translation of the Korán.

otherwise might have been, by the prospect of the labours and difficulties that lay before me. The main events of these first two years of my reign I have already described. What remains may be summarized as follows:

(1) As soon as the new Minister had been appointed, I consulted him about the settlement. After reading all the papers connected with the scheme, he expressed his agreement with the decision which I, in consultation with the Judicial Minister and others, had come to, namely, that, for the present, a short-term settlement should be carried out, and that during its operation, the records should be corrected and verified, so as to form the basis for a more permanent system to be established at some future date. A period of five years was therefore fixed for the new scheme; and, together with the necessary instructions, I published a list of the remissions which were to be made in each district. This measure gave the greatest satisfaction to the farmers, and many pressing applications for land were made. In carrying it into effect, I received valuable advice from Major Impey, who took a special interest in revenue work, and whose views on all matters connected therewith were invariably sound and far-sighted.

(2) To procure seed grain had always been one of the cultivators' chief difficulties. Their inability to recover payment, or to get any satisfaction out of an appeal to the courts, had forced merchants to give up supplying grain for this purpose. In consequence, advances had to be made by the State, a practice which, owing to mismanagement and oppression on the part of district officials, benefited neither the exchequer nor the agricultural community. This arrangement I cancelled, and I issued an order limiting the rate of interest which *mahájans* were to demand for any grain they advanced, securing for them a legitimate gain without throwing too heavy a burden on the cultivator. At the same time it was notified that applications to the courts, arising out of grain transactions, could be made without the payment of court fees.

(3) A fund was established for the purpose of enabling poor students to study in the Agricultural College at Cawnpore.

(4) The management of reserved and protected forests was

altogether changed, and two new officers were appointed to the department. The right of the villagers to take fire-wood and timber for building purposes remained unaltered. Jungle growing in close proximity to villages was cut down, and many fertile tracts of land were cleared and thrown open to cultivation. Forest rules had been made during Colonel Ward's ministry, but they had never been enforced, and the department had been administered with waste and extravagance, while many of the finest forests in the State had been ruthlessly cut down. With a view to restoring these, and to conserve those that remained, new and strict regulations were framed, and everything possible was done to prevent the funds of the department from being misapplied or misappropriated.

(5) Reforms were made in the Post Office, and new stamps, ranging in value from a quarter of an anna up to one rupee, were issued.

(6) Changes were made in the administration of each of the three *nizámats*. The pay of *tahsíldárs* was increased in proportion to the importance of the *táhsíls* over which they presided. I also appointed a number of *naib* (*i.e.* assistant) *tahsíldárs*, and I endeavoured to select for these posts men who were in receipt of State pensions. I had already inquired into the management of the *síga munásib*, or Pension Department, and I found that its main object was to provide a livelihood for a number of altogether worthless persons. The *mansabdárs*, or pensioners, possessed neither education nor any other qualification for useful work in the world. Their whole lives were spent in idle dissipation, and the only occupation for which they showed any real aptitude was to sit and gossip in their own houses. No one could have blamed me had I, there and then, struck their names off the pay list. I cared little what people might say about me, but I knew that, to men of this stamp, such a course would mean complete ruin. It seemed to me, therefore, that the best thing would be to reduce their stipends and make them do some real work for the remainder. At first the bare idea of work frightened them, and they took every opportunity of shirking and running away. Little by little, however, they began to settle down,

and at the present time there are few amongst them who are not ready and eager to obtain employment, and who are not capable of good and regular work.

(7) That the people of Bhopál had little love for education was only too well known to me; but when I went on tour, and personally inspected the schools of the villages through which I passed, I was shocked at the condition in which I found them. Education on anything like modern lines was non-existent. Its very name seemed to inspire fear. All that it was possible for a student to acquire under the ancient and narrow system of teaching which prevailed was a perfunctory knowledge of the Korán, and the merest smattering of Arabic and Persian. My Mother spent a great deal of money on education, and had the course of oriental study prescribed by the Panjáb University been followed, I have no doubt that considerable progress would have been made. A great many schools were opened throughout the State, and scholarships were founded for the encouragement of students. But the management of such matters was in the hands of men who cared nothing for the work in which they were engaged, and it is, therefore, hardly a matter for surprise that the people showed little desire to make use of the opportunities that were put before them. After my tour was over, I was more than ever convinced that the promotion of education was among the very first of my duties; and, though during these first two years of my reign, few reforms were actually accomplished, extensive plans were put in preparation. What they were, and how they were carried out, I shall describe in a future chapter. I must not omit to mention that in the British cantonment at Sehore there was a good English school, sufficient for all the needs of the town. Since, however, the bulk of the inhabitants were Musalmans, I opened a separate school there for teaching the Korán and other religious books.

(8) The reform of the Judicial Department was not a matter which called for immediate attention. The general incompetency of the *vakíls* who practised in the courts was, perhaps, the most unsatisfactory feature. This was due to the fact that the department imposed no test of efficiency on those who

were allowed to plead, the right to do so being a privilege granted by the Minister to whomsoever he chose. I put an end to this state of affairs by establishing a test which every *vakíl* was obliged to pass, with the result that the old class of pleaders quickly disappeared, and, at the present day, none but qualified men can practise, to the great advantage of the department and of the public of Bhopál.

(9) I have referred in a previous chapter to the police force. The abolition, during my Mother's reign, of the police-stations which had previously existed in the *mufassal* had done much to increase the boldness of criminally disposed persons. During these two years, a number of these stations were re-established in each district, and stringent orders were issued regarding the suppression and detection of crime. The efficacy of these measures may be judged from the fact that, in a single year, the number of crimes reported decreased by 1,582.

(10) There is in Bhopál a church for Roman Catholic Christians. In former times, the priest in charge of it was paid from the *jágír* of Shezád Massih, otherwise known as Balthazar Bourbon.[1] On his death, the payment was continued by his widow Madame Dulhin (at whose instigation the church had been built), and afterwards by her adopted daughter. When the latter died, the *jágír* went to her two sons; and shortly afterwards, when the new administration of *jágírs* came into force, this property reverted to the State, and the sons in question received in its stead a pension of Rs. 4,000 a year. Seeing that the *jágír* now belonged to the State, I sanctioned a permanent grant from State funds for the maintenance of the Roman Catholic priest.

(11) As a result of the reforms in the revenue administration, there was an increase in the receipts for the first year of Rs. 2,72,715, and for the second year of Rs. 6,57,086. At

[1] Balthazar Bourbon, who is referred to in this paragraph, was the son of Salvador Bourbon, who took service in Bhopál in the year 1785. He was descended from Jean Philippe Bourbon of Navarre, a cousin of Henri IV. For a full account of the Bhopál Bourbons, see the *Bhopál State Gazetteer*, pp. 106–8.

the time of my accession, the total expenditure amounted to Rs. 32,85,015. At the end of the second year of my administration it was Rs. 24,37,848, showing a decrease during this period of nearly eight and a half lákhs of rupees.

(12) At the time of my accession, the work of the prisoners in the State jail was confined to the manufacture of rugs and carpets. During these two years, a number of other workshops were opened, and the prisoners were taught to make *daris*, *dosuti*, blankets, *charkhána*, *lungis*, and soap.

In 1320 A.H., plague began to make its appearance in Central India, and alarming reports of its progress were received from Rutlám, Indore, and Hoshangábád. In December 1902, I received information from the Political Agent that some deaths had occurred at Icháwar which gave rise to suspicion. I at once sent Kushál Dás Joshi, Assistant Surgeon, to make investigations. On his return, he reported that the deaths were due to pneumonia. But as plague undoubtedly existed at Narsinghgarh, Rámgarh, and Indore, three States bordering on Bhopál territory, I had little doubt in my own mind that the Assistant Surgeon had mistaken pneumonic plague for ordinary pneumonia. Quarantine regulations were immediately issued, and special officers appointed to see that they were carried into effect. At the same time, precautionary measures began to be enforced in the city of Bhopál and other places. These measures were of a very stringent nature, and caused the greatest alarm amongst the people. As soon as this became known to me, as it very soon did through the numerous petitions that came pouring in, I sent the following urgent order to the Nasír-ul-muhám :

" Your letter, with the petition signed by many nobles and other persons of account has reached me. Similar petitions, bearing the signatures of hundreds of the leading citizens of Bhopál, have also been forwarded to me, and I enclose them for your perusal. From these petitions, it is manifest that the issue of plague regulations has caused the wildest consternation and alarm, and with one voice the people are protesting against the severity of the measures which they imagine are to be enforced. By the favour of the Almighty, there has not been, up to the present time, a single authenticated case of plague in the State, and we trust that the same Divine Power will protect us in the future. Let a proclamation be made assuring the people in my name that they shall be subjected to no treatment which is in any way opposed to their customs, their habits of life, or their religious convictions. In no case shall the regulations enforced be more stringent than those usually adopted during outbreaks of small-pox, or similar epidemics. The rules relating to persons entering or leaving infected areas shall be the same as those that have been in force on previous occasions, and they shall be required to take only such precautions as they are already accustomed to. Let a copy of these instructions be sent to Doctor Kushál Dás Joshi with directions that if, which God forbid, any sign of plague should manifest itself, the matter shall at once be reported to me, and that until both he and the Yunáni doctor, who has had experience of plague in other localities, are assured that the disease is actually present, and until my own express sanction has been obtained, no new regulations shall be brought into operation. Do your best to explain to the people that damp and dirt have been proved by experience to be the most fruitful sources of this disease. Cleanliness is enjoined by the laws of God and the Prophet, and affords the only safe protection. Hence it is incumbent on every person to pay the strictest attention to the condition of his house, his dress, and his person. Make arrangements for the thorough cleansing of every quarter of the city, and daily, and in all humility, make prayer and supplication to God."

It was whilst I was on tour during the following year, that this terrible scourge made its first appearance in the city of Bhopál. Here, too, preventive measures caused more dismay than the disease itself. The people were like little children, terrified at being ill, but far more terrified at the idea of having to swallow bitter medicine.

Special measures were now being taken by the Government of India, and in many places quarantine regulations were in force. In Bhopál every precaution that was taken, every beneficial order that was passed, and every remedy that was recommended, served to increase the general panic. Whilst I was in camp, hundreds of petitions reached me, all betraying the same state of helpless terror. From the way in which they were worded, it was plain that the writers were utterly unnerved by fear. I again sent instructions to the city, pointing out the urgent necessity of allaying the panic and restoring confidence. I also dispatched the Revenue Minister from Ghairatganj, where I was encamped, to Bhopál, that he might render assistance to Sáhibzáda Obaidullah Khán, who was directing operations there. This was not the first plague campaign in which the Minister had taken part, and he was consequently able to devise measures suited to the temperament and condition of the people. Sáhibzáda Obaidullah Khán, in accordance with instructions received from me, met the Political Agent at the Sadar Manzil, and informed him of the steps that had been taken. The latter expressed his approval, and the same day held a meeting at the palace for the purpose of devising fresh plans for the suppression of the disease, and the tranquillization of the people. A second proclamation was issued, which had a very beneficial effect, and at my own suggestion, it was arranged to build camps outside the city for the reception of plague cases.

On reaching Deorhi, I asked Colonel Weir to meet me, and we had a long consultation. He explained to me the great benefit of inoculation; but at that time the newspapers were full of an unfortunate mishap which had occurred in the Panjáb, and this aroused so much fear in the minds of the common people that the adoption of this remedy became a very difficult matter. It must be remembered that for eight years plague had been raging in Bombay, and daily, during this period,tales of distress flew inland in all directions, every additional mile embellishing them with new horrors. Then came the news that the Panjáb was attacked, and, after the Panjáb, Mysore and Allahábád In a few weeks, the disease broke out at Hoshangábád, on the very borders of the State. Rájgarh was attacked, and Narsinghgarh, and cases were reported in Sehore. With every fresh advance, the alarm of the people increased, and when, at last, the dreaded enemy appeared in their very midst, their terror was well-nigh unbounded.

There are certain drugs whose immediate effect is to aggra-

19

vate the pain which they ultimately remove. The action of calamities is somewhat similar: they very often restore the calmness which their approach disperses. As the people of Bhopál were called upon to face a calamity that was altogether new to them, it seemed to me that the wisest plan was to interfere with them as little as possible, and to avoid taking any step which would be likely to feed their agitation. Doctor Weir, to whom I expressed my views, fully agreed with me on this point, and I therefore wrote to Sáhibzáda Obaidullah Khán and told him to adopt only the mildest measures, and I advised him to practise himself the same precautions that he was trying to persuade others to adopt; for nothing does more to reconcile common people to unpleasant regulations than seeing them publicly carried out by their superiors.

One of the most effective means of dealing with an outbreak of plague in a city is to prevail upon the inhabitants to evacuate the affected quarters. I did my utmost to persuade the people of Bhopál to adopt this course, and I wrote as follows on the subject to the Revenue Minister:

"With the assistance of the leading citizens, you are to make it known in every quarter of the town that the health and well-being of the inhabitants is my sole object in urging the adoption of this measure, and that no orders will ever receive my sanction the execution of which would involve injury to their feelings or violate their privacy. Every sick person who vacates his house will be provided with quarters elsewhere for himself and those who have charge of him. The State will supply him with the necessary means of conveyance, and will be responsible for the safety of his house, and any property he may leave in it. Poor people will be given quarters in the Kundha Farhat Afzah, and *purdah* women will be housed within the Farhat Afzah garden. Other houses in Jahángírábád have been cleaned and emptied, among them the Bárah Mahal, Nawáb Manzil, Parden Manzil, and the stables of the *deorhi khâss*, where patients can be accommodated with their relatives and attendants. Let suitable quarters be provided for people of all classes, and let arrangements be made so that medical attendance, both English and Yunáni, may be easily available. I send herewith a list of prominent and influential persons who should be placed in charge of the *mahals* in which they reside, and who should endeavour, by reasoning and persuasion, to reconcile the people to these arrangements. If the names on the list are not sufficient, you may, in consultation with Munshi Kudrat Ali Sáhib, add others. In my name, bid all the people with tears, and repentance, and submission, pray to the God of mercies that this scourge may be removed, not only from their own midst, but from every afflicted city in India. Tell them that although necessity compels me to be away from them, they must not suppose that I am either ignorant of, or indifferent to, their misfortunes, or that a single moment passes in which their health and welfare are not in my mind. Tell them also that at all times my prayers are joined to theirs."

Instructions were issued to the sanitary authorities to spare no expense in coping with the epidemic, and on the advice of the Minister a sum of Rs. 26,000 was placed at their disposal. The Imperial Service Lancers were sent into camp at Islámnagar, about six miles from the city, and urgent orders were issued to the surrounding *tahsíldárs* for the supply of provisions and fodder. A new graveyard was made outside the city for the burial of those who died of plague, and many other active measures were taken to check the spread of infection. But I did not stop here. I caused sacrifices to be offered, and prayers to be made in all the mosques. For every religion which claims to be of divine origin teaches the efficacy of prayer in times of trouble. In the religion of Islám this doctrine is specially emphasized, and all true Musalmans believe that he who remembers God, and goes to Him in his distress, and prays that the burden of his misfortunes may be removed, will have light and comfort poured into his heart. "Shall not men's hearts," says the Prophet, "rest securely in the meditation of God?" The Holy Korán tells us that pure thoughts and a tranquil mind can overcome all ills, and that patience and courage are given to those who submit to His guidance; for, "He directeth whom He pleaseth, and best knoweth those who will submit to be directed." These and many other passages, specially suitable for times of affliction, are to be found in the Korán and in the Sayings of the Prophet, and

I caused a large number of them to be printed and circulated amongst the people.

The outbreak in Hoshangábád was very severe, and the disease began to spread rapidly in the southern district of the State. Several of the *mustájirs*, who came to me in camp to get their leases, were attacked by fever, and within two, or, at the most, three days their deaths were reported to me. In many places that I visited my presence gave the people so much confidence that they laid aside their fears, and readily followed the advice which at every audience or durbar I was careful to give them. Whenever their villages were attacked, they abandoned their houses and took refuge wherever they could find a temporary place of shelter. This plan invariably proved successful, and was soon adopted in every village where the disease broke out. On reaching a new camping-ground, my first inquiry was always the same: "What is the state of your village?" Sometimes I received the answer, "Rám ki día hai," that is, "God has blessed it." At other times the answer would be, "The plague came, but we obeyed the Sirkar's order and left our village, and now God has blessed it." So much did my presence comfort them, that as soon as they heard that I was about to move my camp, they came and implored me not to depart. "Our Mother," they would say, "must not leave us. For twenty years we have been longing to see the Sirkar's face." At the same time, distracted letters would reach me from another village, "Will not the Sirkar come to us? The plague is spreading from house to house." Many and strange were the petitions which these simple and ignorant villagers sent to me. All I could do was to give them such consolation and encouragement as seemed best suited to their understandings, and urge them to listen to the advice that I was sending them.

As reports from the city were daily becoming more unsatisfactory, I determined to return there myself, that I might put some heart into the people, and see that everything possible was being done to help them. But my anxieties proved too much for my health, and I was forced to spend a month at

Samarda for rest and change. Nawáb Nasrullah Khán, as I have already said, retired to his own *jágír* at Diwánganj, about six miles from Samarda, and Sáhibzáda Obaidullah Khán joined me at the latter place with his family. Up to this time, my second son had remained in Bhopál; but the disease had now taken such a hold on the town, that the risk which he ran by staying there was more than a mother's feelings could endure. Moreover, I was anxious that every one who could possibly do so should leave the city, and I hoped that, if my son set the example, others would follow it.

Both the Political Agent and Doctor Weir were desirous that I should not hasten my return to Bhopál. I knew, however, that every day my presence was becoming more necessary. The disease was still raging, and the preventive measures were causing more and more suspicion and discontent. This was due partly to ignorance, but much more to the action of certain ill-disposed persons who, ever on the watch for an opportunity of stirring up the people against their rulers, deliberately set themselves to misrepresent every step that was taken to check the progress of the disease. Amongst ignorant people, false and malicious rumours find ready credence, and in their then state of panic the people of Bhopál were ready to believe anything. To restore confidence and tranquillity, to avoid giving fresh opportunities of slander to evil-minded persons, and, at the same time, to safeguard, as far as possible, the lives of the people, was a task of no small difficulty.

As soon as I had recovered my health, I returned to Bhopál, and took up my residence in the Hayat Afzah garden. I suspended the orders concerning inoculation, the burning of infected houses, and compulsory evacuation. Whitewashing and other means of disinfection were employed where possible, and every measure that the English and Yunáni doctors advised, provided that it could be carried out without offending the people, was given effect to. For the rest, I joined with my subjects in prayer to Him who is greater than all physicians, and, at last, through His infinite mercy, our prayers were answered, and the disease disappeared from our midst as suddenly as it had arrived. My grateful thanks are due to Major Impey and Colonel Weir, not only for the assistance they rendered me at this time, but for the unfailing consideration and sympathy with which they treated my subjects.

THE HAYAT AFZAH GARDEN.

p. 294]

CHAPTER X

THE ANNIVERSARY OF MY ACCESSION

IT has always been the custom in Bhopál to celebrate the anniversary of the ruler's accession, the chief feature on such occasions being a State durbar, in which the nobles and officials assemble to do homage and offer their congratulations to the reigning chief. I was anxious to uphold this ancient custom, and at the same time, if possible, to turn it to some practical account. To this end, I directed that, before the date of the anniversary, every department of the administration should furnish a report of its work during the previous twelve months. These reports it was my intention to review in my durbar speech, and at the same time, or, if necessary, at a second durbar, to make mention of, and to reward the services of such officers as had displayed conspicuous diligence or ability. It had been my intention to celebrate my first anniversary in this fashion, but, as my readers know, the events which preceded it rendered this impossible. It was, therefore, all the more necessary that the second anniversary should be duly observed, especially as the year preceding it had been marked by so many administrative changes and reforms.

Accordingly, on the 17th of Rabi-ul-awwal, at eight o'clock in the morning, I held a durbar at the Sadar Manzil, which was attended by the nobles, *jágírdárs*, and principal civil and military officers of the State. My speech which, owing to the number of subjects I had to refer to, was necessarily long, was as follows:

"I render thanks to Almighty God for the protection which

He has vouchsafed to me during the past two years of my reign, and I pray that He will continue the same during the year that He has permitted me to enter upon to-day. Many of you are aware that when, on the 28th of Safar, 1319 A.H., my revered Mother departed this life, and the government of the State was placed in my hands, the condition of affairs was such as to cause me the gravest anxiety and apprehension. The population of the State had decreased by thirty *per cent.*, and nearly fifty *per cent.* of the lands available for cultivation were lying fallow.[1] All the many gardens created by Nawáb Sikandar Begam, at the cost of much labour and thought, were become, through neglect and bad management, little better than barren wildernesses: irrigation had been abandoned; and, such was the state of the treasury, that little or nothing could be done to relieve the general depression; and not only in agricultural matters, but in every branch of the administration, progress and reform were at a standstill.

"It was with these difficulties in his mind that, at my accession durbar, Colonel Meade, Agent to the Governor-General in Central India, said that 'to restore the government to a state of efficiency, the greatest prudence and foresight will be required. But you have the great satisfaction of knowing that the wise council of Nawáb Ihtishám-ul-mulk will always be at your disposal.' His words gave me great comfort, and I vowed that, by God's help, I would strive to overcome my difficulties and prove myself worthy of the trust to which I had been appointed. Although the untimely death of my beloved husband overwhelmed me in grief, yet it pleased God to keep alive in me the spirit of my forefathers, and to give me strength to cope single-handed with the evils of the administration and the grievances of my people. To complete my loneliness, Maulavi Abdul Jabbar Khán, pleading old age and a desire to retire from active life, resigned his position as Minister of the State.

"The whole government was in need of reorganization, and as it seemed to me practically impossible for a single Minister to exercise effective control over all its branches, revenue,

[1] The Bhopál State has an area of 6,900 square miles. Between the years 1880 and 1902, the portion under cultivation decreased from 2,751 to 1,737 square miles. During the last ten years, a gradual increase has taken place. In the year 1891 the population of the State was 952,486. Ten years later it had fallen to 665,961. (See chapter i. of the *Bhopál State Gazetteer*.)

civil, and military, I determined to revive an old system, and to divide the ministerial office into two parts, and place a separate officer in charge of each. My friends, Mr. Bayley and Major Impey, were both kind enough to approve of my plan, and they have my cordial thanks for the consideration they gave to it. As a result of this division of labour, the work of the ministry is now carried on with greater ease, greater speed, and greater thoroughness. There will, in future, therefore, be two Ministers, the *Moin-ul-muhám* and the *Nasír-ul-muhám*; the former to be in charge of the Revenue Department, and the latter of the Police and the Judicial Department. The office of *Moin-ul-muhám* has been given to Munshi Mumtáz Ali Khán, on two years' probation. He was previously in charge of the administration in the Rámpur State, where he was reported to be a skilful and experienced officer. In consequence, he was selected to fill a similar post in Burhánpur, where the finances were in much the same state of confusion as was the case in Bhopál at the time of my accession. The post of *Nasír-ul-muhám* is still vacant, but I hope that a suitable appointment will be made shortly.

"My investigations into the working of the Revenue Department convinced me that the thirty years' settlement was resulting in heavy loss to the State. Although this settlement had been officially sanctioned, it had been carried out in a most imperfect manner. Very few *mustájirs* had been granted leases, and there were very few applications for land, most of the villages being administered on the *khám* system, with no fixed rate of assessment. These and various other troubles had arisen owing to the fact that the twenty years' settlement had terminated, and no permanent arrangement had taken its place.

"These matters I placed before the *Majlis-i-mashwara* for consideration, and the council came to the conclusion that a long term settlement was highly undesirable. About the same time I read, in the *Government of India Gazette*, Lord Curzon's resolution dealing with the question of land settlement; and the views expressed in this resolution, combined with the opinion of my council, confirmed me in my belief that the long system would prove injurious alike to the cultivator and to the State. At this juncture, Munshi Mumtáz Ali Khán joined his appointment as *Moin-ul-muhám*, and, by his advice, I decided to institute a temporary settlement for five years, and I issued orders accordingly.

" A beginning was made in the southern and eastern districts, and, no sooner was the new system introduced than there was an instant and eager demand for land. Nearly all the *khám* villages were converted, and assessments were fixed, so that *tahsíldárs* could no longer raise or lower them at will. Both the people and the State began to recover from the previous depression, and it is now abundantly clear that, under this system, the cultivator, being relieved of his anxieties, can devote himself with zest to the development of his holding, to the profit both of himself and the State. In establishing this system, Munshi Mumtáz Ali Khán rendered me great assistance, and I hope that, in extending it to the remaining districts, I shall find his services equally valuable. In recognition of the work he has accomplished, I take this opportunity of presenting to him a *khilát* of five pieces, together with this silver inkstand, and a thousand rupees in cash.

" For some years, *mustájirs* had experienced great difficulty in obtaining grain for sowing purposes. Owing to the bankrupt state of the cultivators, *mahájans* refused to supply it, while, through the incompetence and dishonesty of district officials, the State received practically no return for the tons of grain it was forced to advance. At the same time, seeing that the *mahájans* held aloof, other persons began to demand a hundred or a hundred and fifty *per cent.* profit on every transaction. Last year, therefore, instructions were given to Munshi Kudrat Ali Khán, Assistant Revenue Minister, to re-establish the system by which, in former years, advances had been regulated,[1] and to impose a limit of twenty-five *per cent.* on the interest to be demanded. Munshi Kudrat Ali Khán carried out my instructions with ability, and I am quite satisfied with the settlement he has made. For this service, I now present to him a *khilát* of five pieces.

" Munshi Muhammad Altáf Husein, Superintendent of Customs, has been for many years in the service of the State. In the reign of my Grandmother, he received a *khilát* and other favours in reward for good service. For this reason, as well as by the advice of the late Nawáb Sáhib, I reappointed him to his old office which he had given up towards the close of my Mother's reign. By his skilful management the revenue from customs, which had greatly diminished during the time

[1] Advances are usually made in the months of October and November, and are recovered at the time of the *rabi* harvest in March or April. Interest is sometimes paid in cash, but more often in kind.

of his predecessor, has been raised to Rs. 83,000. Such satisfactory work deserves recognition. I therefore present to Munshi Muhammad Altáf Husein a *khilát* of five pieces, and, in addition, he will receive an increase to his salary of Rs. 50 per month.

"Other officers connected with the Revenue Department I must refer to on another occasion, after I have received the reports which are still outstanding. As this is the first occasion on which such reports have been called for, there is, perhaps, some excuse for delay; but I trust that, in future, heads of departments will see that they are submitted with more punctuality.

"In the middle of the last hot weather I sent Nawáb Nasrullah Khán and Sáhibzáda Obaidullah Khán on tours of inspection through all the districts of the State. In the accomplishment of this undertaking they displayed energy, tact, and insight, and they were able to acquaint me with the needs and grievances of the people in every part of my territory. In the course of their tours they heard no less than 2,300 petitions, every one of which was the subject of careful inquiry. Later, I went on tour myself in the southern and eastern districts to inspect personally the condition of the villages and the people. As a result of the tours previously made by my sons, I found the cultivators everywhere happy and contented. By the favour of the Almighty, the season has been a good one, so that these two districts are doubly fortunate. Whilst I was in camp, as you know, plague made its appearance in this city, and I had to concert measures to allay the confusion and alarm which followed upon the outbreak. I also sent Munshi Mumtáz Ali Khán to Bhopál to direct operations and assist in restoring confidence. The people were temporarily reassured by his presence; but the circulation of a number of false and malicious rumours soon reduced them to a worse state of panic than before. At last, to comfort my subjects, and to silence these evil tongues, I had to cut short my tour, and return to Bhopál. I thank God a thousand times that He has had mercy on His servants, so that there is not a trace of the disease left in the city. I earnestly pray that He will continue to protect us from its ravages in the future. I must not forget to offer my thanks to Colonel Weir for the efforts he made, whilst I was still in camp, to quiet the fears of the people, and for the able measures he adopted to meet this terrible emergency. I am equally grateful to Major Impey for his assistance. On many occasions he showed his sympathy for the people by accompanying Colonel Weir on his visits to the plague hospitals. Doctor Kushál Dás Joshi, Hakím Syad Núr-ul-hasan, and Miss Blong, the lady doctor, all rendered valuable service, and Mr. Cook, who was in charge of disinfecting operations, was indefatigable in the discharge of his duties.

"The police stations which were established in the *mufassal* by my Grandmother, and also by my Mother, were afterwards abolished by Maulavi Abdul Jabbar Khán, and in consequence dacoities and cattle thefts became much more numerous than they had hitherto been. These police stations I restored according to the original system, and during the past year the number of serious crimes committed has been comparatively small, and in nearly every case the perpetrators have been captured and brought to justice. I appointed Munshi Abdul Kayúm Khán Superintendent of Police on probation for a year; and so well did he perform his duties that I confirmed him in his post, and increased his salary by Rs. 25 per month. I have every confidence that his work in the future will prove equally worthy of commendation.

"I must not let this occasion pass without referring to that great event which filled with joy the heart of every loyal subject of the Empire—I mean the royal durbar that took place at Delhi to celebrate the Coronation of His Majesty King Edward VII. The graceful and kindly courtesy of Their Royal Highnesses the Duke and Duchess of Connaught and of Their Excellencies Lord and Lady Curzon, who presided over that magnificent assemblage, made an impression on my heart that nothing can ever obliterate. All the arrangements connected with my visit to Delhi were in the hands of Munshi Israr Hasan Khán, and were carried out by him in a manner that left nothing to be desired. This officer also holds the appointment lately created for the collection of arrears of revenue, and, from the reports that he has already submitted to me, I can see that he is rendering the State valuable service. As a mark of my appreciation he is presented with a *khilát* of five pieces.

"I will now pass on to the Military Department. Here also I have to make mention of several officers, chief amongst them being Háfiz Muhammad Hasan Khán, Nasrat Jang, Mír Bakshi of the State army. He is an old and faithful servant of whom the State is justly proud, for he has served no fewer than four successive Begams. In every appointment he has filled he has displayed the same high sense of duty, while loyalty and integrity have characterized all his dealings with the ruler and her Government. During the troubles of the year 1273 A.H. (1857), he gave many proofs of his courage and faithfulness, which were duly recognized by the Government of India, and the medal which was awarded him after the restoration of peace is a mark of the high estimation in which his services were held. He was received with honour at the coronation durbar, and the State had again reason to be proud of her servant. That I, too, may show my appreciation of his high qualities and meritorious services, I present to him with my own hand this *khilát* and sword.

"Rulers of Bhopál in the past have always prided themselves on their faithfulness to the British Throne, and I am proud and thankful to be able to follow in their footsteps. It is a source of great gratification to me that the regiment of Imperial Service cavalry, which is so worthy a memorial of my Mother's loyalty, has had, in my own reign, an opportunity of showing its efficiency. It also gave me the greatest pleasure to learn that the officers who had the honour of being called to take part in the celebration of His Majesty's Coronation in England impressed the people of that country by their soldierly qualities and bearing, and that, at the durbar at Delhi, the Victoria Lancers not only proved themselves to be a smart and highly disciplined body of men, but were able to render valuable assistance to the Government in carrying out the military arrangements of that great ceremony.

"The Victoria Lancers are prepared at any moment to take the field in the service of the Government of India, or the Empire. But it is my desire that, not this regiment only, but all the forces of the State, should be raised to such a standard of efficiency that they may be ready and fit for active service should the need for their assistance ever arise. To this end, I have already commenced the re-organization of two squadrons of State cavalry and two companies of infantry, which I have distinguished by the name, Fauj Ihtirámia. The men composing this force have been carefully selected, and the pay of the *sowárs* has been increased by two rupees *per* month. I have much pleasure in congratulating the officers and men of the Victoria Lancers on the high reputation their regiment has won, and I hope that they will not only maintain this reputation, but will strive day by day to enhance it.

"I close my speech with the prayer that the Almighty God will keep me and my children true to the loyal traditions of our race, that He will teach us to act with wisdom, justice, and sympathy, towards those over whom He has set us in authority, and that He will ever vouchsafe to my State and my people the blessings of prosperity and peace. Amen."

OFFICERS OF THE BHOPAL VICTORIA LANCERS.

p. 302]

CHAPTER XI

THE BIRTH OF BIRJIS JAHAN BEGAM

THE third year of my reign was marked by a very happy event. On the 17th of Rabi-ul-awwal, I received the joyful intelligence that in a few hours I should have the happiness of being a grandmother, for my second son, Sáhibzáda Obaidullah Khán, was about to be blessed with a child. The tidings brought new delight into my heart, which had been well-nigh broken by the cares and sorrows that every succeeding year had brought with it. There are many things in which our human natures take pleasure, but there are no joys more potent to dispel grief than those which have their origin in our children. My readers can well imagine the hope, the fear, and the joy, which filled my heart during the remainder of that day and the night which followed.

At six o'clock the same morning, I had been informed by the State Vakíl that the Political Agent desired to see me on matters of importance, and that he would arrive the next day from Sehore by the morning train. Early on the 18th, therefore, Major Impey drove to the Sadar Manzil. As my little grandchild was expected to arrive every minute, and many *purdah* ladies were assembled in the palace, I received his visit in my private office. After a brief conversation I said to him, "My son, Obaidullah Khán, is preparing to receive a new guest to-day." He expressed great pleasure at the news, and in his turn informed me of a circumstance fraught with, if possible, greater happiness, not to me only, but to my family, and, indeed, to my whole State. He was the bearer, he said, of an autograph letter from His Imperial Majesty King Edward VII., thanking me for the casket and address which I had presented through His Excellency the Viceroy at the Imperial

Durbar, and in which I expressed my loyalty and that of my subjects to the British Throne, and offered my congratulations on His Majesty's coronation. As I took the letter into my hands, I expressed my deep and sincere gratitude for the royal favour thus graciously bestowed upon me. "This is the first time," I said to the Political Agent, "that such an honour has ever been conferred on the State of Bhopál. A *kharíta* from His Excellency the Viceroy is always announced by a salute of thirty-one guns. This is a letter written by the King's own hand. Would it not be fitting to make known so high a favour to my subjects by a royal salute?" The Political Agent told me that this depended entirely on my own will and pleasure. Then, knowing that I should that day have many ceremonial duties to perform, he brought his visit to a close, and having received *'itr* and *pán*, drove back to the Lál Kothi. Immediately he had gone I returned, with the letter in my hand and joy in my heart, to the inner apartments. "Now," I said to myself, "I shall certainly see the face of the child; and this letter shall be the first thing in the world, saving only the presence of Him who protecteth all, to overshadow it."

I was, throughout the day, in a state of considerable anxiety owing to the absence on sick leave of Miss Blong, the lady doctor. She knew my family well, and her kindness had gained her the affection of all classes of the people. She was a noble-minded and sweet-tempered lady, and by her tact and ability had done more to improve the Lady Lansdowne Hospital than any of those who had preceded her. She treated her patients with great kindness, and women of the better class never hesitated to go into hospital, or to persuade their friends to do the same, for they knew that their prejudices would be considered, and their privacy strictly guarded. At this time, Miss Maclaren was acting for Miss Blong. She had not been long qualified, and had come out from England only a month previously. My anxiety was increased by the fact that she was not acquainted with the Urdu language, and I was, consequently, the only person in the palace who could make her understand. When I reached my daughter-in-law's room, I found that Miss Maclaren had already arrived, and within a few moments of my entry Sáhibzádi Birjís Jahán Begam was born. My desire was accomplished, for the royal letter was in my hand, and it was the first thing in the world to cast its shadow upon the head of the new-born child. As I gazed upon my little grand-daughter my eyes filled with tears of gratitude. Love for their children is common to all mothers, be they rich or poor, noble or of low degree. But now this natural affection filled my heart more than it had ever done before. The whole palace was filled with joy, and on all sides blessings and salutations were exchanged. While congratulating my son on his happy fortune, I did not forget to render thanks to God for His mercies.

The eldest child of the holy Prophet was his daughter Fatimah; and hence every pious Musalman regards himself as specially favoured when his first-born is a girl. In my own family, this had been the case for no less than four generations. It seemed like a decree of Providence, and my son's joy was as great as my own. According to custom, orders were given that a salute of five guns should be fired from the Fatehgarh fort. It was arranged that the Political Agent's salute should be fired first, then the royal salute in honour of His Majesty's letter, and lastly, after an interval of five minutes, the salute announcing my granddaughter's birth. This prolonged cannonade commenced at nine o'clock, and for more than half an hour the guns continued to boom forth their glad tidings to the city.

I shall always regard this day as one of the brightest in my life. Nobles, officers of the State, and citizens, came in large numbers to the Sadar Manzil to rejoice with me, and congratulate me on the double blessing which God had bestowed on me, for they felt that the joy and honour which the day had brought belonged not to me only but to themselves as well. As is usual on such occasions, official intimation of the Sáhibzádi's birth was sent to the Political Agent, and to the Agent to the Governor-General in Central India.

Among those who had special cause to be thankful for the events of this day was one Mullah Abdul Husein, who had been dismissed from the service of the State for falsifying accounts. On hearing the joyful news, he came to the gateway of the Sadar Manzil, and, with long and loud lamentations, supplicated my favour. "Was I not the faithful servant of the Sirkar's mother? When the Sirkar was little did I not carry her in my arms, and have I not carried in my arms the Sirkar's children? However unfaithful I have been in the Sirkar's service, yet it is just to remember that I was loyal to the Sirkar's mother. I thank God that I have lived to look on the third generation. Have pity on my old age and remember my past services. Whatever wrongs I have done, I confess them all. In this time of happiness, let me be forgiven." His request was granted, and he was reinstated.

On the 24th of Rabi-ul-awwal, the *akíka* ceremony took place. The day was observed as a public holiday, all the offices being closed. At four o'clock in the afternoon, the Sáhibzádi was carried to the durbar hall of the Sadar Manzil, where were assembled the nobles and chief officials of the State. The proceedings were conducted in the same manner as on the occasion of my own *akíka* ceremony. The centre of the hall was occupied by a silver throne covered with a golden cloth, on which a richly embroidered cushion was placed for the reception of the heroine of the occasion. The Sáhibzádi's head was shaved by Amu Khalífa, and, during the operation, she lay on the lap of Begam Ayah, who seven years before had performed the same office for Sáhibzáda Hamidullah Khán. I myself chose the name Birjís Jahán. According to the custom of the State, five prisoners were released from jail, amongst them being the two sons of Rao Mazbút Singh, a *jágírdár* of Nai Garhia, who, in my Mother's reign, had been sentenced to ten years' imprisonment for dacoity. Six years of this term were still unexpired, but as they were men of good family I trusted that this act of clemency would induce them to lead better lives in the future. In this expectation I was disappointed, as will appear in a later chapter.

On the following day, beneath a large *shamiánah* in the palace square, a feast was given to all those who had attended the *akíka* ceremony, and letters and telegrams were sent to all my European friends acquainting them with these happy occurrences. I received many kind replies; amongst them being letters of most hearty congratulation from Colonel Barr, Mr. Bayley, and Colonel Meade. How intimately Colonel Meade was connected with my family my readers will have seen in previous chapters. That his friendship for us had not lessened since his departure from Bhopál, is manifest from his letter, which ran as follows:

"THE RESIDENCY, BARODA.
"*August 14th*, 1903.

"MY DEAR FRIEND,

"I have had a letter of yours by me for some time, and must no longer delay in writing to you. In the first place I must offer you my most hearty congratulations on the birth of your granddaughter Birjís Jahán. I hope she may grow up wise and good like her illustrious ancestors, including Your Highness yourself. I hope I may have the good fortune to see her, for I have, as you know, met five generations of your family: the Kudsia Begam, the Sikandar Begam, Shah Jahán Begam, Your Highness, and your family. Now this is the sixth generation. That Your Highness's descendants may increase and multiply, and that you may be happy and prosperous, is the wish of all your friends, including Mrs. Meade and myself. . . . Do you intend to proceed to Mecca this year? If so, let me know, and Mrs. Meade and I will go to see you off. We are going to Simla on the 20th for a short visit, and will return here. Now farewell. Mrs. Meade joins in best wishes and kindest remembrances. Give my best salams to your two sons, and believe me,

"Yours Sincerely,
"M. J. MEADE."

Mr. Bayley's letter was no less kind:

"THE RESIDENCY, INDORE.
"*June 18th*, 1903.

"MY DEAR BEGAM SAHIBA,

"Ordinarily I should hesitate to offer my congratulation to the Ruler of a State on the birth of a granddaughter, but ladies have in the past and in the present played such a distinguished part in the history of Bhopál that I feel I can safely tell Your Highness of the great pleasure with which I have just heard from Major Impey of the birth of Sáhibzáda

Obaidullah Khán's daughter, and wish long life and happiness to the new Sáhibzádi and to all your family.

"I have been meaning for some days to thank Your Highness much for your letter of the 1st June. I have, however, put off doing so in the hope of being able to write about the gentlemen whom you named as possibly suitable for the Judicial Assistantship. I made inquiries from the Government of Bengal . . . but the reply was not satisfactory. . . . His Honour the Lieutenant-Governor of Bengal kindly offered to give me names of more suitable candidates, and I have asked him to do so, but have not yet received a reply. I have also made inquiries about Dr. Sirajul Hasan, but no answer has come as yet. As soon as I hear I will write to Major Impey, giving him all particulars. It is, I quite agree with Your Highness, of the utmost importance to get a good Judicial Officer as soon as possible, and I am very sorry that there has been so much delay in the matter.

"I was very glad to hear that you had made so successful a tour, and I am sure that it will have been of great benefit to Your Highness's subjects. I continue to get excellent news of Mrs. Bayley and my daughter, who will, I hope, return to Indore on the 1st November.

"With kindest regards and all good wishes,

"Yours very Sincerely,

(*Signed*) "CHAS. S. BAYLEY."

Those of my readers who have perused the earlier part of this story are fully acquainted with the family troubles and difficulties which darkened so large a part of my life. Nor will they have forgotten the events connected with the marriages of my sons, which cast so heavy a cloud over our happiness on that occasion. It is the natural desire of parents to see their sons and daughters married, and still more pleasing to them is the arrival of grandchildren, for only then do the younger parents realize the depth of the love by which their own lives have been surrounded. After twenty-seven years of grief, I was once again tasting the sweets of happiness. For the first time in my life I had the opportunity of arranging a ceremony in a manner according with my own wishes and with the dignity of my family. The sincere goodwill and enthusiasm displayed by all classes of my subjects gave me the greatest satisfaction. Guns were fired off on all sides, and I was the recipient of a large number of congratulatory odes. Many persons begged that they might be permitted to present *jora*, and with such earnestness did they petition me that I found it almost impossible to deny them. Eventually I accorded permission to a few nobles and men of position to present *jora*, while others were to bring only a *kurta* and *topee*. In every case I stated that extravagance was to be strictly avoided.

In spite of my attempted denial, for a whole month a continuous stream of people arrived with their gifts, and every one of them received entertainment in the hall of the Sadar Manzil. Every noble and official in the State, each according to his means or his inclination, made his presentation. Of all the *jora*, none were more elaborate than those presented by Munshi Mushták Ali Khán, the late Revenue Minister, and Munshi Israr Hasan Khán, Deputy Judicial Minister.

On the 18th of Rajab, Nawáb Nasrullah Khán, with much pomp and magnificence, presented *jora* to me, to his little niece, and to his two brothers. A procession consisting of the State cavalry, a troop of the Victoria Lancers, a regiment of infantry with band, and a number of nobles and State officials riding on elephants, was formed to convey the *jora* to the Sadar Manzil. The Nawáb Sáhib invited me to the Ali Manzil to see the procession start, after which I returned to the Sadar Manzil to await its arrival with my son, Obaidullah Khán. It reached the palace exactly at five o'clock. The majority of those who accompanied it were given seats in the Moti Mahal, while the Nawáb Sáhib, with the more important members of the company, entered the Sadar Manzil. The presentations were then made in the usual ceremonious manner. In addition to her *jora*, Sáhibzádi Birjís Jahán Begam received from her uncle a number of valuable jewels.

On the 19th of Rajab, *jora* were presented by myself and Sáhibzáda Hamidullah Khán. As before, they were carried in procession from the Ali Manzil to the Sadar Manzil. At three o'clock a distinguished company, including a number of ladies, assembled at the former place, where they partook of tea prior to the departure of the procession at four o'clock. The route lay through the Báb Shahi, past the opium go-down and the Pukhta Pul, and thence through the Badwára gate to the palace. Police lined the road on either side, and between each pair of men was a *sowár* of the irregular cavalry. Elephants bearing the *máhi marátib* led the procession, followed by the Imperial Service cavalry. The band of the State troops came next, then a regiment of State infantry. Following this were a number of bullocks laden with fruits, and goats with gilded horns and brightly coloured *jhools.* Behind all these came a double line of tray-bearers carrying the *jora.* An elephant loaded with *khichri* followed the *jora,* and last of all came those who had been invited to take part in the procession, riding on elephants or in gaily decorated carriages. As before, on the arrival of the procession, the chief guests assembled in the Sadar Manzil, and the remainder in the Moti Mahal. The band took up its position in the courtyard, and enlivened the proceedings with bright music.

As soon as every one was seated, I took my place in the assembly, and gave permission for the distribution of *jora* to commence. First of all, Sáhibzáda Obaidullah Khán rose and handed one to Nawáb Nasrullah Khán, after which the latter handed others to his two brothers. Munshi Mansab Ali then called out the names of the other recipients, and as he did so each came forward and received his *jora* from the hands of Munshi Israr Hasan Khán, or the Kámdár of the *deorhi khāss.* Those assembled in the Moti Mahal received theirs from the Naib Kámdár. After all the distributions had been made, flowers and *'itr* and *pán* were distributed. This office was performed by Sáhibzáda Obaidullah Khán, as all present were now his guests, my share in the afternoon's entertainment having ceased at the Ali Manzil.

According to Indian custom, this ceremony, which is called *chhathi,* is usually performed by the bridegroom's maternal grandfather; but in Bhopál it is always undertaken by the mother or the father-in-law. Notwithstanding this, my late husband's family did everything they could to show their joy, and Khurshia Ali Khán and others sent *jora* from Jalálábád to the Sáhibzádas and to Birjís Jahán Begam.

There is little more to be told. A monthly allowance of Rs. 250 was sanctioned for the maintenance of the Sáhibzádi, and *jora* were distributed to the servants of the *deorhi kháss* and the *daftar inshah*. The entire cost of these celebrations amounted to Rs. 6,880.

CHAPTER XII

PROGRESS AND REFORM

To commemorate the great durbar held at Delhi in honour of His Majesty's coronation, the Government conceived the happy idea of presenting gold and silver medals to the principal retainers of ruling chiefs, and to other nobles and persons of distinction, who had attended the durbar. Medals, of which the design had been approved by the King, were accordingly struck, and dispatched to India for distribution. Five of these were sent to the Political Agent for distribution in Bhopál, two of them being for my elder sons, and the remainder for any three of my retainers whom I chose to select. After some consideration, I decided that these three should be awarded to Sáhibzáda Hamidullah Khán, Munshi Mumtáz Ali Khán, Revenue Minister, and Munshi Isrár Hasan Khán. I selected the Sáhibzáda on account of his having acted as page of honour to His Excellency the Viceroy, Munshi Mumtáz Ali Khán on account of his high office, and Munshi Isrár Hasan Khán in consideration of the fact that all the arrangements connected with the visit to Delhi were in his hands, and the comforts and conveniences we enjoyed, both when travelling and while staying in Delhi, were due to his excellent management.

As many of my subjects were anxious to hear the contents of the letter which I had received from His Majesty the King, I arranged to hold a durbar at which, after the presentation of the medals, the royal missive should be read aloud. The ceremony took place at the Sadar Manzil, and Major Impey opened the proceedings with a brief speech, in which he pointed out the unique character and high significance of the Coronation Durbar. He spoke of the loyalty I had displayed in

THE DURBAR MEDAL.

p. 312.

postponing my pilgrimage to Mecca so as to be able to be present in the assembly, and congratulated me on having had the honour of receiving an autograph letter from His Majesty the King. He then presented the medals, after which, my own speech, containing an Urdu translation of His Majesty's letter, was read by the Naib Mír Munshi. It was as follows:

"Major Impey, Ladies and Gentlemen,—First of all, I render thanks to the all-powerful King of Kings who has placed me under the benign protection of the British Government; secondly, I thank that Government for maintaining me, its subject ruler, in honour and dignity more than all my predecessors; and lastly I offer my sincere gratitude to His Majesty King Edward VII. for vouchsafing to accept the address which I presented through his Viceroy at the Delhi Durbar, and for his gracious condescension in writing to me with his own hand to acknowledge my humble tribute, and the sentiments of loyalty I ventured to express. Great as this honour is, I feel that I am honoured still more by the words which His Majesty has deigned to address to me. No occasion could be more suitable than the present for reading to you this royal letter, for it will enable you to realize how abundant is his kindness to those who are his loyal subjects. His Majesty has written as follows:

"'BUCKINGHAM PALACE.
"'*March 30th*, 1903.

"'YOUR HIGHNESS,

"'The address which Your Highness has been kind enough to send on the occasion of my Coronation, has been received by me, and it is with great pleasure that I accept this token of Your devotion and loyalty.

"'Trusting that Your Highness is in the enjoyment of good health,

"'I remain,
"'Your Highness's Sincere friend,
(*Signed*) "'EDWARD R. AND I.

"'HER HIGHNESS THE BEGAM OF BHOPAL.'

"This is the first time that such a mark of favour has been bestowed on a ruler of Bhopál. I shall be very grateful to my friends Mr. Bayley and Major Impey if, through their means, I can convey to His Majesty some idea of the delight and gratitude with which I have received this letter. Perhaps these gentlemen could also inform His Majesty that, on the very day on which his royal communication was placed in my hands, a daughter was born to my son Sáhibzáda Obaidullah Khán, as though Providence had decreed that her birth should take place on a day so signally honoured. I shall always regard my granddaughter Birjís Jahan Begam as one on whom heaven has looked with special favour.

"These medals, which have been sent by the British Government, and which Major Impey has just presented, are yet another instance of that Government's generosity, in return for which it behoves me, and you who have received these medals, to show our heartfelt gratitude to His Majesty the King, to the Government of India, and to His Excellency the Governor-General.

"In conclusion, I pray God to keep me and my children true to the loyal traditions of our ancestors. I pray that Their Majesties the King and Queen may enjoy ever increasing prosperity, and I an ever increasing share of their royal favour."

At the end of this speech, garlands and *'itr* and *pán* were distributed, and the durbar came to an end. Sáhibzáda Hamidullah Khán did not receive his medal at the durbar. As it was awarded in consequence of his having acted as page to His Excellency at the royal Chapter, the Political Agent presented it to him in the evening at a special meeting held at the new Kothi. On receiving it, the Sáhibzáda, who was only seven years old, expressed his thanks in the following little speech, which he read himself:

"I am very thankful to God for allowing me, although I am so young, to receive such a big honour. I had the honour of going to the coronation durbar at Delhi, where His Majesty was represented by the Viceroy of India, and I was made His Excellency's page. To-day, His Majesty has sent me this beautiful medal. I am very grateful indeed to His Majesty and to the Viceroy and to Major Impey. How glad I should be if Major Impey would tell His Majesty and the Viceroy of my gratitude!"

Every one present was astonished that so young a lad was able to face this ordeal without faltering, and his speech was greeted with loud applause. "He has inherited the family gift," I heard Major Impey remark, "and will one day make a good speaker."

All the more urgent administrative reforms having been accomplished, I now had leisure to turn my attention to the Judicial Department. As it is to this branch of the government that people look for the protection of their rights and the redress of their grievances, it is essential that it should be administered by men of experience and ability. It was, of course, impossible to make sweeping changes in every office of the department. I therefore retained, for the time, those officers with whose work I was more or less satisfied, and dismissed or transferred the remainder. The Deputy Judicial Minister was one, Ináyat Husein Khán. He was a pensioner of the British Government, under which he had served as a Deputy Collector; and now, owing to advancing years, his duties were become too heavy for him. Moreover, he had not that knowledge of legal affairs which the holder of such a post ought to possess. To replace him I selected Munshi Isrár Hasan Khán, who, having held the post of Superintendent of Police in the reign of my grandmother, was well acquainted with the people of Bhopál. He had now, for two years, been engaged in the collection of arrears of revenue, and I had every reason to be satisfied with his work. On this account, as well as on account of the services he had rendered to the British Government both as *tahsíldár* and Deputy Collector, I considered him fully qualified for important judicial work. He was appointed on a salary of Rs. 400 a month, and took charge of his duties on the 25th of Rabi-ul-awwal, 1321 A.H. The post of *Sadar-ul-mohám*, or Sessions Judge, before whom a very large number of cases come up for appeal, was given to Mr. Sulaiman, barrister-at-law, and that of City Magistrate, which also demands sound legal knowledge, to Mr. Jamshidji, B.A., B.L.

On the legislative side, my chief reform consisted in the appointment of a Legislative Council. Such a council had existed in my Mother's reign, but the then Minister, Munshi

Imtiyáz Ali Khán, so controlled its powers that it was to all intents and purposes non-existent, nor did it show any signs of returning to life under his successor, Munshi Abdul Jabbar Khán. My grandmother, Nawáb Sikandar Begam, was the first ruler of Bhopál to cause the laws of the State to be codified. Her revenue code, containing rules of assessment for *názims* and *tahsíldárs*, was well suited to the needs of her day, and copies of it are still kept in the offices of every district and *tahsíl*. My Mother, in the early part of her reign, devoted much attention to legislative work. She framed the *Takiat Shah Jaháni*, or laws of Sháh Jahán, for regulating the procedure in the Courts of Justice, which are still in force. For a time, she conducted the revenue administration in accordance with the regulations drawn up in the previous reign. But during that troubled period, when the destinies of the State were controlled by Nawáb Sidik Hasan Khán and Munshi Imtiyáz Ali Khán, the *Dastur-ul-amal*, or revenue code of Nawáb Sikandar Begam, was entirely abandoned, and in its place a set of regulations was drawn up which, in theory, guaranteed prosperity to the cultivator and wealth to the State, but which, when put in practice, brought both cultivator and State to the verge of ruin.

No civil or military codes existed, though from time to time various regulations had been issued. A code was prepared by Munshi Imtiyáz Ali Khán, but it was nothing more than a copy of rules in force in British India. Munshi Abdul Jabbar Khán achieved nothing in this respect beyond issuing a number of miscellaneous regulations. The necessity for a code embodying all the laws in force in the State was, therefore, abundantly manifest, for when the laws of a country are in a state of confusion and fluctuation, there can be neither peace, justice, nor security, for its people. Although I lacked the support of Munshi Mumtáz Ali Khán, I knew that the course I was adopting was the right one, and that no work can be successful which is not carried out on fixed principles. Written and permanent laws undoubtedly limit the powers of those in authority, but there can also be no doubt that they conduce to the security and tranquillity of the community.

Moreover, the policy of investing individuals with uncontrolled authority is one of which I have never approved.

Accordingly, I appointed a special council called the *Majlis-i-mashwara* for the making of laws and regulations, and I selected as its members the ablest and most experienced officers in my service. I was anxious to appoint to this council a certain number of non-official members, men of education and well acquainted with the condition of the people, that they might attend its meetings and take part in its deliberations as representatives of the general public. But, to my great regret, I was unable to find a single person in any way qualified to hold such a position. I then searched amongst the *vakíls* practising in the courts, but even among them I could find no one with the qualifications I looked for. However, I knew that *vakíls* would probably be better acquainted with the people than other non-official members of the community, and that being legal practitioners they must necessarily possess some knowledge of law; so I at last decided to select my non-official members from this class. One of those selected, the late Maulavi Abdul Azíz, was appointed secretary to the Council. The procedure was to be as follows: Any law formulated in my office, or by either the Revenue or Judicial Minister, was to be drafted by a secretary familiar with the subject dealt with, and was then to be placed before the *Majlis-i-mashwara*. After passing through the council, it was to be submitted to me, and after receiving my signature it would become law.

On the 5th of Jumádi-ul-awwal, 1321 A.H., I issued letters of appointment to the members, and before the beginning of the month Safar, in a chamber of the Sadar Manzil, set apart for the purpose, the sittings of the *Majlis-i-mashwara* commenced.

The Yunáni system of medical treatment has been practised in India for centuries past. This system originated with the Muhammadans, and was introduced by them into India, where it greatly developed, and found many able and famous exponents. Unfortunately, it has suffered from the indifference and neglect which, of late years, Muhammadans have shown towards the sciences in general; and, at the present day, its light seems in danger of being extinguished altogether. The country still contains people who, despite the vast progress which Western medical science has made, seek relief from Yunáni medicines, and, in cases of serious illness, put their faith in the diagnosis and treatment of Yunáni doctors. Nevertheless, as I have already said, this science is rapidly disappearing from our midst, and I believe that, if it were not for the existence of a few well-known physicians, it would ere now have become obsolete. I may say that it is due to the efforts and skill of two of these physicians, Hakím Ajmal Khán Sáhib and Hakím Abdul Azíz Khán Sáhib, that I myself am alive at the present day.

In its solicitude for the health of the people, the Government of India has established hospitals in every corner of the land, all of which are under able management. But if, in addition, some support could be given to Yunáni methods, we should have still greater reason to be thankful. This treatment has been followed by the people of Bhopál for many generations, and the State still maintains a Yunáni doctor in every *tahsíl*. Until recently, these were men who had undergone no regular training, nor were they required to possess any special qualifications; hence, very little reliance could be placed on their treatment. Of surgery they were as ignorant as though it had no connection whatever with a doctor's duties; and whenever anything in the nature of a surgical operation was necessary, the patient was handed over to the tender mercies of the local *hajjám*. Nor are they much better educated to-day. They regard their offices as hereditary, and their treatment often does far more harm than good.

Nawáb Ihtishám-ul-mulk took a great interest in medical science, and often spoke with regret of the neglect into which the Yunáni system had fallen, and, had his life been spared, he would, undoubtedly, have done all in his power to revive and advance it. When the untimely death of my daughter Asíf Jahán Begam occurred, I made up my mind to set up some lasting memorial to her. I had turned over many schemes, and at last, remembering how much she suffered, and calling to mind my late husband's projects, I decided to open a memorial school to give instruction in the Yunáni treatment of diseases as well as in surgery, where students might qualify themselves for the appointments mentioned above. It did not take long to carry my scheme into effect, and on the 11th of Jumádi-ul-ákhir, 1321 A.H., the school was opened by my son, Nawáb Nasrullah Khán, in the presence of a large and influential gathering. The proceedings began with an address by Syad Muhammad Núr-ul-hasan, chief Yunáni medical officer, which was as follows:

"It is not so very long ago, that the Yunáni medical system was in a highly flourishing state. To-day, we see its prestige rapidly and steadily declining. If we are content to remain idle, and give no thought to the causes which have led to this decline, we shall very soon find that this valuable science is altogether lost to us; indeed, to many of its secrets we have become strangers already. There are, however, many people who still have faith in the Yunáni treatment, on account both of its simplicity and its safety. The medicines employed are compounded of the properties of fruits, flowers, seeds, roots, and other vegetable products. Narcotics and intoxicants are rigorously excluded, except in cases of the most urgent necessity; even ointments and liniments for outward application are entirely free from such constituents; and should a patient by mistake drink these preparations they will do him no harm; while of other medicines, though he should take twice or thrice the quantity prescribed, no ill effects will ensue. There can be no doubt, therefore, of the simplicity and safety of this system. It deals with the causes, symptoms, and treatment of diseases on fixed and sound principles. But Yunáni doctors are hampered by one serious defect, namely, their inability to perform surgical operations. The subject is fully dealt with in Yunáni literature, but that is of very little advantage if it leads to no practical result.

"If we wish to revive this valuable science and bring its methods up to date, the only way in which we can do so is to provide practical instruction in all its branches, commencing with the very rudiments; and our object must be not only to teach students the use and effect of medicines peculiar to the Yunáni system, but to familiarize them with the many appliances which modern research has placed at the doctor's disposal. It was, as you know, one of the most cherished desires of the late Nawáb Ihtishám-ul-mulk to revive and encourage the study of this science, for, in addition to the interest which he took in other subjects, he made, during the long illness of his beloved daughter, Sáhibzádi Asíf Jahán Begam, a special study of medicine and surgery, according to both Eastern and Western methods. And, being endowed with mental powers of an unusually high order, he acquired so deep a knowledge of these subjects, that his opinion was listened to with respect by English and Yunáni doctors alike, few of whom could diagnose a disease with greater accuracy, or prescribe more effectual treatment. It is a misfortune we shall never cease to regret that he did not live to see the accomplishment of a single one of the many admirable plans he had formed for improving the administration of the State. May God grant rest to his spirit in the gardens of Paradise!

"Of one of these plans we are privileged, through the generosity and energy of our noble ruler—may her prosperity be everlasting!—to see the realization to-day. This school, which is about to be opened, and which is to bear the name Madrissa Tabia Asifia, she has established to perpetuate in the hearts of her people the memory of her beloved daughter, and its object is to provide instruction in and to encourage the study of those branches of medical science of which I have been speaking. May God reward our kind ruler for the boon she is conferring on us, and may He ever add to her wealth and honour!

"I hope that this school will promote with equal success the study of both the Eastern and the Western science, and that it will, thereby, tend to reconcile conflicting opinions, and lead to mutual understanding and co-operation. Teachers in both branches have been appointed, and there will be other persons in charge of the scientific apparatus, the library, and the office. The governing body will consist of Her Highness's three sons, Nawáb Nasrullah Khán, Sáhibzáda Obaidullah Khán, and Sáhibzáda Hamidullah Khán, and all matters relating to its management will be decided in accordance with their views. Doctor Weir, the Agency Surgeon, whose skill and kindness are so well known to us all, and whose attitude towards the Yunáni school has always been one of friendly sympathy, has promised us, from time to time, the benefit of his valuable advice and suggestions. The *madrissa* will be inspected by the Assistant Surgeon of the English Hospital, and by the principal Yunáni doctor. In conclusion, I pray God that, under the fostering care of Her Highness and her three sons, the Madrissa Tabia Asifia may long continue to flourish."

At the conclusion of this address, my son Nawáb Nasrullah Khán spoke as follows:

"I am very grateful to my revered Mother for allowing me to have the honour of opening this useful institution. You will all, I am sure, agree with me that in establishing this school, and thus manifesting her solicitude for the health and welfare of her people, Her Highness has earned our heartfelt gratitude. The purposes for which it has been founded have been admirably explained to you by Hakím Núr-ul-hasan, and I need not, therefore, repeat them. To combine under one roof instruction in both the western and the eastern medical sciences, is a plan which, in the present time, should have for our country the most useful results; and I am sure that every one, no matter what his own opinion of the Yunáni system may be, will sympathize with the objects which the Madrissa Asifia is intended to fulfil. I am very grateful to Colonel Weir for having promised us the assistance of his advice, and I very much regret that urgent business has prevented his being present here to-day.

"As it was largely by the advice of Doctor Kushál Dás and Hakím Núr-ul-hasan that Her Highness decided that the memorial to her daughter should take this form, I trust that both these gentlemen will take an interest in the school, and do all they can to promote its welfare. Since it has been founded in memory of our beloved sister, it is unnecessary for me to say that I and my two brothers will spare no effort to make it a success. In conclusion, I pray that God will vouchsafe to Her Highness continued health and prosperity, and that He will long spare her to rule over us."

About this time, many complaints reached me that the Yunáni medicines procurable in the bazars were of very bad quality. Although regulations were in force against the selling of inferior or adulterated drugs, I thought it better to devise some new means of checking the evil, and I placed the matter for consideration before the *Majlis-i-mashwara*. The Council suggested that a store for the sale of medicines, which should be under the supervision of the principal Yunâni medical officer, should be opened by the State, and advised the selection of some trustworthy person as store-keeper, to whom an advance of Rs. 1,000 should be made to enable him to lay in the necessary stock-in-trade. I approved of this plan, and no time was lost in carrying it into effect. The store became a branch of the Madrissa Tabia Asifia, and, by supplying reliable medicines, soon forced every dealer in the city, who wished to compete with it, to do the same; and I heard no more complaints.

CHAPTER XIII

EDUCATIONAL PROGRESS

FEMALE education is a subject in which I take a deep interest, and I have always resented the unjust attitude which the sterner sex have adopted towards it. The idea of educating girls as well as boys was not new to the people of Bhopál, nor had they ever displayed towards it any serious opposition; but, so far, its application had been limited to the teaching of the Korán, and the rudiments of the Urdu language. Here and there, girls were to be found who had been taught by their fathers or brothers to write. But for a girl to advance beyond this, or to attend a school, was still looked upon as a dangerous innovation. With ideas of this description, I have no sympathy whatever; for I believe that a half-educated person is often in a worse case than one who remains altogether ignorant. A mere smattering of Urdu with nothing to follow it is little better than useless. A girl's education, if begun at all, should be carried far enough to produce some practical result, and, in addition to book-learning, should provide her with a sufficient knowledge of household management and other feminine occupations to make her independent and happy in her future life.

After much consideration, I determined to open a school which should provide instruction on the lines I have indicated. At first, knowing as I did the prejudices of the people, I feared that the daily journey to and from school would prove an insuperable difficulty. Nevertheless, I decided to make known my intention; and for this purpose, on the 1st of Rajab, I called a meeting of the chief State officials and leading citizens, and deputed Munshi Imtiyáz Ali Khán, Minister of the State, to take the chair. When the object of the meeting was explained, many of those present declared themselves in sympathy with it, and several excellent speeches were made, in which the speakers expressed their gratitude to me, as well as their readiness to send their daughters to school. There were others who disapproved; but they remained silent, and finally my scheme was accepted, partly because its advantages were obvious, and partly because it emanated from the ruler of the State. As I had anticipated, the opposers were mainly influenced by *purdah* considerations; but I had already devised means for meeting any difficulties that might arise in this connection, for I recognized as fully as they did the necessity for safeguarding a custom to which Musalmans in every part of the world attach so much importance. A still more formidable obstacle was the difficulty of obtaining qualified teachers. A European mistress was not likely to have that command of the Urdu language which is essential to one who has to teach little children, and even though she possessed the required fluency, her accent could not be as pure, nor her mode of expression as idiomatic, as would be the case with a person speaking her mother tongue. There was yet another difficulty, and that was the absence of any model on which to frame a course of study. The British Government had done all that a generous and sympathetic Government could do to promote female education in India, both by establishing *zenâna* schools, and by promising assistance to similar institutions maintained out of local funds. But the British Government cannot be fully acquainted with the social and religious needs of our race, nor have we any right to expect it to supply them. The framing of a course of study for Musalman women must be the work of the educated section of the Musalman community; nay, more, it must, if it is to be done in a thoroughly satisfactory manner, be the work of a committee formed of educated Musalman women, for the female temperament and character can be understood by women, and by women alone.

Although I knew of no course of study which could serve as a guide to me in my undertaking, I resolved to get the school started; and to make a beginning I caused classes to be opened in a house adjoining the Táj Mahal. In addition to the teaching of the Korán, instruction was to be given in Urdu, arithmetic, geography, and elementary domestic economy. The opening ceremony took place on the 1st of Rajab, 1321 A.H. The school, which was named the Madrissa Sulaimánia, was decorated for the occasion, and the road leading to it was gay with flags and garlands. The guests included the principal Musalman ladies in Bhopál, and most of the girls who were about to enter the school. A number of *jágírdárs* and State officials were also invited, and these were given seats in the *mardána*.

Forty girls attended the school during the first year, all of whom were under ten years of age. There were three teachers, Mughláni Khánim, Nazír Bí, and Zánib Bí. Two of these had been educated in their own homes in Bhopál, and the third came from Delhi. Maulavi Sayad Muhammad Razwi, a respected and worthy servant of the State, was appointed manager. Closed conveyances were provided to take the girls to and from school, and an old and trustworthy sepoy was selected as caretaker. The teachers appointed were sufficient for the needs of the school in its early stages; but the scarcity of qualified mistresses is still the chief difficulty in the way of more advanced study.

From the commencement of my reign, it had always been my desire to set up some form of local self-government, and thus to admit my subjects to a share in the conduct of public affairs. Experience has shown that the adoption of this policy generally tends to the enlightenment and progress of a community, and is regarded as one of the most valuable privileges that a government has to bestow. But if local self-government is to prove a blessing and not a curse, it is essential that the community on whom it is conferred should contain a respectable percentage of educated and capable men.

When, with these ideas in my mind, I passed to the consideration of the people of Bhopál, I was reluctantly forced to the conclusion that there was scarcely one amongst them who could be described as a well-educated man, or who could safely be entrusted with work of an administrative nature. Nevertheless, with a view to awakening in them some interest in matters immediately connected with their own welfare, I issued, before setting out on my pilgrimage to Mecca, a notification appointing a municipal committee to administer the affairs of the city, but with powers sufficiently restricted to prevent any serious mismanagement. At the same time, a Municipal Act was passed defining the powers of the committee, and the nature of the control to be exercised by the ruler of the State.

The city was divided into sixteen circles, each of which was represented by two members, and four other members were chosen to represent the court *vakíls*, the bankers, the State officials, and the *jágírdárs*. Amongst its other duties, the Municipal Committee was responsible for the weekly publication of the State *Gazette*, in which the orders of the government, as well as its own proceedings, were notified. The first number of the *Gazette* was issued on the 17th of October, 1903 (15th Rajab, 1321 A.H.). On my return from Mecca, a full report of the working of the municipality was submitted to me. Considering the short time the committee had existed, the report was more satisfactory than I could have expected.

Previous to my accession, I was given, as I have already mentioned, no share in the affairs of the State, so that I had ample time to devote to the training of my children. In accordance with Muhammadan custom, the education of my youngest son, Sáhibzáda Hamidullah Khán, began when he was four years, four months, and four days old. In many families, such an event would be signalized by great rejoicings, but, in the days of which I am speaking, all the ceremonies in my family were celebrated as quietly and simply as possible ; and on this occasion little else was done beyond distributing presents and sweetmeats amongst the servants of my *deorhi*. The Sáhibzáda's training was commenced in a manner suited to his tender age. The custom, so common in many well-to-do Muhammadan families, of entrusting the early training of children to nurses is one

SAHIBZADA HAMIDULLAH KHAN.

p. 326]

that I have never myself adopted; for, even at the present day, it is impossible to find Indian nurses sufficiently experienced or trustworthy for so responsible a duty. I trained my children partly on old and partly on modern lines, but I never found an Indian tutor capable of taking complete charge of them. Those who taught my two elder sons were men of undoubted attainments, but they were altogether unacquainted with modern methods, and their work would have been attended with little success without the supervision of my husband or myself. No tutor could have given to my second son the training which he received from his father, and it was his father who, though not himself *háfiz*, taught him the greater part of the Holy Korán.

My youngest son's first lesson book was the *Kaidah Baghdádi*, and he received verbal instruction in prayer, fasting, and other religious and moral exercises. The early education of his two elder brothers had been conducted on the same principles, and in his case, as in theirs, the strictest attention was paid to conduct and manners, than which, in the training of the young, nothing is of greater importance. After finishing the *Kaidah Baghdádi*, the Sáhibzáda commenced the *First Urdu Reader*. This I taught him myself, as well as the Korán, which he began to read at the same time. Other text-books soon followed, and finding that I had not leisure to teach them all, I began to look out for an assistant. My choice fell on Maulavi Muhammad Husein Khán, a man of upright character, and well skilled in the interpretation of Persian literature. He had previously read Persian with Sáhibzáda Obaidullah Khán, and his teaching was both sound and thorough. Handwriting Hamidullah Khán learnt from his two brothers, and, after my accession, my husband appointed one, Pandit Deo Dutt, to teach him English. He had by this time finished twenty chapters of the Korán, and, before the death of his father, he had completed the whole book, and had commenced its translation. My public duties had now begun to take up more and more of my time; and, being anxious that my son's education should be conducted in a systematic and regular manner, I appointed Munshi Liákat Ali, M.A., a graduate of the Muir Central College, Allahábád, to teach him English, Urdu, and arithmetic. I still continued to supervise his studies, and he used to come and say his lessons to me whenever I had time to hear him. Lessons in riding and shooting he received from his brothers, and he still continued the study of the Korán.

Nothing does more to strengthen the character of a child and stimulate his faith than to read the Holy Book with a translation. For a considerable time, I undertook entire charge of this branch of my son's training, but after the death of the Nawáb Sáhib, my work increased to such an extent that I was obliged to engage a special teacher. During my journey to Mecca, I again took the work in hand, and together we completed the translation of four chapters. After our return to Bhopál, this work had to give way to other subjects, and though from time to time the Sáhibzáda returned to it for his own pleasure, the book has not yet been finished. I trust the regard which he has for his religion will induce him to complete the translation in the manner I had originally planned.

In spite of the appointment of Munshi Liákat Ali, it did not seem to me that my son was making satisfactory progress. Moreover, I was anxious that his training should be continued on more up-to-date principles than had hitherto been the case. His Excellency Lord Curzon had recently written to me asking my views regarding the education of the sons of chiefs. After perusing this letter, to which I replied as well as I was able, I seriously contemplated sending my son to the Mayo College at Ajmere; but further reflection convinced me that he was still too young for the life at a public school. The Daly College at Indore, which had been founded in memory of Sir Henry Daly, a former Agent to the Governor-General, and which promised so many advantages to the Chiefs of Central India, was just then in a very precarious condition; indeed, there seemed every likelihood that it might have to be closed. Eventually, however, the chiefs awoke to a sense of their responsibilities, and the college was reorganized, and placed on a firm and satisfactory basis. I have no doubt that my son could have been well trained at the Daly College, and that he would have enjoyed there many advantages that private tuition can never supply. But I had to think not only of my own son, but of the sons of the nobles and *jágírdárs* of my State; and I knew that in any efforts I might make for the education of the latter, the example of the Sáhibzáda would be of very real assistance to me.

I determined, as a preliminary measure, to engage the services of an English tutor, and I made many inquiries on the subject amongst my English friends. Major Manners Smith, the Political Agent, recommended the appointment of Mr. C. H. Payne, M.A., a graduate of Merton College, Oxford; but, before anything definite could be decided, Major Manners Smith was transferred to Nepaul, and it was not till some months later, when Captain Luard became Political Agent, that Mr. Payne's appointment was finally settled; and on the 1st of November, 1905, the Sáhibzáda's work under an English tutor commenced.

CHAPTER XIV

THIRD YEAR'S ADMINISTRATION

TOWARDS the close of the previous chapter, I referred to a scheme I had in contemplation for the education of the sons of the nobles and *jágírdárs* of the State. This scheme now took a definite shape; and, on the 25th of Rajab, 1321 A.H. (17th October, 1903), I had the satisfaction of laying the foundation stone of the Alexandra Nobles School. It will not be out of place if I give a brief account of the considerations which led me to found this institution.

As my readers can imagine, it was both a trouble and a grief to me that out of all my subjects, 660,961 in number, I was unable to find a single one who was a graduate of a university; and this, in spite of the fact that, in my Mother's reign, the State had offered free grants to any students who were willing to continue their studies after completing the primary course. Even in the city itself, although there was a High School maintained at considerable cost to the State, there were not two dozen persons who had passed the Matriculation examination.

But it was the backwardness of the upper classes, particularly of the *jágírdárs* and others in receipt of large pensions, that I viewed with the deepest concern. The prejudice which these people displayed against modern education was far stronger than that of any other class of the population; while their bigoted adherence to worn-out customs and ideas, their indolence, and their reckless extravagance on the occasion of marriages and other festivals, was exercising a most baleful influence on the social life of the State.

In the large majority of Native States, near relatives of the ruling prince receive grants of land or money for the maintenance of themselves and their families. As generation succeeds generation, and the kinship between the descendants of the original stipendiary and the ruler becomes more remote, the amount of the maintenance is proportionately decreased, while with every succeeding generation it has to be divided amongst a larger number of claimants. Thus, it is no uncommon thing to find the descendants of a man, who enjoyed a revenue of a lákh of rupees, living on an income of five rupees a month. Nay more, he may even be found in the garb of a beggar, and parading a name once borne by a noble house to advertise his degrading trade. Shameful as such cases are, they are too often regarded with indifference, and the warning which they speak passes unheeded. Idleness and waste are the children of ignorance; and when we think of such circumstances as I have just described, we realize how grateful we ought to be that God has placed our country under the control of a power that is a true friend to learning and enlightenment, and able and willing to do more for us than we are disposed to do for ourselves.

In placing the means of education within reach of the peoples of India, the British Government has not neglected the interests of the ruling chiefs and the aristocracy. Those who are to inherit ruling powers may do well to study at one of the Indian universities, but in their case something more than this is necessary. They require, if they are to administer their States on wise, economic, and just principles, a thorough training in administrative methods. To meet this want, the Government of India established certain colleges specially designed for the sons of chiefs and nobles, and in many ways the scheme has proved a great success. But the course of study at present followed in these colleges, though well suited to those who are to become rulers or to inherit wealthy estates, does not provide an adequate training for younger sons who are not so fortunately situated, and who will have to make their own way in the world.

His Excellency Lord Curzon took a deep interest in all matters affecting the welfare of the chiefs and aristocracy of India. In addition to instituting many reforms in the chiefs' colleges, he established the Imperial Cadet Corps, with the double object of reviving the military spirit for which in the past this class of the community has always been distinguished, and of opening up to the younger sons of noble families a useful and honourable career. Lord Curzon did much for India, but there is nothing for which he will be remembered with greater gratitude than for his work in connection with the chiefs' colleges and the formation of the Cadet Corps.

But the *jágírdárs* of Bhopál showed no inclination to take advantage either of the chiefs' colleges or of the existing means of education which the State afforded, and at times I felt inclined to give way to despair. At last, after much consideration, I decided to establish a special school for the *jágírdár* class, and to send my own son, Sáhibzáda Hamidullah Khán, to be educated in it; for I knew that my enterprise would have little chance of succeeding unless I led the way myself. But for my desire to use my son as an example to my own subjects, I should, in all probability, have sent him to the Daly College at Indore, or to the Chiefs' College at Ajmeer.

The new school, named after our beloved Queen Alexandra, was commenced shortly before I started on my pilgrimage to Mecca. The building was designed by Sir Swinton Jacob, and was estimated to cost Rs. 1,53,241. On the advice of the Political Agent and Mr. Cook, the State Engineer, a site was selected near the Lady Lansdowne Hospital on the road leading to the railway station. A large number of people were invited to witness the laying of the foundation stone. The Honourable Mr. Bayley was, unfortunately, unable to be present; but Major Impey and many other European and Indian friends were kind enough to accept my invitation. The ceremony took place beneath a large *shamiána* gaily decorated with flags and flowers. The road leading to it was also decorated, and was lined on either side by the Imperial Service cavalry and portions of the State cavalry and infantry. The ceremony was performed at five o'clock in the afternoon, and I opened the proceedings with the following speech:

"Ladies and Gentlemen,—The means of progress and

enlightenment which our country enjoys under the benign rule of the British Government is one of heaven's most precious gifts. The unceasing solicitude of that Government for our moral and intellectual development has at last opened our eyes to the true value of education, and made us eager to reap the advantages which its acquirement guarantees. It is to this new light that has been kindled in our hearts that my own desire for the educational progress of my people owes its existence.

Although but a short time has elapsed since my accession, and the greater part of that time has been occupied with administrative work, yet the question of public education has not been lost sight of. Two new schools have been opened: the Madrissa Asifia, which provides instruction in surgery and in the Yunáni and English systems of medicine, and the Madrissa Sulaimánia for the education of the daughters of *jágírdárs* and other well-to-do persons; while steps have been taken to improve the many schools that exist in the State for boys of the poorer class. As yet, however, no satisfactory provision has been made for the sons of nobles and *jágírdárs*, and a school in which a high-class education can be obtained is a very urgent need. It is of such a school, to be called after our beloved Queen Consort, the Alexandra Nobles' School, that I am about to lay the foundation stone to-day. In this school, students will receive a modern education combined with religious and moral instruction, and I trust the system will be fruitful of the best results.

"I desire to express my gratitude to Sir Swinton Jacob for the able manner in which he has executed the design of the building, and to Major Impey and my other friends for their kindness in coming to take part in this ceremony. In conclusion, I pray for the long life and happiness of His Majesty the King, and for the strength and permanency of his government in India."

The foundation stone was a large block of marble. I lowered it to its place by means of a pulley, after which it was fixed in position by Major Impey. *'Itr* and *pán* and garlands were then distributed, and the assembly dispersed.

I will close this chapter by referring briefly to the remaining matters which occupied my attention during the third year of my reign.

(1) The five years' settlement was completed, and remissions were made to *mustájirs* amounting to Rs. 5,55,473. More reforms were made in the Police Force, and the number of district constables was largely increased. Previous to this, two companies of State infantry had been permanently attached to the force, which now numbered 2,500 of all ranks, giving one policeman to every three square miles. The cost of maintenance amounted to Rs. 1,91,268, in addition to which a sum of Rs. 30,000 was sanctioned for the building of police-stations. These arrangements proved very effective, and there was a considerable decrease in the number of crimes reported.

(2) The administration of forests showed very little improvement. The expenditure incurred had been heavy, but the income was still exceedingly low.

(3) Since my grandmother's day, an institution known as the Victoria School had been in existence, in which poor girls of the city were given elementary education and instruction in various handicrafts. This school was in charge of a European lady, Miss Beers, and an assistant named Tara Bai. Amongst other subjects, silk embroidery was taught. This work had lately been introduced from England, and was at this time a favourite occupation in Indian zenánas. Another school was opened by my Mother for orphans, and was called the Madrissa Bilkisi, being in memory of my eldest daughter, Bilkis Jahán Begam. My Mother took the greatest interest in these schools, but during the ascendancy of her later Ministers, they were allowed to fall into a very unsatisfactory condition. When I inspected them after my accession, I found that both maintained a large staff of teachers, while the total number of pupils was less than sixty. I was much grieved at this state of affairs, and I caused the schools to be thoroughly reorganized and placed under new and efficient management.

(4) This year, when I was preparing for my journey to Mecca, plague again made its appearance in Bhopál, to the great alarm of the people. Remedial measures on an extensive scale were taken, and were this time accepted with very little opposition. The people showed no objection to disinfecting

their houses, and many were inoculated. The Municipal Committee took vigorous measures for cleansing the town, and great tact and energy were displayed by Nawáb Nasrullah Khán, who directed operations in my absence. He, Major Impey, and Colonel Weir were all inoculated, and by their example, many others were encouraged to adopt the same precaution.

(5) Grass of a superior quality grows very abundantly in the State of Bhopál, but up to this time, it had been a source of very little profit to the State. With a view to preventing the waste of so much valuable produce, I sent two men to Ambála to receive instruction in the subject of grass-farming.

(6) As I have mentioned in an earlier chapter, the State army lacked both organization and discipline, and, like every other department of the State, was badly in need of reform. This year, the reconstruction of the entire force was taken in hand. A beginning was made with the cavalry. The regiment known as the Surkh Wardi was split up into two parts, which were called thenceforward the Risála Ihtirámia, and the Risála Intizámia. New uniforms, at a cost of Rs. 13,514, were provided, and the *sowárs* of the Risála Ihtirámia received an increment of two rupees a month to their pay.

(7) The engine at the waterworks had for some time required a new boiler, and many of my officials advised me to defray the cost by levying a water tax. Mr. Cook, State Engineer, advocated this tax very strongly. He had been placed in charge of the waterworks by the Nawáb Kudsia Begam, and was, therefore, a very old servant of the State. Indeed, he had passed forty years of his life in Bhopál, and was well acquainted with its history. He understood, too, my financial difficulties, and it was for this reason that he pressed me to levy the tax in question. I refused, however, to consent to the measure, and a sum of Rs. 35,682 was sanctioned from State funds for the purchase of a new boiler.

(8) For the upkeep of district roads and Dák Bungalows a yearly grant of Rs. 27,663 was made, though, during this year, as much as Rs. 32,218 was spent, while a further sum of Rs. 59,603 was devoted to buildings alone.

(9) The experience of the last two years had shown me that the majority of the State offices were in very bad order, and many reforms were needed. I therefore gave my attention to this matter, and in the course of the year, reforms were carried out in the office of the Bakshi-gari and the Accounts Office.

(10) The rate of exchange for Bhopál copper money was constantly varying, which was a source of great trouble to the poorer classes and loss to shopkeepers. This matter also was attended to during the year, and a fixed rate of exchange was established.

(11) I have said before that the state of the Judicial Department was not such as to cause me any serious anxiety. But justice should be administered in such a manner as to inspire complete confidence in the public mind, and before this could be the case, various reforms were called for. I kept a constant watch on the procedure in the different courts, in addition to which I heard, personally, every appeal that was made against the decisions of the Ministers' courts; and, now that the ministerial powers were divided between two officers, it was still more necessary that I should hear such appeals; for my doing so not only reconciled people to the decisions of the lower courts, but it caused those who presided over these courts to exercise greater care in the conduct of cases that came before them. It is, of course, impossible to give a decision that will please both plaintiff and defendant. But the judge who puts aside every consideration save that of doing justice, and gives his judgment accordingly, will certainly succeed in pleasing the community at large.

(12) Not infrequently cases arise which require the issue of a *fatwa*, or ruling from the Korán, and these are referred for decision to the State *Kázi* and *Mufti*. Trouble had often arisen owing to differences of opinion between these two officials, and in such cases it had been customary to refer the question at issue to the ordinary courts, where the decision, though it might be just, lacked the weight of a religious decree. I therefore established, at a cost of Rs. 11,644, a *Majlis-ul-ulámа*, or Court of Theologians, in whose presence all such cases were to be tried, and, in the event of a difference

of opinion between the *Kázi* and *Mufti*, were to be decided by the opinion of the majority.

(13) Though my pilgrimage to Mecca occupied nearly a quarter of this year, some idea of the work I got through may be gathered from the fact that I passed orders on 31,213 papers.

CHAPTER XV

THE *HAJ*

ALTHOUGH I have fully described my performance of the *haj* in *The Story of a Pilgrimage to Hijáz,* I do not feel that any account of my life can be complete which does not contain a reference to this important episode. As my readers know, the desire to visit the shores of Hijáz, and the holy cities of Shírab and Bathah, had long held possession of my mind, and that, but for the durbar in honour of His Majesty's coronation, this desire would have been accomplished in the second year of my reign. Now, however, I had received the definite permission of the Government of India to make the pilgrimage, and nothing remained but to prepare for my departure. With the assistance of His Excellency the Viceroy, Mr. Bayley, Agent to the Governor-General in Central India, and Major Impey, the details of my journey were satisfactorily arranged, and the Turkish Government undertook the responsibility of protecting my caravan in Arabia. I knew that my second son, Sáhibzáda Obaidullah Khán, was anxious to accompany me, and on the 27th of Jamádi-ul-awwal, I sent him the following official communication: "I intend very shortly to go on a pilgrimage to the holy places. If you are willing to accompany me, you will be good enough to send me as early as possible a list of the persons of your *deorhi* whom you propose to take with you, in order that their travelling allowances may be settled, and other necessary arrangements made for them on the journey."

During my absence, the management of the affairs of the State was entrusted to Nawáb Nasrullah Khán, and to facilitate his work, and to enable him to carry on his duties in an efficient manner and with credit to himself, I issued an order defining his powers, and setting forth in detail the procedure to be followed, and the policy to be adopted in all transactions connected with the administration. Special instructions were given in regard to the hearing of appeals, the appointment, transfer, or promotion of State officials, the maintenance of order, the granting of leases and contracts, the management of State funds, correspondence with the supreme Government, and the entertainment of political officers and other distinguished guests.[1] This was the first time in the history of the State that the powers of the Chief had been delegated to the heir-apparent, and I was very anxious that my son should prove himself worthy of the responsible position in which I was placing him.

During the period of my mourning, I made two wills, one dealing with public and the other with private bequests. The sudden death of my husband had reminded me with terrible force of the uncertainty that surrounds our earthly existence. Life perishes as easily as a bubble breaks. He is wise who constantly bears this in mind, and regards the world but as a waiting-room from which, at any moment, he may be summoned to the real life beyond.

> "This life of the world is nothing but a sport and a play; but, verily, the abode of the next world, that is life,—if they did but know!"[2]

When a sudden calamity brings us face to face with the power of God, it is impossible that our hearts should not be filled with awe; we should not be human were it otherwise. But this was not the only reason for my taking this step. The making of a will is commanded as a duty, and in the Sayings of the Prophet it is stated that he who neglects to do so will rise dumb from his grave. The will relating to public bequests was witnessed by the Minister, the *Kázi*, and the *Mufti*; and the two latter, together with my three sons, were appointed its custodians. The private will I entrusted to a

[1] A *verbatim* copy of these instructions is to be found in *The Story of a Pilgrimage to Hijáz*.

[2] The *Qurân*, translated by E. H. Palmer.

confidential officer of my household, with instructions that, in the event of my death, it was to be handed over to Nawáb Nasrullah Khán.

The Government of India kindly deputed Major Macwatt of the Indian Medical Service to accompany me as far as Jedda, and obtained for me several concessions connected with quarantine regulations. By the rules of International Law, I was bound to submit to quarantine, but I was allowed to undergo detention at Bhopál instead of in Bombay, and at Bu Said instead of at Kámrán. I had already sent my own agents to Bombay to engage a steamer for me, but they informed me that they could not hire any boat suited to my purposes for less than one and a half lákhs of rupees. I then obtained permission from the Government of India to entrust the matter to Major Impey. He accordingly went to Bombay, and in conjunction with Captain Goodrich, Director of the Royal Indian Marine Dockyard, who knew every ship connected with the port, a highly satisfactory arrangement was made. When Major Impey came to see me on his return he said, "Your Highness will, I am sure, be glad to learn that the ship that has been engaged is named the *Akbar*, so it must surely be the right ship to take you on your way to the house of Allah Akbar." I answered that the omen was an excellent one, and I hoped that I should have the good fortune to perform the *haj-i-akbar*.[1] A day or two later, Sáhibzáda Obaidullah Khán and Munshi Isrár Hasan Khán went to Bombay to inspect the ship, and to purchase the various necessities for the voyage.

Since the day on which I took the reins of the administration into my hands, I had passed no measure to which I had not given careful consideration, or which I did not think would conduce to the welfare and happiness of my people. But the responsibilities of a personal ruler are heavy; and

[1] Of the many rites connected with the performance of the *haj* none are more essential than those which take place at Arafat on the 9th day of Zil Hijjah. Should this day happen to fall on a Friday, which is always regarded as an auspicious day, the pilgrim is said to have performed the *haj-i-akbar*, or the great pilgrimage.

THE NISHAT AFZAH GARDEN.

p. 340]

being fully conscious of the weaknesses of my human nature, I did not doubt that my administration had been far from blameless. I therefore thought it my duty, before setting out to visit the Holy Shrine, to ask my subjects to pardon any faults which, unwittingly or otherwise, I might have committed. So, on the 14th of Rajab, in the Asifia mosque, built in memory of my daughter, and completed only two weeks previously, I publicly asked my subjects to forgive my shortcomings, and exhorted my Ministers and other officers of the State to deal leniently and justly with my people in my absence. That I received the forgiveness I asked for was manifest from the fervent prayers that were made for my safe return.

Two quarantine camps were made ; one for my followers at Díp, about twelve miles from Bhopál, and the other in the Nishát Afzah garden for myself and my retainers, who numbered about a hundred. We entered this camp on the 27th of Rajab, and on the 2nd of Shábán (October 28th), left by special train for Bombay. This train had been thoroughly disinfected, as had also the carriages attached at Díp containing the remainder of the party, and we reached Bombay the next morning at seven o'clock. We were met by Nawáb Nasrullah Khán, who had gone to Bombay a day before us, the Political Agent, the Secretary to the Government of Bombay, Captain Goodrich, and many European and Indian gentlemen. A guard-of-honour was also present, and a salute was fired from the fort. Our train drew up close to the wharf alongside which the *Akbar* was moored, so that we were able to go on board without further delay. At noon, we left our moorings and dropped anchor in the harbour. Nawáb Nasrullah Khán came on board at four o'clock to bid us farewell, and an hour later the anchor was weighed. Our pilgrimage had commenced, and, chanting the words *Bismillah mujarha o mursáha,*[1] we gazed on the fast receding shores of our native land.

At the time of our departure, Birjis Jahán Begam was just five months old, and she had, perforce, to be left behind. I prayed to God to protect her in my absence, and placed her in the joint charge of Nawáb Nasrullah Khán, Munshi Isrár

[1] *i.e.* "In the name of God we moor it, and in His name we set it afloat."

Hasan Khán, Munshi Mumtáz Ali Khán, Munshi Nasír-ud-dín, and the lady doctor, with instructions that I was to be kept constantly informed as to her welfare. It pained me very much to leave her, but I grieved still more for Sáhibzáda Obaidullah Khán and the Sharia Dulhan, who had chosen to endure the pangs of separation from their beloved child rather than leave me to go on my pilgrimage alone.

Although this was my first experience of a sea voyage, I felt none of the discomforts of sea-sickness ; but many of those who accompanied me, including my second son, suffered considerably.

On the 21st of Shábán, we reached Bu Said, an island opposite to the port of Jedda, where we expected to be put in quarantine. We cast anchor at eleven o'clock in the morning, and the following day Mr. Devey, the British Consul at Jedda, came on board and informed us that, as we were able to show a clean bill of health, he had moved the Sublime Port to forgo the quarantine restrictions ; but it was not until seven days later that Major Macwatt received a letter from the Consul, stating that the exemption had been sanctioned. The next day I received a visit from Ali Yamani Beg, Acting Governor of Jedda, his Deputy, Faík Beg, a medical officer, and a *bim báshi* (*i.e.* a military officer). The Vice-Consul[1] acted as interpreter, and the Governor inquired after my health, and expressed the hope that our voyage had been prosperous. He then told me that His Majesty the Sultan had given strict orders for my safe conduct from Yembu to Medina, and that a detachment of seven hundred troops with two guns was to be placed at my disposal. This force, however, was

[1] At Jedda there is a Muhammadan Vice-Consul, who is appointed by the British Government to assist any Muhammadan subjects of Great Britain who pass through the port on their way to Mecca. At this time, the post was held by Khán Bahádur Muhammad Husein Khán, and I am sorry to say that I heard many complaints against him. He was generally supposed to be in league with the Sharíf of Mecca, and to be responsible for most of the inconveniences which pilgrims had to endure at the hands of the latter and the Sheikhs of Mecca. My own experience certainly justified this supposition, as may be gathered from what I have written in *The Story of a Pilgrimage to Hijáz.*

not due to reach Yembu until the expiration of the period of quarantine, so he suggested that, instead of delaying my departure, I should make up my escort from the troops stationed at Jedda and Yembu.

Sáhibzádas Obaidullah Khán and Hamidullah Khán paid a return visit to the Governor of Jedda on my behalf, and I arranged for the dispatch of fifty of my followers in advance to Mecca. On Friday, the 29th of Shábán (2nd November), having taken on board two hundred Turkish soldiers, we left for Yembu, arriving at noon the next day. I went ashore in a *purdah* boat which, under the directions of Sáhibzáda Obaidullah Khán, the Captain of the *Akbar* had made ready for me. We were received by the Governor, Sadatlu Mustafa Effendi, and a guard-of-honour, and a salute of twenty-one guns was fired by the port battery. According to Turkish military etiquette, it was necessary that I should review the guard-of-honour. To accomplish this I was given a seat in a window from which I could see the men march past. When this had taken place, Major Macwatt made a short speech, in which he said that any steps taken to promote the comfort and secure the safety of Her Highness the Begam of Bhopál would help to strengthen the friendly relations that existed between the British and Turkish Powers. In reply, the Turkish officers gave hearty assurances of their desire to serve the Begam, and to protect her from all dangers.

The next morning, Major and Mrs. Macwatt returned to Jedda; and, a day or two later, my caravan set out for Medina. At the moment of our departure, the officer commanding the escort called his men to attention and spoke to them as follows: "My children, the Begam of Bhopál is a Musalman. She is visiting your country for the purpose of performing the holy pilgrimage. It behoves you, therefore, to do your utmost to serve and protect her. This is the order of your Sultan. See that you acquit yourselves worthily of the task entrusted to you, and remember that by the smallest deviation from duty you will incur the displeasure of your master, and bring discredit on your country." When we were on the march, my palanquin was surrounded by my own soldiers, the Turkish troops marching on the flanks and in the front and rear of the caravan. At night, our camp was surrounded by a ring of sentinels, posted at intervals of ten paces; and each man stood with his rifle loaded and his back to the camp. After gunfire at 9 p.m., no person was allowed to enter or leave the lines.

Whilst we were encamped at Ain-i-hamrah, our caravan was fired upon by a party of Bedouins, and a letter was received from a Bedouin Sheikh threatening to oppose our march to Medina unless his demands for money were gratified. When Sáhibzáda Obaidullah Khán told me of this letter I said, "Life is of more consequence than property; let him have what he asks for." But the Sáhibzáda had plenty of courage, and the idea of submitting to a demand of this nature was by no means to his taste. I told him to consult with Himli Effendi, the officer commanding the escort, which he accordingly did. Himli Effendi was equally opposed to submission, so we determined not to pay a single *pice*. Every preparation was made to ward off an attack, and we passed the night in much anxiety. The course we had adopted was evidently the right one, for the Bedouins, seeing that we were not to be cowed, thought better of their enterprise, and left us unmolested; and in the morning we resumed our march.

The country through which we were passing was mountainous and rocky, and, in consequence, some changes were made in the disposition of our escort. My own body-guard was strengthened, and a sharp look-out was kept on all sides. The men of the advance-guard climbed every hill on either side of our route, and signalled to us with flags when we were to advance. At one o'clock, a number of Bedouins were seen on a rocky emminence in front of us, and a few moments later they commenced firing on us. Sáhibzáda Obaidullah Khán narrowly escaped being hit, and a number of bullets passed close by my palanquin. They continued firing for some time, but fortunately no damage was done. As soon as the danger was past, I sent for Hilmi Effendi and thanked him and his soldiers for the manner in which they had protected us. In reply he said, "Your Highness is a distinguished lady, and the ruler of a State under the protection of the British Empire. We have received orders to guard you and your people, and you must therefore look upon me as your servant, and my men as your children. They will serve and obey Your Highness with the same zeal as your own troops." By sunset we reached Bír Abbas, where we encamped.

On the morning of the 11th Ramazán, my son told me that a Turkish officer with 300 men and a battery of artillery was approaching from Medina to welcome us. I directed him to go forward with two other of my officers and meet them. After formal greetings had been exchanged, the officer in command, being informed that my caravan was close at hand, halted his men and awaited my approach. As soon as my palanquin reached the spot, the soldiers presented arms and the artillery fired a salute of twenty-one guns. The noise of the salute caused no little confusion in the rear part of the caravan, where it was believed that we had been attacked by Bedouins, and many of the men came galloping in our direction, anxious to take part in the supposed affray. After a brief halt, we continued our march to Bír-i-darwesh, and encamped there for the night.

The next day, we came to Bír Ali, where many of my people climbed a high hill and obtained their first sight of Medina. We were all greatly refreshed at this place by a delightful perfume which pervaded the atmosphere, but for which we could discover no means of accounting. A few miles beyond Bír Ali, the holy city came clearly into view. When I first beheld it my heart was filled with rapture, and involuntarily I cried out, *Allah'm sal áli Muhammad o' áli ál Muhammad o bárak o salam.*[1]

At nine o'clock in the evening, we halted at Bír Urwah, which is less than two miles from Medina, and many of the chief people of the city came out to see me. Sáhibzáda Obaidullah Khán was so impatient to visit the Holy Shrine that he set out within an hour of our arrival, and returned at two in the morning. As dangerous tribes were known to be in

[1] *i.e.*, "May God send blessings on Muhammad, his children, and his followers."

the neighbourhood of Bír Urwah, extra precautions were taken for the night, and the sentries were instructed to be more than ever on the alert. At eight in the morning, the son-in-law of the Sheikh-ul-haram, or Guardian of the Holy Places, came to call upon me, and in the course of conversation he told me that His Majesty the Sultan had sent repeated instructions that the Begam of Bhopál was to be rendered every assistance during her sojourn in Medina. We left our camp at nine o'clock, and as we neared the city, many people came out to gaze at us. Soon after starting, we were met by a detachment of Turkish troops, and a company of slaves playing music. Outside the Arab gate, I was welcomed by the Governor of Medina, Izzatlu Hasan Muzafa Pasha. He was accompanied by the Treasurer of the Sacred Haram and a body of troops with artillery and band, and a salute was fired in my honour. Close to the gateway, a tent had been pitched, and here I alighted with the Sáhibzádas, and the chief nobles of Medina were introduced to me. On this occasion I made a short speech, in which I expressed my gratitude to His Majesty the Sultan for the honourable reception I had been accorded in his country, and for the trouble that had been taken to provide for my safety and comfort. I also offered my sincere thanks to the Governor of Medina, to the Sheikh-ul-haram, and to all the other nobles and officers who had shown me courtesy, or rendered me assistance, since my arrival in Arabia. In conclusion, I referred to the valuable services rendered to me by the men who had composed my escort, and to the courage and coolness they had displayed in the face of danger.

When this ceremony was over, I re-entered my palanquin, and my caravan passed through the gateway into the city. We stayed a few moments at the mosque of the Prophet, and then went on to the house which the Sharíf of Mecca had engaged for my residence. This house was a long distance from the Holy Shrine, so, after a few days, I removed to another more conveniently situated, which the Sheikh-ul-haram was kind enough to engage for me. On the fourth day, I visited the Shrine, and performed the essential rites. The Sheikh-ul-haram was good enough to reserve a place for me in the *masjid* somewhat apart from the other women worshippers, and here I said my prayers daily as long as I remained at Medina.

The Sheikh-ul-haram and other distinguished persons invited me to accept their hospitality, and the ladies of their families visited me. The dinners and other entertainments which I attended were for the most part after the European fashion, and I have fully described them in *The Story of a Pilgrimage to Hijáz*.

It had been arranged that I should proceed from Medina to Mecca *viâ* Yembu and Jedda, and arrangements for a steamer to meet me at Yembu had already been made. I now decided that, instead of returning to Yembu, it would be safer to make the journey to Mecca by the Sultani road, and the Sheikh-ul-haram, whom I consulted, was of the same opinion, and advised me to await the arrival of the Syrian *mahmil*,[1] and to accompany the caravan which was about to convey it to Mecca.

The change in my plans was communicated to His Majesty the Sultan, and he at once sent orders to Abdur Rahman Pasha, Keeper of the Sacred Curtain, to make arrangements for my safe conduct. A strong force was detailed for our escort, as the Bedouins on the route were assuming a threatening aspect, and our departure was fixed for the 27th of Zikád. Abdur Rahman Pasha reached Medina on the morning of the 27th. He came to visit me on his arrival, after which I paid a farewell visit to the Holy Shrine, and in the afternoon, having said the *asar* prayer, we set out once more on our travels.

[1] The word *mahmil* signifies a litter borne by a camel. The sacred *mahmil* consists of a square *amári*, or canopied litter, in which is carried the cloth covering for the Caaba. This covering, which is changed once a year, comes annually from Constantinople. It is carried on a camel in a *mahmil*, and is in charge of the Syrian caravan. "The caravan goes first to Arafat, and, after performing the ritual of the *haj*, repairs to the Caaba, when the *mahmil* is placed in the Syrian courtyard. The old covering is then taken off and the new one put on. Of the old covering, the embroidered curtain hanging against the entrance of the Caaba, and the 'waistband' into which the names of the Turkish sovereigns are woven, become the property of the Sharif of Mecca. The residue is distributed equally between the Shaibi Sáhib, the eunuchs, and the servants of the Caaba. Underneath the outer covering of the Caaba there is another inner covering. This is changed only on the accession of a new Sultan." See *The Story of a Pilgrimage to Hijáz*, pp. 120–1, and the illustration on p. 44.

Before leaving Medina, we assumed our pilgrim dress,[1] though this is not usually done until Rabík is reached. During the journey, Abdur Rahman Pasha showed me much kindness, and took every precaution necessary for the safety of our caravan. He begged me to occupy his own tent, which I at first declined to do; but as he made the offer with so much politeness, and evidently considered the arrangement advisable, I felt bound to comply with his wishes, and another tent was made ready for his own accommodation.

Although we had a strong force to guard us, we were by no means free from anxiety. During the first three stages we encountered no dangers of any kind; but, shortly after we had set out on the fourth march, a sudden attack was made on us from a hill overlooking our route, and many bullets came whistling past us. Our escort behaved with great steadiness and courage. The guns were brought to bear on the spots from which the firing proceeded, and the attack lasted for nearly two hours. Finally, the hill was carried by assault, and the Bedouins were dispersed. In this affair, Sulaiman Agha, a Turkish officer who had accompanied us from Jedda, was killed, and we heard that the Bedouins lost several of their number. Before the commencement of the fight, Abdur Rahman Pasha had placed me in his own palanquin, for it was against the Bhopál caravan, and my palanquin in particular, that the attack of the Bedouins was directed. By the grace of God, all my followers came through this danger safely, and, without further adventure, we entered Mecca on Tuesday, the 6th of Zil Hijjah (23rd February, 1904).

His Excellency Ahmad Rátib Pasha, the Vali of Hijjáz, and

[1] The ceremony of putting on the sacred dress, or *ihrám*, is as follows: "After performing the *ghusl* (total ablution) and the *wazu* (partial ablution), the men cover the upper part of their bodies with a sheet, and wrap another round their lower limbs. They keep their heads bare. The women, after bathing and performing ablution, continue to wear their ordinary dress, but do not cover their faces with a veil. The use of perfumes, eating spiced food, paring the nails, oiling and combing the hair, painting the eyes with *surma* (powdered antimony), applying *missi* to the teeth, wearing more ornaments than usual, beautifying the hands with henna, conjugal intercourse, killing any living creature, and indulging in mirth and amusement, are forbidden to those in *ihrám*."—*The Story of a Pilgrimage to Hijáz*, pp. 83-5.

His Highness Aun-ur-rafík Pasha, the Sharíf of Mecca, with a Turkish guard-of-honour, met us outside the city, and a salute was fired. To return this courtesy, I sent my sons the next day to call, on my behalf, on these two personages. Whilst at Mecca, I received visits from the Grand Sharíf and his wife, Abdur Rahman Pasha, Governor of Damascus, Sheikh Muhammad Salih Shaibi, Keeper of the Holy Key, and other persons of importance. The visits of the two former I returned in person. Here, for the first time since our departure, we received letters from Bhopál. On the 8th of Zil Hijjah, I set out for Arafat, and on the 9th, I performed the *haj*. We also made pilgrimages to Mina and Muzdalifa, and, on the 12th, returned to Mecca. I shall not attempt here to describe the origin and significance of the *haj*, as I have dealt with the subject at length in *The Story of a Pilgrimage to Hijáz.* A few words, however, in explanation of this important ceremony will not be out of place.

We are told in the Holy Korán how Abraham was led to a belief in God, how his faith was first awakened by the sun, the moon, and the stars, whose brilliance he ascribed to the power of a Supreme Being, and how, as he watched them disappear, he would cry out from the depths of his heart:

> "Praise be unto Thee; we have no knowledge but what Thou teachest us, for Thou art knowing and wise."[1]

Having found out the unity of God, he taught his faith to the people. He taught also how He should be worshipped, and on the very spot where, in the days of Adam, the first House of God had been raised, he laid the foundation of the Holy Caaba. Since the time of Abraham, the Caaba has been many times reconstructed, but despite the lapse of centuries, and the clouds of ignorance by which, from time to time, the world has been darkened, the custom of the *haj*, which originated with the raising of the first House, has survived, with few modifications, to the present day.

Muhammad—God's peace be upon him!—was born in

[1] Sale's translation of the Korán.

610 A.D., and was a direct descendant of Abraham, the Friend of God. Of the importance in his eyes of the performance of the *haj*, and of the new rites connected therewith, which, through the inspiration of the Almighty, were prescribed by him, a full account is contained in the Holy Korân. Because of these things, and because of the good which accrues from it, both in this world and the next, the pilgrimage to Mecca is regarded by the true Musalman as transcending all other obligations. The *haj* prayers are the same that were uttered by Abraham himself, and the dress of the patriarchal age is the dress of the pilgrims to-day. The meeting together year after year of a vast concourse of people composed of many races, differing from one another in appearance, language, manners, and habits, yet all, from the highest to the lowest, clad in the same humble garb, and all bent upon accomplishing the same holy purpose, is not only a remarkable phenomenon, but one that has a far-reaching influence on the social and political life of the Islamic world.

Our caravan started on its homeward journey on the 22nd of Zil Hijjah. His Excellency Ahmad Rátib Pasha provided us with the necessary military escort, and we reached Jedda in safety on the following day. The *Akbar* lay at anchor in the harbour, and the same *purdah* boat in which we had landed was in readiness, so I, the Sharia Dulhan, and my two sons, went straight on board. The same evening, we telegraphed our safe arrival to Abdur Rahman Pasha, Ahmad Rátib Pasha, and the Sharíf of Mecca.

As I have already mentioned, it had been arranged that we should travel from Medina to Mecca *viâ* Yembu and Jedda, and an Egyptian steamer, the *Behara*, had been chartered for the journey between the two latter places. The change in my plans necessitated the cancelling of the contract for the hire of the *Behara*. This I had been able to accomplish through the kind mediation of His Highness the Khedive, and on the eve of my departure, I requested the British Consul to convey to His Highness my grateful thanks for the assistance he had rendered me.

On the 8th of Muharram (March 20th), the *Akbar* entered

Bombay harbour. Major Impey, Nawáb Nasrullah Khán, with Birjis Jahán Begam, and several of the officials of the State, had come to Bombay to welcome us. Major Impey was the first to come on board and congratulate me on my safe return from the *haj*. He was soon followed by Munshi Isrár Hasan Khán and my little granddaughter. I found the latter looking strong and well, and I rejoiced to find that all the fears I had entertained on her account had proved to be groundless. During my long wanderings, the affairs of the administration, and the knowledge that plague had again made its appearance in Bhopál, had kept my mind in a state of constant anxiety, but my chief concern had always been for the welfare of Birjis Jahán and my son Nawáb Nasrullah Khán. It was not till eight o'clock in the evening that the latter came on board. I described a few of the main features of our pilgrimage to him, and then the three brothers sat together and talked far into the night. In the morning, the *Akbar* was taken alongside the wharf, and at eight o'clock I went ashore. A guard-of-honour was present, and the usual salute was fired.

I had decided to make a short stay in Bombay, so I drove from the wharf to Muzafa Hall, where arrangements had been made for my lodging. Nawáb Nasrullah Khán and forty of my retainers remained with me, and the rest of the party, with Sáhibzáda Obaidullah Khán, left by special train for Bhopál. Whilst in Bombay, I went to see a large weaving factory and various other places of interest. I also received a visit from His Highness the Mahárájah of Baroda.

On Saturday, the 12th of Muharram (April 3rd), I left by special train for Bhopál, where I arrived at three o'clock the next day. Many nobles, *jágirdárs*, and high officials of the State, were present at the railway station, and I received them in the State waiting-room. Nawáb Nasrullah Khán had made grand and extensive preparations for my reception. The whole city was decorated, and the road from the station to the palace was gay with flags and triumphal arches. Special trouble had been taken in the adornment of the Sadar Manzil and the Humáyun Manzil. The State troops, with the *máhi marátib*, conducted me in procession to the palace, and salutes were fired by the artillery and the guns of the Fatehgarh fort. The road along which the procession passed was crowded with spectators, and happiness was apparent on every face. These decorations and the illuminations which took place in the evening were undertaken by the State. The next day, on his own behalf, Nawáb Nasrullah Khán entertained us in a most sumptuous fashion at the Shaukat Mahal, and at night the palace and the adjoining buildings were again illuminated.

On the 27th of Muharram, another procession was formed to convey to the Asifia mosque the sacred relics we had brought back with us from Hijáz. This was the occasion for further rejoicings, and the day terminated with a grand display of fireworks. Thus, in the space of five months and ten days, by the grace and favour of Almighty God, my holy undertaking was successfully accomplished.

THE SHAUKAT MAHAL.

P. 352]

CHAPTER XVI

THE YEAR 1904

ON the very day that I reached Medina, that is, on the 12th of Ramazán, 1321 A.H. (December 2nd, 1903), a son and heir was born in Bhopál to Nawáb Nasrullah Khán. In accordance with the usual custom, a salute of five guns was fired from the Fatehgarh fort, and the State troops assembled in front of the Shaukat Mahal and fired a *feu de joie* in honour of the happy event. The nobles and chief officials also assembled at the palace to offer their congratulations. The tidings were communicated to me by cable, and I was asked to select a name for the new-born child. There is no line of telegraph to Medina, and the cable reached me ten days after its arrival at Jedda, whence it was brought to me by a camel *sowár* dispatched by the British Consul.

When any good fortune befalls a Musalman whilst in the holy city of Medina, he regards himself as specially blessed, and my own joy on the receipt of this welcome news was more than I can describe. I prayed that the child might grow strong and prosper, and I placed an offering of almonds and dates at the holy shrine. The Sáhibzádas too rejoiced greatly, and we all sent telegrams of hearty congratulation.

I chose the name of Habibullah Khán for my new grandson, for the same name had been given to the blessed Prophet himself, in whose holy city I was then sojourning. In the absence of any rapid means of communication, a considerable time elapsed before the cable containing my wishes reached India. By the desire of the grandfather, the *akíka* ceremony took place on the fourteenth day, and was performed in a very simple manner. It is necessary that some name should be given at this time, so the child was called Abdullah. The *akika* ceremony is strictly enjoined by the laws of Islam, and it should take place on the seventh, fourteenth, twenty-first, or fortieth day. For a son, two goats are sacrificed, and for a daughter one; and when the head of the child has been shaved, the hair is weighed against gold, which is distributed amongst the poor. These rites were duly performed, but the rejoicings connected with the ceremony were postponed until my return. My cable arrived on the seventeenth day, and the child was then given the name Muhammad Habibullah Khán.

It was the 17th of Muharram when I entered Bhopál after my return from Hijáz. Family affection is, indeed, a wonderful thing. How my heart expanded with joy when I came back to my dear son and my two grandchildren! I am very thankful to God who, of His goodness, has given me both grandsons and granddaughters. Of the Begams of Bhopál I am the only one whom He has blessed with male issue. I hold myself very fortunate in this earthly life in that He has chosen me for this manifestation of His bounteous kindness, and in my prayers I repeat the words of Hazrat Sulaimán (on whom be peace!):

> "Lord! stir me up that I may be thankful for Thy favour wherewith Thou hast favoured me and my parents; and that I may do right to please Thee; and make it right for me in my offspring; verily, I turn repentant unto Thee; and, verily, I am of those resigned."[1]

Shortly after my return, the nobles and prominent officials of the State assembled at the Sadar Manzil and presented to me addresses of congratulation both on my safe return from my travels, and on the birth of my grandson. All begged permission to present *jora*, and I dealt with this request in the same manner as on the occasion of the birth of Sáhibzádi Birjis Jahán Begam. On the 11th of Rabi-ul-awwal, Sáhibzáda Obaidullah Khán presented *jora* to his little nephew, the proceedings being as grand and ceremonious as when Nawáb Nasrullah Khán made a similar presentation to Birjis Jahán

[1] The *Qurân*, translated by E. H. Palmer.

Begam. On the 12th of the month, the postponed *akíka* festivities took place, and on the 18th, *jora* were presented by myself and Sáhibzáda Hamidullah Khán. All these ceremonies were conducted in the same manner as at the birth of my granddaughter, and for the maintenance of Sáhibzáda Habibullah Khán a monthly allowance of Rs. 250 was sanctioned.

Since my return from Hijáz, I had been anxious for an opportunity of meeting Lord Curzon, and about this time, I learnt that His Excellency was going to England, and that, on his way to Bombay, he would pass through Bhopál. It was arranged that I should meet His Excellency at the railway station; and, on the day appointed, the station buildings were decorated with flags and flowers, and the platform was carpeted with scarlet cloth. A guard-of-honour was provided from the Risála Ihtirámia and the Imperial Service Lancers, and the State band was also in attendance. I awaited His Excellency's arrival in the State waiting-room, and my three sons were with me. There were also present on the platform Syad Nasír-ud-dín Ahmad, Judicial Minister, Munshi Mumtáz Ali Khán, Revenue Minister, Munshi Syad Kudrat Ali, Assistant Revenue Minister, and Munshi Isrár Hasan Khán, Assistant Judicial Minister. The special train reached the station at three o'clock, and His Excellency's saloon stopped immediately in front of my waiting-room, and, as he alighted, the band played the National Anthem, and a salute of thirty-one guns was fired from the Fatehgarh fort. His Excellency shook hands with me; and then, turning towards my youngest son, who was standing near me, said, "I am glad to see my little page." He then entered the waiting-room, where he remained in conversation with me for nearly half an hour, after which he re-embarked on his train, and left for Bombay. As I had just returned from the *haj*, our conversation was mainly on the subject of my travels.

This year, on the happy occasion of his birthday, His Majesty King Edward VII., Emperor of India, conferred upon me the title of Knight, Grand Commander of the Indian Empire, and the fact was notified in a *Gazette Extraordinary*, issued by the Government of India on June 24th, 1904. His Excellency Lord Curzon, Viceroy and Governor-General of India, communicated the news to me by telegram, and I at once dispatched the following reply:

"I thank Your Excellency most heartily for your congratulations, and I beg that Your Excellency will make known my gratitude to His Majesty the King for the honour which he has so graciously bestowed upon me, and which I value most highly."

I desire to say here how warmly I appreciated the many letters and telegrams of congratulation which I received from my friends, both English and Indian, on this occasion, and particularly those from Mr. Dane, Foreign Secretary, General Beatson, Colonel Barr, Resident in Hyderabad, Colonel Robertson, Resident in Mysore, Major Daly, Agent to the Governor-General in Central India, His Highness the Mahárájah Sindhia, the Nawáb of Lohári, Major Manners Smith, Political Agent at Sehore, Mr. Lang, a former Political Agent, and Colonel Weir, Civil Surgeon at Sehore.

I had endeavoured to educate my two elder sons in such a manner as to fit them for the positions they would have to occupy in the world; but, from the first, both displayed a strong inclination for a military career. It was natural that they should inherit the warlike instincts of their race, and the more so as these had been so strongly developed in the person of their own father. My eldest son, seeing that he was heir-apparent, I felt bound to train to the management of civil affairs. The case was different with my second son; and in view of the keen interest he had always taken in anything connected with soldiers and their duties, I formed the intention of entering him in the Imperial Cadet Corps. Colonel Meade was strongly in favour of this course, but circumstances arose which prevented me from putting my plan into execution, though it was some time before I altogether abandoned it.

On my return from Hijáz, I received a *kharíta* from the Government of India on the subject of the Imperial Service Troops, and the idea suggested itself to me that my son could not do better than join this service, as it offered scope for his abilities and tastes, as well as opportunities for displaying his loyalty and devotion to the interests of the Empire. Moreover, I was not entirely satisfied with the condition of the Victoria Lancers, and I was anxious to see the regiment in charge of an officer of true military instincts, and on whom I could place full reliance. In the skirmishes with the Bedouins which had taken place during our journey to Mecca, Sáhibzáda Obaidullah Khán had given ample proof of his courage and coolness in the presence of danger, and as I knew that he possessed the other qualities that I looked for, I decided that he was well fitted to command the Imperial Service Troops in Bhopál. Mr. Bayley and Major Manners Smith gave the proposal their hearty approval, and at once entered into correspondence on the subject with the supreme Government. Lord Ampthill, who, in the absence of Lord Curzon, was acting as Viceroy of India, expressed his cordial appreciation of the step I contemplated, and readily accorded his sanction; and, on August 24th, 1904, I was officially informed by Mr. Bayley that Sáhibzáda Háfiz Háji Muhammad Obaidullah Khán Sáhib Bahádur was appointed Honorary Colonel of the Imperial Service Cavalry in Bhopál.

To show the satisfaction which this announcement gave me, and to give some encouragement to the young Colonel, I held a state durbar in honour of his appointment. Twenty-seven European ladies and gentlemen accepted my invitation to be present on the occasion, amongst them being the Honourable Mr. Bayley, General Beatson, Inspector-General of Imperial Service Troops, Major Manners Smith, V.C., Political Agent, and Major Stainforth, Inspecting Officer of Imperial Service Troops in Central India. The durbar was also attended by the officers of the State army, and a large number of nobles and State officials. Mr. Bayley reached Bhopál at eight o'clock in the morning, and although his arrival was private, there was a guard-of-honour on the platform of the railway station, and an escort was provided by the Ihtirámia Horse, and the Victoria Lancers. Munshi Mumtáz Ali Khán and Munshi Nasír-ud-dín Ahmad, the Judicial Minister, welcomed him on behalf of the

State, and conducted him to the Lál Kothi. Here a second guard-of-honour was stationed, and presented arms as the carriage drove up to the entrance, and a salute of twenty-one guns was fired from the Fathgarh fort.

At eleven o'clock, Mr. Bayley and the other European guests proceeded to the Sadar Manzil, and on their arrival at the palace a salute was again fired. At the first gateway they were received by Sáhibzáda Obaidullah Khán, and at the entrance to the durbar hall by Nawáb Nasrullah Khán. The arrangements of the durbar had been admirably carried out by Munshi Isrár Hasan Khán, under the supervision of the Nawáb Sáhib. The ladies were accommodated in the arched gallery overlooking the hall. My own seat was in a screened doorway connecting the hall with an inner apartment. On my right were the seats of the European officers and the officers of the State army, the former in the first row, and the latter in the second. On my left were my three sons, the Revenue and Judicial Ministers, and the *sirdars* and officers of the State.

When all were assembled, I opened the proceedings with the following brief speech:

"Mr. Bayley, Ladies and Gentlemen,—My chief object in holding this durbar is to manifest my appreciation of the permission which, at the instance of my kind friends Mr. Bayley and Major Manners Smith, has been accorded me by His Excellency the Viceroy to appoint my son, Sáhibzáda Muhammad Obaidullah Khán, Colonel of the Imperial Service Troops in Bhopál. Although the regiment of Lancers which the State maintains was established in the reign of Nawáb Shah Jahán Begam, yet, having no male issue, my Mother never experienced the feelings of pride and pleasure which are mine to-day. I give thanks to God that He has vouchsafed to me the privilege of dedicating a son of my own to the service of the British Government, and I pray that he may never cease to do his duty in that service with loyalty and devotion. For the double boon which the Government has conferred upon me, first by acknowledging my eldest son, Nawáb Nasrullah Khán, to be heir-apparent, and granting him the title of Nawáb, and now by permitting me to appoint my second son to an important post in its service, my gratitude is more than I can express. I desire to acknowledge my indebtedness to Mr. Bayley and Major Manners Smith for so ably representing my proposal to His Excellency the Viceroy, and for obtaining for it His Excellency's approbation and sanction. I also desire to thank them for honouring me with their company at the marriage festival of my sons, and again on this occasion. I am equally indebted to General Beatson for his kindness in coming to take part in these festivities, and thereby adding largely to our pleasure.

"To complete this ceremony in a fitting manner, I now direct Nawáb Nasrullah Khán, on my behalf, to fasten to his brother's waist the sword which, as the emblem of bravery, I now present to him to mark the commencement of his military career. From this day forward, Sáhibzáda Obaidullah Khán will hold the rank of Colonel commanding the Bhopál Victoria Lancers, and all matters connected with the regiment will be referred to him for orders. I trust that, with God's help, he will prove himself an efficient servant and loyal defender of the British throne."

As soon as I had finished speaking, Mián Ikbál Muhammad Khán, an officer of my body-guard, handed to Nawáb Nasrullah Khán a sword, the hilt of which, as well as the scabbard, was set with precious stones.[1] The Nawáb Sáhib took it and fastened the belt about his brother's waist, and then handed to him the letter announcing his appointment. When this had been done, Sáhibzáda Colonel Obaidullah Khán rose and said:

"I have not words to thank Your Highness for nominating me for the office of Colonel of the Imperial Service Troops in Bhopál, and for the opportunity thus afforded me of proving my loyalty to the British Government. Nor can I adequately express my gratitude for this sword which Your Highness has presented to me, or for the honour which my brother, Nawáb Nasrullah Khán, has conferred upon me by fastening it with his own hands to my side. I am deeply sensible of the honour done to me by the presence here to-day of Mr. Bayley and

[1] This sword was a gift from Her Majesty Queen Victoria to Nawáb Shah Jahan Begam, and was formally presented to her by Lord Lytton on the occasion of the Imperial Assemblage at Delhi in 1877. See p. 89.

Major Manners Smith, and I am equally grateful to General Beatson, my superior officer, for the kindness he has displayed to me, his subordinate, by coming to witness these proceedings. I am sure I may look to him and to Major Stainforth for assistance and support in the performance of my new duties. This is the first time that a member of the ruling family in Bhopál has entered the service of the Government of India, and I pray God to help me to act up to the loyal traditions I have inherited from my ancestors."

Sáhibzáda Colonel Obaidullah Khán then asked permission to take his seat amongst the military officers on the right of the durbar, as a token of his admission to their rank as a member of the Imperial Service Troops of the Indian Empire. This done, Colonel Obaidullah Khán received the cordial congratulations of his many friends, and with the distribution of *'itr* and *pán* the durbar was brought to a close.

A review of the State troops and a gymkhana had been arranged for the afternoon, but owing to a heavy downpour of rain these had to be abandoned. In the evening, I entertained my European guests at a banquet at the Lál Kothi. As usual, I joined the party at dessert, and after the royal toast had been honoured, I proposed the healths of Mr. Bayley and General Beatson. The toast was enthusiastically received; and in reply, Mr. Bayley said:

"Your Highness, Ladies and Gentlemen,—When Your Highness a little while ago asked me to ascertain whether the appointment you proposed to make would be acceptable to the Government of India, I felt sure that no apprehension need be entertained as to the answer which would be given. It was, nevertheless, with the greatest gratification that I received a letter in which His Excellency the Viceroy instructed me to convey to Your Highness his cordial approval of the suggestion and of the motives which had prompted it. The rulers of Bhopál have never failed to come to the fore when any question of loyalty to the British Crown has arisen—to do so has been the traditional policy of the ruling house for the last hundred and twenty years—and the outcome of Bhopál's participation in the Imperial Service movement has been that fine body of cavalry, the Victoria

Lancers. It has been, from the first, the hope and desire of the Government of India that the Princes should be personally associated with the Imperial Service Troops which they maintain. Bhopál, as every one knows, has prospered for many years past under a succession of able female rulers, and it has been merely the accident of sex which kept Her Highness the late Begam and Your Highness from assuming the actual command of your troops. In the action which you have taken, you have displayed your own loyalty and devotion to the Empire, and you have given to your son the opportunity of earning the highest distinction which is open to the scion of any princely house."

General Beatson then delivered a long and interesting speech, which was listened to with close attention. In the course of his remarks he said:

"It is a matter of pride to me that I am connected with the British General who, when operating near Bhopál with a force to prevent the irruption of the Pindári free-booters into the Deccan, was the recipient of the first overtures made towards an alliance with the British by Nawáb Wazír Muhammad Khán. Little did I think, when in the old Irish home, I gazed at Sir Barry Close's picture, the representation of a sturdy warrior with a kindly sunburnt face, his sword at his side and a treaty in his hand, that I should one day stand in the very honourable and important position I now do, endeavouring with all my heart and mind to knit closer the ties of friendship he began so long ago. In the intensely critical moments of the Indian rebellion, the great Sikandar Begam ruled the destinies of Bhopál. Throughout that terrible time, she bore herself true to the splendid traditions of her family, upholding truth, honour, and loyalty, under conditions of difficulty and temptation few can imagine. A grant of territory, honours, and her recognition as 'ruler in her own right,' followed these services. In 1868, when Sikandar Begam passed to her rest, she was succeeded by her daughter Shah Jahán Begam, and recently by Your Highness, who have both so steadily maintained the reputation of the State for good administration and undeviating loyalty. During Your Highness's journey to Mecca and Medina, you had an opportunity of seeing the effects of misrule, and must have fully realized in your passage through a country devoid of railways, roads, and all the ordinary comforts of civilization, where both life and property are ever in danger, the inestimable benefits conferred on this country by the *pax Britannica*. It was to help to maintain this land in peace that the Shah Jahán Begam, in 1889, offered troops for the defence of the North-West frontier, but it was not until 1892 that the Victoria Lancers were reorganized and embodied as an Imperial Service Corps. Your Highness will be glad to know that they are becoming day by day more efficient, and it was a great pleasure to me at my last inspection to find a batch of recruits of an excellent stamp drawn from your own territory. I have this year been able to report a great improvement in musketry; whilst in signalling the corps can hold its own with the best regiments in the Indian Army. This morning, Your Highness has nominated your son the Colonel Commandant, and I should like to assure you how welcome that appointment is. In making it we realize with joy your desire to keep in closer touch with your regiment, and we would beg of you to make every possible use of it for State purposes. The employment of detachments in State work from time to time will give officers and men chances of showing their ability, of grasping initiative, and of assuming responsibility. It will enable your State to be controlled by fewer irregular troops, and thus lighten your military budget. The scheme of an Imperial Service force drawn from the States was devised, not only to provide an addition to the Indian Army, welcome though that be, but it was hoped that it would give an outlet for the energies of the scions of princely and noble families, and enable them to follow the service of the sword by which so many of their forefathers won their properties and undying fame. Your Highness's nomination of the Sáhibzáda Obaidullah Khán as Commandant of your Victoria Lancers is, therefore, a most desirable step in the right direction, which will, it is hoped, be followed by other rulers."

At the conclusion of this speech, I distributed garlands and *'itr* and *pán* amongst my guests, and then bade them farewell. Mr. Bayley left for Indore the same night, and General Beatson and the other guests departed the following morning.

The first period of the history of Bhopál—*i.e.* from 1120 A.H., when the State was founded by Dost Muhammad Khán, to

SAHIBZADA COLONEL OBAIDULLAH KHAN.

p. 362]

the commencement of the reign of Nawáb Sikandar Begam in 1260 A.H.—was one of almost uninterrupted warfare. Each successive ruler spent his life at the head of his forces, either making war on his enemies, or defending his territory from their attacks. And if the record of progress made in these hundred and fifty years is brief, the victories that were gained, and the deeds of valour that were done, brought undying honour to the State.

The last occasion on which the troops of Bhopál were actively engaged was during the Mutiny in 1857. At such a critical juncture, the presence of a woman at the head of affairs would not, ordinarily, be supposed to make for the stability of a State, or the security of its people. But in the veins of Nawáb Sikandar Begam ran the blood of her warlike ancestors, while her troops were still animated by the spirit of former days. And thus it came to pass that Sikandar Begam proved herself equal to the emergency she was called upon to face, and showed that a woman, though born for the gentler duties of domestic life, may yet be endowed with qualities which render her as competent as any of her stronger brethren to lead and to rule.

Storms are followed by calms, and since the year 1857 the States and peoples of India have enjoyed a period of peace and progress without parallel in the history of their country. Under the supremacy of the British Government, they are in possession of freedom and security such as the rule of no other power in the world could give them. The last ten years of the reign of Nawáb Sikandar Begam were years of prosperity and tranquillity; and when, in 1868, the days of her life were completed, she bequeathed to her successor territories richer, better administered, and of far wider extent, than she or any of her predecessors had inherited.

Unhappily, the generation that succeeded to this rich inheritance paid little attention to the opportunities for progress and improvement which it offered. By nature prone to indolence and pleasure-seeking, the people of Bhopál came to regard the indulgence of these habits as the goal of their existence. Not only were they incapable of work, but they showed no desire to overcome their incapacity; and the result has been that in every branch of the State service, and in the military department in particular, practically all important posts have had to be filled with strangers from without. Since the day I assumed charge of the administration, nothing has caused me deeper anxiety and distress than this innate apathy of my subjects, which makes it impossible for me to employ them in any important duties, civil or military.

As I thought over these matters, I saw plainly that, without a good education on modern lines, no man can qualify himself for the higher grades of civil employment. But it seemed to me that it should be a comparatively easy matter to train any man to be a soldier provided there be in him a spark of military spirit. The first step I took in this direction was the appointment of my son to the command of the Imperial Service cavalry, and to the general control of the forces of the State. Other military posts were given to various relatives of my family; and in the following month, that is, in September 1904, I opened a military riding school, in which the sons of nobles and other persons of position, who were physically fit for a military career, might receive instruction, and qualify themselves for superior posts in the service. Up to the present, the school cannot be said to have been a success. It has been open for five years, but the people have shown little inclination to take advantage of its existence. I trust that, by degrees, the influence and example of my son will bring about a better state of things.

On the 15th of August, 1904, I received a letter from the Honourable Mr. Bayley, Agent to the Governor-General in Central India, stating that it would give him great pleasure if I would spend a few days as his guest at Indore. I gladly accepted his kind invitation, and my visit took place in the first week in November. I set out on the 5th of the month, taking with me my three sons and, by special request from Mrs. Bayley, my little granddaughter Birjis Jahán. Mr. and Mrs. Bayley entertained us with the utmost kindness and cordiality, and, as long as we remained at Indore, did everything in their power to render our visit enjoyable.

In the month of September my grandson Habibullah Khán

fell seriously ill, and for some time I feared that my projected visit would have to be abandoned. The child was suffering from pneumonia, and for some time his condition was very critical. By the grace of God, however, combined with the skilful treatment of Miss Blong, the lady doctor, and Major Grant, the Agency Surgeon, the disease took a favourable turn, and, by the end of October, he was so far recovered that I felt there was no necessity to alter my plans.

We reached Indore on the 6th of November, and were met at the railway station by Mr. Bayley, the Resident at Indore, and other European officials, who gave us a most hearty welcome. A salute of nineteen guns announced our arrival, and we drove to the bungalow of Mr. Keely, First Assistant to the Agent to the Governor-General, which that officer had been kind enough to place at our disposal, and in which every arrangement had been made for our accommodation. I shall never forget the thoughtful kindness and unbounded hospitality of Mr. and Mrs. Bayley. We visited many places of interest in and around Indore, and, in spite of his heavy duties, Mr. Bayley always accompanied us. On the evening of the 8th, he gave a banquet in our honour at the Residency, to which all the English ladies and gentlemen resident in the Station were invited. At the conclusion of dinner, the toast of His Majesty the King having been duly honoured, Mr. Bayley, in the following very kind words, proposed my health:

* "Ladies and Gentlemen,—You have just joined me in drinking to the health of His Majesty the King-Emperor. I feel sure you will all agree that no toast could be more worthy to follow than the one I am about to propose—the health of Her Highness the Begam of Bhopál, a loyal representative of His Majesty's subject rulers in India. I have, on several occasions, had the honour of proposing Her Highness's health, and it is a duty I always perform with increasing pleasure; for it is my experience—and I think it is the experience of every one who has the pleasure of Her Highness's acquaintance—that to know her better is to respect her more. And for this reason: we find out, as our acquaintance grows, not only that she is a lady richly endowed with the graces and finer virtues of her sex, but that, in her

capacity as ruler, she can vie in ability and energy with any chief in India.

"The loyalty of the rulers of Bhopál to the British throne is so well known that it may seem superfluous to give any account of it. But the story is one which repetition can never stale. It has its commencement in the days when India was tasting the first-fruits of British rule; for it was in the reign of Auranzebe that Her Highness's famous ancestor, Dost Muhammad Khán, in the manner common to those days, established his authority in Bhopál and the surrounding districts. On his death, the lands over which he held sway became the centre of revolutionary warfare, and, during the next hundred years, the little State was all but swallowed up by its powerful neighbours. Then came Wazír Muhammad Khán, a worthy descendant of Dost Muhammad, who succeeded in reconquering the territories which his predecessors had lost. In 1809, he endeavoured to form an alliance with the English; but, at this time, British policy, as far as Native States were concerned, was one of strict non-interference. Wazír Muhammad's overtures were, therefore, rejected, and he was left to fight his battles alone and unaided. For nine months he was besieged in his capital; but at last his enemies, disheartened by want of success, abandoned the siege in despair.[1] Wazír ruled wisely, and in 1817, when the British were engaged in the subjugation of the Pindáris, negotiations for an alliance were again opened, and in the following year a treaty was signed. This took place in the reign of Nazar Muhammad Khán; and, from that day to this, the conditions of the treaty have been faithfully observed by both parties. Nazar Muhammad died shortly after the treaty was concluded; but his policy of loyalty has been firmly adhered to by the four successive Begams who, since his day, have guided the destinies of the State. The names of the Kudsia Begam, the Sikandar Begam, Nawáb Shah Jahán Begam, and Nawáb Sultán Jahán Begam, will ever be associated in the English mind with deeds of friendship and loyalty. In the dark days of the Mutiny there was, in the whole of India, no firmer friend to the British throne than Nawáb Sikandar Begam. We all earnestly hope that Nawáb Sultán Jahán Begam may live long to follow in the footsteps of her ancestors. We have, to-day, received a fresh example of her loyalty. She has, as I think you all know, just announced her intention of adding to the strength

[1] See Appendix G.

of the Imperial Service troops which the State already maintains. To this force she has recently appointed her second son, Sáhibzáda Obaidullah Khán, Colonel Commandant; and I take this opportunity of offering to the Sáhibzáda, as well as to Nawáb Nasrullah Khán, who during Her Highness's recent pilgrimage to Mecca, has carried on the administration of the State with ability and success, my hearty congratulations and good wishes.

"I know that the toast I am proposing needs no further word from me to commend it to your acceptance. But I find it difficult to stop giving expression to the pleasure which Her Highness's presence as my guest has given to me. The occasion is certainly a notable one; for not only is this the first time that Her Highness has visited Indore, but it is the first time that such a visit has ever been paid by a ruler of Bhopál. The pleasure of entertaining Her Highness is one to which Mrs. Bayley and I have long been looking forward. It is a pleasure we should appreciate at any time, but, in the present instance, we feel specially grateful to her for accepting our invitation; for she has done so at considerable personal inconvenience, and in spite of the heavy anxiety which the recent illness of her grandson has caused her. I am glad to say that this anxiety is now passed, and that her little patient is well on the road to recovery. As I have already said, this is the first visit Her Highness has ever paid to Indore. I should like to say, in conclusion, that I sincerely hope it may not be the last; and I can assure her that there is no place in India where she may count upon a warmer welcome. Ladies and Gentlemen, I ask you to drink to the health of Her Highness the Begam of Bhopál."

In reply to these kind words I said:

"Ladies and Gentlemen,—It is not possible in a few words to tell you how greatly I appreciate the kindness with which, from the time I reached Indore up to the present moment, my distinguished host and hostess have overwhelmed me. My gratitude to Mr. Bayley for the manner in which he has referred to the loyalty of myself and my family to the British throne, is more than I can express in words. It has always been the good fortune of the Bhopál State to possess a true friend in the Agent to the Governor-General for Central India. The real value of such friendships

I have fully realized only during my own reign, which began, as you are aware, during the Honourable Mr. Bayley's tenure of office. The friendly hospitality which he has extended to me and the kind words he has spoken about my family in his speech to-night, are things I shall remember as long as I live. Ladies and Gentlemen, I propose the health of my kind friends Mr. and Mrs. Bayley. I pray that God will grant them health and happiness, and I pray that He will grant long life to his Majesty the King, and everlasting prosperity to the British Empire."

We left for Bhopál the following morning, and, although our departure was private, Mr. Bayley and many other gentlemen came to the railway station to bid us farewell. We took away with us the happiest recollections of our visit, and of the spontaneous hospitality of our kind host and hostess.

APPENDICES

APPENDIX A

The troops of the Indore cantonment were the first to revolt in Central India. They murdered several Europeans, and this obliged Colonel Durand, Agent to the Governor-General, Mr. Shakespeare, Mr. Stockley, and Colonel Trevor to go to Sehore, *viâ* Ashta, along with their wives and children. But the Bhopál contingent at Sehore contained a large number of *purbiahs*, or natives of eastern Hindustán; and as these men had been induced to join the rebellion, all the officers above-mentioned took refuge in Bhopál. Nawáb Sikandar Begam treated them with great kindness, and sent them (with the exception of Colonel Trevor who remained with the Sehore troops) in safety to Hoshangábád. About the same time the doctor of the Gwálior contingent, Captain Carter, commanding the detachment at Augar, Captain Macdougal, second-in-command, Major Macpherson, Captain Le Marchand of the Artillery, Mrs. Burton, Mrs. Harrison, and Mrs. Hayman, with their children and some servants (27 persons in all), had been forced to quit Indore, and had taken refuge in Orchode, a small village in the Jáwar *pargana* of the Bhopál State; and they thanked God that they had reached a place of safety, for they knew that Nawáb Sikandar Begam was their friend. There the *Tahsíldár* supplied all their wants, and offered to send a letter for them to the Political Agent at Sehore. A letter was accordingly dispatched to Major Rikardes, the then Political Agent, and he, after consulting Nawáb Sikandar Begam, informed them that they should proceed directly to Hoshangábád, and should on no account come to Sehore. The State provided them with provisions and clothing, as well as twelve elephants for the journey. These acts of kindness greatly pleased them, but they could not understand why they were not allowed to go to Sehore. They questioned the Muhammadan messenger who brought the letter, and he related to them all that he had heard, telling them how all the Europeans had gone to Hoshangábád by the advice of the Begam, and that the Political Agent was himself preparing to start when his answer was written. He also told them that her Highness the Begam had herself undertaken the responsibility of preserving order at Sehore. They accordingly set out, and reached Ichắwar at 11 o'clock at night, and the gate of the Fort was at once opened to them. The next day, they went on to Larkui. Here they were met by a man named Kandan Singh, who told them, with many threats, that he was a spy in the service of the Mahárájas Sindhia and Holkar, and that he had had strict orders not to allow any *Feringhi* to pass that way alive. "Behind yonder hillock," he said, "are stationed five hundred men under my command. Three days ago the Resident of Indore passed this way, and he had to give me five hundred rupees, besides a large number of swords and guns, before he was allowed to proceed on his way." The European party, on hearing this, were greatly astonished. They possessed neither money, arms, nor, what they regretted much more, any means of punishing the man for his treachery. It afterwards transpired that Kandan Singh was a brother of Dulip Singh and Narpat Singh, Jágírdárs of Larkui. The object of these men was merely to plunder. But the fear of having their *jágír* confiscated, and of even heavier punishment to follow, caused them to abandon their evil designs, and the party journeyed on unmolested till they reached Budhni, where they crossed the Narbadda, and arrived safely at Hoshangábád. Here they met Major Rikardes, Captain Tod, Colonel Holland, and, to their great joy, Captain Harrison also. All thought that the latter had been murdered, and the greatest compassion had been felt for Mrs. Harrison, who was of their party, and who had given birth to a child twelve days before their arrival at Hoshangábád. Soon after these events, the Indore troops induced the Sehore contingent to break out into open revolt. Nawáb Sikandar Begam at once sent a force to Sehore, which took possession of the Government treasury, and kept the mutineers in check until the arrival of British troops. The men of the contingent were then made prisoners, and the ringleaders hanged. At Bairasía, Bábu Shab Rao Sáhib, Superintendent of Police, was murdered at the instigation of Sarfaraz Khán, a Resident of Rahatgarh, and Namdar Khán Pindára. The Bhopál troops captured these men along with Fázil Muhammad Khán, Jágírdár of Ambapáni, in a small village near Rahatgarh. They were handed over to the British General, and were hanged at the Fort gate. Their *jágírs* were confiscated. Nawáb Sikandar Begam, besides doing her utmost to preserve order within the boundaries of her territories, sent provisions to a number of Europeans who had taken refuge at Kálpi, and dispatched her soldiers to Ságar, Chandheri, Jhánsi, and other parts of Bandalkand, to help in the restoration of order. On many occasions these troops displayed great bravery; and on November 29th, 1858, the Agent to the Governor-General expressed, through the Political Agent, his great appreciation of the valuable work they had done. It was acknowledged in all dispatches and Government reports that, during the Mutiny, no ruler had remained a firmer friend to the English than Nawáb Sikandar Begam, and that the State had done signal service to British rule.

APPENDIX B

THE marriage agreement was as follows:

I, Ahmad Ali Khán, the son of Báki Muhammad Khán, of Jalálábád, in the district of Muzaffar Nagar, inasmuch as Her Highness Nawáb Jahán Begam, Ruler of Bhopál, has, with the approval of her Nobles, Jágírdárs, Ministers, and the members of her family, consented to my marriage with Nawáb Sultán Jahán Begam, Heir-apparent of the State, do hereby promise that I will abide by the conditions stated in this agreement. I further declare that I have signed this agreement of my own free will in the presence of the undersigned witnesses according to the custom of the State. I declare myself to be morally and legally bound by it, and in the event of my infringing it, or any of its clauses, I shall be answerable for the same to her Highness Nawáb Shah Jahán Begam, the Ministers of the State, and the Political Agent in Bhopál.

(1) I, being a Muhammadan of the Sunni sect, do promise that I will never, for any reason whatever, change my religion; and that if at any time, whether of my own accord, or at the instigation of others, I depart from this promise, my marriage shall be declared null and void.

(2) I agree to pay two crores of rupees as *mihr-i-muajjal*, this amount having been fixed in the presence of the Kázi, and other witnesses. I promise to pay this sum either in full, or by instal-

ments, on the demand of either Nawáb Sultán Jahán Begam, or of Nawáb Shah Jahán Begam. In the event of my failing to do so, I shall be liable to the forfeiture of my *jágír*.

(3) I promise always to fulfil, to the best of my ability, all the duties of a husband, and that I will not interfere in any way with my wife's *jágír* or other personal property. I promise to love and cherish my wife, and to do my best to live in harmony with her. In case of my failing in any or all of these things, it shall be in her power to bring about a separation.

(4) I promise that I will not take a second wife without the express permission and approval of Nawáb Sultán Jahán Begam. I shall have nothing to do with the marriages of any children, whether male or female, that Nawáb Sultán Jahán may give birth to; the decision in such matters resting wholly and unconditionally with herself and her mother, the Ruler of the State.

(5) I agree to manage my *jágír* in accordance with the laws of the State. If I violate any of them, my *jágír* shall be liable to confiscation, in which case I shall receive a fixed income from the State in its stead.

(6) I promise to treat the nobles, Jágírdárs and officers of the State with respect and courtesy. I will endeavour to act upon any advice that they may give me, and to do nothing that may give them offence, or lead to disorders in the State.

(7) I will not retain in my service any person to whom the Ruler of the State or her Ministers may take exception, or who is reputed to be ill-disposed towards the State, or the British Government.

(8) I will endeavour always to keep my expenditure within the limits of my income. In the event of my falling into debt, such debt shall be liquidated from my own *jágír*, and not from the coffers of the State.

(9) I promise that I will not permit any of my relatives or personal friends to interfere or take part in the affairs of the State without the permission and approval of both Her Highness Nawáb Shah Jahán Begam and Nawáb Sultán Jahán Begam.

(10) I will, as in duty bound, honour and respect Her Highness the Ruler on all occasions, public or private.

(11) I authorize Her Highness Nawáb Shah Jahán Begam to decree a separation should there be serious disagreement between my wife and myself. That is to say, if, which God forbid, such disagreement should arise, the word of Her Highness

shall be sufficient to part us, and there shall be no need of public proceedings.

Dated 15th Rajab, 1289 A.H.

(*Signed*) AHMAD ALI KHAN.

SEAL

Seal of Ahmad Ali Khán

20th Rajab, 1289.

Signatures of witnesses:

BAKSHI MUHAMMAD HASAN KHAN.
LATIF MUHAMMAD KHAN.
THAKUR PARSHAD, *Accountant.*
MATTU KHAN, NAWAB BAKSHI.
MAJID MUHAMMAD KHAN.
MUNSHI BANSI DHAR.
THE POLITICAL AGENT IN BHOPAL.

APPENDIX C

AT the celebration of the Diamond Jubilee in London, the royal escort, by the special desire of Her Majesty the Queen, included a number of officers belonging to the Imperial Service Troops, one officer being chosen from each State. Bhopál was represented by Major Mirza Karím Beg, and the contingent, which was under the command of Major Drummond of the Central India Horse, sailed for England on the *Persia*, and reached London on May 22nd. During their visit to England these officers had the honour of waiting upon His Royal Highness the Prince of Wales, His Royal Highness the Duke of Connaught, and Lord George Hamilton. In the course of conversation, the latter said, " It was Her Majesty's intention to meet all the Chiefs of India at this time; but, owing to the famine which prevails in India, this could not be accomplished. I assure you all that your presence has given great pleasure to the people of the United Kingdom." On a subsequent occasion, Lord George Hamilton entertained the contingent at luncheon. The Jubilee procession took place on June 24th. Her Majesty was seated in a carriage drawn by eight horses, on either side of which rode officers of the Indian Army. The distance covered was eight miles, and twenty thousand troops lined the route. The officers of the Imperial Service Troops rode immediately in front of the royal carriage, and, together with the Ambassadors, saluted Her Majesty as she entered Buckingham Palace at the close of the procession. It was officially stated that seventy lákhs of people assembled to witness this pageant.

When Her Majesty drove out on July 1st, the officers of the Imperial Service Troops formed her sole escort. They were afterwards received and entertained by Her Majesty at Windsor Castle. Before their departure from England, they attended a levée in London. Each officer, as his name was called, approached Her Majesty and presented his sword to be touched, their homage being graciously acknowledged. On July 7th, Major Karím Beg was decorated by the Queen with a medal, and a few days later, at the Military Tournament, he received a sword from the Prince of Wales as a prize for tent-pegging.

APPENDIX D

The State, for administrative purposes, is divided into three districts, viz. *Nizámat-i-mashrík*, *Nizámat-i-magríb*, and *Nizámat-i-anúb*. Each *Nizámat* comprises nine *tahsíls*.

Each *Nizámat* is in charge of a *Názim* who is the Chief Revenue Officer, District Magistrate, and Civil Judge. He is assisted by *tahsíldárs* in charge of *tahsíls* who are first- and second-class magistrates and *munsifs*. Other officers are the *kánungos*, *patwárís*, and inspector of police.

Each village of any size is a community in itself, having its own artisans, the carpenter, blacksmith, and leather worker, who are paid by a share of the village grain at each harvest. Other members are the village servants, such as the *nai* or barber (a most important individual, who besides his technical duties acts as go-between in arranging marriages), the *dhobi* or washerman, and the *chaukidár* or village watchman. Over the whole community is the *patél* or headman, who is responsible for the proper condition of the village and assists the *mustájir* in collecting the revenue. He is assisted by the *patwári* or village accountant and register-keeper. (*Bhopál State Gazetteer*, Vol. III.)

APPENDIX E

In the *Táj-ul-Ikbál*, Nawáb Shah Jahán Begam thus describes her visit to Calcutta and her presentation to the Duke of Edinburgh :

"On the 1st of December 1869 A.D. or the 26th Shaban 1286 A.H., Colonel Thompson, the Officiating Political Agent, in accordance with instructions from the Agent to the Governor-General for Central India, wrote to the effect, that I was invited to attend the Durbars of the Governor-General and of the Duke of Edinburgh, and to be present by the 26th of the month. With the greatest pleasure I started from Bhopál on the 17th December or 14th Ramzan 1286 by post stages for Hoshungabad, and took rail at Nursingpur for Jabalpur, where I again took rail on the 23rd of December, arriving at Calcutta on the 25th of December. On the 29th December, or 25th Ramzan of the same year, I had the honour to pay my respects to the Prince and to the Governor-General, both of whom treated me with great consideration; and on the 31st of December I took part in the Chapter, held by the Prince, for the Star of India. Afterwards, on different days, these two exalted personages honoured me with return visits at my residence, and visits were courteously interchanged with the Governors of Bombay and Madras and the Bishop of Calcutta and other gentlemen of distinction. The Theatre, Magazine in Fort William, the Citadel of Calcutta, the Museum, and Mint, were also visited by us. We also witnessed a review, and on the 14th of January 1870 A.D., or the 11th Shawal 1286 A.H., I paid a visit to the steamer commanded by His Royal Highness, and at all the above places the English Government caused me to be received with the full honours due to me."

APPENDIX F

MR. T. H. THORNTON, in his work entitled *General Sir Richard Meade*, referring to the State of Bhopál, writes:

"Bhopál is, next to Hyderábád, the most important Musalman State in India, with an area not far short of Holkar's, a population of nearly 1,000,000, and a military force of about 2,000 infantry, 8,000 cavalry, and 69 guns. Its ruling family is Afghán, descendants of Dost Muhammad Khán, a distinguished officer of the Moghul Emperor Auranzeb, and it was represented at the time of Meade's appointment by Shah Jahán Begam, the daughter of Sikandar Begam, G.C.S.I., who, after the death of her worthless husband in 1844, and the usual family dissensions, was appointed Regent by the British Government in 1847.

"Under the advice of a former Agent, Sir Robert Hamilton,

she had introduced an excellent system of administration, and both mother and daughter proved themselves staunch friends of the British Government in 1857. In recognition of her services the mother was appointed a Knight Grand Commander of the Star of India, and Bhopál received an assignment of territory confiscated from the neighbouring State of Dhár, which had rebelled."

APPENDIX G

THE following is a brief summary of the history of Bhopál, from the foundation of the State in 1707, to the reign of Sikandar Begam:

Dost Muhammad Khán, the founder of the Bhopál State, was an Afghan belonging to the Mirázi Khél, a branch of the Aurakzais of Tirah. He migrated to India in 1696, and after
1707 to 1726 serving under various chiefs and military leaders, and meeting with many adventures, was nominated superintendent of the district of Berasía, where he settled, and was joined by the members of his family. On the death of the Emperor Auranzeb in 1707, he became practically independent, and added to his territories Jugdespúr (renamed Islámnagar), Gunnúr, Bhilsa, Ichávar, and other places. He founded the city of Bhopál, and surrounded it with a wall which is still standing. He made the city his headquarters, and built the Fatehgarh fort. Towards the end of his reign, his territory was invaded by the Nizám of the Deccan, and, to avoid defeat, he was forced to surrender his son, Yár Muhammad Khán, as a hostage. Dost Muhammad Khán died in 1726, aged sixty-six years, leaving behind him a powerful and well-established principality.

Dost Muhammad Khán was succeeded by his son Yár Muhammad Khán, who reigned sixteen years, and added to his dominions, Sewáns, Udayapúr, and Pathári. His
1726 to 1742 chief minister of state was his uncle, Akil Muhammad Khán, a man of high character and ability. The latter was killed in a riot during the Holi festival in 1742, and Yár Muhammad Khán died the same year.

On the death of the Nawáb, his brother Sultán Muhammad Khán claimed the throne. The rightful successor was Fáiz Muhammad Khán, the son of Yár Muhammad, and he was
1742 to 1777 supported by the Nawáb's widow, the Mahji Sáhiba, and by Baiji Rám, the Minister. The contending parties had recourse to arms, and after several severe conflicts,

the succession of Fáiz Muhammad was secured. Fáiz was a religious recluse, and left the administration of the State to the Mahji Sáhiba and his ministers. Of these there were, in the course of his reign, no less than six, four of whom were murdered. The fort of Raisen was annexed to Bhopál during this reign.

Fáiz Muhammad left no children and was succeeded by his brother Hayat Muhammad Khán. He, too, was a religious recluse, and took little part or interest in the affairs
1777 to 1808 of the State, which was ruled by successive ministers. Amongst the latter, the most famous were Faulád Muhammad Khán and Chhoté Khán. Faulád was minister in 1778 when Colonel Goddard, on his famous march from Calcutta to Bombay, passed through Bhopál, an occasion still remembered with pride by the people of the State.[1] The chief event in the ministry of Chhoté Khán was the desperate attempt made at his overthrow by Sharíf Muhammad Khán, a grandson of Dost Muhammad. The struggle was a long one, and in the end Sharíf Muhammad was killed. Chhoté Khán was an able minister, but the frequent attempts made on his life led him to regard all Patháns with dislike and suspicion. He died in 1795. The following year, Muríd Muhammad Khán, another grandson of Dost Muhammad, was appointed minister. His rule was characterized by oppression and tyranny; and the heir-apparent, Ghaus Muhammad Khán, with the assistance of Wazír Muhammad Khán, a son of Sharíf Muhammad above referred to, sought to bring about his downfall. Muríd called in the aid of Sindhia, promising to make over to him

[1] Referring to the reception which Colonel Goddard met with in Bhopál, Sir John Malcolm writes as follows:

"The inhabitants of that country are justly proud of the part their prince took on this occasion; and with reason, for it was bold and decided beyond what their condition warranted. Every aid required was freely given by the petty State; and from the certificates still preserved by some of the villages, it would seem that all ranks behaved in the most friendly manner to a body of men who prized such conduct more from having elsewhere met with nothing but hostility. That the remaining part of the march of the Bengal detachment, after it passed the Nerbudda, was unobstructed, may in some degree be ascribed to the line taken by the Patans of Bhopal, whose conduct on this memorable occasion established a claim on the British Government that merited all the notice which it has since received. In an official abstract made from the correspondence of General Goddard, it is stated that every effort was made to render the Nabob of Bhopál hostile to the English, but in vain. He remained true to his first promise of friendship, though many of his fields and villages were, in consequence of his fidelity to his engagements, plundered by the Mahrattas."

in return the fortress of Islámnagar. This fortress was occupied by Moti Begam, the sister of the Nawáb, who refused to surrender it, and when the Mahrattas arrived to take possession, she resisted them with so much determination that they were forced to retire, and Muríd made over to them the fort at Raisen instead of that at Islámnagar. At this juncture, Sindhia was obliged to withdraw his forces, and Muríd ended an ignoble career by swallowing powdered glass.

Wazír now became Minister. He recovered Raisen, and other places lost by his predecessor. His growing power soon excited the jealousy of Ghaus Muhammad, who appealed to Sindhia and then to Nágpúr for aid against his Minister. Wazír was forced to withdraw from Bhopál, and the city was occupied by the Mahrattas. He, however, soon returned, and after a daring assault, recovered the town and fort. Ghaus Muhammad, finding himself powerless in the hands of his Minister, retired to Raisen, and Wazír Muhammad became, from that time, the ruler of the State. In 1812, the forces of Sindhia and Nágpúr made a combined attack on Bhopál. Wazír defended his citadel with great bravery and skill for nine months, at the end of which time the siege was abandoned. In 1811, Wazír had endeavoured to form a treaty with the English, whom he always regarded with friendship and admiration. Unfortunately, his overtures were rejected, and though he never ceased to court an alliance, he died before his hopes could be fulfilled.[1]

1808 to 1816

Wazír was succeeded by his son Nazar Muhammad Khán in 1816, the title of Nawáb still remaining with the dethroned Ghaus Muhammad. In 1818, Nazar married the Kudsia Begam, the daughter of Ghaus Muhammad, thus uniting the two branches of the family. The same year, after the subjugation of the Pindaris, in the accomplishment of which Nazar rendered valuable assistance, negotiations for an

1816 to 1868

[1] Wazír Muhammad's defence of Bhopál ranks amongst the finest military achievements recorded in the whole course of Indian history. The besieging army is said to have numbered close upon 70,000 men. Wazír had but 10,000, and of these, 4,000 were cavalry, who, being unable to procure forage for their horses, left the town ere the siege had well begun. When, at the end of nine months, the enemy withdrew, Wazír had not 200 fighting men left. The following extract is taken from Major William Hough's *Brief History of the Bhopál Principality* (published in 1845): "Captain James Grant Duff, in his history of the Mahrattas, speaks of the 'heroism of Vizier Mohamed in the gallant defence of Bhopál.' Another authority

alliance with the British were successfully concluded. The treaty, a copy of which may be found in the *Bhopál State Gazetteer*, was ratified by Lord Hastings at Lucknow on the 8th of March. Nazar Muhammad's death, the result of an accident, took place the following year, and deprived the State of a gallant soldier and a wise and high-minded statesman. Nazar left only one child, a daughter, named Sikandar Begam. With the sanction of the British Government, it was settled that Munír Muhammad Khán, the nephew of Nazar, should succeed, under the regency of the Kudsia Begam. Munír, however, quarrelled with the regent, and was eventually compelled to resign in favour of his brother Jahángír Muhammad Khán. In 1835, Jahángír married Sikandar Begam. Shortly afterwards, he quarrelled with his wife, who, with the Kudsia Begam, had to seek refuge at Islámnagar. Both parties took to arms, and after a fierce encounter at Ashta, the British Government stepped in to restore order. The Kudsia Begam retired into private life, and Jahángír was entrusted with full powers. He died in 1844, and the Government proclaimed Shah Jahán Begam, his seven-year-old daughter, chief of the State, the Sikandar Begam with her uncle, Faujdár Muhammad Khán, being appointed joint regents. As might have been expected, this arrangement soon gave rise to further dissensions, and the British Government again intervened. As a result, Faujdár Muhammad resigned all share in the administration, and for the next twenty-two years, the State remained under the sole and able direction of the Nawáb Sikandar Begam. (C. H. P.).

states that 'the siege of Bhopál, in 1813–1814, is one of the most remarkable of the time, and the conduct of the chief, whose garrison at the commencement of the siege did not exceed 8,000 or 10,000 men,—is the theme of praise and admiration of the Muhammadans of India.'

"The circumstances of this celebrated siege are of so remarkable a character, that the reader of the military exploits detailed by the various Muhammadan and Hindu historians, will fail to find the relation of any siege which so well deserves to be held up to the example and admiration of future ages. It is famed for the skill and talent with which the plan of defence was formed, and for the courage and gallantry with which it was carried into execution."

GENEALOGICAL TREE OF THE BHOPAL FAMILY[1]

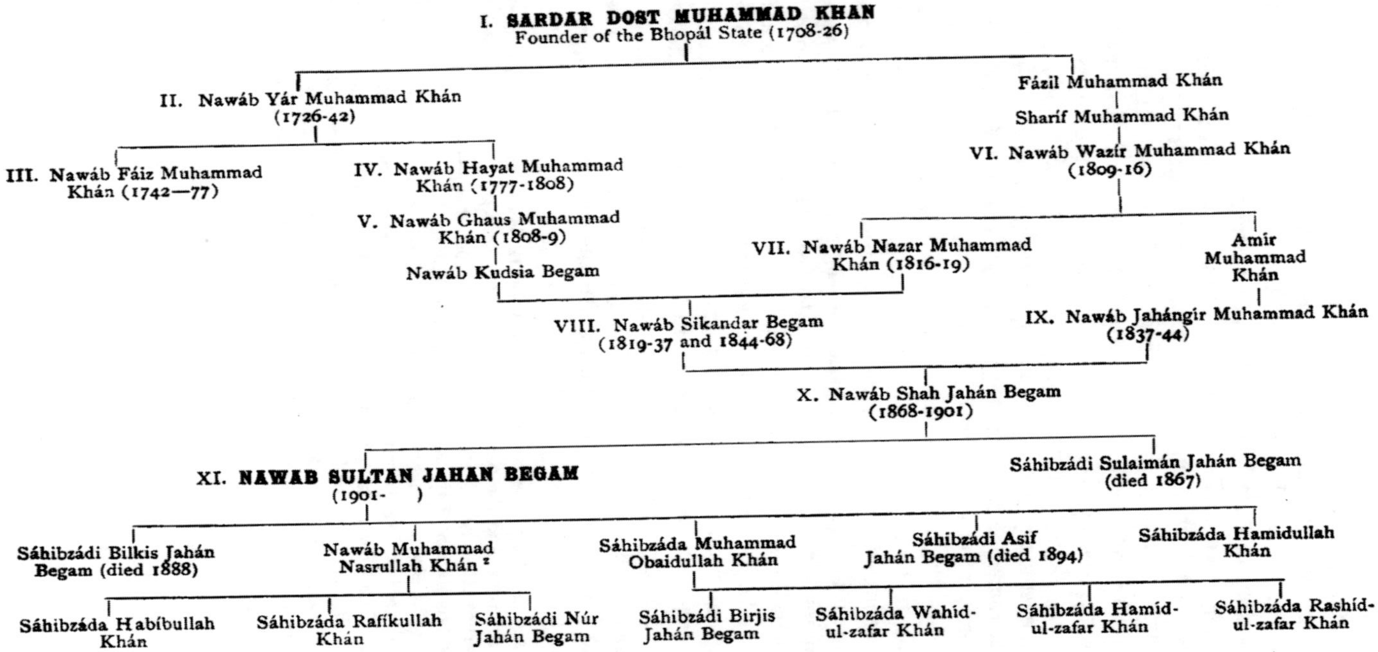

[1] Adapted from the tree given in the *Bhopal State Gazetteer*.

[2] Now heir-apparent.

INDEX

Abdul Jabbar Khán, Maulavi, 174, 205, 225, 228, 239, 260–1, 316
Abdul Kayúm, Captain, 230, 254
Abdul Latíf Khán, 104, 123
Abdul Rahím Sáhib, 162–3
Abdur Rahman Pasha, 347–8
Adil Muhammad Khán, 36–7
Agra, 43, 89
Ahmad Ali Khán, Nawáb, 42–62, 79, 80, 94, 214–8, 228–37, 253–4, 257, 296, 318–20
Alamgír Muhammad Khán, 72, 95, 192
Ali Bayázid Khán, 32
Ali Hasan Khán, 137, 191–3
Altáf Husein, 298
Argyll, Duke of, 15
Asif Jahán Begam, 96, 162–6, 239, 319

Bagh Muhammad Khán, 32
Bahádur Muhammad Khán, 32–4
Bairasía, 11, 22
Báki Muhammad Khán, Nawáb, 7, 24, 26, 28, 34–9, 94
Báki Muhammad Khán, 44
Balthazar Bourbon, 286
Bannerman, Colonel, 114–7
Barr, Sir D. W. K., 19, 61, 175–7, 243
Bayley, Mr. C. S., 19, 254–8, 263, 307, 357, 360, 365–8
Beatson, General, 357, 361–2
Bilkis Jahán Begam, 75–6, 98–100, 129–33, 135–40, 206
Birjis Jahán Begam, 305, 341
Blong, Miss, 233, 304
Bombay, 341, 351
Bourbon, Joan, 132–3

Calcutta, 71–5, 105–8, 129–31
Canning, Lord, 12
Cawnpore, 181
Chhoté Khán, 377
Close, Sir Barry, 361
Connaught, Duchess of, 270–1
— Duke of, 268, 270
Cook, Mr., 114, 135, 335
Crosthwaite, Sir R., 19
Cunningham, Sir J. D., 18
Curzon, Lady, 181, 185, 270
— Lord, 181–5, 212–3, 265, 268, 270–1, 331, 354

Daly, Sir H., 14, 19, 64, 82–3, 90–2, 109–11, 116
Dane, Doctor, 135, 190, 233
Delhi, 11, 82–9, 265–74
Dost Muhammad Khán, 366, 376
Dufferin, Marquis of, 129–30, 140
Durand, Sir H. Marion, 15, 18
Durand, Sir H. Mortimer, 130–1

Eden, Captain, 15, 18
Edinburgh, Duke of, 374
Edwards, Captain G., 159–60
Elgin, Countess of, 170–2
— Earl of, 168–72, 180–1

Fáiz Muhammad Khán, Nawáb, 376
Faujdár Muhammad Khán, 8, 14, 18, 41, 379
Faulád Muhammad Khán, 377
Fázil Muhammad Khán, 21, 36, 41

Gadhi Ambapáni, 21, 36
Ghaus Muhammad Khán, Nawáb, 34, 377, 378

Goddard, Colonel, 377
Griffin, Sir Lepel, 15, 19, 116, 121, 125–8, 202, 224

Habíbullah Khán, Sáhibzáda, 353
Háfiz Ahmad Raza Khán, 103–4
Hafiz Muhammad Hasan Khán, 17, 36, 45, 125, 142, 300–1
Hamidullah Khán, Sáhibzáda, 166, 232, 272, 278–80, 312, 314, 326–9
Hamilton, Sir R., 8, 15, 19
Hastings, Marquis of, 379
Hayat Muhammad Khán, Nawáb, 377
Henvey, Mr. F., 19, 145
Himli Effendi, 344
Hoshangábád, 81
Husein Khán, Munshi, 18, 45
Hutchinson, Captain, 11, 15, 28

Ihtishám-ul-mulk, Nawáb. *See* Ahmad Ali Khán, Nawáb
Impey, Major L., 242, 263, 283, 294, 299, 313, 340
Imtiyáz Ali Khán, 125, 157, 172–4 202, 225, 316
Indore, 366–8
Islámnagar, 34, 376
Isrár Hasan Khán, Munshi, 124, 245, 268, 276–7, 300, 312, 315

Jabbalpúr, 10
Jagva Bapu, 33
Jahángír Muhammad Khán, Nawáb, 8, 14, 33, 379
Jalálábád, 43
Jedda, 342

Karím Beg, Major, 161, 374
Kincaid, Colonel W., 79, 82, 202
Kudrat Ali Khán, Munshi, 263, 267, 274, 298
Kudrat Ullah Khán, 218
Kudsia Begam, Nawáb, 9, 11, 45, 46, 52, 54, 59, 77–9, 97, 101–3, 379

Lála Naubat Rai, 37
Lang, Major J., 194, 205, 207, 210, 235, 239, 242
Lansdowne, Marchioness of, 152, 155–6
— Marquis of, 147–55, 157–8
Lawrence, Lord, 12, 14
Lytton, Countess of, 86–8
— Earl of, 83–8, 112

Mackenzie, Miss, 163–4
Macwatt, Major, 340, 342–3
Malika Bíbí, 39
Mattu Khán, Captain, 45
Mayo, Earl of, 199–200
Meade, Colonel M. J., 61, 156, 163, 165, 207–8, 219–20, 296, 307
Meade, Sir R., 11, 15, 18, 19, 30, 375, Ap. E.
Mecca, 12, 239, 348–50
Medina, 345–7
Muhammad Jamál-ud-dín 16, 29, 49, 56, 58–9, 103, 144
Mumtáz Ali Khán, Munshi, 263, 276, 297, 312
Murawwat Muhammad Khán, 17, 35
Muríd Muhammad Khán, 377

Nasír-ud-dín Ahmad, Maulavi, 264
Nasrullah Khán, Nawáb, 76, 91, 118, 186–8, 220–22, 230, 245, 251, 299, 309, 321, 338, 351, 359
Nazar Muhammad Khán, Nawáb, 33, 378
Northbrook, Lord, 65, 67, 73, 75
Núr-ul-hasan, Sayad, 319–20

Obaidullah Khán, Colonel Sáhibzáda, 89, 95, 118–9, 145–6, 186–8, 229–30, 245, 248, 251, 278–80, 289, 299, 357–60
Osborne, Colonel W. W., 30, 46, 53, 79
—Mrs., 53–4

Patiála, Mahárája of, 11
Payne, Mr., 329

Raisen, 279–81
Rája Kishen Rám, 17
Ripon, Lord, 105–7
Roberts, Field-Marshal Lord, 141–2

Sadar Muhammad Khán, 34
Samarda, 61, 163–4, 293
Sehore, 175
Shah Jahán Begam, Nawáb, 4, 15, 28–31, 44–62, 64–6, 69–74, 80–5, 95–6, 107, 115–6, 129–33, 136–7, 148–50, 169–70, 175–6, 179–83, 186–7, 189–94, 197–202, 212–3, 216, 374
hams-ud-dín, Munshi, 37–8
Sherman, Mr., 177
Sidik Hasan Khán, 17, 45, 49, 53–60, 69–71, 78–80, 85, 91–7, 103–4, 120–4, 136, 142–5, 174, 201, 223–4
Sikandar Begam, Nawáb, 5–16, 21–8, 33–6, 40–4, 83, 92–3, 209, 316, 363, 369, 379

Táj Mahal, 206–7
Thákúr Parshád, 277

Umrao Dula, Nawáb. *See* Báki Muhammad Khán, Nawáb

Wales, H.R.H. the Prince of, 63–75
Ward, Colonel C. I. H., 104, 123–4, 172, 224
Wazír Muhammad Khán, Nawáb, 10, 32–4, 213, 366–7, 377–8
Weir, Colonel, 289, 294, 320

Yár Muhammad Khán, Nawáb, 376
Yembu, 343, 347